DR LYNNE MILLWARD

SOCIAL RESEARCH METHODS

Richard M. Hessler
University of Missouri

SOCIAL RESEARCH METHODS

Richard M. Hessler
University of Missouri

WEST PUBLISHING COMPANY
St. Paul • New York • Los Angeles • San Francisco

Copyeditor: Marilynn J. Taylor
Composition: Northwestern Printcrafters, Inc.
Artwork: Precision Graphics
Cover and Interior Design: Lois Stanfield

COPYRIGHT ©1992   By WEST PUBLISHING COMPANY
                  50 W. Kellogg Boulevard
                  P.O. Box 64526
                  St. Paul, MN 55164-0526

Printed in the United States of America

99 98 97 96 95 94 93 92   8 7 6 5 4 3 2 1 0

Library of Congress Cataloging-in-Publication Data

Hessler, Richard M.
   Social research methods / Richard M. Hessler.
      p.   cm.
   Includes bibliographical references and index.
   ISBN 0-314-93107-4
   1. Social sciences—Research—Methodology.   I. Title.
H61.H48   1992
300'.72—dc20   91-32286
                                                    CIP ∞

Contents in Brief

Contents

Preface

■ Methodology and theory are the core disciplines of any science. This particularly is true of the social sciences. If you learn sociological methodology and theory well, you can master any of the subspecialty areas, such as criminology or medical sociology, in very short order. There have been times in the past when I was asked to teach a subject in sociology in which I had never read. Because I was well-grounded in methodology, I was able to critically sort through the literature and find empirical research worth teaching about. Theory helped me put the various findings into a larger context and to synthesize, that is, create new insights out of old interpretations. I can recall many instances where I was able to guide students onto new research paths because I knew enough theory and methodology to do some creative sociological imagining.

This book was born out of my deep respect for and appreciation of sociological methodology. I have benefited enormously from my methodology training. The potential to solve incredibly vexing social problems or to set social policy agendas is yours for the mastery of methodology. The production and control of sociologically useful knowledge derives from methodological knowledge.

As is true with any important knowledge base, the temptation is there to produce a cookbook of facts, a compendium of methodological techniques. Such methodology books exist and, in fact, serve a useful purpose. Technical know how is fifty percent of doing methodology. The other half is thinking methodologically. I believe that thinking outweighs technical learning.

This book stresses methodological thinking, not at the expense of technical knowledge by a long shot, but styles of methodological thinking is what you will get the most of in this book. My reason for this emphasis is simple. Mere technicians know how to perform certain procedures but have problems deciding which is the most appropriate technique to use, especially in the face of new situations. The researcher who knows how to think methodologically will be in the best position to select the most effective techniques, to actually design the research strategy, rather than just implementing it. Knowing how to set up research so that you are able to evaluate techniques and decide when to use them is the highest form of methodological knowledge to which this book aspires. To paraphrase Abraham Kaplan's law of the instrument, give a small boy a hammer and everything he encounters gets pounded regardless of need. The methodologist armed only with technical knowledge faces a similar fate.

Part I of this book thinks through the basic issue of what scientific research ought to be like and how to decide whether what you do as a scientist is ethical or not. While there is no one best way to do science, there is a standard of thinking that all science aspires to, and Part I discusses that standard.

Part II focuses on styles of measuring social reality. The discussion begins with measurement theory, then takes the student through methodological decisions made about indicators, scales, questionnaire and interview schedule construction, sampling, and interviewing. I try to lace the discussion with personal experiences with a view to giving the student a glimpse of what goes on backstage, behind the scenes of polished research reports and journal articles. Methodologists at work is a theme that runs throughout the book.

Part III centers on when and how to use experimental, survey, case study, and observational research designs. Again, the emphasis is on decision making and thinking out the strengths and weaknesses of various approaches, given the constraints posed by theory and the research problem. Boxes describing the work of other sociologists pursuing such important research problems as AIDS, social inequality, and voting behavior, are some of the examples of the uses of different research designs.

Part IV covers data reduction and analysis, the knotty problem of how one decides what to do with data once in hand. Description and analysis are the two main goals, and qualitative and quantitative data present the researcher with very different issues when deciding how to pursue those goals. Here, as is true of measurement and research design, I urge the student to think in a balanced fashion. Rather than accepting the black-or-white, quantitative-or-qualitative data analysis thinking popular in the methodological literature, I try to show the student how to think in ways that balance and combine the strengths of both forms of data.

The instructor's manual contains student research project ideas and data analysis technologies that provide an opportunity to think methodologically in real research situations. These ideas have worked well for me for more than twenty-five years of teaching research methodology, and I hope they work as well for you. Computers play a prominent role in research and have since the early 1950s. Several of the assignments give the student hands-on experience with some of the latest computer techniques.

This book emphasizes the thought processes involved in doing methodologically sound research. In this, it is a relatively unique methodology book. There are tremendous opportunities for young methodologists to really make a difference in the quality of life for people the world over. There is so much social scientific research that needs to be done. The burgeoning ranks of the elderly, war, the decline of community and social support, AIDS, poverty, racism, and sexism are only a few of the explosive social problems advancing on all of us. I am certain that if solutions are in the future, they will come from people like you who are well versed in methodology and thus capable of creatively defining research problems, designing and conducting definitive studies, and translating sound analyses into policy.

I deeply appreciate the superb editorial direction of the people at West Publishing Company. Namely Tom LaMarre and Bernice Carlin who handled the acquisitions and the development of the text. Emily Autumn, the production editor, supervised the copyediting and made many valuable, substantive suggestions that I heeded. Liz Grantham of West handled the publicity and Lucinda Gatch produced the software plan for the instructor's manual. Judy Elam and Kathy Yardley, of the University of Missouri, Columbia, typed three revisions, a marathon test of skill and patience, which they survived intact. Special thanks go to my wife, Anne Dietz Hessler, to my children Amy Gundy, Peter, Angela and Birgitta Hessler for their support and research help, and to my parents, Hugh and Doria Hessler, for all they have done for me.

The following reviewers read (and in some cases re-read) the manuscript in its various stages. I thank them for their many suggestions, corrections, and encouragement.

Marion E. Bihm, *McNeese State University*
Leonard Bloomquist, *Kansas State University*
Robert L. Caine, *Georgia State University*
Scott Eliason, *University of Iowa*
Dula J. Espinosa, *Arizona State University*
Ronald A. Farrell, *University of Nevada—Las Vegas*
Wolfgang Frese, *Mississippi State University*
Billy Johnson, *Central State University—Oklahoma*
Michael B. Kleiman, *University of South Florida*
Michael Leming, *St. Olaf College*
Judy Linneman, *Texas A & M University*
Jeffrey C. Salloway, *University of New Hampshire*
Richard Shaffer, *California Polytechnic State University—San Luis Obispo*
R. N. Singh, *Texas State University*
Rick L. Slavings, *Radford University*
Michael Stuart, *California State University—Fullerton*
Alton Thompson, *North Carolina State University*

Introduction

Research methodology is the science of *how* to make research decisions, and it includes the practice of evaluating the goodness or badness of decisions made in the course of doing research (see Figure 1). Think of research as a series of interrelated decisions, each one building upon the other. Note from Figure 1 that there is a bouncing back and forth between some of the stages of research. For example, you may define the problem tentatively and then revise your definition after conducting an extensive review of the literature. Similarly, you will want to go back to the literature once you have formulated your theory, clarify definitions and hypotheses, and then reformulate the theory. The point is that the stages are interdependent, that is, decisions at one stage affect the next and so forth. The researcher then is in a position to evaluate the worth of each decision and of all the decisions taken as a whole. Methodology is the body of knowledge utilized in deciding how worthy the decisions are.

■ Methodology

This body of knowledge called research methodology is not something that social scientists have invented out of the blue and in the abstract, removed from the real world of research. Just the opposite is true. Research methodologists use their own research and the research of many other social scientists to arrive at rules for conducting research. These rules are nothing more than conventional ways of doing research. They tell the researcher that he or she "ought" to do the following under certain conditions. There is nothing sacred about the rules. Their value is that they have helped enough researchers get valid answers to research questions that the community of social scientists agrees that the rules work. They may not agree forever, in which case the rules are changed to some—it is hoped—that work better.

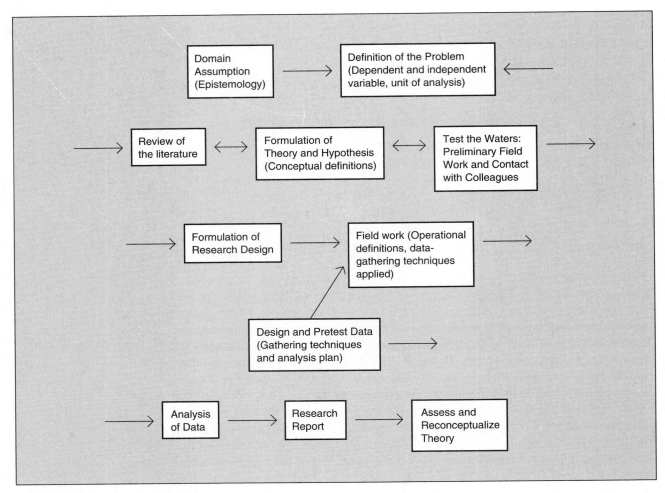

Figure 1 ■ The Research Process

■ *Domain Assumptions*

In addition to developing conventional wisdom about methodology, many social scientists identify themselves and are identified by others as working within certain theoretical "domains." Another way of approaching this issue is to ask the social scientist what his or her "domain assumptions" are. It is incredibly difficult to avoid such categorization so that most active researchers are known not only for the substantive area of their research, for example, political sociology or medical sociology, but also for their answers to the questions: "How do I know when I know something?"; "What are sociological facts?"; "What is my view of human nature?"; "What is the best research program given the research problem?"; and "Does my research add or subtract from the sum total of sociological knowledge?" Such names as "number-cruncher survey researcher," "soft data qualitative methodologist," "Marxist," "symbolic interactionist," or "positivist" are shorthand descriptions of the relationship between theory and methodology. We will spend the rest of this book expanding upon this discussion.

The first chapter addresses the social scientific (epistemology) question of what knowledge is. This will be tough going because it is a philosophy of science issue that has proved frustrating to some of the greatest thinkers the world has known. But, as methodologists or researchers, we cannot ignore this question and hope to do scientific research that is worth anything at all. Without an answer to the question of what knowledge is, we would be unable to specify what kind of data to collect and why one would consider the data at all. In short, scientific investigation must start with the researcher's basic assumptions concerning what knowledge is. Such assumptions form the foundation for the definition of the research problem and all the design decisions that follow. In presenting the philosophy of science foundation for research methodology, we will draw heavily upon the work of D. C. Phillips (1987), Earl Babbie (1986), Hans Zetterberg (1965), Robert Brown (1963), Sam Stouffer, et al. (1949, 1950), Max Weber (1949), Karl Popper (1961), and Morris Cohen and Ernest Nagel (1934). It is hoped that the reader will come away from this chapter with a clear understanding of the process by which observations of social action are explained and verified as truthful, as well as having acquired insights into how to think methodologically.

Throughout the remainder of the book, the reader will be challenged to think methodologically rather than simply being exposed to methods or techniques for doing research. Specific techniques, important and effective as they are, come and go as our technology and knowledge base change. Turning then to something of more lasting value, the goal for this book is to provide the student of methodology with a guiding philosophy of science principles and styles of methodological thinking that in turn will enable the student to conduct sociologically and practically relevant research. Certainly, specific techniques are presented throughout the book, but much of the writing provides examples of methodological thinking. What the researcher assumes about the nature of social reality, either tacitly or explicitly, exerts a strong influence on the types of research problems chosen for study, the theories used to explain the problems, and the research design decisions made. It is hoped that the reader will gain from this book the methodological thinking skills necessary to creatively approach research problems with competence in using and even creating theory and techniques that are in harmony and work together.

Part One

SETTING THE STAGE:
PHILOSOPHY OF
SCIENCE CONCEPTS
FOR THE METHODOLOGIST

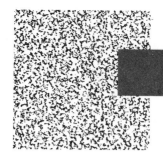

Chapter One

THE LOGIC OF
SOCIOLOGICAL KNOWLEDGE

▌ *This chapter attempts to show that the definition of the research problem is the first and most important step in sociological methodology. This is where you select the variables that you will measure and analyze. Beginning with this precept, the reader gets on a tour of the types of explanations involved in problem solving. The goal here is to get the student to evaluate the scientific adequacy of the types of explanations discussed with a view to developing a "sociological imagination" in approaching research problems. Concepts and theory are discussed and then the battles over what constitutes sociological knowledge are examined. Positivism with its search for ultimate truth is subjected to intense criticism with the help of Thomas Kuhn* (The Structure of Scientific Revolutions) *and the concept of paradigm shift. The goal in this chapter is to get the student to question what is meant by scientific knowledge and truth and then to address the core characteristics of sociological research. The chapter concludes with a discussion of the relationship between theory and method.*

Why has AIDS spread from homosexual and intravenous drug user populations into the heterosexual population? What are innovations in sport and why do they occur? Is the fact that women live longer than men due to genetics and/or to sociological factors? Do highly successful intercollegiate sport programs bring academic success to colleges and universities? Why are the United States and South Africa the only modern Western industrialized countries that do not have a national health system? Why is the national high school dropout rate 40%? Why are 50% of all newborn infants in inner cities delivered by unwed girls fifteen years of age or younger? Why is the gap between wealthy and poor growing in all countries of the world? These are a few important questions that can be answered only by summoning the logic of sociological research-based knowledge. Without sociological research, one person's guess is as good as another's and personal opinion rules.

But how does one do research on these questions? Do you develop a theory (explanation) or go out and collect boxcar loads of data? Where does the interested researcher begin?

Karl Popper (1949) said it well when he identified the definition of the **research problem** as the indisputable beginning of all social research. He cautioned researchers to always consider the research problem first before deciding whether or not sociological knowledge has happened and if an explanation can be trusted as true. In Popper's own words:

> Science, we may say, is confronted with problems, at any moment of its development. It cannot start with observations, or with the "collection of data," as some students of method believe. Before we can collect data, our interest in *data of a certain kind* must be aroused: *the problem always comes first*. The problem in its turn may be suggested by practical needs, or by scientific or prescientific beliefs which, for some reason or other, appear to be in need of revision (p. 121).

◼ *Nonscientific Explanations*

Let's start with Popper's notion of prescientific beliefs. Our goal in this regard is to demystify the discussion of scientific logic or explanation by grounding it in everyday experience common to all of us. Simply put, each of us has knowledge of everyday life that, with a little research methodology applied to it, could become scientific knowledge.

One of the few universal characteristics of people is a strong desire to explain things going on around them. People are universally inquisitive and strive to find and explain patterns they observe in themselves and in others. Once patterns are observed, efforts are made to explain them and even to predict these regularities.

Much of this human activity occurs outside the realm of science and is called common sense. The following is an example of this human activity. As a freshman high school track athlete, I considered myself a sprinter. In my neighborhood, I had never lost a race shorter than one hundred yards, so I knew that I would work out with the sprint team and race the shorter distances. The coach seemed to go along with my thinking, and I worked out with the sprinters. I noticed that most of the sprinters were black, but I let it go at that and did the workouts along with the best of them.

The first race was a junior varsity one hundred-yard dash. I finished next to last in my heat and was depressed. The same thing happened the next race and the one after that. I observed that most of the people beating me were black, just like my teammates, and when the coach moved me up to the half mile, I noticed that my teammates and the people I raced against were mostly white. Thus, I concluded that black athletes were better sprinters and whites were better middle-distance and distance runners. This conclusion was based on empirical observations and was backed up by other track athletes I talked with about it.

From this observation, I began to develop an explanation or theory. I turned to biology and the field of genetics, which seemed to satisfy the major criteria of scientific theory, namely that the theory be objective, simple, and cover adequately the observations under question. Objectivity involves the issues of values and assurance that the scientist's values are not influencing the acceptance or rejection of the theory. Simplicity, or the principle of parsimony, means that you get by with the minimum number of concepts and propositions and that your logic is clear and unambiguous. Coverage is adequate when you are able to apply the theory successfully to new cases of the problem under investigation. Certainly, my confidence in the genetic theory was solidly grounded in the cannons of science, thus I could close the book on the problem of explaining black athletic supremacy in the sprints.

INADEQUACY OF NATIVE COMMONSENSE INQUIRY

The central flaw with the above native explanation was discovered by Karl Popper and discussed in his classic book *The Logic of Scientific Discovery* (1957). Popper rejected the prevailing view that explanations or theories that seemed to be supported every time someone turned around and made an observation were the most scientifically valid theories. Using our example, no one observed white sprinters who could compete successfully with black sprinters. All black sprinters were faster than white sprinters. In fact, the theory went beyond the sprints to include all team sports that had more than 10% black athletes playing. In those sports, blacks were clearly superior to whites in almost every situation of comparison.

Popper turned the scientific tables and came up with a central principle of science that we subscribed to in sociological **methodology**. Rather than setting up a study to try to prove that a theory or explanation is true, one must strive to prove the theory false. Instead of searching for events that confirm your theory, you should do all in your power to find events that disprove it. On of the biggest mistakes a scientist can make is to collect observations with the goal of proving the theory behind them. In this sense, the scientist is in danger of paying attention only to observations that confirm the theory and ignoring or missing those that refute it. The essence of science, then, is to set your observations up in such a way as to maximize the chances of refuting your explanation or theory. In the case of our example, a good scientist would expand the observations beyond just athletes but would certainly include all athletes, black and white. Once done, the scientist would discover that there is as much variation in athletic ability among blacks as there is between black and white athletes.

In other words, there are as many poor athletes, proportionally speaking among blacks as there are poor athletes among whites. Why then are black athletes so far and above white athletes? Why are black athletes better sprinters? The answer obviously has nothing to do with genetic differences between white athletes and black athletes, this we know from the expanded observations.

Rather, the difference probably has something to do with racial discrimination and stereotyping by the larger dominant white society, which controls how blacks are viewed and treated. Consequently, black athletes have to be better than white athletes in order to succeed in sports. For this reason, society will tolerate a mediocre white athlete much more easily than it will a mediocre black athlete. In sociological terms, we have a situation in U. S. sports of unequal treatment for equal ability. If blacks are to succeed, they have to excel far beyond the performances of the white athletes. This is an alternative explanation to the genetic differences one.

In order to maximize the chances of rejecting our new explanation, we need to expand the data or observational base to include what methodologists call the universe, that is, all blacks an all whites. We would draw a sample from the white universe and one from the black universe and compare the two samples on measurements of various physical attributes that we think are related to athletic performance. When we do this, we discover that there is as much variation within the white sample on weight, percent of body fat, height, and so on as there is among blacks. Furthermore, the variation within each group is greater than the differences between them. If our explanation was false, that is, if blacks really are physically superior to whites by birth alone, then the research subjects in the black sample would be physically similar to one another and, as a group, would be better suited for athletics physically than the whites. Obviously, we failed to prove ourselves wrong so, for the moment at least, the unequal treatment for equal ability explanation stands.

■ *Types of Methodologically Sound Explanations*

Science, in the words of Abraham Kaplan (1964), is "a social enterprise, in which data are shared, ideas exchanged, and experiments replicated. It is precisely the accumulation of empirical evidence which shapes a welter of diverse opinions into scientific knowledge common to many minds" (p. 36).

The philosophy of science is a discipline that has produced useful principles to help us understand science and the forms of explanation, including some basic assumptions that make up the philosophical underpinnings of theory. But first, we must reject as too stringent the logical positivism[1] concept called the verifiability principle. This is not a rejection of positivism, just one of its principles. Verifiability claims that if you cannot measure it (verify it), then you cannot use it in scientific explanation. If it is unmeasurable, it is not a candidate for scientific study (see page 13 for an expanded discussion of this point).

This is erroneous because there are very powerful and productive theories the bases of which cannot be measured directly but that, nevertheless, explain very important observable reality. One example from physics is the theory of black

---

[1]Positivism is a theoretical branch of methodology that subscribes to the view that "if you can't measure it, you can't know it."

holes. No one has yet been able to measure a black hole, but still the theory of what black holes are and how they work is a powerful explanation of the gravitational events surrounding stars and their light. Also, a theory or explanation must be written in such a way that the theory can be rejected or disproven.

Scientifically sound explanations begin with scientifically sound problem definitions. We will discuss the strategies for defining research problems later in this chapter, but for now, we need to know that the problem statement establishes the context, substance, and scope of the explanation. Research problem statements set the stage for the theory or **explanation.**

Robert Brown's work *Explanation in Social Science* (1963) is a classic discussion of the types of explanations extant in the social sciences. Brown rejects descriptions and classifications that do not have "why" as part of their task as not being true explanations. Thus, pure description may be necessary in working toward explanation, but it should not be considered adequate methodology in and of itself. The types of explanations covered here are: genetic explanations, intentions, dispositions, function explanations, and empirical generalizations.

GENETIC EXPLANATIONS

Genetic explanations include: (1) the beginning or origin, (2) the description and (3) explanations of the development of some event, process, group, or so on. A relatively new area in sociological methodology called sociohistorical analysis is a type of genetic explanation. For example, a genetic explanation of European peasant unrest during the sixteenth century would start with the problem statement, "What was the origin of sixteenth century European peasant unrest, and what were the sociological structures and processes associated with this unrest?" The origins of the unrest included the demise of the feudal system in which peasants were oppressed but also were protected from the hardships of independent living. Also, the wealthy classes gained more wealth very rapidly, while rising costs and inflation reduced the economic power of the peasants. Finally, relative deprivation set in as the peasants looked at the rapid gains in wealth of the wealthy folks around them and felt left out, alienated, and deprived by comparison.

Obviously, the explanation is date dependent, that is, it is pertinent to the sixteenth century. Sociological concepts and hypotheses are involved, but they are superseded by the fact that the event and conditions are unique. While the sociological reasoning may be applied to all sorts of other situations of unrest, the reasons contained within a genetic explanation are pertinent only to the specific historical event under investigation.

INTENTIONS

This type of explanation, according to Brown, involves the motives behind the actions under investigation. In simple terms, the researcher who is operating within the intention realm will assume that intentions have a direct effect on behavior and then seek to uncover intentions. While Brown discounted this type of explanation as not very well utilized by social scientists, recent methodological developments in voting behavior research have placed intention explanations on the same shelf with other methodological tools (Granberg, 1988). This work stems from Martin Fishbein's (1963; 1980) theory that was a solution to the problem of attitudes versus deeds, that is, what people say and what they actually do being different. Fishbein theorized that behavioral intentions are a better prediction of behavior than are attitudes. Intention is influenced by attitude, but behavior follows directly from behavioral intentions. Intention is an important tool in understanding behavior in various other domains of social psychological research as well (Biddle, Bank, and Slavings, 1987).

DISPOSITIONS

Disposition explanations focus on tendencies and abilities of individuals or groups to act in certain patterned ways. For example, consider the statement "Jones was disposed to increase his income by taking on more malpractice cases." Disposition explanations are a bit more powerful than intention explanations because they focus on recurrent behaviors or tendencies, rather than a given intention that may occur only once. In other words, intention explanations may or may not represent patterned or recurrent behavior, whereas disposition explanations do in fact represent stable and consistent patterns or tendencies in the way people do things or in their abilities to do things. When using a disposition explanation, the researcher may be able to uncover the specific goals or intentions behind the patterned activity. If so, then the researcher has both intention and disposition explanations in hand. But it does not work the other way around. Intention explanations always include goals or objectives, but those goals, and therefore the intention explanation, may be a one-time transitory event, observed now an never again. For example, one can explain the increase in medical malpractice claims by citing the tendency of insurance companies to engage in a profit cycle of raising premiums, expanding coverage, and settling claims out of court. One could add an intention explanation by investigating and bringing into the picture the motives of lawyers, arguing that they are members of an income-maximizing profession and, hence, will take advantage of any funds made available by insurance companies. However, from knowing the intention of the lawyer to make a lot of money, we do not automatically know the disposition to make that money by suing doctors.

FUNCTION EXPLANATIONS

Function, one of the most widely used of the types of explanation defined by Brown, exists when the researcher asks, "What role or function does x play in the maintenance of y as a system?" According to Brown, function explanations accomplish three things for the sociological methodologist: (1) they state or define conditions necessary for the existence of a social system; (2) they emphasize the importance of the conditions for the system; and (3) they allow the methodologist, by isolating and describing the function of things, to essentially design practical ways to preserve and enhance the system under investigation. Good examples of function explanations can be found in anthropology, where ethnographers isolate a particular type of relationship, for example, the nondisciplinary relationship between uncles and nieces and/or nephews, and explain the existence of the relationship in terms of its positive impact on the social equilibrium of the family group.

EMPIRICAL GENERALIZATIONS

This type of explanation is a law-like statement about the relationship between two or more objects, states, or events. For example, we might state that for all human groups, the greater the extensiveness and intensiveness of face-to-face interaction, the greater the sentiments of liking among the members, which in turn promotes more interaction. In shorthand, for all A, if A has the property B and B has C, then A has the property C. This is a general law-like statement that can be used to explain the existence of A. In our example, the existence and maintenance of the group is explained by the general sociological principle (law-like statement) that sentiment and interaction are always mutually interdependent and reinforce each other. Note that this conclusion is not logically necessary, that is, the statement that the existence of the group is a consequence of the interaction and sentiment process is not true based on logic alone. We are not able to deduce the existence of the group on the logical fit or relationship between the principle and the group's existence. Rather, it is based on empirical grounds, that is, we developed the explanation and law-like generalization from observing or studying many groups over time and analyzing how these groups maintained their existence. Obviously, if the explanatory principle is to qualify as a law-like empirical generalization, we must be able to find it in every case of a group maintaining its existence over time.

Deduction, then, is a type of logical argument that starts with an empirical law and then proceeds to draw a conclusion about a particular phenomenon. The conclusion is logically necessary (automatic), given the law and the premise connecting the phenomenon and the law.

Induction starts with particular phenomenon and then tries to develop empirical laws. The conclusions are not logically necessary but are based on empirical observations. Both styles lead to empirical generalization.

It is possible but not very likely in sociological methodology to extend empirical generalizations and create laws. Laws are deductive explanations deduced from invariable universal statements about the relationships among properties. The existence and validity of the explanation depends on logic alone, not empirical verification.

■ *Concepts and Theory: The Core of Explanation*

Theories are explanations or answers to a research question. You start with a problem, usually do some preliminary observing to check out your thinking, then begin the painful process of developing an explanation for the problem. Conversely, theory produces new research problems. **Concepts** are the building blocks of the theory. They are basic to any explanation.

While concepts are abstract ideas and therefore not observable directly, they point the way to measuring and ultimately categorizing phenomena. When we get right down to it, most of the words in our language are concepts. Without them, we would be unable to communicate. For example, *nutrition* is a concept, an abstraction that categorizes literally dozens of other concepts and perhaps hundreds of behaviors. Subsumed under this concept is the word *food*. Taken together, these two terms enable human beings to survive through recognizing and distinguishing the edible from the inedible, the nutritional from the nonnutritional. Thus, concepts are the very essence of knowledge and understanding. They are abstract creations of human beings useful for understanding and explaining the real world.

Theory is another word for explanation. Research begins with a question, and theory is the attempt to answer the question or to explain the research problem. Theory consists of three basic components: (1) concepts; (2) propositions or statements linking the concepts together; and (3) rules for connecting concepts with the observable world (measurement). Carl Hempel used a network model to define theory:

> A scientific theory might therefore be likened to a complex spatial network: its terms are represented by the knots, while the threads connecting the latter correspond, in part, to the definitions and, in part, to the fundamental and derivative hypotheses included in the theory. The whole system floats, as it were, above the plane of observation and is anchored to it by rules of interpretation. These might be viewed as strings which are not part of the network but link certain points of the latter with specific places in the plane of observation (1952, p. 36).

Figure 1-1 represents this spatial network. The concepts are linked together by propositions that describe how the concept operates and how the operation of one concept affects the other concepts. Also, a few of the concepts are generalized (D, E, and F) by rules that tell the researcher what to observe and how to observe it. Referring to my own research on the rural elderly, I developed a theory that contains several concepts. For the sake of this example, I will mention only a few of the concepts and show how they are linked by proposition statements. The concepts are age, gender, sense of self-worth, social networks, health status, and mortality. Mortality is the dependent variable, that is, the research problem to be explained. The research question is, "What are the sociological factors involved in the prediction of mortality?" Social networks are defined conceptually as primary and secondary social interaction patterns that can be characterized in terms of their intensiveness and extensiveness. Primary interaction patterns consist of family members and friends, whereas secondary social networks consist of formal organizations. Health status is defined as perceived physical and emotional functioning relative to one's peers and in a more general sense. Mortality is defined as the occurrence of death. Age is the most powerful predictor of mortality. The older a person is, the more likely it is that the person will die. Females live longer than males primarily because females are more involved in social networks. As

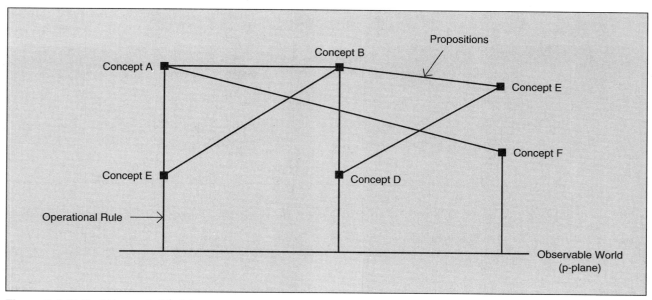

Figure 1-1 ■ Carl Hempel's Model

individuals age, family and other primary networks play an increasingly prominent role, signaling to the elderly that their independence is waning. Secondary
networks provide individuals with a greater sense of self-worth than family because secondary networks involve free choice as to membership, incorporate a
wider, more heterogeneous group, and have less dependency interactions. Highlighting one of the propositions, "gender-secondary social network," this would
read: Women are more involved in secondary social networks than men. This
"gender effect" is associated with lower mortality among women. Social networks
and interaction, particularly in secondary networks, are associated with living a
longer life. Poor health is associated with an increased risk of death, but the existence of social networks mitigates the effects of health status. Regardless of
health status, individuals embedded in extensive and intensive social networks
face less risk of death than those who have small or no social networks. This is
because social networks provide material and social support that cushion the impact that poor health has on the risk of mortality. Figure 1-2 describes the theory.

Here we see the concepts health, social networks, and mortality linked together by propositions to produce a coherent explanation of mortality. Not every
concept in the theory is measured, that is, not all of the concepts touch down to
the p-plane. Nevertheless, since most of the concepts touch down (are measured),
the theory is very concrete. The fewer concepts that touch down in a theory, the
more abstract the theory is. Another way of describing the extent to which the
concepts are measured is through the use of the terms *middle range* and *grand*.
A middle-range theory has lots of its concepts measured, whereas the grand theory has only a few of the many concepts that are measured. Several theories in
particle physics have no concepts actually measured, and yet the theories are

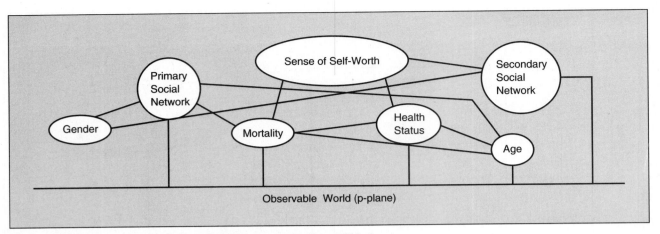

Figure 1-2 ■ Theory for Predicting Mortality among the Rural Elderly

very productive in terms of generating research and for explaining observed reality. How abstract a theory is has little to do with its scientific merits.

■ *Domain Assumptions*

Of great importance to sociological methodology is the question of the proper or best theory of social reality. Tackling this brings us to a very interesting point about theory and concepts, which is that the answer to the question depends on the basic assumptions (also called "**domain assumptions**") of the sociologist. If the sociologist assumes that his or her methods and explanations are as scientifically sound as any of the physical sciences, then the best theories should establish or utilize social laws. Society and its inhabitants should follow social laws just like molecules follow physical laws. Emile Durkheim was a firm believer in the assumption that the methods of physical science would yield sound research and theories in sociology, simply because he viewed social phenomena as following social laws. According to Durkheim, theories should contain social laws and thus ought to predict social phenomena as well as explain it. Durkheim believed that he had discovered the social law that suicide rates are determined by the degree of social cohesion or integration in the society or group under investigation.

In contrast, there are social scientists who assume that social laws should not be a part of theory and, hence, that explanation cannot include prediction of behavior or of social processes. Standing in between these two positions is Max Weber, who allowed the possibility that social laws exist and that the techniques of physical science are useful to sociologists. However, Weber viewed the measurement of concepts in the physical sciences as being indirect in the sense that the researcher had some artificial physical measuring instrument between himself or herself and the phenomenon being studied. Theories containing this type of measurement, according to Weber, may contain laws and predict events, but the scientist is removed from the subject being investigated and thus cannot understand or explain the subject fully.

Weber viewed a full explanation or understanding as coming from sharing the perspective with the subject, something that is impossible when measurement occurs through such instruments as microscopes or questionnaires. Weber came up with a method for tying concepts to the observable world, a method that he called **verstehen**, a German word meaning "to understand." In the social sciences, the researcher is able to "take the perspective" of the research subjects, to empathize with the way they experience the social world, because the researcher is a member of the social world, too, and experiences very similar things. The goal of theory, according to Weber, is to understand the meaning associated with social behavior, in short *verstehen*. Measurement, then, could yield data in the form of numbers gathered from a questionnaire or in the form of observational notes that the researcher has written after "walking a mile," so to speak, in the shoes of the subjects.

▪ *Positivism and other Epistemological Battles*

There are many faces of positivism, but all of them are relatives of the founders who are called *logical positivists*. Carl Hempel from philosophy, Otto Neurath in economics, and Kurt Godel, the late mathematician at the Institute for Advanced Study at Princeton, were all logical positivists. Godel was the clearest example of this school of thought, this epistemological[2] position. Godel claimed that numbers are real, that they really exist in an objective way, independent from the observer or user. As we know, numbers are highly abstract concepts. We cannot find one in nature, and all we see are representations or pictures of them, such as written numerals. But Godel argued that numbers were real, objective, existing in nature. What this view accomplished and essentially what **logical positivism** accomplished is the point that no scientific concept, no research idea, is so abstract that it cannot be measured or observed. If you have a concept that cannot be measured or that does not represent so-called objective reality, you have religion or metaphysics and not science. Thus, to a positivist, all the concepts in a theory are measurable, that is, they all touch the p-plane either actually or potentially.

PRINCIPLE OF VERIFIABILITY

The principle behind this point is called the **principle of verifiability**. This principle states that a concept is meaningful only if it can be seen or measured empirically. Measurement or observation is considered absolutely necessary in order

---

[2]A branch of philosophy that focuses on the definitions of knowledge and attempts to answer the question, "How do you know that you know?"

to verify or refute a scientific theory or explanation. Thus, a statement such as "women live longer than men because women have more extensive social networks" is scientifically meaningful only if it can be measured and verified empirically (being verified by observation and/or measurement). This insistence on observation or measurement is the crux of logical positivism.

Behaviorism is a form of positivism. It is psychology's contribution to the principle of verifiability. John Watson (1948) was the founding father of this highly coherent version of positivism. Mental processes, such as cognition, conscience, consciousness, reflection, and other events of the mind, were not considered appropriate subject matter of the scientific study of psychology. Only observable behavior—better yet, only behavior observed in controlled laboratory settings— was considered the real subject matter for the science of psychology. Watson and his followers truly believed that behavioral psychology was no different than what at the time was considered to be the best experimental natural sciences, especially physics. Theories based on carefully controlled observations and verified as such were considered true beyond a doubt. Little did Watson and his followers know what would become of physics and its pure science approach when laboratory physicists observed things that simply did not fit the most widely accepted theories. More about this a little later.

CRITIQUE OF POSITIVISM

Popper, whom we heard from earlier in this chapter, produced an important criticism of positivism. Whereas the positivists insisted that **scientific observation** was purely objective, that is, completely unaffected by knowledge, Popper said that observation was clouded by the predispositions of the researcher. The positivists argued that the researcher can be confident that a theory is true when all the observations ever performed verify or support the theory. Conversely, Popper pointed out, the researcher cannot conclude that a theory is false when observations do not fit the theory, that is, when things observed do not do what the theory predicted they would do.

This point is part of a larger epistemological battle in science over the efficacy of theory based strictly on induction or observational evidence. David Hume, back in the eighteenth century and followed by Popper much later, blasted the positivist assumption that all things not yet observed will fall neatly in line with the things already observed. Both men argued that even if pure objective observation were possible, the researcher cannot have confidence that theory based on the observations will cover all future observations of the same phenomena. In short, you cannot rely strictly on observations to develop scientific theory. And here is the epistemological battle. The positivists argue that science is strictly objective; Popper and Hume countered that science is partly subjective. The researcher cannot be confident that science has an objective foundation, and yet theory must be verified or falsified by testing it empirically. The researcher brings a particular set of personal experiences that is completely subjective to the scientific enterprise. This personal subjective background influences the way the observations are conducted and even how the researcher interprets the observations.

This is a radical criticism of positivism because it says that objectivity is only partly possible. At best, the researcher may be able to control the subjective aspects of thinking, but the researcher cannot get rid of the bias. Observation, and even theory, cannot be purely objective or value neutral. Even if this were not the case, the researcher still is faced with the possibility that the relatively small number of observations made do not represent all the existing objects or even the undiscovered objects under study. Always lurking around the corner might be the observation that just does not fit.

A good example of this, where a widely respected theory suddenly could not explain some new observations, comes from that reputed bastion of science, physics. Ed Regis in *Who Got Einstein's Office?* (1988), his superb philosophy of science book on the Institute for Advanced Study at Princeton University, wrote about the physicists Chen Ning Yang and Tsung Dao Lee who discovered that a particle called the K-messon violated the hallowed law of conservation of parity. Freeman Dyson, one of the giants of the quantum physics revolution, wrote: "Nobody has had any success in classifying the known particles, or in predicting the properties of the unknown ones. Nobody understands why such and such particles exist, why they have the particular masses that are observed or why some of them strongly interact and some do not". The inability to explain these particles did not result in the demise of the theory. Physicists working on these anomalous observations simply tried to define the problem away by arguing that the K-messon was really two particles that behave differently from one another. Most physicists believed in the law too strongly to seriously question it in the light of strange observations.

But Yang and Lee held their ground, arguing that the law was predicated on limited observations and that it was reasonable to assume that the new observed particles were real and correctly identified. No, they were not about to accept the claim that the K-messon was in fact two particles. Instead, they and their colleagues designed a set of experiments, performed the appropriate observations, and declared that the widely held general law of parity was false and not a general law of nature. For this analysis, Yang and Lee received the Nobel Prize.

■ *Thomas Kuhn and His Concept of Paradigm*

Thomas Kuhn's book *The Structure of Scientific Revolutions* was very troublesome for those scientists who believed, as did the positivists, that there was an ultimate truth out there, a truly objective reality waiting to be discovered through scientific methods. Kuhn said that all scientists, by dint of their socialization and training as scientists, see the subject matter of their science through tinted glasses. These domain assumptions by the scientists about the very nature of their subject matter, about what truth is, and about what they believe constitutes verification serve as blinders (tinted glasses) forcing the scientists to see the world in peculiar ways.

For Kuhn, there was no way to observe reality independent from the values, beliefs, and basic epistemological assumptions (domain assumptions) of the scientists. For example, if the scientist believes that truth is out there waiting to be discovered, this epistemology will determine what kinds of research problems are studied and what kinds of theories are proffered. The goal would be to develop the one true theory. If the scientist believes that all physical properties affect each other in a cause-effect pattern resembling the collisions of billiard balls, that scientist will proceed to define research problems and to explain them in a very different fashion than the scientist who believes that there is a master order to nature, a kind of super unifying law.

Kuhn argued that there could be no one objective true theory but rather multiple theories stemming from the beliefs and assumptions of the scientists behind them. Kuhn brought human beings squarely into the very essence of the scientific enterprise, namely into theory or explanation. Kuhn viewed scientific reality as being made up of multiple **paradigms**, that is, multiple scientific truths. For Kuhn, there is no one true way in science of defining reality or of explaining it. Thus, a paradigm in sociology would be an entire constellation of epistemological assumptions, beliefs in certain theories, values, and exemplars or demonstrated solutions to problems. Scientists who subscribe to the paradigm form a community of scholars, and they tend to cling to the paradigm, even when empirical evidence starts to go against it. Eventually, the inability of the paradigm to handle new findings becomes too embarrassing or politically compelling to the community of scholars, and they overthrow the paradigm, a process that Kuhn calls "paradigm shift." Two examples of paradigm shift in sociology occurred in medical sociology and the sociology of poverty. For more than two decades, researchers in medical sociology developed theories about disease, illness, and sickness and conducted research on the process of becoming ill, physician-patient relationships, and rehabilitation, all with the domain assumption that the physician's definition of health and illness was the one correct definition. This domain assumption eventually was recognized and defined as "the medical model." At this point, medical sociologists began to question the medical professions' definitions. Hospitalizations began to be viewed as a power play where patients are striped of their basic identity, for purposes of social control, as opposed to the medical model view of "doing what is best for the patient." Human behaviors defined by doctors as sicknesses were scrutinized in a new light, and medical sociologists evolved a new powerful concept called "medicalization of deviance." This concept viewed the medical profession as moral entrepreneurs constantly striving to define deviant behaviors, for example, alcoholism or homosexuality, as diseases, thereby creating new medical vistas to conquer and, of course, new sources of income. This paradigm shift from the medical model to the social control of patients model led to great breakthroughs in research agendas and findings.

The poverty paradigm of the 1950s and early '60s viewed being poor as an individual responsibility. The domain assumption was that opportunities abound and people are poor because they have individual-level character flaws, for example, they are too lazy or unintelligent, that prevent them from taking advantage of the opportunities. Of course, this paradigm fit well with the larger U.S. value of individualism. The paradigm shift occurred when sociologists began to question the domain assumption in light of research evidence that showed that poor people wanted desperately to work and that even working was not enough. The new paradigm identified the larger United States and world economic system as the "cause" of poverty, and such theoretical concepts as "structured inequality," "blaming the victim," and "cycle of poverty" were introduced into the analysis of poverty. The domain assumption shifted from individual fault to system fault.

Of course, this view of science as a collection of value-laden communities is at odds with the mode of science as uniform, coherent, objective, value-neutral, and working toward the ultimate truth about a very objective reality. Kuhn's paradigm view of science stood the scientific community on its head, and the reaction to his work was almost violent in its opposition. But it made perfect sense to Kuhn, especially given what he had learned from Aristotle's *Physics*. If one judges Aristotle's conclusions from the Newtonian physics paradigm, he appears to be a complete moron. Aristotle, a most brilliant thinker, concluded among other things that heavier objects fall faster than light objects. And yet, from the perspective of his paradigm, Aristotle was perfectly correct in his conclusion about the behavior of physical objects.

Ed Regis (1988) quoted astrophysicist John Bahcall on the question of whether or not scientific truth is possible. "I personally feel it is presumptuous to believe that man can determine the whole temporal structure of the universe, its evolution, development and ultimate fate from the first nanosecond of creation to the last ten years on the basis of three or four facts which are not very accurately known and are disputed among the experts. That I find, I would say, almost immodest." Theory? "Interesting intellectual exercise but nothing to be worried about." And this coming from one of the finest physical scientists alive.

If the reader still feels compelled to think of scientific truth about some objective reality as possible, then one more example from quantum physics is in order. According to mainline theory in physics, objects such as a wristwatch should not exist. This is because atoms that make up things in the real world should not exist. According to theory, the electron that moves around the nucleus in an orbit should dissipate away its energy, slow down, lose its orbit, and ultimately collapse in on the nucleus. To avoid this embarrassing situation of having a theory that makes reality impossible, quanta were invented. These smallest amounts of energy have no cause and cannot be predicted. The theory behind quanta says that there are no real objects or things out there, that a single electron can be in two places at the same time, and that quanta communicate with each other. Empirical testing apparently has upheld or verified the laws of quantum physics, and confusion about scientific truth reigns supreme. Instead of a "paradigm shift" occurring, quantum physicists simply invented a concept that then enabled them to preserve their beloved theory. The physicists had become "true believers" in their theory, a most dangerous stance for a scientist to take. Again, if the emphasis had been placed (correctly, I might add,) on trying to disprove the theory, a paradigm shift would have occurred, possibly for the greater good of physics.

■ *Core Characteristics of Sociological Research*

Given the philosophy of science principles discussed above, we turn now to the core characteristics of sociological research that meet the standards of science. Core characteristics are those parts of scientific inquiry that are absolutely necessary, in some degree, in order for the research to be considered scientific. Please remember these characteristics are ideal typical, that is, they are what the ideal scientific method should be. These core characteristics are: (1) public verification; (2) objectivity; (3) control; (4) isolation of independent factors; (5) generalization; and (6) creativity, imagination, and the ability to wonder.

Of course, the real world of research involves lots of compromises with the ideal. Thus, the very first point is that we have a continuum of sociological science, ranging from the ideal "pure science" to the other extreme of "quasi-science," which is not quite science and not quite native human inquiry and probably not something whose findings you would want to trust.

Pure Science |——————————————| **Quasi-Science**

Particular sociological studies would fall somewhere between the two end points, depending on the extent to which the core characteristics were present.

PUBLIC VERIFICATION

Suppose only I am able to replicate my research because I have neglected to specify and document all the methodological decisions made. If so, then I have failed to provide for public verification, a very important core characteristic of science. In order to meet this standard, one must write down and publish all the procedures and methodological decisions made during the course of the research. The researcher should leave a paper trail that any other researcher, knowing nothing about the study, could pick up and essentially reproduce it. In the case of survey research, for example, the data could be sent via electronic mail on the computer to another distant researcher, analyzed, and interpreted in the same fashion. This characteristic of public verification makes it possible to double check the work of others to verify its soundness or to caution other researchers about its flaws.

Another way to achieve verification is through theory. A theory is verified if it hangs together logically, that is, if the propositions connecting the concepts and telling the researcher how to get from one concept to the other follow each other according to the rules of logic. If the rules of logic prevail, then the theory is verified. Any researcher should be able to replicate the verification procedures.

OBJECTIVITY

Objectivity exists when the researcher controls his or her emotions and values by not allowing them to influence the decisions made in the course of a study. This is not to say that the researcher is or can be value neutral. Max Weber (1949) pointed out the futility of insisting that scientists are value neutral. In fact, today Weber's position is even more significant, given the vast number of social scientists working in the public policy area. When Weber wrote his essay "The Meaning of 'Ethical Neutrality' in Sociology and Economics," the majority of sociologists were working in university settings and not in the value-loaded world of government bureaucracies and applied social research. In Weber's words,

> What is really at issue is the intrinsically simple demand that the investigator and teacher should keep unconditionally separate the establishment of empirical facts (including the "value oriented" conduct of the empirical individual whom he is investigating) and his own practical evaluations, i.e., his evaluation of these facts as satisfactory or unsatisfactory (including among these facts evaluations made by the empirical persons who are the object of investigation).

Weber recognized that the very nature of the particular problem investigated was evidence that the researcher has values and that these values have a vital role to play in teaching and research. However, Weber insisted that the researcher be up front and public about his or her values, even going so far as to warn the scientific community and students when he or she was evaluating or placing value on something. Also, Weber was insistent that those values had to be controlled and not mixed with methodologically scientific decision making.

CONTROL

In the ideal world of core characteristics of sociological research, studies should be tightly controlled. Control involves time, the independent variables (causes), extraneous variables, measurement, the researcher's values, and the documentation of all the decisions made in the course of the research.

Various research designs, as we shall see in a subsequent chapter, are successful in varying degrees with these forms of control. Longitudinal designs take time into consideration by measuring at various points in time, rather than only once. Time is important to control or to take into consideration because the researcher needs to establish which factor or variable came before the other in time in order to argue to prove that one factor was the cause of the other. Here we are using the term *cause* rather loosely in that we are seldom in a position in the social sciences to establish that a particular variable is a necessary and sufficient cause of another variable. In the social sciences, we work with infinite chains of relationships that are very complex and interrelated. To isolate one or two variables as the cause, even assuming that they are measured in a valid and reliable fashion, is foolhardy.

Nevertheless, with the above point as a warning, we use the concept "cause" as the ideal toward which all analysis aspires. Also, using cause and effect helps us keep our thinking straight as we set up analysis plans and try to construct theory or explanations. To say that x causes y is to say that x occurs before y in time, that there are no significant other causes that overshadow x, and that whenever x is present y will follow, for example, $x \rightarrow y$.

In controlling for extraneous factors, if through theory you have isolated the variables that you hypothesize as explaining the problem or dependent variable, then you want to be sure that you have taken into consideration all the variables that are not hypothesized as significant but that may be involved in "causing" the dependent variable. Standardizing the research subjects or using statistics are two of several methods designed to achieve control over extraneous factors.

Measurement should be objective in the sense that all of the decisions to create observational tools, classify, and otherwise operationalize the concepts must be written in such a form that any researcher could read and follow the rules for measuring the concepts. Also, concepts must be defined conceptually (abstractly) and operationally (the rules for measuring the concepts) in a precise and conventional (accepted by your colleagues) way.

The researcher must tell others whenever he or she is speaking or arguing along value lines, but most important, the researcher must control personal values and not allow value judgments to enter into the research (Weber, 1949). An unfortunate example of how *not* to conduct sociological research. Project Camelot (Horrowitz, 1970), stands out. Camelot was a Central Intelligence Agency-funded project that used sociological survey research as a front to gather intelligence on the revolutionary mood and potential of peasant communities in South America. This violation of the value-control norms became so pervasive that Alvin Gouldner was inspired to write *The Coming Crisis of Western Sociology*, in which he argued that all sociological methods and theory are contaminated by values and ideology. I am not as gloomy, but Gouldner certainly identified a problem for scientific sociological research.

The only exception to this general principle of controlling values in research is evaluation research, where the basic task is to place a value or to judge some program, institution, or event. Otherwise, the researcher who wants to stay scientific and objective must follow Weber's advice and keep personal values out of research decision making and writing. Social scientific research is not the place for grinding axes. The real business of science is to do your level best through design to reject your explanation or theory, rather than to set things up in such a way that you cannot help but be correct.

ISOLATION OF INDEPENDENT FACTORS

Through theory and other empirical research (the literature), the researcher is able to state what the most likely "casual" variables are for the particular effect being studied. In methodological terms, you pick out the independent variables that you think explain the dependent variable, that is, the problem being studied. This terminology is a bit confusing at first. I remember thinking when first exposed to independent/dependent thinking, that being independent should rule out the variables being related to the dependent variable. After all, if it is independent from the dependent variable, then one must search for another variable for the problem variable to be dependent upon. Just remember that the problem to be explained (the effects) is called the dependent variable, because it depends on other variables for its existence. Independent variables (the causes) explain the dependent variable and, as such, should be closely related to the dependent variable. They are independent of each other—conceptually, a state necessary for precise concept differentiation. The concepts in a theory must have precise definitions (boundaries) so that the research is able to distinguish one from the other.

Theory helps the research zero is on a few of the literally hundreds of potential independent variables. Remember the principle of parsimony? It tells the researcher to seek out the simplest explanation. Thus, the more the researcher can narrow the search and select the most relevant independent variables, the better the research will turn out. It is theory that enables the researcher to narrow the focus in this way.

GENERALIZATION

Generalization is the process of going from the particular to the whole, from specific instances to a principle or law that incorporates the particulars into a larger whole. An important goal of any science is to arrive at general laws that can explain a wide variety of events or behaviors simply. A general law in sociology might be George Homans's "mutual dependence of interaction and sentiment." This says that sentiments of liking are associated with wanting to interact, which in turn produces greater sentiments of liking and so forth, in a circular fashion. Any interaction pattern in any group ought to be covered by this law in the sense that the researcher should be able to use the law to explain why any group maintains itself. Another example of this process is Fred Davis's (1963) study of the social-psychological impact of a life-threatening illness (polio) on fourteen children and their families. Davis conducted open-ended interviews with the afflicted children and their parents. He repeated the interviews several times over a twenty-four month period. From the specific details of each child's experience along with the family response, Davis formed a theory or "general law" that explained the "passage through the medical crisis" as a series of stages of development (prelude, warning, impact, and inventory). The particular crisis experiences of the fourteen families were different. For some, it took one day to move from the onset of symptoms to the diagnosis. For others, it was a week. Regardless, the "general" crisis experience, the stages, was shared by all fourteen families. Generalization, then, extends the time, location, and population. In the Davis example, the time is extended from the particular instances (one day from symptoms to diagnosis to one week) to the general (go through first stage regardless of the time from onset of symptoms to diagnosis). Likewise, the same is true of location and population. In Davis's own words:

> Does the study have relevance beyond the specific patterning of events comprising paralytic polio as such? I believe that it does. In analyzing the relatively long-term involvement of fourteen families in the social vicissitudes caused by this particular disruptive experience, we are perforce inquiring into such generalized matters as the perception of sudden crisis by families. . . . Although it is true that the precise manifestations of these events and problems will vary with the nature of the crisis or family situation, there are enough structural and [procedural] similarities to contribute to our knowledge of general conditions, provided that the generic properties of these various crisis are so delineated as to make comparisons possible (p. 8).

In short, the particular time, place and population are extended to cover all families experiencing crisis any time, any place. This is a generalization. Unfortunately, the social sciences have few such laws, which suggests that social scientists need to work harder to design and conduct studies that will produce general laws.

CREATIVITY, IMAGINATION, AND THE ABILITY TO WONDER

Above all else, good competent science is open to innovative ways of thinking and conducting research. This is a real problem in research because of the power of convention. Why do so many sociologists use the .05 level of confidence? The reason is that all the other sociologists do it, so it must be correct. It is strictly conventional.

There is merit to being conventional in science, for without it, we would have a chaotic and nonreplicable hodgepodge of research tools and findings. However, the danger is in becoming complacent with the conventions and thereby losing track of the creative dimension of science. Closely associated with creativity is the ability of the scientist to wonder about conventional wisdom and about anomalous empirical data. When faced with some cases that deviate from the vast majority, it is tempting to push the deviant cases aside, dismissing them as mere aberrations or exceptions. Long ago in sociological methodology, there was a technique called "deviant case analysis." Over the years, we have lost sight of this valuable tool, which plays a very important role in creating a critical mind-set in tune with wondering about things

Finally, there is sociological imagination. C. Wright Mills (1959) defined the sociological imagination. "Personal troubles," problems under the control of the individual, were distinguished from what Mills viewed as the proper domain of sociology, namely "public issues." Issues are beyond the individual's control, but they affect everyday life. Personal troubles is the domain of psychology, and public issues require the sociological imagination. Irving Jumping Eagle's personality conflict with his boss is now amenable to sociological analysis. However, the 50% unemployment rate among Native Americans is a sociological problem. Mills saw the sociological imagination as that bent of mind that transformed personal troubles into public issues. Mills viewed the sociological imagination as asking how action is patterned or recurrent in a society, how a given society is part of a larger historical context, and how people's private lives are constrained by impersonal forces beyond their control.

■ Relationship between Theory and Research Methodology

Robert Merton (1959) wrote a classic statement on the relationship between explanation and research, between theory and methodology. He discussed various ways theory and research benefit each other. It is only through theory that the researcher has any idea what to study and how to turn observations into precise classifications, that is, measurement. Just as everyday concepts define the way we conduct our everyday lives, so do scientific concepts guide research decisions. Second, theory helps the researcher avoid the trap of concocting an explanation after the facts have been gathered. This is a problem commonly seen in sociology, where huge data files are massaged until, as one colleague once said, "the data confess," that is, until the researcher comes up with a plausible explanation. This is not, in and of itself, a methodological error, for after all, theory often emerges from data that simply do not fit the existing models. However, it is infinitely preferable to have a theory, or even a rough theory, that you attempt to test. Third, Merton pointed out that theory helps to increase the productivity of research by providing generalized laws and concepts that allow the researcher to house a wide variety of observations under one explanatory roof.

On the other side of the coin, Merton showed how research helps theory. First, the unexpected or unanticipated finding (serendipity) can initiate new theory, a process that has occurred many times over in the social sciences. Sam Stouffer, Paul Lazarsfeld, and their colleagues (1949) studied the morale of U. S. soldiers during World War II and found, unexpectedly, that morale was lower in units with high promotion rates and lower in units where promotions were few and far between. The researchers conceptualized (invented a concept) an came up with "relative deprivation." Soldiers who did not get promotions felt deprived in situations where others were getting ahead, whereas not getting promoted was taken in stride when others were not getting promoted either. One feels deprived only relative to situations of good fortune of which you are not a part. This powerful theoretical idea later was applied to explain the paroxysm of violence that destroyed portions of Watts and other urban ghettos in 1968. Second, new research findings exert pressure on the scientific community to reformulate theory.

Thus, there is a symbiotic relationship between theory and research. Theory gives us the tools for judging the methodology and methodology, the tools for testing theory. These two aspects of science are absolutely interdependent.

Frank Westie (1957) wrote an excellent paper using the example of the relationship between social class and racial prejudice. He demonstrated how the researcher between social class an racial prejudice. He demonstrated how the researcher can take a bewildering array of theoretical propositions and make some coherent theoretical sense out of it through empirical research. His methodology is worth noting here: (1) list all the theoretically predicted empirical relationships, for example, "The upper class is least prejudiced"; (2) for each empirical relationship, list all the possible explanations; (3) conduct a study to see which of the predicted empirical relationships really exist; (4) cast out the supposed empirical relationships that failed to survive the empirical test, along with the interpretations attached to them; and (5) do further research in order to select the best explanations attached to the surviving empirical relationships. This is a method for developing theory from **empirical data**. You start with theory, generate many alternative explanations, conduct empirical research, reassess the theory, collect more data, reassess, and so forth. Theory and data feed each other in a cycle.

■ The Definition of the Research Problem

Scratch the surface of any genuine research and you will find a well-formulated research problem at its beginning. No problem, no research. The research problem is the starting point of all sociological research. If you botch the research problem, you are in deep trouble.

Formulating a research problem, like other methodological decisions, is something that can be done well or poorly. The odds are in favor of poorly because of the fact that stating the problem is exceedingly difficult intellectually and is fraught with dangers as a consequence. Fortunately, there are some excellent methodological warnings and advice that have evolved over years through the trials and errors of sociologists. A quick look at the warnings and advice is in order.

REJECT TRIVIA

A research problem is trivial when: (1) the subject matter of the research is trite or uninteresting sociologically, for example, "Should men's pajamas have buttons or not on the fly?"; or (2) there is a lack of depth of inquiry of the research problem. The latter is the more important danger of the two. If you want to be trivial, you should ask the research question in such a way that you do not seek to explain *why* something occurs. You might settle for describing the origins of the consumer movement in health, for example, but you would not go after why that consumer movement exists in the first place. In my own research on the rural elderly, the research problem went well beyond stating the significance of social isolation in predicting mortality. Sure, I found that social isolation was a strong predictor of death, but the research problem would be poor methodologically if it stated, "What is the predictive power of social isolation for mortality?" Here the problem does not take us anywhere sociologically, and hence, it is trivial. It would not be trivial to ask, "What is the role that social isolation plays in mortality and *why* does isolation affect mortality in that way?" Here, we are interested in trying to puzzle out the cause of mortality, rather than describing it or even predicting it per se. Thus, a well-formulated research problem ought to contain some element of *why*, which is the researcher's way of serving notice to the scientific community that he or she is going to interpret or explain some data pertaining to a problem.

SIMPLE SENTENCES

Start the definition of the research problem with a simple question or declarative sentence. Either will do fine. For example, my puzzlement about why some elderly individuals lived many years and other died relatively early in their retirement led to the research question, "What are the sociological factors associated with longevity among the independently living rural elderly of Missouri?" Or, I could have stated, "The purpose of this proposed study is to determine the factors associated with longevity among the independently living rural elderly of Missouri." Notice that these two statements: (1) are complete sentences; (2) are simple sentences; (3) contain the dependent variable or the focus of the problem, longevity; (4) state limits on the research population, in this case, the rural elderly living on their own in Missouri; and (5) are relatively general statements.

SUBPROBLEMS

Once the first sentence is out of the way, the task is to clarify and specify the research problem. Now you will need to write some simple sentences that break the general problem statement down into its components or subproblems. This is getting down to the specifics of what you intend to investigate. In the case of the rural elderly study, you might start the second sentence of the problem definition with, "More specifically" or "Specifically." The second sentence might read, "Specifically, the purpose of this study is to monitor and explain the effects of social cohesion on longevity, comparing men and women over time." At this point, you will introduce the main independent variable (the "cause" in cause-effect thinking) if your research problem is advanced enough to draw on a theoretical model. Remember, it is legitimate to have an exploratory research problem in which the purpose is to develop the problem theoretically, in which case you might not have subproblem statements with independent variables. Also, in qualitative sociology, the goal may be to interpret observable reality, in which case the research problem would probably emerge over the course of the observations and interpretations. Nevertheless, the vast majority of empirical research in sociology follows the above approach with a problem statement and subproblem formulation at the beginning of the research.

It is a good idea to clarify the subproblem statement as much as possible. In the above example, the statement might read: "Does the absence of social cohesion pose a risk of increased mortality for the elderly? What are the effects of changes in social cohesion associated with the aging process on longevity? Do men and women differ significantly in the quality of social cohesion and in the changes in cohesion that occur during the aging process?" Notice here that we are pushing for answers as to why longevity varies between men and women in addition to trying to understand more generally the role that social cohesion plays in how long rural elderly individuals live. You can make a list of the key variables that we think explain longevity, the dependent variable.

VALUES

The research problem should be stated in an objective fashion. By doing this, the researcher meets the criteria of science, which calls for objectivity, some form of replicable measurement, and public verification. This does not mean that the researcher is value neutral or that his or her values do not enter into the research problem. The very fact that I chose the rural elderly to study was predicated on my values as a scientist and citizen. Values are always present in sociological research. However, one must not allow those values to enter into the actual formulation of the research problem.

For example, a value-loaded way of asking a research question might be: "Why college athletes should be allowed to choose freely whether they will be tested for drug use." Or "Why the president's war on drugs is doomed to fail." The first problem statement is a normative or value statement that begs the question of mandatory drug testing of college athletes. The use of the word *should* is a dead giveaway. Words such as *would*, *should*, *ought*, *must*, and so on have no place in a statement of a sociologically valid research problem. The first example tells the reader that the researcher values freedom of choice and that the research most probably will be set up to prove the point. The second example tells the reader that the researcher's mind is made up, that what will follow will be a series of unbalanced arguments and possibly data to support the researcher's personal values. In both cases, the warning flags are flying, and methodologically astute researchers will avoid paying any attention to such research problems.

KEEP IT SOCIOLOGICAL

The sociological imagination is very difficult to acquire, but it is a surefire means for ensuring that the research problem is sociological and thereby amenable to sociological theory and methodology. Time and time again, I have had to reject students' research problem statements because they focused on individual issues and explanations, rather than on group-level problems. Seeking to explain why immigrants value education above wealth is a sociological problem. Trying to explain why one immigrant does this is not a problem for sociology. Social structures such as class, status, and power; institutional relationships such as education or religion, sex roles, social movements, professions, all are examples of the appropriate sociological focus of research problems. Individuals' personality, motives, and attitudes are perfectly appropriate subjects for psychology but not for sociology.

■ *Conclusions*

This chapter is abstract and difficult out of necessity. The world of sociological research has a complex philosophical core that the researcher must heed. Methodology is the science and art of evaluating the worthiness of the research problem and the research design decisions. Unless one is grounded in the philosophical principles behind decisions, it is impossible to measure anything in the social world.

The image of the dispassionate value-neutral social scientist working within perfectly objective rules of scientific procedure is challenged in this chapter. What the scientist accepts as knowledge, what he or she admits as fact, depends on the scientist's philosophy of knowledge (epistemology), also called "domain assumptions." Some sociologists think that facts exist independent from the scientist. All the scientist does is discover this objective reality. Others think that social reality is constructed by the theories of sociologists. In this fashion, the scientist creates fact, rather than discovers it.

The implications for methodology and research are far-reaching. The objective fact scientists (positivists) probably will gravitate toward large-scale survey research designs with fixed-choice items. The scientists who believe in socially constructed reality (phenomenologists[3]) more likely will use observation participant-observation designs with open-ended measuring techniques. Furthermore, the subject matter of science, both physical and social, throws the occasional curve ball that the prevailing theory is unable to handle. Scientists who fail to recognize the fact that they are human beings with philosophies and values that affect their scientific work may hold on to their theories at all costs and end up striking out. Others who recognize the philosophical core of their work stand a better chance of benefiting from anomalous findings through advances in theory and methodology. As Karl Popper pointed out, you never achieve objective proof of a finding, because Mother Nature reserves the potential for throwing a curve that does not fit the established pattern of findings. You never can be sure that you have measured all relevant variables and observed all relevant cases.

The reader might be tempted to conclude that sociological science, or any science for that matter, is not possible. Applying the same philosophical reasoning to this point, one might conclude that no one has shown this to be true, nor would cases where science was shown to be impossible necessarily deter one from trying to do science. There are core characteristics of science that we should adhere to, such as being aware of our philosophical assumptions, documenting our procedures, and so forth.

Finally, the interplay between theory and methodology was elaborated in order to stress the point that intellectual discovery and growth occurs partly as a result of theory and in part to research. One cannot exist without the other.

GLOSSARY

behaviorism   a form of positivism in which observable behavior, not emotions, attitudes, cognition, and other mental phenomena, was considered the only scientifically legitimate subject matter of psychology.

concept   an abstract idea used to categorize phenomenon; the building block of explanation.

deduction   a form of explanation in which the conclusion follows logically from a law and the premises connecting the phenomenon being explained with the law; going from the general law to the specific phenomenon.

---

[3]For more on this, see Holzner, Burkart. *Reality Construction in Society*; Cambridge, Mass: Schenkman Publishing Co. 1968.

domain assumptions   the values, beliefs, and philosophy of knowledge (episte-mology) of the researcher.

empirical data   information that has been observed or measured and that is capable of being verified by others.

explanation   the reason given for an occurrence of the research problem and past research findings, usually forming a theory.

generalization   the process of deriving a principle or law that applies to a phenomenon from specific instances of that phenomenon.

induction   a form of explanation in which the conclusion is not logically necessary but is based on observations; going from the specific phenomenon to general law.

logical positivism   a school of thought comprising a branch of methodology whose adherents argue that scientific knowledge must be obtained using the techniques of physical science, especially measurement and general laws.

methodology   the science of how to make research decisions and the tools for evaluating these decisions.

objectivity   the ideal state of research when the researcher recognizes his or her biases and values and does not allow them to influence research decisions.

paradigm   similar to domain assumption, involving the values, epistemology, favorite theories, and exemplars or tested explanations of a group of scientists.

principle of verifiability   from logical positivism stating that a concept must be measured (verified) in order to be of value to science.

research problem   a question raised about some aspect of reality. The problem is the dependent variable, the variation of which you are trying to explain.

scientific observation   any act of measuring the real world using the principles and tools of science, including the physical senses of the observer.

theory   an explanation of a research problem made up of concepts linked in logical relationships by propositions and laws. A theory is "grand" or very abstract if few of the concepts are actually measured. A theory is "middle range" if several of the concepts are measured.

verstehen   a German word used by Max Weber to describe the goal of sociological research and theory, which is to understand social meaning and motives.

FOR FURTHER READING

Campell, Norman. (1952). *What is science?* London: Dover.

Hoover, Kenneth R. (1988). *The elements of social scientific thinking* (4th ed.). New York: St. Martin's Press.

Kaplan, Abraham. (1964). *The conduct of inquiry: Methodology for behavioral science*. San Francisco: Chandler.

Phillips, D.C. (1987). *Philosophy, science and social inquiry: Comtemporary methodological controversies in social science and related applied fields of research*. New York: Pergamon Press.

Weber, Max. (1949). *The methodology of the social sciences*. (Edward A. Shils and Henry A. Finch. Trans. and Eds.) New York: Free Press.

Zetterberg, Hans L. (1965). *On theory and verification in sociology* (3rd enlarged). New Jersey: Bedminister Press.

Chapter Two

RESEARCH ETHICS

■ *This chapter begins with a study of the Institutional Review Board, an institution designed to protect the safety of human research subjects. This study provides a lead-in to ethical theory. The chapter concludes with applications of ethical theory to some notoriously unethical sociological studies. The goal is to expose students to a double bind ethical problem common to sociological research, force them to think things through with appropriate ethical principles, then to apply this knowledge to major sociological studies presented throughout the text.*

Ethics is a branch of philosophy that applies principles in order to decide whether human conduct is good or bad, harmful or beneficial. Applied to sociological inquiry, **research ethics** helps one decide which research roles are appropriate and which ones are not.

Sociology is a diverse profession with many conflicting views of appropriate research roles and behavior. This diversity has resulted in some members of the profession doing research and writing reports that other members find morally offensive. Each of the social sciences has a code of ethics that the members of the professions are bound to follow. The American Sociological Association code is reproduced in Appendix A. Ethical principles underlie these codes, principles that govern not only research and teaching by professionals but also have great importance for everyday life.

This chapter starts with an analysis of a study of the Institutional Review Board (IRB), the main organization that decides whether or not sociological research is ethical. I decided to start with this real world example rather than with a more abstract discussion of ethical principles because the example contains many ethical principles and dilemmas. Next, three basic ethical theories that form the basis for the principles are discussed. The chapter concludes with the application of the ethical principles to some notorious social science research.

■ *IRBs and Clandestine Research: A Study*

In 1974, the National Research Act (Public Law 93-348) was passed. This law created the National Commission for the Protection of Human Subjects of Biomedical and Behavioral Research. The work of this commission led the U.S. Department of Health Education and Welfare to establish regulations for IRBs. IRBs were authorized to review all proposed research where there was any hint of harm to the subjects. Again in 1980, new IRB regulations were established by the department, newly reorganized as the Department of Health and Human Services (HHS). The new rules allowed an IRB to exempt social science research from compliance with the IRB process only if no potential harm to the subjects could be found or established. Also, if the research was conducted from an institution that did not receive federal HHS funds, then IRB scrutiny was not necessary. So the main criteria for acceptance or rejection of a study by an IRB was nothing more or less than the potential risk to the subjects.

Thus, all institutions receiving federal money, especially research institutions such as universities and medical schools, were required to establish an IRB process. Typically, this involved a board made up of members of the faculty, in the case of the university with a director and regularly scheduled meeting times. Boards range in size from seven to fifteen members, and quite typically, there will be a dozen of more proposals to review in the course of any given month. Most of the IRB members are experienced researchers who have methodological expertise. If the university has a biological or medical sciences division, then it will have two IRBs, one for the medical sciences and one for arts and sciences.

With this background in mind, John Galliher, a professor of the faculty of the University of Missouri-Columbia, engaged in a debate in the sociological literature about the American Sociological Association code of ethics (1973), particularly concerning the protection of human subjects. Galliher argued that protection in the form of confidentiality did not extend to actors who are involved in government, business, or other organizations in ways accountable to the public. Extending this concept of the public figure to public agencies, John Galliher and Richard Hessler (1983) decided to study the extent to which IRBs conformed to their mandate to protect human subjects and to test the extent to which **clandestine research**, that is research which by its very nature must remain hidden to the subjects, was possible under the IRB mandate.

INFORMED CONSENT

We were aware of several classic studies in sociology. that would never have been completed if an IRB, nonexistent at the time, would have insisted upon informed consent. La Piere's (1934) observational study of hotel and restaurant owners' and workers' reactions to racially mixed customers (Richard La Piere and his research assistants) or Laud Humphreys' (1970)[1] observational study of homosexuality in the public restroom would never have gotten off the ground. If the researchers had to get the subjects to read and sign a consent form describing the substance of the study and all the potential risks involved, the studies would either have been incredibly biased or the subjects would have refused to participate. In either case, the IRB requirement to obtain informed consent would have rendered the research worthless. Other studies in similar circumstances are Tittle and Rowe's (1973) study of cheating by students while grading their own tests, the Schwartz and Skolnick (1962) study of employment agency discrimination against pseudoapplicants with bogus criminal records, and the Chambliss (1978) study of organized crime in Seattle using participant observation and informants. All would have failed if they had been required to get informed consent forms signed.

According to federal regulations, informed consent means that the researcher must get the respondent to sign a form that provides a written explanation of the purpose of the study, a description of the **risks**[2] and benefits to the subject, an offer to answer any question that the respondent might have concerning the methods of procedure, purpose, and so on, and a caveat that the respondent is free to refuse to participate in the study by withdrawing consent at any time. Thus, informed consent is predicated on the principle of providing the respondent with the opportunity to freely choose to participate with full knowledge and with the absence of pressure tactics of any kind. Regarding pressure tactics, I am reminded of the birth of one of my daughters in 1973 at a major university teaching hospital. The physician in charge was conducting research on digestion in infants and asked my wife and I if our daughter could be in his study. The procedure involved ingesting supposedly safe levels of radioactive isotopes and then having Xrays taken of the digestive tract. He offered a years' supply of infant formula free of charge as a reward. Of course, we refused, but this was done without any description of the risks because this occurred prior to informed consent and IRBs. I thought at the time how difficult it would have been then, and perhaps even now, for a low-income mother and father to refuse the doctor. It is likely that the parents would not know what the risks were, but even if they knew, the fact that they had received free medical care for the birth of the child because of their income status plus the doctor's offer of free infant formula for the entire year following the birth would make it very difficult to turn down the offer. In short, the reality of poverty, the power of the doctor, the knowledge gap, and the obligation incurred as a result of charity medicine essentially create a form of coercion and a restraint against free choice.

---

[1]Laud Humphreys observed gay sex in public restrooms. He acted as a watchdog, warning the gay participants if the police showed up. Humphreys recorded license plate numbers and tracked the gay men to their homes where, under a false pretext, he obtained background information about them.

[2]Risk is calculated by figuring in the *odds* that *x* will occur and the *consequences* of its occurrence.

Informed consent was developed in response to the dangers posed by this type of biomedical research. Most notably, it was a result of the Tuskeegee syphilis experiment in which men with syphilis were not told that they had the disease and were left untreated until they died from it in order to study the entire course of the disease. The risks in biomedical research and the ability of subjects to understand them are qualitatively different than that found in social scientific research. Murray Wax (1977) an Joan Cassell (1978) have pointed out that because the federal regulations were developed in response to the dangers posed by biomedical research, informed consent may not be appropriate or necessary for the social sciences, especially in studies where the researcher has very little, if any, control over the research setting. It may be inappropriate to ask a researcher to get informed consent forms signed when he or she has nothing to do with the risks or benefits to the subjects because there is no researcher control over the research setting. Laud Humphreys had no control over the public restrooms he observed in; hence, he was not responsible for any risks to the subjects caused by their sexual activity. The doctor with his offer of infant formula is not the same as Laud Humphreys watching and recording activities beyond his control. However, it is Laud Humphreys's responsibility to make sure that the confidentiality of the subjects is not violated or that the knowledge gained through his observations is not used to harm the subjects. More will be said about confidentiality later in this chapter.

Cassell and Wax (1980) edited a superb special issue of *Social Problems* in which the ethical problems and principles associated with field research were discussed. They pointed out that the utilitarian basis for informed consent, namely the benefit/risk ratio, is problematic for the social sciences because the potential harms and benefits in the biomedical sciences are qualitatively different in the social sciences. Benefits and risks are usually physical in biomedical research, but they may be economic, social, or psychological in social science research, and they might stem from the application of the knowledge gained either by the subjects, the researcher, or the larger society. In a very real sense, knowledge is power and can be used to help or to harm.

THE STUDY

Galliher (1980) has taken the position that the rights of advantaged or powerful individuals to be informed about research ethically can be violated if by doing so the research benefits the disadvantaged or powerless. For Galliher, the principle of informed consent may be valid for research involving the poor, or "studying down" from the researcher's social status, but not for studying the rich, or "studying up." In order to extend this principle, Galliher and I reached into the world of IRBs with a proposal designed to test the mandate of IRBs concerning informed consent.

A research proposal was written with the specific aim of studying IRB reaction to a study that invariably placed subjects at risk. We were not serious about the written proposal in the sense that we were not actually planning to carry out the proposed research. In short, the written proposal sent to the IRB was bogus. Our true intention, which was to study the IRB, was kept hidden from the IRB until the data gathering was complete. Seven colleagues, senior faculty members at major universities across the United States and Canada, were invited to participate by sending the proposal through their university IRBs. Only two colleagues agreed to participate. The reasons given by those who declined ranged from fear to unease about the fact that we would be deceiving the IRBs.

The proposed research that the IRB reviewed was a study of discriminatory practices within public and private firms. The proposal sent to the IRB involved a study in which a white female, a white male, and a black male, all confederates (part of the study), would respond to seventy-five firms that had advertised jobs for unskilled workers. All three confederates would contact each firm in a randomized order of appearance. By design, some of the firms would have government contracts. The resumes of the three confederates would be identical except for a portion of the job interviews where they would be randomly assigned either a record of criminal conviction or of hospitalization for mental illness. We planed to test the extent to which sexism, racism, and discrimination against ex-convicts and ex-mental patients existed in the firms. The hook was that the proposal guaranteed to make public the names of the firms and the outcomes associated with those firms. Unlike in other research, we planned to describe the identity of the subjects, in this case, the firms.

There were other studies of employment discrimination that we cited, but none of them proposed or actually made public the identities of the agencies involved. Clearly, we were in uncharted water. Even more clear was the fact that observational research was the only effective approach to our particular research problem and that the study could not be done if informed consent was imposed by the IRB with the identity of the confederates and the purpose of the study being made known to the subjects. Finally, if discrimination was found, the possible violation of civil rights laws as well as the inherent immorality of the discriminatory behavior made it difficult, from the risk/benefit model, for the IRB reviewers to reject the plan to divulge names. We were prepared to argue that we as researchers were protected by the First Amendment to the U.S. Constitution and that we were obligated, from a risk/benefit model, to turn in unethical and illegal practices against the public good. No external funding was sought, and we proposed to get underway immediately pending IRB approval, conditions that necessitated quick and decisive IRB action. The board could not approve the proposal with the hope that it would not be funded and hence would not be carried out.

FINDINGS

One midwestern state university IRB reviewed the proposal and, on March 21, 1980, rejected it. The letter of disapproval read, in part:

> The committee believes there are risks for the firms to be included and possibly for the employes and the University. In light of these risks, the committee is not convinced that the potential benefits of the project merit approval. Some committee members expressed concern that the focus of the project appears to be law enforcement rather

than research. Others suggested that review by University legal counsel would be helpful in order to clarify any risks to the University itself.

It was immediately apparent to us that the IRB had overstepped its bounds and had moved well beyond its federal mandate to protect human subjects. Now it appeared that the university had become a research subject at risk along with firms that might have broken the law. Also, the IRB committee ruled that our proposal was law enforcement rather than research. This, too, is an extension of its mandate, which is to determine risk, not scholarship.

A colleague at a southeastern state university also submitted the proposal. That IRB rejected it, too, and the letter from the committee chair stated the following reasons for the rejection:

1. the apparent lack of measures to protect personnel department people from being "sacrificed" when the findings are released (i.e., become "news");[3]

2. and to protect confederates against lawsuits instituted by the firms studied.

The committee members also questioned scholarship in terms of their concern that the confederates would not receive adequate instruction as to how to behave and therefore there was the possibility that they might behave abrasively or condescendingly.

REACTIONS OF PROFESSIONAL ASSOCIATIONS

Once the rejections were in hand, we turned to three major professional organizations that serve the social sciences: the American Association of University Professors (AAUP), the Society for the Study of Social Problems (SSSP), and the American Sociological Association (ASA). We were trying to determine what type of support, if any, we could expect from our professional associations.

AAUP

The AAUP washed its hands of the matter and stated in a letter: "The committee appears to have exercised its authority consistent with its own guidelines, and those guidelines occasion no concern under this Association's principles."

SSSP

The chair of the SSSP committee on Standards and Freedom of Research, Publications, and Teaching responded: "The university would be a party to deception, since the proposal indicates publicizing the names of employers found to discrim-

---

[3]The research subjects' interests were taken to heart here.

inate. It was the consensus of the committee that no assistance was possible under these circumstances." The chair of the committee requested further information about the IRB's response. Upon receipt of that, the chair commented that the issue of deception could be overcome if the subjects were debriefed after the employment interviews. This procedure is done all the time in experimental research that requires naive subjects. Under the condition of informing the subjects once the research ends, the chair felt that the IRB could not forbid the study on the grounds of deception alone.

One member of the committee compared our proposed research to Laud Humphreys's (1970) public restroom ("tearooms") study:

> Suppose that Laud made public the names of individuals who frequented the tearooms? Certainly these people were involved in illegal acts (as are the employers who discriminate). Wouldn't your research set a precedent that would justify "blowing the whistle" on any illegal "actor," whether that actor was an organization or an individual, powerful or powerless?

To this last commentary, Galliher and Hessler wrote:

> The most interesting feature of the last commentary is that it places all law violators and all law violation on the same moral plane. Yet, numerous survey have shown that respondents make fine distinctions in the perceived seriousness of various law violations. Presumably, such distinctions would determine whether "blowing the whistle" is seen as necessary. Equating systematic employment discrimination with fellatio may denigrate the importance of the former. There is a special irony that an association that was originally founded to support the study and alleviation of human misery would fail to endorse the right to locate and publicize the sources of this misery (1983).

The ASA was no help, either, choosing to avoid formal action on the matter.

INTERVIEWS WITH IRB MEMBERS

Focused interviews were completed with five of the fourteen members of the midwestern university IRB. We obtained permission from each respondent to quote them. A biologist explained the rejection as follows:

> The whole committee took a very negative attitude because your proposal has a regulatory mood. In fact, one of its stated purposes is the opposite of confidentiality. The fact that it is not the role of a university to act as a regulator was unanimous in the committee, but rather the role is scientific research.
>
> A couple of committee members were concerned that using only three confederates could not control for personality variables which could confound the results. Also, the committee worried about legalities. The Occupational Safety and Health Administration is no longer allowed to make unannounced inspections. And there is the legal issue by using x hours of their time without their knowing it. And if a company is in trouble, they know who did the employment interviewing and might punish them. Our purpose is to protect the university, investigators, and subjects.
>
> Your proposal might be accepted if no company is identified. Or you could select industries that are numerous in the state so they couldn't be identified. Also you could debrief people afterwards and tell them what research they were in.

Thus, the committee defined the proposed research as law enforcement, which the members felt was outside the realm of legitimate university research. If we had argued that lots of sociological studies would not have been possible given this view, for example, Laud Humphreys' research, the IRB members would have come back at us with the point that we were proposing to do bad science with too few confederates to enable us to generalize or to have confidence in the findings. Legal risk to the university was raised as well, indicating to us that the IRB had exceeded its mandate.

The IRB chair had his own view of the reasoning behind the rejection:

> Generally in each science we have a good deal of guidance from the committee member in the discipline where the proposal comes from. We have to go to them for guidance. And we would have to reject something not just if it represents a physical or biological risk but if it is a humanistic invasion such as the case of contacting people who have recently had a death in their family. Deception at times could be permitted with an adequate debriefing. Our purpose is to identify risk but since we are researchers we have a tendency to stray and comment on the experimental design.

The concept "humanistic invasion" was employed here as grounds for rejecting a hypothetical proposed to contact bereaved individuals. Certainly bereavement has become a vital and important research line in medical sociology, hardly the stuff that an invasion would seem to be made of.

The issue of risk to the university was stated most succinctly by the associate dean of the graduate school and an ex officio member of the IRB. In his words:

> The committee was in agreement that your proposal placed individuals at risk— information was gathered and then shared with those that might take legal actions against companies and individuals in the companies. Also there was a possibility that the university as a legal entity was placed at risk by this project. The legal risk to the university got a lot of discussion.
>
> If the Human Subjects Committee (IRB) asks who is at risk and if the answer is, people being interviewed, then it is clearly an appropriate role for the committee to intervene. But if the answer is that the university is at risk for it might be sued, this is a new wrinkle and raises the issue of academic freedom and freedom of speech.
>
> If the resources of the university are used to see if laws are being violated, which law enforcement agencies could use in getting enforcement—is that appropriate use of the university resources? This is not easy to answer. The question is, if the primary purpose of the research is law enforcement, can the university legally support it? But you could argue that law enforcement is merely a fallout of the study, not its primary purpose.
>
> My feeling is that if you want to distribute information that could be used in law enforcement, then your results should be more carefully and fully developed. My own concern was that your sample size was not sufficient to draw statistically significant and scientifically sound conclusions. There were risks that the university might be sued, but on the benefits side I had the feeling that the study was flawed. Yet, as an economist, I feel it is absurd to say that risks can be as easily measured as can benefits. Risks and benefits are worlds apart in kind. So the group of people on the committee must simply make a value judgment.

The lessons learned from this study were: (1) IRBs may extend their federal mandate to include institutions as well as subjects in the calculation of risk or harm from the research; (2) the ethical principles underlying IRB actions are unclear and poorly formulated, resulting in convoluted reasoning by IRB members; (3) IRBs do in fact function as barriers to reform-minded researchers whose research must use deception in order to obtain valid and reliable observations.

In the next section, we will discuss ethical principles that should help resolve the research dilemmas posed by the IRB study, issues such as the researcher's right to know, the subject's right to informed consent and confidentiality, and the paternalism of IRB review.

■ *Ethics: The Harm Principle*

John Stuart Mill (*On Liberty*) developed the harm principle, which is an ethical principle of relevance here. Mill followed the philosophy of **utilitarianism**, which is to say that he used the criterion of usefulness to society as the basis for deciding whether some action was good or bad. But in the pursuit of such useful actions, Mill was not about to allow society or some agent of society to step in and tell an individual what to do about producing socially useful behaviors. Mill valued individual free choice and **functional autonomy**, and he designed his ethics to protect that freedom. However, when some action harmed the society, Mill accepted paternalistic[4] intervention to stop it. In his own words:

> The sole end for which mankind are warranted individually or collectively in interfering with the liberty of action of any of their number is self-protection. That the only purpose for which power can be rightfully exercised over any member of a civilized community, against his will, is to prevent harm to others (*On Liberty*, p. 9).

Mill was convinced that the individual knows his or her best interests and goals better than anyone else might know them. This is an important point, because knowing the best interests of individuals, according to Mill's harm principle, is absolutely necessary prior to establishing whether or not some act is harmful to those individuals. In other words, before one can decide that an act harms someone, one must know the best interests of the individual and must decide that the action impedes or harms those interests.

Furthermore, Mill argued that the whole purpose of the harm principle is to protect free choice and functional autonomy. Again, this principle assumes that individuals have full knowledge about their best interests. If individuals are denied access to that knowledge, for example, then this situation is one that harms the larger group or society, and paternalistic action is justified.

Returning to our proposal to conduct clandestine research, the harm principle offers guidance. First, the IRB members presumed to know what were the best interests of all parties concerned—the researchers, the subjects, even the university. But assuming that the individuals are rational and knowledgeable, they will

---

[4]Action taken against the wills of individuals or action taken in the absence of the individuals' knowledge.

know their best interests better than the IRB members. Second, in order to establish the fact that harm is about to befall one or more of the actors involved, one must know not only the interests but also that the interests are compromised. Third, if research findings might shed light on situations in which individual freedom is compromised because information is systematically hidden from those individuals, then that research activity would reduce harm to the larger society.

Discrimination is clandestine, and those who are discriminated against usually remain ignorant of this fact, thereby rendering them less free to make choices and therefore more likely to continue to suffer harm. In this situation, it is right and good to act paternalistically, which, in the case of our proposed research, involved conducting the study without informing the subjects that they were under investigation. The subjects are perfectly free to stop discriminating since they have full knowledge of their actions. On the other side of the coin, the people who are being discriminated against are probably not aware of it or, if they are, they may not know what to do about it. The researchers certainly know what they are doing and are acting as free, knowledgeable, and autonomous individuals. Likewise for the university, which represents the collective interests of its faculty and administration. In this sense, the basic right to be a free and autonomous individual is contingent upon knowledge. Without it, one is a slave to those with it.

In the case we discussed, the only people without adequate knowledge to be free and autonomous are the victims of the discrimination, a category that probably includes the whole society, which is harmed by this illegal activity. Thus, under the harm principle, the IRB's action would be unethical. It allowed the conditions that were producing harm to continue to exist, thereby creating harm, rather than protecting against it. **Paternalism** is the fatal flaw, for it is virtually impossible for an IRB or any detached institutional group to assess and to know the best interests of subjects and researchers.

■ Exchange Ethics

Exchange methodology may provide us with an alternative to paternalistic ethics. It may be a way out of the box posed by the harm principle and informed consent. The reader should be warned that I have a value position on this matter. In Chapter 1, I warned you about the need to control your values by preventing your values from influencing your methodological decisions. And yet here I am presenting exchange methodology, which is value driven. Control was exercised, but research decisions were affected, for example, censorship, by the values. I suppose the best we can do in an imperfect research world is to strive for perfection and recognize our successes and our failures.

Several years ago, in response to our dissatisfaction with paternalism and the view that the scientist knows best what knowledge is needed, we designed a process whereby the potential subjects or beneficiaries of the research would join the researcher as full-fledged colleagues (Hessler and New, 1972). We developed a methodology that combined a critical view of existing power relationships along with advocacy research in which a solid egalitarian relationship is built between the researcher and the individuals studied. Exchange methodology was the label we gave to this method, because it is based on the gift relationship in which there is both giving and receiving, rights and obligations for all participants in the interaction. For example, if I give you a gift, you are obligated to reciprocate. If you return the favor, your response reinforces my act and makes it likely that the relationship, should it continue, will be one of giving and receiving for the individuals involved. Unlike power relationships, where one party tells the other to do something and the other party complies whether they want to or not, exchange relationships exist because both parties want them to exist and people do things for each other out of a mutual sense of duty.

Exchange methodology gives subjects that same power as the researchers in terms of making decisions about the research. This covers all the research decisions, from the definition of the problem through what to analyze and how to disseminate the findings. J. Thomas May (1979) has made an excellent distinction between exchange as covenant and exchange as contract. As he points out the two processes are first cousins but inherently different. In his words:

> Contracts involve buying and selling; covenants involve giving and receiving. Contracts are external; covenants are internal to the parties involved. Contracts are signed to be expediently discharged; covenants have a gratuitous growing edge to them that nourishes rather than limits relationship. Contracts can be filed away, but a covenant becomes part of one's history and shapes in unexpected ways one's self-perception and perhaps even destiny. . . . The duties of fieldworkers to their host populations—duties to respect confidences, to communicate to them the aims of the research, to protect anonymity, to safeguard rights, interests and sensitivities, to give fair return for services rendered, to anticipate the consequences of publication, to share the results of research with affected parties, and to be sensitive to the diversity of values and interests of those studied—all these duties rest on a deeper footing than contract, on a lower pedestal than philanthropy, and on a more concrete foundation than Kant's universal principle of respect.

Thus, exchange methodology can be thought of as an ethic of covenant. It allows the researcher to learn firsthand what the best interests of the subjects might be, although one always runs the risk of having participants in the exchange group who do not represent the larger world of research subjects. Nevertheless, the exchange means that representatives of the subjects design the study, along with the researcher, which gives them in-depth knowledge about the research. Assuming that the representatives reflect the best interests of the research subjects, no harm should come of the research. Also, with a stake in the study and by dint of the representatives' approval, the researcher can be reasonably confident that the study will be of some benefit to the subjects. The principle of free choice and functional autonomy among researchers and subjects is upheld by this approach. In Boston's Chinatown, we formed a research committee consisting of community residents, my research assistant, and me. Research design was done by the committee members, and all research decisions were discussed and decided by the members. In short, the local residents had the power to control the study, including censorship over any written documents on the study produced by the researchers.

Advocacy research means that the researcher strives to do research that will improve the conditions or meet the best interests of the subjects. In the case of exchange methodology, we adopted the goal of the Boston Chinatown community to have a more accessible and culturally empathetic health care system. All of our research efforts were geared to accomplish that goal.

Advocacy researchers are in the business of gaining the best scientific knowledge possible and then applying it to improve society. This is not as simple as it appears because communities are very complex, with lots of factions and competing values and goals. Improving the quality of life in one quarter usually is accomplished at some cost to another quarter. The researcher can only trust that the exchange approach puts him or her into adequate touch with the subjects so that the least harm is done along with the greatest good possible. Some harm is inevitable, however, given the complexity of the social world, but the altruistic nature of exchange methodology should minimize the harm.

It is very tempting to give up on scientific objectivity by grinding an ax for the subjects. But in order to remain consistent with the ethical principles of least harm and exchange, in addition to the commitment any good scientist makes to seek the truth, this must not happen.

Again, we must return to the all-important principle of autonomy borne out of knowledge. The community is better off knowing nothing than to think it knows something true that is in fact false. Of course, it is best off with knowledge gained from accurate and valid results derived from intellectually honest research. Indeed, as we have discussed in Chapter 1, objectivity does not mean value-free research. We know that value-free research is impossible and in fact applaud exchange methodology as an excellent means to integrate the subjects' and researchers' values into the acts of defining the research problem and setting the policy goals. But those same values that guide the formulation of the problem and the policy goals must not affect the other stages of research. The researcher absolutely must control his or her values in the course of designing the study, interpreting the data, and drawing conclusions. If you allow your values to intervene explicitly, you run the risk of being discredited as a scientist.

■ The Right to Know

Sociology and all the sciences exist in part because society values knowledge for its own sake. If knowledge were valued only for its social utility, then much of what has been accomplished in scientific research would not have been supported and hence would not have occurred. The bottom line is that society supports research because it values knowledge as an end in and of itself. It may seem strange to be arguing this point in light of all the pressure on researchers today to come up with solutions to the problems that plague humankind, but it is true.

◼ *Project Camelot: A Case of Social Science Gone Bad*

We have a right to know for the sake of knowing, but this right is not absolute. Rights can be assigned priority rankings, some being more important than others. The right to free choice, to personal autonomy, and to protection from harm clearly take priority over the right to know.

Project Camelot is a case in point. Camelot was a study sponsored by the Central Intelligence Agency (CIA). It had a sound sociological foundation in that it was a massive survey conducted by sociologists at several major U.S. research universities and designed to test the self-fulfilling prophecy theory of W. I. Thomas. The research targets were peasant communities throughout Latin America. The core of the survey consisted of a series of future events. These futures were presented to peasants who were asked to rank them in terms of how likely they thought the futures were and how desirable they were. The researchers claimed that Thomas's anticipation theory was the reason behind gathering the data. They promised peasants that their answers to the questions would be kept strictly confidential in the sense that the identities of the villages and even countries would be kept secret. The fact that the CIA funded the research also was kept secret. The researchers used their university affiliations to identify sponsorship that involved several major prestigious U.S. universities. Unfortunately, what the researchers were up to was not at all what was presented to the public. They were out to define or locate hot beds of revolutionary potential in the villages by identifying groups of peasants who identified futures as very likely and very undesirable. The researchers were prepared to turn over to the CIA the names of the villages and the peasants. This was cut short when an anthropologist from the University of Pittsburgh inadvertently spilled the beans to a university official in South America. The projected was unmasked.

Project Camelot represented a low point in social science research ethics (Horowitz, 1965). Clearly, the clandestine nature of the research was necessary in order to complete the research. But the autonomy of the subjects was severely threatened by the proposed disclosure of their attitudes concerning their future status. Confidentially was essential for the safety and freedom of the subjects. I am certain that if the Camelot researchers had utilized the exchange methodology, the subjects would have made the point perfectly clear.

It seems to me that the exchange methodology solves or at least addresses some of the ethical issues that we have discussed. It can be considered an ethical principle because it ensures that the subjects remain autonomous, knowledgeable, and, within the bounds of good science, free to choose any direction they believe necessary to meet the needs of the community. If the community representatives are on the ball, any harm caused by the research should be more than offset by the knowledge gained. In the case of Boston's Chinatown, the community health survey that was completed in six months produced widespread interest within the greater Boston medical community to do something about the serious health problems and socioeconomic barriers to medical care experienced by the Chinatown residents. Maternal and child health screening, cancer detection, and immunization programs were launched rather quickly after the findings were made public.

Exchange ethics comes at a price for the researcher. There may be data that the researcher desperately wants to have but that the community representatives are not interested in obtaining. It happened to me with the Chinatown study. I wanted to know about the intergenerational relationships because I had learned from my research assistant, a Chinatown resident, that the young people were fighting with the elders over Western influences. The community representatives told me that they did not want the outside world knowing about this, mainly because the community was dependent on tourism. The restaurant business was viewed by the residents as the economic life blood of the community and any adverse publicity that might have reduced the tourist trade was just not worth it, even though the researcher made a compelling sociological argument for including intergenerational conflict. Also, there was the possibility that the community residents would censor the written word. Fortunately, we had worked out our differences and had reached mutual understanding well before any data were published. Nevertheless, the threat of censorship was real, and many of our colleagues told us after the study was complete and the publications out that they would not have worked under the exchange conditions we negotiated.

Censorship threatens the scientists' right to know. It is unethical, given the harm principle and the knowledge factor associated with it. If knowledge is necessary in order for informed consent to mean anything, then any act, including censorship, that stifles knowledge is unethical.

It is unlikely that censorship would occur if a strong exchange relationship has been forged and maintained throughout the research. Certainly, it is less painful and more productive sociologically to work out the boundaries of what can and cannot be published well in advance of the actual writing of papers and reports. As long as the researcher knows in advance what is off limits, he or she can freely decide to go ahead with the research, renegotiate the limits, or give up on doing the study, if it should come to that point.

■ *Freedom to Choose and Researcher Intervention*

We are beyond the point in social science research where a researcher can allow subjects in serious lie-threatening trouble to go unattended. There are instances from the not too distant past where studies were completed with subjects in such extreme poverty that death from starvation was fairly common yet completely avoidable. Colin Turnbull (*The Mountain People*, 1974) studied a tribe in Uganda where food was waylaid by corrupt officials. The resultant starvation caused social chaos and the eventual destruction of tribal life. To sit impassively taking notes may have been scientifically sound, but ethically, it was unforgivable. The principle of individual free choice demands, in situations like Turnbull's, that the researcher stop all research and work to put the knowledge gained toward alleviating the conditions that are threatening the people. In Turnbull's case, immediate pressure should have been brought to bear on the corruption that was causing the starvation. Of course, the study would have ended at that point, since the researcher would have changed the entire social system through his intervention. This would not necessarily have meant the end to any possible research, but the original research problem, which was predicated on objective and unobtrusive observation, would have been finished. In its place, the researcher could monitor the process of intervention and evaluate the impacts that such intervention might have had on the tribe. The focus would change from a basic research problem, that is the effect of food deprivation on the social order, to a policy research question having to do with the uses of research. In any case, the threat to the autonomy and lives of the people demanded immediate intervention. Knowledge, as we know, is of great value but not of absolute value.

This situation in which Turnbull found himself is by no means unique. Lest we throw stones in glass houses, I too found myself in a similar situation to Turnbull's, and I want to disabuse the reader of any notion that Turnbull was evil or in a minority.

In my case, I was appointed to a research team under the aegis of the U.S. Agency for International Development. There were several U.S. social scientists on the team, and we were sent to Ecuador for four weeks of intense field work among the small farmers in the Andes mountains. Very early into the field work, I became aware of significant corruption in the government that was seriously compromising the lives of the peasants. The more I worked, the clearer the patterns became. I knew that there were powerful forces within the Ecuadorian government that could act to resolve the corruption, but colleagues on the research team advised me to do my job and to keep quiet. They were convinced that any whistle-blowing would hinder the progress being made in the relationship between Ecuador and the United States. They argued that disclosure would make life much worse for the peasants. I should have told the peasants, at the very least, if in fact I had subscribed to the ethical principle of free and autonomous research subjects. Instead, I went on with my field work, wrote up an objective report on the work limited to what I had been asked to cover, not on what I had discovered about corruption, and went home. Subsequent events, that is, a failed attempt in Ecuador to have a free election, led me to question the wisdom of my colleagues and the lack of courage on my part to intervene in the plight of the peasants.

■ *Conclusions*

Scientific research must attend to the problem of doing science within an ethical framework. In this chapter, we have argued that the harm principle is a key ethical principle for the social sciences. This principle depends on a free, autonomous, and fully knowledgeable public, in the ideal situation, and research that disrupts this freedom must be considered suspect ethically. We rejected Kant's idea that there exists some absolute standards of right and wrong, the categorical imperatives as he called them, and instead turned to exchange methodology as a means to negotiate standards of ethical conduct in research. This approach seems best for considering the harm principle and the principle of research subject autonomy carefully while negotiating the particular ethical issues, such as confidentially, censorship, the right to know, and so forth.

The key to understanding this chapter is to realize that there are no absolute ethical standards and consequently no absolute answers to the problems that have plagued social scientific research throughout its brief history. The challenge for researchers is to anticipate ethical problems before they emerge and to design into your research a system for addressing the ethical issues. With increasing pressure on the social sciences to come forth with solutions to massive social problems, such as drug abuse, family violence, sexually transmitted diseases, academic cheating, and so on, the research we do will be more invasive, more explosive politically, and more susceptible to ethical problems. Lots of work is needed, work such as the exchange methodology discussed in this chapter, in order to construct a powerful and effective ethical system for research in the social sciences. Students need to use their sociological imaginations to design research that will test existing ethical standards and produce innovative solutions for rectifying failures uncovered in those standards.

GLOSSARY

clandestine research   studies in which the intent of the researchers and perhaps even the identities of the researchers are hidden from the subjects and public.

exchange methodology   an approach to research where the subjects are given power equal to the researcher to make research decisions.

functional autonomy   a state in which the individual has full knowledge about his or her best interests an can act freely on those interests.

paternalism   a system of authority in which individuals' needs are defined for them and their conduct is regulated against their wills and/or in the absence of individuals' knowledge.

research ethics   a system of philosophical principles, including moral principles, values, duties, and rights, that the researcher can use to develop rules of conduct and to discern good research from bad research.

risk   grounded in benefits versus costs, risk is a status defined by the odds that something harmful will occur and the consequences of such an occurrence.

utilitarianism   an ethical principle that evaluates the worth of something in terms of its usefulness, seeking the greatest good for the largest number of people.

FOR FURTHER READING

Hammett, Michael P., et. al. (1984). *Ethics, politics and international social science research: From critique to praxis*. Honolulu, Hawaii: Hawaii University Press.

Kimmel, Allan J. (1988). *Ethics and values in applied social research*. Newbury Park, Calif.: Sage Publications.

Nejelski, Paul (Ed.). (1976). *Social research ethics: An examination of the merits of covert participant observation*. Cambridge, Mass.: Ballinger.

Nejelski, Paul (Ed.). (1976). *Social research in conflict with law and ethics*. Cambridge, Mass.: Ballinger.

Reynolds, Paul Davidson (1979). *Ethical dilemmas and social science research: An analysis of moral issues confronting investigators in research using human participants*. San Francisco: Jossey-Bass.

Part Two

METHODOLOGY FOR IMPROVING THE QUALITY OF SOCIOLOGICAL OBSERVATIONS

Chapter Three

MEASUREMENT

▊ *The philosophy of science basis for measurement is discussed prior to launching into the long-standing debate over quality of data versus quantity. Measurement is tied to the problem definition and analysis plan, and then validity, reliability, and levels of measurement are discussed. The most important part of this chapter is the section dealing with the links between measurement, theory, and analysis. This brings the reader back to the basic methodological tenet of the fit between the research problem and specific procedures for conducting research.*

Without measurement, we are stuck with theory alone to provide us with explanations of things, events, and people. Such a fate would be depressing to researchers who, as good scientists, strive to prove that their theories are false. Measurement is defined broadly as the classification of cases according to some rule. The rule should specify what qualifies as a case, what property or properties of the case are involved, and how to apply the rule to the properties in order to classify the cases. Measurement is the means that researchers use to transform concepts into observations. It provides a bridge between the abstract world of theory and concept and the more concrete world of people, things and events.

In this chapter, we will discuss the philosophy of science basis for measurement in the social sciences along with the long-standing debate concerning the quality versus quantity dimensions of measurement. Also we will discuss the levels of measurement, the rules associated with the levels, and techniques for achieving those levels. Techniques for determining validity and reliability are presented. The link between analysis and measurement is discussed in terms of achieving the most productive, precise, and meaningful level of measurement given the analysis plan.

51

■ *Philosophical Basis for Measurement*

Measurement would be absolutely meaningless without what is called **"Measurement/reality isomorphism."** Isomorphism means similarity of form. This philosophy of science principle requires that the measurement rules and the results of measurement, that is, numerals, numbers, or names, mirror what we think is really out there in the world. Thus, in measurement we hope to achieve a classification scheme that is identical to the "true" scheme in the real world existing outside of our measurement efforts.

As we know from Chapter 1, it is likely that there is no "truth" or reality independent of observation or measurement. Nevertheless, we need to assume that there is such an objective reality for the sake of understanding the philosophical basis for measurement. The "true" value of whatever it is you are measuring, for example, the social status of college professors, is what you hope your measurement reflects. When you say that you have measured social status, you must assume that your measurement is identical or nearly identical to the true status of college professors. Measurement is considered an approximation or estimate of that elusive ideal truth.

■ *Measurement and Meaning*

I was told the following story by the late Paul Lazarsfeld who at the time was trying to teach a number of us first-year graduate students at the University of Pittsburgh some of the finer points of measurement. Apparently, the noted sex researcher Alfred Kinsey was confronted by one of the male subjects in his study of male sexual behavior who demanded to know why, no matter what he said, all Kinsey cared about was "How many times?" Through this story, Lazarsfeld taught us that there was more to measurement than counting. Lazarsfeld, one of the most outstanding quantitative sociologists who ever lived, told us to never allow counting to get in the way of the pursuit of meaning. Ed Suchman, another excellent methodologist and colleague of Lazarsfeld's, drew the model shown in Figure 3-1 on the board to back up the warning about number crunching:

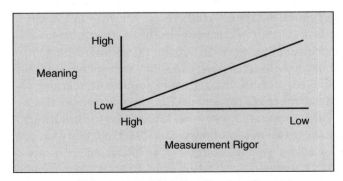

Figure 3-1 ■ Suchman's Model on Number Crunching

Measurement and meaning are in a **dialectical relationship**. As one gets better (more precise), the other gets worse. If measurement rigor is high in the sense that the researcher simply counts, nothing more, then meaning is low. All the researcher knows is that fifteen runny noses came through the medical clinic door on Monday, whereas forty-five came through on Tuesday. What may be more meaningful here would be to measure the pathways that the fifteen patients took to get to the clinic or to try and understand why anyone would seek medical care in the first place.

The point here is that measurement can become an end unto itself. The researcher can become very smug scientifically and cease to search for alternative explanations simply because there are lots of numbers compiled in the computer ready to count. We can lose sight of the principle that measurement is a means to an end and that it serves theory and explanation first and foremost. Ricky Slavings at Radford College suggested that I reread A. A. Milne's (1954) classic *Winnie-the-Pooh* for insight into this phenomenon of reifying method. In Milne's words:

> Here is Edward Bear, coming downstairs now, bump, bump, bump, on the back of his head behind Christopher Robin. It is, as far as he knows, the only way of coming downstairs, but sometimes he feels that there really is another way, if only he could stop bumping for a moment and think of it. And then he feels that perhaps there isn't.

Measurement serves theory and explanation by fulfilling the following functions: (1) Measurement creates standard units that allow scientists to compare and study seemingly different objects, processes, or events. For example, if we measure social class by using education, income, and occupation, then we have a standard unit that allows us to compare individuals from all walks of life; similarly, standardization allows scientists to compare different studies of the same research problem as variables. (2) Measurement makes it easier to analyze things, that is breaking things down into their component parts. It does this by allowing the researcher to divide and subdivide the objects of study into smaller and finer distinctions. Breaking something down into its smallest divisions is very helpful for understanding how it works. (3) By measuring the properties of variables precisely, we are able to statistically relate those variables in order to test the extent to which the variables are related. This improves our chances of contributing to the growth of theory and thereby adding to the sum total of scientific knowledge. This is part of a larger advantage of measurement, which is that, at a certain level, it allows the researcher to use mathematics as a tool of analysis.

▪ *Quantitative and Qualitative Measurement*

In the past, social scientists created a distinction between qualitative and quantitative measurement. Once these two dimensions of measurement were set apart from one another, the scientists involved waged a war of sorts over which dimension was inherently better. The quantitative folks argued that assigning real numbers to things was the only legitimate function of measurement. Anything else, such as naming something "far" or "wide," was just too vague and value-loaded to be called scientific measurement. The qualitative side argued that social reality was too complex to be turned into numbers. They insisted that the meanings imbedded in social reality only could be grasped by measurement techniques that helped the researcher see the social reality through the eyes of those being studied. It just so happened that these techniques of observation/participant observation yielded narrative accounts full of direct quotes and descriptions of observed behavior that the proponents argued could not be turned into numbers without destroying the essence of its meaning.

One of the classic studies that relied solely upon **qualitative measurement** was Erving Goffman's (1961) study of St. Elizabeth State Mental Hospital in Washington, D.C. For one year, Goffman stalked the wards of the hospital observing the interactions of the staff and seven thousand patients. Through this observational research, Goffman wrote hundreds of pages of field notes, that is, qualitative eyewitness accounts of what he observed. Nothing was standardized in his measurement. If you or I observed the same scene, our field notes would be slightly different from Goffman's and different from each other's. Nevertheless, Goffman uncovered much of what we currently know about institutionalization as well as enhanced our understanding of the conflict between the needs of the mental patient and the goals of "the medical model." Goffman's discovery of "the underlife" of the institution stimulated organization researchers to consider "informal" levels of organization, a major theoretical and empirical breakthrough.

On the quantitative side of the ledger, Michael Harrington used U.S. census data on income, education, occupation, and other demographic indicators to write his trail-blazing analysis of poverty in the United States (*The Other America*). His study raised the level of the nation's awareness of poverty to the point that Congress passed legislation establishing the Office of Economic Opportunity, the Department of Housing and Urban Development, and the War on Poverty was launched.

This debate has been unfortunate because it is based on the false premise that qualitative and quantitative measurement represent two distinct dimensions or facets of measurement. Clearly, both approaches are meritorious scientifically. Paul Lazarsfeld, often mistakenly identified as a true believer in **quantitative measurement,** set the record straight on the futility of this distinction in a brilliant essay with Allen Barton called "Qualitative Measurement in the Social Sciences" (1971). Lazarsfeld worked his entire life to clarify the language of social research through precise quantitative measurement. He believed that clear, unambiguous, and quantitative measurement of individual motives or attitudes would provide us with the data needed to understand the deterioration of community structure and thereby to reverse it. However, he was convinced that qualitative measurement was the methodologically sound way to begin to work toward the ideal of precise quantitative measurement. The key contribution that Lazarsfeld made here was to reject the distinction made previously in quantitative versus qualitative. Lazarsfeld viewed measurement as having only one dimension, not two. Qualitative and quantitative differed not in kind but in degree or level. In his and Barton's words:

It should be realized that systematic study can be carried on in the social sciences as elsewhere by many devices which are less precise than strict quantitative measurement but nonetheless far better than unaided individual judgment. It is the contention of this chapter that there is a direct line of logical continuity from qualitative classification to the most rigorous forms of measurement, by way of intermediate devices of systematic ratings, ranking scales, multidimensional classifications, typologies, and simple quantitative indices. In this wider sense of "Measurement," social phenomena are being measured every day by both theoretically oriented and applied social researchers.

For Lazarsfeld and Barton, something measured was *more* or *less* qualitative or quantitative, not a case of either/or. They proposed a range definition whereby there are degrees of quality or quantity along a single dimension of measurement called "level of measurement," which we will discuss fully in the next section of this chapter.

Lazarsfeld and Barton believed that scientific research has a type of life cycle with stages of development. The early stages of research should involve concept building and theory construction. This can best be accomplished by using qualitative methods first, then, once the concepts are clearly delineated and the researcher knows which variables are key to explaining the problem, quantitative methods are appropriate. In the early stages of research, the inquiry must be exploratory, rather than theory-testing. Research questions should be asked in a way that will elicit qualitative answers. For example, rather than asking, "What is the relationship between educational level and career choices?", we should ask, "What are the pathways that people take in choosing a career? What do they do in deciding?" Thus, qualitative methods should be more heavily used in the early stages of research and quantitative methods toward the mature and later stages. Of course, combining the two methods is desirable for any given study, but the emphasis on one or the other would shift depending on the developmental stage of the research and the problem. In the words of Lazarsfeld and Barton:

> Before we can investigate the presence of absence of some attribute in a person or social situation, or before we can rank objects or measure them in terms of some variable, we must form the concept of that variable. Looking at the material before us in all its richness of sense-data, we must decide what attributes of the concrete items we wish to observe and measure: Do we want to study "this-ness" or "that-ness," or some other "-ness"? The precise origin of our notion of this-ness or that-ness may be extremely varied, but it usually seems to involve combining many particular experiences into a category which promises greater understanding and control of events. . . . When we have formed some such category, we may then break it down into component elements upon which to base research instruments—instructions to coders, ranking scales, indicators.

▪ *The Unit of Analysis*

A key to understanding and working with measurement is the concept of **unit of analysis.** The unit of analysis is the person, event, or social structure that the re-

Unit of Analysis	Examples
Individual	Female heads of households
Group	Families in poverty
Organization	Major research universities
Social Artifact	Women who manage
Country	U.S., Canadian, and Swedish medical care systems compared

Figure 3-2 ■ Examples of Units of Analysis

searcher actually measures. For example, I have been studying aging for over twenty years using a panel of seventeen hundred elderly persons. These individuals are living independently in their own homes and are scattered over sixty-four small towns through the state of Missouri. The unit of analysis is the individual, elderly person, not the household or town. I obtained information about the household but only through the individual respondent. In other studies, the family may be the ultimate unit of analysis, or it might be an entire county. Also, the unit can shift within a single study, with the researcher moving back and forth from the individual to organization to social structure (see Figure 3-2). For example, Swigert and Farrell (1976) studied the relationship between structured inequality, homicide, and the law. The unit of analysis included the individual (homicide rate) and the organization (U.S. criminal justice system). The unit of analysis depends on the research problem and what the researcher is trying to explain. One way to determine what the unit of analysis might be is to locate the object in the dependent variable within the statement of the problem. In the case of Goffman's research, the problem was to explain the moral career of the mental patient. Here, the unit of analysis is the mental patient. If the research problem reads, "What is the effect of family financial status on family violence?", the unit of analysis is the family.

■ *Levels of Measurement*

Measurement was defined at the beginning of this chapter as the classification of cases according to some rule. The rule will determine what level of measurement you achieve, be it nominal, ordinal, interval, or ratio level.

A key to understanding the **level of measurement** is theory. The more developed the theory in terms of clearly defined concepts and precisely stated propositions, the more detailed and precise the rules for measurement can be. In other words, theory and concept definition determine the level of measurement one can achieve. For example, if you have decided to study the role of the immigrant but very little research or theory exists on this problem, you will have to settle on rather broad and vague rules of measurement because you do not have a very clear picture what it is about being an immigrant that you desire to measure. You probably have some leads based on general sociological theory, in this case it might be role theory, but the finer empirical details, relationships, and the theoretical rationale are just not available to enable you to zero in and to measure the most relevant aspects of being an immigrant. In this situation, you need to do qualitative exploratory research in order to first define the relevant concepts. At this stage of the research, you would be using categorical rules that would yield nominal levels of measurement. You would be in the business of finding out what the process of being an immigrant is all about, rather than testing a precise hypotheses about specific aspects of becoming an immigrant. Once the theory is spelled out and the concepts are clearly defined, then more precise measurement is in order. An excellent example of this is Paul Lazarsfeld's qualitative analysis of his own immigration to the United States from Austria (Lazarsfeld, 1968).

There are four principles of measurement that need to be recognized at this point.

PRINCIPLE 1: MEASUREMENT/THEORY SYMBIOSIS

Measurement and theory have a symbiotic relationship. Each depends on the other in order to advance scientifically. There has to be at least some minimal presence of one if the other is to grow. In the total absence of theory, the researcher would be unable to decide what to measure. Similarly, without measurement, theory would remain an untested curiosity. Even in exploratory qualitative research where the objective is to define a research problem more clearly, the researcher observes and records only a small portion of the total interaction occurring. What is the basis for this selectivity? Theory is the answer. Even if the theory is in its infancy, it is the only scientifically acceptable basis for measuring one thing opposed to another. Out of the infinite number of measurements possible, the researcher has no way of deciding what to include and which items to exclude without help from theory. In all research situations, quantitative or qualitative, of all the words and deeds observed, the researcher invariably will narrow the focus and decide to measure only a small sample of the multitude.

PRINCIPLE 2: DEFINE THE UNIT OF ANALYSIS

Reflect on the statement of the problem and define the object of your analysis. This is the irreducible entity that constitutes the object of your analysis. The unit of analysis is the noun that completes the sentence. "The purpose of this study is to explain the membership patterns of women who join pro-choice and anti-abortion organizations." The unit is individual women.

PRINCIPLE 3: USE CONCRETE CATEGORIES

The third principle is that measurement should start with very concrete categories that are directly observable as part of everyday life. These categories would be very specific and limited to the things measured; hence, the researcher would not be able to generalize very much based on the results of the measurement. For example, I might begin my research on the question of why so few black women played intercollegiate basketball in the sport's formative years by measuring and classifying players by race and teams by wins and losses, the proportion of black men playing at the same schools as the women's teams, and classifying the towns that the schools are located at in terms of the proportion of blacks residing there. These are concrete measurement categories. As research on a particular problem advances, the emphasis shifts from description, exploration, and theory building to analysis and theory testing. Here, measurement should use more abstract categories, and the goal should be to generalize as widely as possible.

PRINCIPLE 4: DISCRIMINATE

Measurement must discriminate among the research cases. Numbers or categories should yield unambiguous classification. Any given case should fall into one and only one category, and all the cases in the study should be classifiable under your measuring instrument.

NOMINAL LEVEL OF MEASUREMENT

Again, there are four levels of measurement: (1) nominal; (2) ordinal; (3) interval; and (4) ratio. As one moves from nominal to ratio, the quality of the data changes from categories to real numbers that can be added, subtracted, and generally subjected to any manner of statistical manipulations.

   Nominal measurement involves naming something and providing rules for categorizing things under that name. Our everyday language is loaded with nominal categories that make communication and action possible. Think of the difficulty if one had to start fresh with no language. The problem would be to communicate in order to survive. One would have to name things and create categories to place those things in. Learning needs language with categories, for without them, there would be too much information for our brains to process.

   The **nominal level of measurement** is not much more complicated than everyday language. When we name something and provide rules for categorizing things relative to the name, we have achieved the nominal level of measurement.

   There is neither order nor degree to things measured nominally. There are just names and the rules for placing objects, people, or actions under those names. There are two important rules to keep in mind when designing a nominal measure. First, the categories must be mutually exclusive. This means that any given unit of analysis (the objects of study) must fit into one and only one of the nominal categories. There is no room for ambiguity here. Something is categorized in one and only one category, or the measure should be discarded. The second rule states that the nominal categories must be exhaustive. This requires that all the cases measured can fit into one of the categories. If the nominal categories can

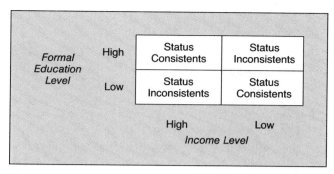

Figure 3-3 ∎ Property Space

handle each and every case, then the categories are exhaustive. This is the operationalization of the fourth principle of discrimination.

All of us have had to fill out forms that measure social background information. Such items as sex, race, place of birth, religion, and marital status are clear-cut nominal measures. There is no inherent or researcher-designed order to the categories for any of these variables. All individuals classified as Protestant are the same in this regard, as are all individuals classified as Catholic. Neither of those categories is higher or stronger or more of some particular quality than the other. They are just names, not rankings. It is futile to use math with the nominal level, for to do so would yield meaningless results, such as "the average gender."

Typologies are a powerful form of nominal level measurement. Types such as "the organization man," "the authoritarian personality," and "the Protestant ethic" are classic sociological examples of nominal categories that have had a profound positive effect on the growth of theory. Allen Barton developed a methodological tool called "property space" that is of great help to the researcher who is trying to build nominal categories. It is a simple strategy in which the researcher puts together two variables and the "space" created by the juxtaposition of the variables demarcates the **ideal type** categories (see Figure 3-3).

The categories are called ideal types because, strictly speaking, they are not fully exhaustive or mutually exclusive, and they exist only in the imaginary world of the researcher. It may sound strange but ideal types are very useful for creating theory or explanation, even if they are not very good for classifying things. Max Weber, the principal architect of ideal types, once defined ideal types as "useful fiction." You will not find the Protestant ethic or the spirit of capitalism in their pure ideal form, but the ideal type helps the researcher sort out the qualities or characteristics to be measured in later studies. The ideal type is a mini-theory that not only explains social action but also serves as a measurement standard against which researchers can evaluate their findings.

ORDINAL LEVEL OF MEASUREMENT

When the operational rules or measurement yields a rank order of some sort, the **ordinal level of measurement** is in effect. This is a higher level than the nominal

Years Completed

0

1–7

8–11

12

13–15

16

17–19

20 +

Figure 3-4 ■ Level of Formal Education:
Last Year of School Completed

because it allows the researcher to make judgments about something being "greater than" or having "more of x" than something else. This means that you create variance through measurement with a view to explaining that variance. This is especially handy when the study has generated lots of data on many subjects. More importantly, some research problems are at the stage where theory is developed enough to be tested. With that goal in mind and given large numbers of variables and cases, the ordinal level of measurement is a welcome addition to the methodologist's tool kit.

Educational level is an ordinal level variable if the rule tells the researcher to measure education by asking the respondent to indicate the appropriate category of formal schooling completed.
As Figure 3-4 shows, education measured in this fashion results in a ranking of the respondents from no school through graduate Ph.D. By doing this, the researcher knows that any given respondent who answered the question correctly has more or less or the same education as any other given respondent. All the respondents can be ranked relative to each other. It is possible to rank them in terms of more or less. What is not possible is to be able to tell precisely how much more or less the differences or rankings are. At the ordinal level, we know that John Jones has more education than Ivan because John checked off "16" whereas Ivan has indicated "13-15." We know that John is ranked higher, that he has more education than Ivan, but we do not know exactly how much more of it he has. Social class, occupational prestige ratings, self-ratings of health into excellent, good, fair, and poor, and age categories that the respondent is asked to choose from are a few other examples of ordinal level measurement. The categories are not standardized or equal units, and they yield rankings that can only be discussed in terms such as higher, lower, more, less, higher, and so forth.

INTERVAL LEVEL OF MEASUREMENT

The **interval level of measurement** specifies that you use standardized categories that have equal appearing intervals between them. Income is an equal-appearing interval level of measurement, and temperature is an example from the physical sciences. With income, one hundred dollars is twice as much as fifty dollars. Zero is a real value, and all of the numerical values correspond to real numbers. Fifty-five dollars is exactly ten dollars more than forty-five dollars, and so forth. For example, a person with an IQ score of one hundred is fifty interval units "higher" than a person with a score of fifty. However, it is not sound methodological to conclude that the person with the score of one hundred is twice as smart as the person with the fifty score.

RATIO LEVEL OF MEASUREMENT

The **ratio level of measurement** has all the attributes of the nominal, ordinal, and interval levels plus the property of an absolute zero point. This is of greater relevance to physics than sociology.

To sum up, the nominal level of measurement produces categories of general names under which the researcher groups the relevant cases. There is no order or degree of the property being measured. Ordinal level gives you a rank order, but you are unable to specify the precise difference of magnitude between the ranks. Interval also yields a rank order but with the added property of allowing the researcher to determine the precise interval between the ranks. **Transitivity** means that the levels of measurement themselves are ranked, with interval being the most detailed and nominal the least. Thus, one can move from the interval level to the other levels but not the other way around.

■ *Transitivity*

The ordinal, interval, and ratio levels make it possible to use correlation-based statistics without violating their assumptions. The principle of transitivity makes it possible to transform interval into ordinal or nominal, and ordinal into nominal, but it does not work the other way. If the research problem warrants it and the researcher can afford it, it is best to write rules of measurement that yield the highest level because one can always transform levels downward from interval to nominal (see Figure 3-5 on page 62). However, invariably the researcher will lose information in moving from interval to ordinal to nominal.

■ *Validity*

Measurement should yield valid results. The issue here is, "Does the measure capture what theory and the concept are about?"

The key to understanding what **validity** is and how to judge it resides in the question, "Validity for what?" This question tells the researcher that validity can be evaluated only if there is a clear idea of what was supposed to have been mea-

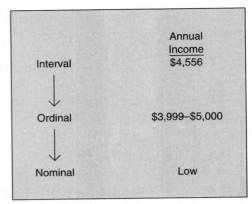

Figure 3-5 ■ Transitivity and the Loss of Information from Interval to Nominal Levels of Measurement

sured. Put another way, the question reads, "Does the operational definition measure what it was designed to measure?" "Does my alienation scale measure alienation?", for example.

In order to answer this question, the researcher is required to have two definitions. The first is the definition of what was supposed to have been measured. This is the concept and its conceptual, abstract definition. Again, we return to the first steps of the research process and see the importance of clear conceptual definitions, for without them, you cannot assess validity. The concept to be measured and its definition is the first requirement for determining validity. Second, the researcher must have a clear operational definition of the rules for measuring the concept. Both of these definitions, the conceptual and the operational, must be written down and documented for others to view as well.

Basically, all of the different techniques for determining if the measure is valid or not stems from the process of comparing the conceptual definition against the operational definition.

Figure 3-6 presents the ideal situation of a perfectly valid measure along with the possible sources of invalidity. The solid circle is the conceptual definition and the dotted one is the operational definition. Model A is perfection with the operational definition measuring exactly what it was intended to measure, nothing less and nothing more. Model B represents a validity problem in which the operational definition is too narrow for the concept as defined. In this case, the measure covers only part of what you intended to cover, but it does so too narrowly. Model C shows the opposite problem, where the operational definition is too broad for the conceptual definition. Here, you are measuring what you intended to measure plus things that you did not intend to measure. The operational definition is invalid because it covers more ground than you intended it to cover. Model D represents a validity problem where the operational definition is tangential to the concept. In this case, the measure covers only a piece of what you intended to measure, leaving a good bit of the conceptual definition unmeasured.

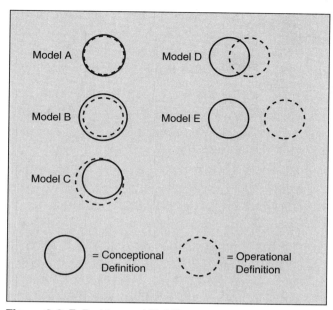

Figure 3-6 ■ Problems of Validity

Finally, Model E is perfectly invalid in that there is no correspondence at all between the conceptual and operational definitions. The two are not even close.

Keeping these sources of invalidity in mind, let us turn to three basic techniques for assessing validity. These techniques are: (1) face validity; (2) predicting to a criterion—internal construct validity; and (3) predicting to a criterion—external construct validity.

FACE VALIDITY

The simplest and consequently the weakest method for determining validity is to see if the measure has validity "on the face of it." This involves nothing more than the researcher, singly or with the help of others, sitting down and comparing the conceptual definition with the operational definition. If the measure looks like it measures what it was designed to measure, it is deemed valid by the researcher. This process should take place during the design phase of the research before doing any field work. One would hope that all researchers would conduct a face validity check at the very minimum.

PREDICTION TO A CRITERION: INTERNAL CONSTRUCT VALIDITY

A more powerful technique than face validation is to design your measures in such a way as to have other independent measures that theory and research experience tells you ought to be related to the measure you are trying to validate.

For example, if you have several questions that are supposed to measure the respondents' perception of their health status, you could ask the respondents also about the number of work days lost, days spent in the hospital, and the number and purpose of visits to physicians. If on the basis of the responses to the perceived health measure you could predict the responses to the other measures, assuming of course that days lost and so on are independent (of the main measure) indicators of health problems, then you have predicted to an internal criterion, and your measure can be said to be valid. It is internal because the criterion is part of the date of the study, rather than external to it.

PREDICTION TO A CRITERION: EXTERNAL CONSTRUCT VALIDITY

If the measure is valid, the acid test is to find some surefire indicator of the concept that exists out in the social world, independently of the study variables. An example of this would be to measure preparedness for college using the Scholastic Aptitude Test, an inventory designed to measure ability or potential to succeed in college. Armed with scores, you would predict future college performance. The future actual performance in college is the external criterion. Another example comes from a colleague of mine who designed a scale measuring attitude toward abortion. My colleague predicted that people who had strongly favorable attitudes toward abortion would be members of formal organizations that favored women's rights to have an abortion. Conversely, respondents who were strongly opposed to abortion would be members of various anti-abortion organizations. The memberships are independent of the scale and are extremely valid criteria. If the scale is valid, it should allow one to predict outside criteria.

■ *Reliability*

Reliability is the extent to which you would get the same results if you repeated the measure again and again. Reliability is the test of a measure's consistency over repeated applications. It is another piece of measurement strategy whereby the researcher tries to design questions or indicators which represent accurately the concepts. Reliability says very little about validity, that is, whether or not the items really measure what you intended them to measure. A scale can be perfectly reliable, but it can be measuring the wrong thing, for example, a bathroom scale that is properly calibrated but set five pounds too light. Measures can be reliably invalid, but reliability is a necessary condition for validity. The best possible situation is to have both valid and reliable measures.

How does the researcher check for reliability? There are several techniques, the the following four are presented here because they are effective and practical. (1) Repeat the item. This is a little like trickery because you sneak the same item into another location in the questionnaire or interview schedule and hope that the respondent does not notice that he or she has answered it already. Theoretically, if the respondent gives the same response to both items, the item is reliable.

(2) Test-retest, in which you simply repeat the measure at two points in time. If you get different results, you have to decide between the possibility that the measure is unreliable or that the respondents have changed somehow. This is the problem of deciding whether you have real change or an unreliable instrument. (3) The split-half technique, in which you design double the number of items that you really need to measure the concept, administer all of the items, then split them in half and compare the two halves. For example, if you settle on a twenty-item scale of mental illness, you would design forty items, administer them, randomly split them into two groups of twenty each, and then compare the two. This is an indirect method for determining if your instrument yields consistent readings. (4) Test theory, which is a statistical theory for estimating reliability. In order to use test theory, you must assume that error is random, not systematic. Also, you must obtain at least two distinct measurements or observations of the concept being studied.

■ *Links between Measurement, Theory, and Analysis*

Methodology is a science of research decisions. It provides the researcher with rules and norms for evaluating the decisions behind the design and implementation of research. In this most fundamental way, methodology is a tightly linked human system. The decisions made at one point are intimately affected by previous decisions that, in turn, affect later decisions.

Measurement is valid only in the light of theory. Without concepts and their definition, at some minimal level, it is impossible to design valid measures. Similarly, the plan for analyzing data dictates what level of measurement you need to achieve. Also, the analysis plan is a strategy designed to answer the research question. Theory guides this strategy by helping the researcher formulate hypotheses, which are hypothetical answers to the research question. For example, if I am starting out to answer the research question, "What are the sociological factors associated with longevity among the rural elderly?", I will turn to theory to help formulate a set of answers (explanation) to the research question. In my search for an explanation, I will read other studies and theoretical works. Finally, I will settle on a theory that involves the relationship of the individual to the social system at the most general level. This tells me that I am going to have to go beyond the individual in measurement.

One of the concepts that comes up in the literature over and over again as a predictor of good health and longevity is social networks (see Salloway and Oberembt, 1976). This concept is defined in terms of formal networks, such as measurements in formal organizations, and informal networks made up of nuclear family, other relatives, and friends. The theory about social networks is very complex, but one of the basic hypotheses is that the more extensive and more intensive the networks, the better the health and the greater the longevity.

Many other hypotheses are derived about the relationship between networks, age, health, and gender. Thus, I know that I must measure these concepts and that I must design an analysis that will allow me to study the interrelationships among these concepts. I plan to use regression analysis on certain variables, which means that I must achieve at least the ordinal level of measurement for those variables. Now I can design the questions and their response categories with some confidence that I will be able to address the research question and that I will be able to assess the validity of my measurement in the process.

If I am a clever methodologist, I will borrow the measures used by the other researchers ahead of me who have studied the problem of longevity and health using social networks as part of the theory. Of course, this assumes that the conceptual definitions employed by the other researchers are acceptable to me and that they suit my particular research needs as well. A word of advice here: put down on paper the outlines of the tables you plan to fill with data. This is called dummy analysis, and it is a useful tool to help the researcher decide which are the appropriate concepts to measure and what level of measurement to seek.

■ *Conclusions*

Measurement is the classification of cases according to some rule. It is the only means that we as researchers have to transform our theories into observations of social structure and process. Measurement is the procedure by which concepts are operationally defined or, in other words, reconceptualized. The validity of measurement is dependent on how well the researcher defines the concept and then on how well the rules for operationalizing the concept work. One strives for a perfect fit between the concept and its measure, that is, the measure measures only the concept, nothing more and nothing less. This is called isomorphism, and a fierce debate exists about the proper role for qualitative and quantitative measurement relative to isomorphism, of the fit between concept and meaning.

I must conclude that measurement and meaning are in a dialectical relationship. The more stringent the rules, that is the more finely tuned the measurement, the less likely it is that the researcher will measure the deep meanings in social reality. Furthermore, there is a similar tension between validity and reliability. There must be a happy middle ground, but I cannot dictate what that ground is or what steps to take to stand on it. This is where the art of research comes to the fore, and the researcher must bring ingenuity and creativity to the measurement enterprise. The rules of measurement are only conventional, not absolute, and the researcher's task is a tough one. Guided by theory and the work of other researchers, the best you can do is to ensure that your concepts are the most powerful explanatory factors possible, that they are well defined, and that you know where you are going with the analysis. That is the bare minimum. Armed thus, you need to define measurement rules that get the job done parsimoniously, validly, and, most important, in a fashion that yields the maximum sociological explanation and meaning. All the handbooks (Miller, 1977) extant cannot take the place of the researcher really knowing the problem, mastering the literature, and exercising his or her sociological imagination.

GLOSSARY

dialectical relationship   a relationship between opposites such that they interact at each other's expense, for example, pleasure/pain, love/hate, cost/benefit, quantitative measurement/meaning.

ideal type   also called typology, ideal type is a "useful fiction" at the nominal level of measurement created out of the property space of two intersecting variables.

interval level of measurement   a level of measurement in which the rules provide for a rank order among the cases being measured with equal interval size between the ranks.

level of measurement   the state of classification (nominal, ordinal, interval, ratio) achieved in measurement.

measurement   the classification of cases according to some rule that specifies which property of the cases to measure and how to measure that property. The operational definition of a concept is measurement.

measurement/reality isomorphism   the "true" value of what you are measuring, existing independent of your measurement, is matched by the value derived by your measure.

nominal level of measurement   a level of measurement in which the rules provide for categorizing cases and giving them names or labels.

ordinal level of measurement   a level of measurement in which the rules provide for a rank order among the cases being measured in terms of unknown interval size between the rank.

qualitative measurement   measurement in which the rules permit the researcher to use primary narrations, direct observations, and secondary documents to measure the cases.

quantitative measurement   measurement in which the rules assign real numbers to the properties of the cases.

ratio level of measurement   a level of measurement similar to the interval level plus having an absolute zero point.

reliability   a state of measurement, based on repeated measurements, in which the operational definition (measure) is consistent, that is, it produces the same measurements, all else being equal.

transitivity   a principle of logic applied to the four levels of measurement that states that if a property relationship exists between the first element (e.g., nominal level) and second element (e.g., ordinal level) and between the second element and third element (interval level), then the relationship exists between the first element and the third element, for example, nominal < ordinal < interval < ratio.

unit of analysis   the person, event or social structure that is measured.

validity   a state of measurement in which the operational definition (measure) measures the concept precisely as intended.

FOR FURTHER READING

Lazarsfeld, Paul F. (1972). Problems in Methodology. In Paul F. Lazarsfeld, Ann K. Pansanella, and Morris Rosenberg (Eds.). *Continuities in the language of social research* (pp. 17–24). New York: Free Press.

Stevens, S. S. (1946). On the Theory of Scales of Measurement. *Science, 103,* 677–680.

Chapter Four

INDICES AND SCALES

■ *The principles of scaling, such as multiple indicators, the index, transitivity, dimensionality, reproducibility, and levels of measurement, are discussed. Q-Sort, Guttman, Likert, Thurstone, and Ordered Alternative scales are presented using examples from sociological research. The chapter concludes with examples of the application of scales in analysis.*

Quantitative measurement at the ordinal or higher level contains two important principles called multiple indicators and unidimensionality that make the life of the methodologist complicated and interesting. These principles mean essentially that quantitative ordinal or higher-level measurement will produce indices and scales. Partly it is a matter of efficiency and ease of analysis, but mainly indices and scales are developed and used to meet the demands posed by the two principles.

   This chapter begins with a discussion of the principles of multiple indicators and unidimensionality. Next, the terms *index* and *scale* are defined, and then specific index construction and scale construction techniques are discussed.

■ *Multiple Indicators*

As the reader may recall, measurement error is a function of the fit between the concept and the operational definition of that concept. Of course, there are other causes of error, but the main goal is to have a measure that represents the concept perfectly, that is, a measure that does no more and no less than what it was intended to do. In short, a measure that fits the concept exactly.

   In order to ensure this, it is necessary to have more than one **indicator** or item as the measure of the concept. Think of items or indicators as questions in a sur-

Table 4-1 ■ The First Five of Antonovsky's Questionnaire Items

21 Question 1: "When you talk to people, do you have the feeling that they don't understand you?"

Never have this feeling (1)...(2)...(3)...(4)...(5)...(6)...(7) Always have this feeling
No Response (8)
Don't Know (9)

22 Question 2: "In the past, when you had to do something which depended upon cooperation with others, did you have the feeling that it:"

Surely wouldn't get done (1)...(2)...(3)...(4)...(5)...(6)...(7) Surely would get done
No Response (8)
Don't Know (9)

23 Question 3: "Think of the people with whom you come into contact daily, aside from the ones to whom you feel closest. How well do you know most of them?

You feel that they're strangers (1)...(2)...(3)...(4)...(5)...(6)...(7) You know them very well
No Response (8)
Don't Know (9)

24 Question 4: "Do you have the feeling that you don't really care about what goes on around you?"

Very seldom or never (1)...(2)...(3)...(4)...(5)...(6)...(7) Very often
No Response (8)
Don't Know (9)

25 Question 5: "Has it happened in the past that you were surprised by the behavior of people whom you thought you knew well?"

Never happened (1)...(2)...(3)...(4)...(5)...(6)...(7) Always happened
No Response (8)
Don't Know (9)

vey. For example, the concept "sense of coherence" is defined as a perception or belief that the immediate social environment is ordered, manageable, and predictable. Since this perception is manifested in what particular individuals believe about their social contexts, it is necessary to operationalize or measure this concept by going to individuals and recording somehow their beliefs about the predictability, and so forth of their situations. This has been done by Aaron Antonovsky, a medical sociologist who has measured the sense of coherence and found that it is positively associated with health (1979). Antonovsky designed questions that individuals answer as a measure of their sense of coherence. Table 4-1 has a select few of Antonovsky's items or questions (see Appendix C for complete set of items).

Notice that there are several items, all of which are designed to measure the one concept, the sense of coherence. Why not economize and use just one item or question? The answer is that you reduce the chances of undershooting or overshooting the concept by having multiple items. This is because for any given concept, there is a universe of items, literally hundreds of variations and types of measures of the concept, and the best you can do, given time and financial constraints, is to draw a sample of items from that universe. Assuming that probability theory is correct for sampling—that according to the law of large numbers, you are more likely to achieve a true or accurate estimate of social reality out there the larger the number in your sample—you are more likely to measure the concept exactly as you intended to measure it the more items you have in your sample of items. With more than one item, questions that overshoot or measure more than the concept stand a chance of being weeded out or, at least, being canceled out statistically by the items that undershoot the mark. Thus, the competent methodologist always designs multiple indicators for each concept.

■ Unidimensionality

A concept should be defined in such a way that it has an integral part or parts that is its essential meaning. Each part is called a **dimension**. Some concepts have only one dimension, for example, age, defined as that part of an entity extending from its beginning to any given point in time. Here, the dimension is chronological units of time, and there is only one dimension. On the other hand, the sense of coherence concept has three dimensions: manageability, orderliness, and meaningfulness. No matter the number of dimensions, the point is that the set of items or measures for a given dimension must be unidimensional or have only one dimension, ideally the same one as the concept. Thus to have **unidimensionality**, all items in the sense of coherence measure that measure the meaningfulness dimension must measure only that dimension and not order or manageability in addition to meaningfulness.

■ The Index

By combining items of different dimensions into one score, you create an **index**. Much of what I know about index construction comes from a classic practical guide for organizing data so that the researcher knows what he or she is saying and that the researcher has made the most relevant points with the data at hand. The book is *Say It with Figures* by Hans Zeisel, and many of the examples of indices are taken from his superb Chapter 5, "Indices."

Zeisel points out that the researcher must balance or weigh four qualities of the index in constructing one. These qualities are: (1) accuracy; (2) utility, (3) economy, and (4) clarity. Accuracy is really validity, that is, the fit between what the index measures and what it is supposed to measure. In order to test accuracy, the researcher must have some idea, independent of the index, of the status of the entity being measured by the index. Zeisel calls the entity being measured the index object. For example, if you have constructed an index of batting skill, the scores derived from the index ought to represent fairly the batting skills of the baseball players so classified. The independent measure of the index object (batting skill) might come from independent judges of batting skill or from other measures outside of the items making up the index. Utility gets at the issue of the

Table 4-2 ▐ Zeisel Index

Go out together	Almost always	+1
(rather than separately)	Half and Half	0
	Hardly ever	−1
Observe wedding anniversary	Regularly	+1
	Occasionally	0
	Never	−1

practical use to which the index can be put. If the index allows the researcher to draw conclusions that would not have been possible without the index, then utility exists. Or, if the index yields data that can be applied to formulating public policy, for example, the index of socioeconomic status and its role in policy to improve the access of health care for the poor, then the index is useful. The more simple an index, that is, the fewer items and calculations, the more economical it is. However, simplicity comes at the expense of accuracy and, hence, usefulness.

Let's look at an example from Zeisel having to do with the measurement of marital happiness, a sociological phenomenon of great interest today. Clever sociologists like Zeisel begin the task of constructing an index by observing cases of the index object. This means writing up several varieties of specific marriages in the form of detailed qualitative case studies rich with direct quotes. Ideally, you would have a range of marriages, some where the husband and wife indicate that they are extremely happy, others where the couples are miserable, and some in between. You can then scan the cases for telltale features that appear to be associated with happiness or unhappiness. These features will become the items in your index. List all the items, then assign each one a positive, negative, or neutral sign ($+$, $-$, 0), depending on what they indicate about marital happiness. Zeisel constructed a simple index of marital happiness. (See Table 4-2.)

Note that each item has the same weight or value as the others in terms of contributing to the total score, meaning that the items making up the index are of equal importance in measuring marital happiness. If you calculate the arithmetic mean by dividing the sum of the single scores by the total number of observations, the score ranges between -1 and $+1$, with zero being the middle ground between the two extremes. For example, if three people choose positive indicators, four select negative, and six pick zero, the index score would be:

$$\text{Index Score} = \frac{(+3) + (0) + (-4)}{10} = -0.1$$

The push and pull between efficiency, accuracy, and usefulness makes it challenging to construct indices more complex than the example above. Usually, the more of one factor, the less of the other. Usefulness is sacrificed for economy, and accuracy usually means reduced efficiency. Baseball just happens to be one of my favorite sports and also one of the most statistic-laden activities known to humanity, making it a good candidate from which to draw examples of more complex indices and the dilemmas posed by them. There are many statistics that can be used to describe the batting performance of a baseball player. You have hits, strikeouts, runs batted in, home runs, singles, doubles, triples, runs scored, stolen bases, walks, sacrifice hits, number of times at bat, hits with runners on base, outs with runners in scoring position, outs, and so forth. From all these indicators of batting skill, an index was created called the batting average. It is relatively simple, given the number and complexity of the multiple indicators. It is made up from two indicators, the number of times at bat and the number of hits. The number of times at bat is divided into the number of hits, and there you have batting average, an index of batting skill. It is a highly simple index and certainly useful to sportswriters, managers, and team owners in determining a player's salary, position in the batting order, and so forth. However, its simplicity reduces the accuracy in terms of capturing batting skill. But before we can decide this issue of accuracy, we need to define the concept of batting skill. Let's assume that skill includes not only how frequently a batter hits the ball but also how much of a scoring threat he is. Look at the following 1988 major league players:

Player	Bat. Av.	At Bat	Hits	SO	HR	RBI	Steal	2 B	Runs
Craig Biggio	.211	123	26	29	3	5	6	6	14
George Brett	.306	589	180	51	24	103	14	42	90
Kirby Puckett	.356	657	234	83	24	121	6	42	109
Bo Jackson	.246	439	108	146	25	68	27	16	63

The batting average is only one of nine measures of batting skill represented here. The batting average is simple and consequently very useful. Accordingly, we would rank Puckett first, Brett second, Jackson third, and Biggio, a rookie catcher, fourth. But Jackson is first in home runs (HR) and stolen bases, while Biggio has the fewest strikeouts (SO). Something should be telling us that we might benefit from a more complex index of batting skill, one that might include more of the measures above. For example, we might construct the following indices: Runs Batted IN (RBI)/ Hits (H); Walks (W)/ At Bats (AB); Runs (R)/ Hits; Doubles (2B)/Hits; Home Runs/Hits; Steals (S)/Hits; Runs/At Bats; Strikeouts/Hits; and Strikeouts/At Bats. The composite index pictures looks different from the batting average one.

Player	RBI/H	W/AB	R/H	2B/H	HR/H	S/H	R/AB	SO/H	SO/AB
Jackson	.63	.06	.58	.15	.23	.25	.14	1.4	.33
Brett	.57	.14	.50	.23	.13	.08	.15	.28	.09
Biggio	.19	.06	.54	.23	.11	.23	.11	1.1	.24
Puckett	.52	.04	.47	.18	.10	.03	.17	.35	.13

With more information in the form of indices, we gain perspective on the batting skills of the four players, compared to what we knew from the simplified batting average index. Jackson clearly is the more dangerous of the four in terms of generating runs, home runs, and steals out of his hits, but he strikes out more than the other four. Brett is the second most effective in terms of striking out infrequently and generating RBIs, runs and doubles out of his at bats. Biggio, a rookie with very few at bats, ranks very well on runs, doubles, and steals out of his hits, which indicates that he is a threat to pitchers. He does not hit the ball as often as Puckett, but he is more effective at converting his hits into runs and home runs. Puckett, the player who led the American League in batting average and RBIs in 1988, is not as effective a hitter as his league-leading batting average would indicate.

Clearly, we have gained greater insight into batting skill, but the utility of this more complicated data set is less than the simple batting average. It is difficult for the baseball fan to interpret this more complicated set of indices. Again, an overall index score based on the average of the various indices would be easier to interpret but would hide the more interesting details of batting skill or quality. In short, the accuracy of the index is sacrificed for economy and clarity. Still, there are several important biases in the more complex indices. The quality of opposing pitching, the order that the player enjoys in his team's lineup, and the batting skills of his teammates are important factors that contribute to his batting performance. Finally, the indices are weighted equally, that is, each index has the same value for understanding batting skill as the other indices. We assume that RBI/Hits tells us as much about batting skill as SO/Hits.

WEIGHTED INDICES

Many years ago, August Hollingshead developed an index that was designed to measure the social status of individuals. The index was called the "Two Factor Index of Social Position" and was made up of two items: (1) education; and (2) occupation. The main problem for Hollingshead was to justify theoretically and empirically that these two items were the best indicators of social status, a task that he accomplished. Another problem facing him was the question of weighting, that is, should the items be treated as equals? Is occupation as powerful a determinant of status as education, or does occupational status play a larger role than education level in determining how the larger society assigns status to the individual? One needs sociological theory in order to decide whether to weight items and who to distribute the weights.

The two factor index has values and weights assigned to each of the factors. The education factor is based on the number of years of formal schooling completed. The index values are as follows:

Years of School Completed	Index Value
Professional (M.A., M.E., M.D., Ph.D., LL.B.)	1
Four-year college graduate (A.B., B.S., B.M.)	2
1-3 years of college	3
High school graduate	4
10-11 years of school (part high school)	5
7-9 years of school	6
Under 7 years of school	7

The occupation index was set up in a similar fashion. General occupational categories were defined, and under each category the researcher could find many specific occupations. For example, the category "Major Professionals" had under it accountants, actuaries, agronomists, chemists, lawyers, geologists, university professors, and so on. "Lesser Professionals" included chiropractors, health educators, engineers, nurses, opticians, librarians, finance writers, and so forth. Remember that this index was created in the 1930s and the status associated with various occupations was different than it would be today. The important point is that Hollingshead relied on studies of the relative prestige of occupational groups as the basis for assigning the different index values, similar to the education index in this regard. Specifically, the occupational index was designed as the following:

Occupational Category	Index Value
Higher executives, major professionals	1
Business managers, lesser professionals	2
Administrative personnel, minor professionals	3
Clerical, technicians, small business owners	4
Skilled manual employees	5
Semiskilled employees	6
Unskilled and unemployed	7

With these two indices in hand, Hollingshead used the empirical evidence from the studies at the time that tapped into the way people evaluated education versus occupation. On the basis of this research, he decided to place a higher weight on occupation.

Factor	Factor Weight
Occupation	7
Education	4

Let's assume that the respondent is the manager of a chain grocery store and has one year of college under his belt. The index score would be calculated as follows:

Factor	Index Score	Factor Weight	Score X Weight
Occupation	3	7	21
Education	3	4	12
		Index of Social Position (ISP) Score	33

If you calculated the ISP for several hundred respondents, you would have several hundred ISP scores to contend with. You could use the scores as they are in correlations, where the higher the score, the lower the socioeconomic status. Another way to deal with the final index scores is to group them in some coherent fashion. Since it was designed as an index of social status, Hollingshead created five social classes from one, which is the highest status class, to five, which is the lowest. Now the index scores are grouped into one of the five classes, and the researcher will use the five classes in any analysis. The range of scores associated with each class was designated by Hollingshead based on empirical examples. But in the final accounting, the designations are simply conventions, that is, an agreement among researchers that this is the way we will all group the raw scores. Much of methodology is like this.

Class	ISP Scores
1	11-17
2	18-31
3	32-47
4	48-63
5	64-77

Seymour Parker and Robert Kleiner (1966) refined and added to the original Hollingshead ISP. They updated the occupational status scores based on the changes that had taken place in the relative prestige of occupations since the 1930s. More important, Parker and Kleiner added a third factor to the index, which was income. Their index was called "Social Class Index: Parker and Kleiner," and it looked like this:

Number of Years of Education Completed	Step Number
0-4 years	1
5-8 years	2
9-11 years	3
12 years (graduated high school)	4
13-15 years	5
16 years (graduated college)	6
17 years and over	7

Yearly Income	Step Number
$0-999	1
$1,000-1,999	2
$2,000-2,999	3
$3,000-3,999	4
$4,000-4,999	5
$5,000-5,999	6
$6,000 and over	7

Occupation	Step Number
Unskilled workers	1
Sales personnel, semiskilled	2
Skilled craftsmen, skilled clerical	3
Minor administrative, supervisors	4
Second-line management, college-degree professionals	5
Major administrative, corporate officers	6
Major professionals	7

Unlike Hollingshead, Parker and Kleiner weighted education higher than income, which in turn was rated higher than occupation. Their three factor index was calculated in the following manner:

Education step number is _____ × 4.4 = _____
Income step number is   _____ × 2.5 = _____
Occupation step number is _____ × 1.0 = _____

Sum of the three weighted factors divided by 3
Social Class Index score is _____ .

And so it goes with indices, simple to design and accurate if based on theory and empirical findings from other research. There are a few tricks of the trade to assist the researcher in compiling items and forming an index. First, each item or question going into the index should have roughly half the respondents on the positive end of the answer and the other half on the negative side, assuming that the answer categories are dichotomized, that is, grouped into just two possible answers. This is not a hard and fast rule but a warning to be careful about using items that are "skewed" in the sense that the responses are heavily unbalanced or unlike a normal distribution. Perhaps such items are "too easy" in that no one can say "no" or "yes" to them. Whatever the reason, items that have unbalanced responses should be avoided for index ease. Note that scaling requires an intensity structure to the items, thus unbalanced response distributions are to be expected. If everyone answering the question answers positively or even if 90% are favorable, the question probably should not go into an index. Second, the items making up the index ought to correlate with each other but not too highly. A perfect correlation between education and income, for example, would mean that you could get along just as well with one of the two items as you could using both. Using two items in this case is no better than using just one, so you would be wasting your time and the time of the respondent to ask both questions. Only use additional items if they add to the index in the sense that they contribute to the overall score in a meaningful way. While we have seen that items in an index may be weighted differently, the overall index score represents a fairly simple ordinal level classification of individuals along some structure, such as social class, health status, living conditions, honors and productivity (*The Academic Mind*), or modernization.

There is another technique called scaling that, like indices, is a method for putting multiple items together into one summary-type score. The main advantage of scales over indices is that scales tap what is called the "intensity structure" of the items. This is particularly advantageous in attitude measurement. We will turn our attention to scales.

■ *Methodological Principles of Scales*

INTENSITY STRUCTURE

Scales are used primarily in situations where the researcher needs to build perceived intensity into the questions. This problem can be seen when measuring attitudes where the respondent may have different levels of feeling about different issues or persons. The intensity structure enters the picture if the substance of the questions or items has gradations that are socially inherent. For example, there is an intensity structure to the concept of mathematical knowledge. Obviously, mastering calculus is tougher than becoming competent in algebra, which in turn is harder than being able to add, subtract, and divide. We can say that items that measure all three levels of mathematical knowledge are transitive (A > B > C). If calculus is A, algebra B, and arithmetic is C, then you should be able to conclude knowing only that a person has mastered A, that B and C are mastered as well. There is an inherent intensity structure to the items in the sense that they are interdependent and logically linked in a transitive way. There is an inherent scale to the items.

On a sociological level, we can see the intensity structure in a Bogardus Social Distance scale. Here, the substantive problem is to measure an attitude called racial prejudice. The researcher using this scale should realize that there is an intensity structure built into the substance of the items themselves. The substance in this scale is the distance that individuals desire between themselves and various ethnic and racial groups. The intensity is reflected in the distance from an ethnic group that an individual feels should be maintained. For example, you might write several questions about social distance but design them in such a way that the distance shrinks progressively as the respondent moves from one question to the next. An example might go something like the following: "Please tell me whether you agree or disagree with the following statements: (1) I would allow Cambodians to live in the United States; (2) I would allow Cambodians to live in the same town as I do; (3) I would let Cambodians enter my occupational field; (4) I would live on the same block as Cambodians; (5) I would be willing to live next door to a Cambodian; (6) I would allow my son or daughter to marry a Cambodian." Clearly, the items are transitive and share a racial or ethnic social distance intensity. If a respondent disagreed with the first statement, he or she should disagree with all the rest. This is because the first item is the most "intense" in the sense of intensity of prejudice toward Cambodians. The respondent feels so strongly anti-Cambodian that he or she would be intolerant of even the greatest sort of social distance, namely being in the same vast country with Cambodians. On the other side of the scale, if a respondent agreed to allow a child to marry a Cambodian, surely he or she would be willing to live in the same country or on the same block with Cambodians. The intensity of feeling toward ethnic minority groups is built in to the wording of the questions, and it follows a seemingly logical progression.

On a final note, intensity can be built into the items themselves, such as the above example, or it can reside in the response categories where the respondent is asked to express various degrees of agreement or disagreement. For example, an age stereotyping scale that I have used has several items, one of which is: "People my age are set in their ways." The respondents, very elderly individuals, were asked to respond by picking one of the following response categories: strongly agree, agree, disagree, strongly disagree, and a middle-of-the-road option. Here, the intensity is in the responses, not the items.

ACCURACY

Similar to the index, scales require multiple items in order to present the respondent with the intensity structure and to tap the respondent's degree of feeling or attitude. For this reason, scales are made up of multiple items, which improves the accuracy of measurement. For example, reliability statistics will show higher reliability for each additional item added to a scale, up to the point of diminishing returns. Also, you are more likely to have a valid scale the more items that are included, again up to a certain point of excessiveness. Scales are simply better measurement tools with several component items versus a relatively few items.

EFFICIENCY OF DATA ANALYSIS

Scales are composite measures that allow the researcher to summarize the individual scores of all the component items, and the intensity structure helps the researcher interpret the meaning of the scores. This facilitates data analysis in the sense that instead of item-by-item tallies, you have a single, meaningful score. Also, scaling helps the researcher weed out redundant and otherwise unproductive items, thereby increasing the efficiency of analysis by preventing wasteful questioning, recording, and analysis.

POWER OF DATA ANALYSIS

A well-constructed and tested scale should achieve the ordinal or even interval level of measurement. This is not necessarily the case with an index that may yield numbers that are only partially ordered at best. For example, a crowding index using the number of rooms divided by the number of people is an ordinal level measure, but an index of medical student orientation to science using reading preferences, perceived best role as a physician, and ultimate career plans will yield nominal level measurement. Using such an index, the researcher only will be able to classify the medical students in terms of what types of orientations they have with no order to the types. The advantage of ordinal or interval level of measurement resides in the ability of the researcher to use more powerful statistics, which in turn adds quality to the analysis itself.

DIMENSIONALITY

The scale will have a finite and determinable number of dimensions that form the core of the intensity structure. The dimension is the core content matter of the items that the respondent should recognize and respond to accordingly. If the researcher has designed a sense of coherence scale around the dimension of control, then the items in that scale should all have control as their content and the respondents ought to be able to perceive only the dimension of control as the basic reference or content of the items. Scales allow the researcher to test empirically whether or not the intended dimensions are perceived by the respondents. This is partly a validity issue. Scales help the researcher evaluate validity by yielding clues about how well the respondents saw the intended dimension and, thus, measured what the researcher intended to measure.

■ *Types of Scaling*

SUMMATED RATING SCALES

Summated rating scales, usually used to measure attitudes, have several items of equal attitude intensity. Thus, they do not have the increasing intensity structure built into the items that some other scales have. Consequently, summated rating scales are somewhat easier to design.

The respondents answer with varying degrees of intensity to several items. Then the answers are added up (hence, the term *summated*) and the total score is used in the analysis. The individual attitude scores, assuming that the scale is an attitude scale, comprise a range from the lowest score to the highest one. This range can be thought of as an attitude range representing degrees of agreement or disagreement. The several items making up the scale are assumed to be of equal attitude value, that is, no item is any more intense or powerful than any other item in the scale. Thus, summated rating scales are not really scales of items but scales of responses.

The main advantage of this type of scale is the ease with which the researcher is able to design them. After all, there is no intensity structure to think about and to have to build into the items themselves. The big disadvantage is that this type of scale does not provide the researcher with very good evidence about dimensionality. Consequently, they are more difficult to validate in the sense of demonstrating that there is a particular dimension or dimensions underlying the items and that the respondents respond along those dimensions. If it is racial prejudice that your scale purports to measure, then summated rating would not test the extent to which the items have only the dimension "race prejudice" as reflected in the responses. There is no way to ensure that the scores reflect the fact that when the respondents answered the items, they had the dimension and only that dimension in mind. For example, two respondents might have a score of twenty. In one case, the respondent answered all ten items with racial prejudice as the reference point. The respondent kept the concept in mind for every item answered. On the other hand, the second respondent interpreted some of the items as referring to racial prejudice but viewed others in economic terms. Her score is the same as first respondent's, but it is not equal by any means. If you add up twenty roofing nails to get a score of twenty, there is not much of a comparison with a score of twenty derived by adding ten roofing nails, five carpet tacks, and five thumb tacks. Furthermore, even if the researcher can assure that the respondents perceived the intended dimension, there are numerous ways a given score can be reached. Let's assume that you have twenty items with a simple agree-disagree response category. A score of 5 can be produced through 15,504 different combinations of answers (20!/15!/5!). If you are confident that all of the items have equal attitude value, then it should not matter very much what combination of items might have produced a score of 5. Unfortunately, there is no good empirical way to verify the equality of the items, so with summated rating scales, the researcher is on thin ice in treating similar scores as equally representing a given degree of feeling or attitude. Because of this inherent weakness, other scaling methods have been designed in order to help the researcher build an intensity structure into the items and to test or verify that intensity and, consequently, the dimensionality of the scale as well.

LIKERT SCALE

The **Likert scale** was designed by R. Likert in 1937. There are five categories for responses: strongly agree, agree, undecided, disagree, and strongly disagree. The items or statements are classified by the researcher into those that express an unfavorable attitude and those that indicate a favorable one. There should be approximately equal numbers of items on both sides. Items are reflected in the sense that scores for the favorable items are the opposite of the scores for the unfavorable. If "strongly agree" is assigned a one for the favorable items, then it would receive a four for the unfavorable items. Next, the researcher gives what should be a fairly large number of items to respondents representative of the study population in a pretest. The researcher takes all the high-scoring individuals and the low-scoring individuals and looks for items that do not discriminate between the two groups of individuals. For example, if the high scorers and low scorers respond the same way to an item, that item is thrown out. This procedure helps to eliminate unintended dimensions, but it is no guarantee that you are measuring only one dimension or the intended dimension of the concept. The Likert scale offers some evidence, however, that there is an order or intensity structure to the items.

THURSTONE SCALE

The **Thurstone scale** was designed by L. L. Thurstone in 1929, and it is called the equal-appearing interval scale because it is designed to produce items that have defined and equal intervals of intensity between them.

The process begins with the researcher writing 130 items with varying degrees of intensity of agreement in mind. The next step is to round up fifteen expert judges. If the questions were designed to scale attitudes toward death and dying, then the judges might be physicians or medical sociologists. Each judge rates each item by assessing the extent to which it represents a favorable feeling or unfavorable one. Each judge is asked to sort the items (each item is written on a card) into eleven piles, with the first pile containing those items that express the most unfavorable feeling and on to the eleventh pile, which contains most favorable statements. Then the researcher eliminates those items that received widely different ratings and assigns the median scale position or score (pile number) to the remaining items. For example, item number ten might have been rated as follows:

Pile No.	No. of Judges
1	0
2	0
3	0
4	1
5	2
6	6
7	4
8	2
9	0
10	0
11	0

In this example, item number ten would be given the score of six. Once all of the items are grouped according to their median scores, then the researcher picks two items at random from each of the groups, thus ending up with twenty-two or so items in the final scale.

Thurstone scales have the intensity structure built into the writing of the items, and the judges put the finishing touch on by ordering the items along that structure. However, the question of dimensionality still remains. Thurstone scales do not offer an empirical test of whether or not the particular dimension that the items are designed to measure is indeed the one dimension that the respondents are responding to. The Guttman scaling procedure, discussed next, is a classic procedure for building intensity into the items and for testing the dimensionality at the same time. While newer, more powerful scaling procedures have made Guttman scaling relatively obsolete, I feel that the Guttman model is basic to understanding the more complex scaling solutions to the dimensionality problem.

■ Cumulative Scales

GUTTMAN SCALE

Louis Guttman designed a scaling procedure which uses its own internal logic in order to establish that the items have a coherent and logical intensity structure and that there is one dimension underlying the items. Guttman scales are cumulative because the items have an increasing degree of "difficulty" or "hardness" to them. They follow in steps of hardness from the "easiest" to give a favorable response to through the most difficult or "hardest" to say yes to. Going back to the

Bogardus social distance idea, the easiest item to agree to would be to agree to live on the same planet with Carpatho Russians, while the hardest would be to allow your son or daughter to marry a Russian. Thus, if a respondent said no to the easiest, he or she would surely say no to the most difficult as well. The intensity structure is built into the wording or substance of the items. The criteria used to verify this intensity structure and unidimensionality come from the empirical application of the scale and the way the items work together in the overall respondent answer pattern.

Thus, the two major assumptions underlying the **Guttman scale** are: (1) there is an increasing degree of strength or difficulty to the items (scalability); and (2) there is a single dimension to the items (unidimensionality).

Let's look at an example. First, you must define conceptually the dimension that you are setting out to scale. This is standard procedure for any type of measurement where all roads lead to a solid, clear conceptual definition. If you are trying to build a Guttman scale of attitude toward civil liberties, you would define civil liberties as a first step. Assuming that the definition includes freedom from government interference with the right of free speech, we can identify the key dimension as tolerance toward deviant ideas. Tolerance is the one dimension that will form the substance of the scale items, and the intensity of tolerant or intolerant attitudes toward deviant ideas becomes the pattern for the design of the scale itself.

The next step is to write fifteen or so items about tolerance toward deviant ideas. Remember that you need to build the intensity or difficulty into the items. You can think of this as writing examination questions that range from easy to very difficult. Some Guttman items should be very difficult to answer, that is, favorable responses to them would indicate an absolutely intolerant attitude. Other items would be easier in the sense that favorable responses would indicate some degree of intolerance but also tolerance, and still other items would reflect complete unqualified tolerance. The most difficult items would be questions that only the most hardened intolerant person theoretically would agree to, such as banning all homosexual literature, for example. Other items would be less intense, and still others would indicate a highly tolerant attitude toward deviant ideas. One of these latter items might read, "No matter how much I personally dislike the ideas, under no circumstance should people with such ideas different from my own be prevented from expressing those ideas."

Once the items are written and the response categories designed, you must pretest the scale on a hundred or so individuals similar in as many ways as possible to the population targeted for study. Hence, you will end up with roughly one hundred complete response sets to the Guttman items. The responses to each item must be dichotomized (turned into two categories, such as "agree/disagree") and arbitrarily scored in the sense that the "positive" response means that the respondent possessed the attitude or trait, whereas the negative indicates its absence. Once you decide the scoring, it must be consistent for each of the items.

When you pretest the items, you will end up with one hundred responses, some positive (+) and others negative (−). Rank the items from the one with the fewest number of positive answers to the one with the most positives. Then rank the respondents from the person with the greatest number of positive answers to the respondent with the fewest. The result should resemble the following:

Respondent	Items								
	2	9	1	4	6	3	8	7	5
01	+	+	+	+	+	+	+	+	+
08	−	+	+	+	+	+	+	+	+
07	−	−	+	+	+	+	+	+	+
10	−	−	−	+	+	+	+	+	+
45	−	−	−	−	+	+	+	+	+
32	−	−	−	−	−	+	+	+	+
87	−	−	−	−	−	−	+	+	+
78	−	−	−	−	−	−	−	+	+
22	−	−	−	−	−	−	−	−	+
77	−	−	−	−	−	−	−	−	−

The above example is unrealistic in that the number of items is smaller than the fifteen you would ordinarily pretest and the smaller than usual number of respondents fall into the perfect Guttman scale pattern. However, from it, you can see that the items are ranked from the one with the fewest positive responses (theoretically, the "hardest" item, that is, the one which most clearly and unambiguously separates the people who possess the particular attitude from those who do not) to the one with the most. Note also that the respondents are ranked from the person who had the most positive responses to the person who had the fewest, none in this case.

Each of the ten respondents represents a pure scale type that ranges from the most of whatever attitude the scale is designed to measure to the least. If your scale was measuring tolerance, the respondent 01 would be considered the most tolerant and 77 the least.

ERROR RESPONSES

Error responses are patterns where certain respondents do not fit the ideal typical pattern portrayed above. They are error responses relative to the ideal patterns because the ideal represents perfect scalability and 100% unidimensionality as well, a situation impossible to achieve in the real world of research.

An error is any response that does not conform to one of the scale types. For example, the response pattern, + + − − − + + + +, would have three errors relative to the scale type, + + + + + + + + +. In this case, the negative responses do not fit the ideal pattern, so they are considered errors. However, if you placed the response set in the scale type, − − − − − + + + +, there would be only two errors, namely, the first two positive responses.

This brings us to a couple of more important decisions to be made. First, you should move respondents and their response sets around in order to minimize errors. Once you have the error responses set within the scale types that keep any error at a minimum, then you must count all of the error responses for each item.

If any one item has more than 50% error, that item should be discarded. Remember, you may discard items, not respondents. If an item is discarded, the whole procedure must be done again, including the error calculations.

Fortunately, we have computer programs that do all of this work for you. In the old days before canned computer programs and PCs, researchers had to compute Guttman scales by hand, using cut and paste or the scalogram board, a device similar to the abacus. The computer program will achieve the best combination of items and then will compute the coefficient of reproducibility (C of R), which is the test used to determine whether or not the scale is a Guttman scale. The C of R is computed in the following manner:

$$\text{C of R} = 1 - \frac{\text{Number of Errors}}{\text{\# of Respondents} \times \text{\# of Items}}$$

The C of R will yield numbers ranging from zero to one. The established rule of thumb is that the C of R should be .90 or greater in order to conclude that the scale is unidimensional and scalable in the Guttman way, that is, that you have a Guttman scale.

ORDERED ALTERNATIVE SCALE

Muzafer Sherif and Carolyn Sherif (1969) pioneered the research and theory that led to the development of the ordered alternatives scaling (OAS) method. This type of scale is best suited for research that is based on symbolic interactionist theory. The basic assumptions underlying the **ordered alternatives scale** consist of the following theoretical propositions:

1. Each individual has a frame of reference that functions as the foundation for all thought and action. This frame of reference consists of factors internal to the individual, such as attitudes, motives, and values, and external environmental factors, such as the physical environment, social networks (reference groups), and so forth.

2. Attitudes are very important for the individual in structuring the other components of the frame of reference because attitudes form the basis for evaluating objects and events, for determining whether they are acceptable or objectionable.

3. An object or event forms a domain, for example, the domain of the abortion controversy or the domain of the unification of Germany. Each domain has categories that represent possible or real outcomes. For example, the abortion controversy might be considered as having several faces, including abortion upon demand, abortion only in the case of rape, incest, or danger to the life of the mother, and no abortion under any circumstances.

4. These various categories in any attitude domain are the properties of attitude. As such, they are the evaluative criteria for attitude because it is these categories that the individual reacts to in terms of finding them acceptable, unacceptable, or neutral.

5. This feeling toward the categories is scalable because people have degrees of feeling.

With these points in mind, OAS was developed to scale people's attitudes within specific attitude domains. Because it is assumed that properties of attitudes vary in importance, then the attitude itself must be scalable in terms of the extent to which individuals consider it important for their frame of reference. Methodologically, OAS should allow the researcher to scale attitudes and to determine the degree of involvement of individuals in the attitude.

OAS has what is called the latitude of acceptance, the latitude of rejection, and the latitude of noncommitment. Given a particular attitude domain, individuals are able to look at the categories or properties and decide which ones are acceptable, which are unacceptable, and which ones he or she is neutral about. More specifically, OAS requires that the researcher complete the following steps:

1. Design a set of statements within an attitude domain that span the full range of normal possible outcomes or attitudes in the domain. Usually, this involves nine or more items. For example, an OAS on attitude toward death and dying might include such categories as full knowledge of fatal illness, dying at home, hospice or hospital, terminating heroic treatments, and so forth;

2. Ask the respondent to choose the one statement that is most acceptable, that is which comes closest to his or her own attitude about the category;

3. Then ask the respondent to choose any other statements that are acceptable;

4. Choose the one statement that is considered the most objectionable; and finally,

5. Indicate which other statements, if any, the respondent considers objectionable.

From this exercise, the researcher will be able to scale the respondent's attitudes on the particular issue in terms of the most acceptable, the least acceptable, the latitude of acceptance (all the statements found acceptable), the latitude of rejection, and the latitude of noncommitment. Theoretically, individuals who have a very small latitude of acceptance and a very large latitude of rejection are very involved and committed to that particular category defined as acceptable. Conversely, individuals who indicate a wide latitude of acceptance with very few, if any, categories rejected, would be relatively uninvolved or committed to the issue in question. Thus, the size of the latitude of rejection is most important in determining how strongly individuals feel about some attitude domain. The larger the latitude, the more strongly the commitment to the attitude. According to Sherif and Sherif, strong commitment to a particular attitude means that the person will be very discriminating in the choice of categories, accepting a very few while rejecting most of the other choices. Schematically, this scale type would look like the following:

[A] [NC] [R   ]

_____

Persons who are less committed to the attitude categories and who are less involved emotionally with the attitude domain are less discriminating in terms of committing themselves in accepting or rejecting the objects in the domain, the choices. Thus, their pattern can be represented by:

[A] [R] [NC   ]

_____

One of the practical applications of this technique is that people who have large latitudes of rejection are the very least likely to change their attitudes. If you were trying to convince individuals to vote for a political candidate who supported a woman's right to choose abortion and you measured attitude toward abortion with an OAS, you would be wise to put any efforts to change people's minds on abortion toward those individuals with large noncommitment and small rejection latitudes.

Q METHODOLOGY

Unlike other scaling techniques, **Q methodology** is designed to scale individuals, rather than items. Also different is the fact that Q requires sixty to ninety items, a huge number compared to Thurstone or Guttman scaling techniques. Not only is the size of the item set so much larger than other scaling techniques, but Q also demands that the items contain many dimensions reflecting every conceivable view or position on the topic in question. This scaling technique was invented by Will Stephenson (1953), who applied it extensively in his research at the University of Missouri School of Journalism.

Starting with a carefully defined research problem, for example, the norms governing university professors' thinking concerning the university, the researcher sets out to write sixty to one hundred statements about what a university ought to be and do. This requires thorough coverage of the waterfront in the sense that all possible normative statements, regardless of how bizarre they may seem, must be represented. One way to expedite this stage is to gather normative statements from university professors, administrators, higher education task force members, extremist or radical groups, and anyone else deemed appropriate. Publications about the role and scope of universities also can be screened for content.

The next step, given the example research problem above, is to get university professors to sort all of the statements according to degrees of personal approval or preference. Usually, the degree of approval ranges from zero to ten:

Highly Approve										Highly Disapprove
10	9	8	7	6	5	4	3	2	1	0

The researcher may ask the respondents to put a certain number of the statements in each of the eleven categories, or it could be left to the discretion of the respondents. The advantage of setting the desired number of statements for each of the eleven categories is that a normal curve can be approximated, with very few statements at the two extremes and the largest number between categories 3 and 8. Thus, the researcher would ask the respondents to put five statements in category 10, six in category 9, and so forth.

In short, what the respondents are doing is ranking the one hundred statements from the most to the least approved. Each respondent has a rank order, that is, a particular pattern or way that the statements are ranked.

The analysis is to compare the respondents in terms of their rank orders. Using a rank-order correlation technique, one is able to find clusters of respondents whose rankings correlate highly. The bottom line of Q methodology is to compare the rank orders and to interpret the groupings or clusters of respondents. The way to interpret the results of the correlations is to study the content of the statements that the clusters of respondents have ranked in common. If cluster A, for example, has ranked statements expressing the norm of learning for learning's sake as the most highly approved statements, the researcher might then give a conceptual name to that group, perhaps "traditionalists." Then again, perhaps another cluster centered around the statements having to do with the obligation of universities to train students to get good jobs. Those respondents might be called "instrumentalists," and so it goes. The respondents are classified according to the content of the statements that the classes ranked in common. The respondents who ranked statements similarly comprise clusters or groups of individuals, and the factor analysis is commonly used to derive the clusters.

Q methodology is an excellent technique for building or developing concepts and theory. More importantly, it is a powerful device for monitoring and explaining change in attitudes.

Computerized programs exist that help the researcher design indices and scales. Factor analysis and cluster analysis search large numbers of items in order to select groups of items that "hang together." These groups of items are called common factors or clusters, and the researcher assumes that the items comprising the clusters or factors share properties in common, like items making up an index.

■ *Missing Data*

Missing data can try the patience of even the most even-tempered methodologist. It is a particularly aggravating problem for scales. Missing data is a term that encompasses responses or nonresponses that cannot be analyzed as a category of the variable in question. For example, the Antonovsky sense of coherence items discussed earlier (and in Appendix C) have response categories 1 (never have this feeling) through 7 (always have this feeling) that are analyzed as part of the scale. However, response categories 8 (no response) and 9 (don't know) constitute missing data because neither of those responses fit the scale pattern. They do not add to our knowledge about the respondents' sense of coherence.

If you are adding response categories 1 through 7 for all the items in order to derive a scale score, any item with an 8 or 9 response is unusable. You cannot drop only the items with missing data because the scale is a totality and every item is essential. The only thing to do is to drop respondents who have responded 8 or 9 to any of the items. Obviously, this is not the best eventuality, but it will work. The best strategy is to work on avoiding missing data through careful pre-testing and other field work strategies discussed in later chapters.

◼ *Conclusions*

Indices and scales are used in quantitative measurement as a means of improving the odds that the researcher has measured what he or she has set out to measure (validity). Scales help the researcher assess the extent to which he or she is measuring one dimension, and both indices and scales serve to reduce measurement error by the use of multiple indicators to measure a concept. Analysis is simplified greatly by using indices and scales.

Some scales, such as those of Thurstone and Guttman, are used to measure and classify attitudes while another, the Q methodology, is designed to classify individuals. Indices, too, have multiple uses in measurement. The researcher might construct a general index that would be easier to interpret than a more complicated one with more detailed items. However, the more detailed index would contain more information, albeit with heightened difficulty in interpreting its data.

Finally, scales help the researcher tackle the difficult methodological principles of measurement, such as intensity structure, dimensionality, accuracy, and efficiency of data analysis.

GLOSSARY

dimension   a part or feature of a concept integral to its essential meaning.

Guttman scale   a scaling procedure that uses its empirical application to verify that the items measure one dimension and that the scale intensity structure exists.

index   a single measure comprised of multiple items with multiple dimensions.

indicator   the question or item used to measure a concept.

Likert scale   a scale with one-half of the items expressing a favorable attitude and the other half, unfavorable, with five response categories: strongly agree, agree, undecided, disagree, and strongly disagree.

Ordered Alternatives Scale   an attitude scale, based in symbolic interaction theory, that measures strength of attitude and commitment to it.

Q methodology   unlike any other scaling technique, it scales individuals by grouping them according to their pattern of ranking items.

scale   a cohesive set of items with a graduated intensity structure.

summated rating scales   a type of scale used to measure attitudes by adding the scores of items of equal intensity.

Thurstone scale   a scale using judges to produce items with an intensity structure and equal intervals between the scores.

unidimensionality   one dimension in a concept determined through measurement using Guttman scaling, factor analysis, or other scaling techniques.

FOR FURTHER READING

Lazarsfeld, Paul F., Pasanella, Ann K., and Rosenberg, Morris. (1972). *Continuities in the language of social research* (pp. 1–118). New York: Free Press.

Miller, Delbert C. (1977). *Handbook of research design and social measurement* (3d ed., pp. 86–97). New York: David McKay.

Oppenheim, A. N. (1966). *Questionnaire design and attitude measurement.* New York: Basic Books.

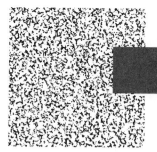

Chapter Five

QUESTIONNAIRE CONSTRUCTION

▌ *Using lots of examples from sociological research, the principles of questionnaire construction are discussed as a basis for deciding upon specific strategies for formats, wording, and relevance for the respondent.*

"Keep it simple," admonished Ed Suchman, my methodology instructor in the graduate program of sociology at the University of Pittsburgh. "If you want to know something, ask," he went on. "There is no mystery to designing a good questionnaire. Know what you want to ask, know how you are going to analyze it, and keep it short."

That was vintage Suchman, one of the founders of survey research and a brilliant practitioner of the art. Because he was so good at designing and carrying out surveys, Suchman tended to assume that survey tasks, such as questionnaire construction, came as easily to others as they came to him. Of course, this assumption was false. After repeated attempts to design a questionnaire, none of us in Suchman's methodology course could keep a straight face when he spoke those words above. No mystery? Who was he kidding?

Fortunately, our incompetence outshone Suchman's brilliance. Rising to the challenge, he presented clear and insightful lectures on questionnaire construction. This chapter is based in large part on Suchman's ideas presented in that methodology class long ago. The rest of it comes from colleagues and my own experiences over the years with questionnaire construction.

The chapter begins with some methodological principles governing questionnaires. Next, techniques and strategies for writing questions and response categories are covered. Finally, formatting issues are discussed, along with methods for ensuring maximum return rates for mailed questionnaires.

91

■ *Methodological Principles*

CONCEPTUALIZATION/RECONCEPTUALIZATION

The great art form called the American quilt serves as a metaphor for the questionnaire. A quilt is a patchwork of myriad different pieces all joined together by some common organizing theme. Each piece has its own symmetry and self-contained beauty. It could stand alone as a work of art. Several pieces make up a square. It too is a self-contained unit. Dozens of squares are joined to form the whole quilt with its big pattern. Every stitch, each piece of cloth, every color has a perfectly logical reason for being included in the whole. If the quilt is to have integrity and symmetry, every little piece must be absolutely necessary. Things added as an afterthought or other interesting but nonessential pieces only detract from the quilt and even can ruin it.

The questionnaire is a patchwork of concepts that have been operationalized. Each concept included should be a logically necessary part of the theory or explanation of the research problem. The researcher should be able to defend each and every concept in terms of how it contributes to the understanding of the research problem. Some concepts are necessary in order to understand other concepts, while others are joined together to form the theoretical argument called the explanation of the problem. Regardless, there should be no concepts in the study that do not have a direct bearing on the explanation.

Each concept is represented in the questionnaire by its operational definition. The reader is reminded that concepts are first defined at an abstract level, then they may be defined operationally or at the measurement level. Depending on how the operational definition is worded, the concept will be measured at either the nominal, ordinal, or interval level of measurement. The operational definition is the reconceptualization of the conceptual definition, which is why we call it the **conceptualization/reconceptualization** process.

The questionnaire is composed of all of the operational definitions. It is the map of the reconceptualization process that the researcher should be able to use as a tool for testing or even constructing the theory. Each **operational definition** ought to refer to a known and necessary concept. Furthermore, since the concepts should form a theory or whole explanation, that is, hang together logically, so too should the operational definitions form a whole fabric. Each operational definition could stand on its own, but the questionnaire is a whole, so all of the operational definitions hang together to produce that whole. For example, my study of the rural elderly had an interview schedule[1] consisting of more than one hundred operational definitions. In spite of the large number of operational definitions (variables), the research problem was simple and precise, namely, an effort to test the explanation that longevity within the context of independent living was "caused by" interaction in social networks. Once the theory was elaborated and the concepts defined abstractly, the explanation used the concepts of net-

---

[1]For the sake of brevity, I use the term *questionnaire* in a generic sense to refer to structured and semistructured interview schedules and self-administered questionnaires.

work participation, health status, socioeconomic status, and life satisfaction as predictors of living a long independent life. This was the theortical coherence, the whole fabric of the questionnaire. All of the operational definitions contributed to the measurement of those key variables. There was no room for thinking, "It sure would be nice to include some consumer economic measures along with attitudes toward the economy." Consumer economic behavior was not part of my theory, which meant that I had no sound basis for including measures of it in the questionnaire.

JUSTIFY EACH QUESTION

The principle is that all operational definitions in the questionnaire must be justified through their role in providing essential measurement for concepts that are fundamental to the theory. The assumption behind this principle is that you really need a theory before setting out to design a structured or semistructured questionnaire. It does not have to be a carefully worked-out theory, but regardless of how rough, you need a theory.

The alternative is to design a questionnaire without the guidance of theory, that is, to create a reconceptualization without the conceptual map. The resulting questionnaire might possibly be exciting and productive of theory building, but the chances are better that it will produce confusion and lots of dead ends. Methodologists call this latter atheoretical approach the "shotgun" or, more prosaically, the "garbage can" approach to questionnaire construction. It is a shotgun or garbage can because the questionnaire is made up of an unconnected smorgasbord of operational definitions. You have a smattering of social class questions, a few mental health items, some questions on attitudes toward death and dying, and so forth. There is no solid rationale or logic for including questions other than personal interest or a researcher's hunch.

Certainly there should be room for hunches and creativity in research but not with structured and semistructured questionnaires. The place for exploration and creative testing is qualitative measurement and case study design, not quantitative measurement and survey design. Structure locks the researcher into a course of action. In the survey with massive numbers of cases and a standardized questionnaire, there is little or no room for changing your mind about questions should they not pan out. The simple methodological truth of the matter is that a questionnaire needs an organizing theoretical theme, a whole picture if you will, and the researcher ought to be able to justify each and every operational definition or question according to its contribution to that theme. If a question does not add to explanation in a known way, then discard it.

THE HUMAN SIDE OF OPERATIONAL DEFINITIONS

The tendency in research circles is to objectify and even reify the operational definitions. By this, I mean that researchers tend to view their concepts and the measures as having inherent or ultimate meaning. Nothing could be farther from the truth. Operational definitions are creations of the researcher, as are concepts.

Recalling that there is a universe of potential concepts that could be used to classify or explain an element of human behavior, so too is there a universe of operational definitions. For example, we observe people purchasing items that seem to have absolutely no practical use. In fact, the purchasers already are overwhelmed with similar items, yet they buy more. You analyze this pattern and conceptualize it as "conspicuous consumption." Another researcher might define it as "social climbing," while still another could see it as "creative waste." The point here is that conceptualization is a judgment call and an artifact of the researcher's mind.

Similarly, reconceptualization can be done any number of ways, depending on the orientation of the researcher. In as much as there are numerous ways to define social processes conceptually, so are there many ways to operationalize concepts. Social class, for example, has been measured using questions about the contents of the respondent's living room, by finding out what the respondent's education, income, and occupational statuses are, and even by asking respondents what social class they think of themselves as belonging to. Another interesting case is the concept age. It has been defined conceptually as chronological age but also as mental age. Operationally, mental age has been transformed into dozens of intelligence inventories. Chronological age may be measured in several ways. I have asked respondents how many years old they were on their last birthday, what their birthdate is, which of several five-year age groups they place themselves in, and even how old they think of themselves as. Health status is similar with many conceptual and operational possibilities. The question, "How is your health generally? Would you say that it is 'good,' 'fair,' or 'poor'?" is one operational definition used quite a bit. Another way is to ask the respondent, "Compared with people your age, would you say that your health is . . . ?". Or, you might ask respondents to go down a long checklist of symptoms, asking them if they have ever had these things and if so, whether they are bothersome now. The point is that operational definitions are the creations of researchers. In as much, they are useful for purposes known to the researcher and dictated by the conceptual definitions, but operational definitions have no meaning beyond this.

MULTIPLE ITEMS REDUCE BIAS

Think of operational definitions or items in a questionnaire as only a sample of the universe of items possible. As we saw above, there are many different ways to operationalize any given concept and the sample of items you choose could be representative of the universe or they could be biased, that is, nonrepresentative. As such, choosing items for a questionnaire is similar to a sampling design problem.

One way to avoid this bias is to have multiple items for each concept measured. Thus, if I am measuring social class, I would strive to have at least two questions for this purpose. Never settle for only one item. This is one case where more is better, up to a point, of course. With three or four items to measure a concept, the chances are better than with only one item of achieving reliability through adequate representation of the universe. With several items, a weakness in one direction has a chance of being counteracted by a strength in another direction. Ideally, one item will pick up where the other left off. But if you use only one item as a measure and it happens to be off the mark, your operational definition is off the mark.

REFERENCE POINTS

The questionnaire is a creation of the researcher's thinking. As a whole product, it represents the researcher's "model" of the research problem. The types of questions asked, the substantive content of the questions, the response categories, and the scope of respondent knowledge required by the questions constitute the researcher's view of social reality, which is imposed on respondents.

Because the questionnaire is an artifact of the researcher's thought processes, it is essential to provide the respondent with as complete a grounding as possible in what the researcher's model or thinking is about. This means two things. First, the respondent should be informed about the nature of the research problem and what the researcher's theory is. Second, each question must be made absolutely clear to the respondent. All vagaries and ambiguities must be excised.

Providing the respondent with a context or **reference point** for each question is the way to accomplish this goal of clarity of items. For example, the question "How has your health been generally?" is lacking in reference points. It would be much clearer to the respondent in terms of how to interpret what you mean by the question, that is, what you want to measure by it, if the respondent was told something about the time frame for assessing personal health as well as the standard to compare his or her health against. Health relative to what and over what time period? It would be a much better question, that is, much clearer to the respondent, if it had been worded, "During the past six months, how has your health been generally compared to people your age?" Similarly, if the question presupposes specific knowledge on the respondent's part, the researcher must provide the bare bones of that knowledge. For example, if you wanted to measure respondent attitudes toward the Supreme Court's *Roe v. Wade* decision, you should provide a brief description of that decision as part of the question. The best safeguard in terms of respondent knowledge is to choose respondents for which the research topic is salient or relevant.

I had an interesting experience this past year as I was doing the final wave of interviews for the twenty-year panel study on the rural elderly. For this experience, I learned that providing reference points can be a problem if not thought out and pretested carefully. In the two earlier interviews, 1966 and 1974, the respondents were asked a series of questions designed to measure stereotypical thinking about the elderly. My hypothesis was that younger people harbored prejudices or stereotypical thoughts about the elderly. It was hypothesized that the young were fearful of growing old and also had very little face-to-face interaction with elderly people. Consequently, it was thought that young people would hold a series of stereotypes about the elderly. Because U.S. society is dominated by youth socially and culturally, the elderly respondents would perceive these stereotypes and internalize them, that is, come to believe them.

I asked the elderly respondents to tell me how they thought about statements that were stereotypes about the elderly. For example, one statement read, "Old people are set in their ways." The respondents were asked to react to the statements with the following direction: "I am going to read some statements about old people. For each statement, please think about it and tell me how *you personally* believe about it. Do you strongly agree, agree, disagree, strongly disagree, or are you neutral on it? A card with the Likert-type response categories was given to the respondent to aid in remembering the choices. Notice that the reference point was "old people," a term that was perfectly appropriate in 1966 and 1974 but not in 1987, when I was doing the last wave of interviews. By this time, elderly people had raised the consciousness of the larger society about using terms that elderly people considered derogatory and barriers toward reaching their goals in retirement. Old had come to mean "used up," something needing to be thrown away.

In order to protect the integrity of the respondents and to show them the proper deference, I changed the wording of these questions. This maneuver was very costly in terms of the theoretical problems it caused. In order to compare the responses to questions from one time period to another, the question must remain the same between the two samplings. Here, I was changing the content of the items, which in turn made it very difficult to attribute change in the responses to anything other than the change in the wording.

In any case, I changed the wording in all the items to read: "People my age are. . . ." The result was interesting. One ninety-five-year-old man stopped me half way through the questioning and said, "I can't answer these questions." Being a good interviewer always alert to tracking down the leads, I reflected on his phrase, "Can't answer these questions?" The respondent replied, "No, I can't because I don't know anybody my age anymore." All of his peers had died, leaving him without a reference group of people his age.

This illustrates the difficulty of providing a meaningful and appropriate reference point and underscores well the need to spend time early in the instrument design phase of the research to pretest the questions and their response categories. I had done this with elderly people representative of my sample, but the problem with the wording was not uncovered before it was too late to do anything about it.

PRETEST

Test the wording of the questions and even the analysis before getting too far into the field work. This bit of advice was imparted by Suchman, who was a master at figuring out the very best measurement strategy for a given research problem. He was a believer in revising.

Suchman's method was to write questions carefully using other people's tested work where possible. Once the questionnaire was together and the usual face validity checks made, Suchman would conduct a conventional **pretest** of the questionnaire. The next step is where his innovative creative genius departed from conventional methodological wisdom. Instead of producing a final clean version of the questionnaire, he would keep the rough draft copy and make enough copies of it to get the research project through two or three weeks of field work. With the rough draft in action, Suchman coded the results as they came into the research office, put them on the computer, and began the basic analysis according to plan. Simultaneous to his checking the answers to the questions, Suchman would call the field work staff into the office to brainstorm over the questionnaire and any other field work issues that might have arisen. If the computer analysis or the discussions with the field workers turned up any problems with question content or wording, Suchman made the appropriate changes. He gave the changes one week in the field, repeated the analysis procedure, and then settled on the final version, assuming the problems had been ironed out to the best of his ability. He knew that perfection was illusory, so his final version was considered to be a compromise sufficient to get the job of answering the research question done.

This approach had an unanticipated consequence of facilitating, speeding up if you will, the writing up of the study's findings. Because the analysis plan was in place and the statistical models ready to go before the field work began, not only was Suchman able to test the utility of his explanatory model before he got too far into field work, but he was also able to get the results into print faster than anyone I have ever worked with or observed. It was as if he had a template for the written report ready to go before generating any of the data.

One example sticks out in my mind. Suchman went to the University of California at Santa Barbara for one year as a visiting professor of sociology. Upon arriving for the fall semester, he required his undergraduate methodological students in sociology to conduct a large survey of a random sample of the entire undergraduate student body at the university. The research problem was to explain the use of marijuana by students. Before he left to return to Pittsburgh at the end of the spring semester, the study was completed, and the results were published as "The Hang Loose Ethic and the Spirit of Drug Use" in the *Journal of Health and Social Behavior*. The field work and the analysis were completed essentially at the same time, thereby expediting the writing of the paper.

COVER THE BASES

Covering the bases is a technique designed to give the researcher the best of all possible questionnaire construction worlds. Simply put, it means using different questionnaire techniques together on the one research problem. Just as the navigator takes three different measures, for example, the sun, the horizon, and time, and brings them together to pinpoint the location of the ship, so too can the researcher use open-ended, fixed choice, statements, and questions all in one questionnaire to good advantage.

STATEMENTS AND QUESTIONS

At one level of questionnaire construction, you have two choices to make. The items in the questionnaire can be written as statements, for example, "People my age are set in their ways," or as questions, for example, "How has your health been generally?" Using both styles in the same questionnaire breaks up the monotony created by relying on only questions or statements, plus it capitalizes on the advantages of each approach. Statements can be tailored to measure sensitive topics but in a nonpersonal, general, and thereby less threatening fashion. The respondent is asked to react to somebody elses' idea rather than answer a pointed question about his or her own views.

OPEN-ENDED AND CLOSED ANSWER CATEGORIES

Also questions can be written without any specific answer categories (open-ended questions), or they may have fixed response categories (closed-answer questions). **Open-ended questions** allow the respondent to answer completely on his or her terms, unencumbered by the researcher's idea of what appropriate answers might be. For example, during the nineteen or so years in which I taught medical students how to do interviews with hospital patients, I advised them to use open questions throughout the interview. The students typically would start with "Tell me, Mrs. Pickering, what circumstances caused you to be hospitalized?" That was it; no response categories were provided in order to channel the respondent's thinking. Rather, the respondent was given a figurative blank page on which to write or state all of the things viewed as important contributions to the hospitalization. In order to get more specific if necessary, the interviewer could probe along certain line, such as, "And what about your husband's part in the decision to come to the hospital?" The key to the open-ended question is to write it in such a way that the respondent has maximum freedom to answer as deemed appropriate. You can use such phrases as, "Tell me about. . . ." Be sure to provide enough lines for the interviewer or the respondent to record the answer. The open question might read as follows: "Tell me about your family."

The **closed answer question** forces the respondent to address the issue in terms that the researcher has decided are important to know. Rather than measuring what the respondent chooses to say about her family, the closed answer question would force the respondent to think about and react to very specific problems or issues of family life. Perhaps the literature has shown that families in which the husband controls the disposition of his income and the wife, her's have higher life satisfaction scores than families where the dual income is under the sole control of one spouse. Under these conditions, the researcher might want to avoid the general "tell me about . . ." in favor of fixed choice questions. Such a question might read, "Which of the following statements best describes the way in which your family income is controlled? 1. Husband has sole control over his pay. 2. Wife has sole control over her pay," and so forth. This approach helps ensure that the respondent is thinking and answering along the lines that you intended. Of course, the open-ended approach provides relatively unstandardized responses, which makes analysis more cumbersome, whereas the closed-ended format enhances your ability to plan out the analysis well in advance of the field work and to analyze the data quickly as it comes in.

Closed-ended response categories ought to conform to the measurement principles of: (1) exhaustiveness and (2) mutual exclusiveness. **Exhaustive response categories** are those in which the researcher is able to fit or categorize every one of the responses. **Mutually exclusive response categories** are those in which the answer selected by the respondent can be put in one and only one category. Thus, the response categories must cover all the responses and do it in such a way that there is no hesitation or uncertainty as to which one of the categories a specific response belongs. The simplest way to ensure that your closed-ended categories are exhaustive is to provide what has been called the "garbage can" category of "Other (please specify) _____ " and the old stand-by, "Don't know." There is some evidence (Bishop et al., 1986) that trying to force respondents into selecting one of the categories that are analytically useful (you cannot analyze "don't know" responses other than to tally how many there are and to see if the question was understood or relevant to the respondents) can backfire with respondents tending to express opinions on things they know nothing about, that is, on issues that are completely irrelevant to them.

There is no simple expedient for ensuring that the categories are mutually exclusive. Pretesting helps decide the issue, along with instructions to the respondent such as, "Please choose the one best response that most nearly describes how *you personally* feel about the following statements."

SIMPLE QUESTIONS

One of the most common mistakes that designers of questionnaires make is to try and cram too much information into any given question. Because of the space and time limitations placed on research, the thinking seems to be along the lines of getting two questions for the price of one.

Usually, this is manifested in the phenomenon known as the double-barreled question. Here, you ask two questions in one sentence. For example, my panel study of the rural elderly involved a very important predictor variable called social networks. This variable was a powerful predictor of longevity, and it involved several qualitatively different types of social networks. These included family of origin, family of procreation, relatives, friends, and formal organization memberships. It turned out that only one type of social network, membership in formal organizations, was a predictor of longevity. If I had created a double-barreled question to save space and time, for example by asking, "Please indicate below the number of times in the last six months that you had face-to-face contact with family members or your associates in your organized groups," I would have been unable to sort out the difference in terms of contact with family and with the organization members. In short, it would have been impossible to decide after the fact whether a response of "ten times" referred to family, organization, or both.

Write questions that have only one dimension to them. This means that you must have a clear conceptual definition first in order to decide whether you have one dimension, and the correct one at that, in your questions. Usually, short, simple sentence questions are a step in the right direction.

NEGATIVE ON THE NEGATIVE QUESTIONS

Reflecting on the double negative problems in questionnaires that I have observed and, yes, even contributed to, I have to agree with the line from *My Fair Lady* where Henry Higgins accuses Americans of not having spoken English for years. Consider the following: "Please read each statement and indicate whether you agree or disagree with it.

     1. Death is not something to fear.
           ____ Agree
           ____ Disagree"

A "disagree" response (double negative: the question and the response are both negative) is difficult to interpret. Is the respondent afraid of death or not? The same problem would occur if the respondents are given "yes" and "no" response categories for a negatively worded question. For example, the question might be worded: "Please indicate how you feel about the following statements by selecting either the 'yes' or 'no' answers provided. Physicians should not be allowed to do the following things:

Perform abortions ____ yes ____ no

Own hospitals   ____ yes ____ no"

If the researcher insists on wording the question negatively, in this case, it would help to change the response categories to read: ____ allow ____ not allow, rather than ____ yes ____ no. The simplest thing is to avoid the double negative and negatively phrased questions.

LEADING QUESTIONS

The term *leading* means that the question is worded in such a way that the respondent is encouraged to answer a certain way. The researcher lets the respondent know through the wording of the question what the "correct" or "acceptable" response is.

Max Weber (1949) warned social scientists about the folly of believing that research could be totally objective. Subjectivity is inherent in the research act. The researcher's values are behind the particular research question chosen for study, and the epistemology subscribed to by the researcher guides his or her formulation of the questions. Nevertheless, we must strive to keep this inherent subjectivity to a bare minimum by avoiding the more blantant mistakes associated with leading the respondent along.

One common mistake is to invoke the name or main idea of some well-known person. If the person is well-respected, then the positive halo effect could be a problem. For example, you might word the question: "Abraham Lincoln's policy concerning congressional power over the president to declare war has never been challenged. Do you agree or disagree with President George Bush's view that the president has the power over Congress to declare war?" On the negative side, if you were measuring U.S. citizens' tolerance toward socialists speaking on the radio, you would be better off providing some general definition of socialist than using some prominent socialist's name in the questions. "Would you allow Fidel Castro to speak on NPR?" might tap how people feel about Castro as a person but miss the mark on how tolerant they are toward socialists.

This principle extends to the use of words or phrases that carry emotional or ideological baggage with them. Terms such as *un-American, liberal, conservative, communist, welfare state, pro-life, drug abuser,* and *anti-religious,* are "loaded" words and dangerous to use without detailed clarification. Other words that have become media cliches should be avoided, such as *yuppie, drug czar,* and *supermom.* Generally, stick to simple English and avoid colloquialisms, slang, media words, and ideologically charged words in writing questions.

On very rare occasions, **leading questions** are necessary and even desirable. Extreme reluctance to answer the questions is one case where leading questions might spell the difference between getting the data or not. I recall being on the receiving end of the leading question tactic back in 1971. I had just completed a study of citizen control in comprehensive mental health centers for the poor. During the course of the research, my colleagues and I had uncovered some graft and nepotism by center administrators. We included these findings along with the analysis of the citizen movement, keeping the identity of the centers confidential as per our promise to the center administrators. The report was published, and it received considerable acclaim.

Not long after its publication, the Center for Responsive Law (a Ralph Nader organization) got into the act. Two Ph.D. researchers from that center called me and began firing leading questions right and left. One of the questions was: "If you are decent at all and supportive of citizen control, you would answer the questions. Who are the administrators?" When I refused to answer, they asked: "Then what is your position on citizen control?" Without hesitation, I vented my anger at being thusly confronted by giving them a long answer, precisely what they wanted of me. Then they asked me to spell out my thinking generally on corruption at the centers, and I bit there, too. Under normal objective questioning, I would never have talked. However, the leading questions got through to me, and I relented.

Another way to use leading questions to get past recalcitrant respondents is to lead with, "Your opposition has said x, y, and z. Now is your chance to put your two cents' worth in. What are your thoughts on x?" Or, if research has shown that most people feel a certain way or do a specific thing, and that behavior or attitude is difficult to talk about because of social taboos, then a leading question can be used to good advantage. Alfred Kinsey, the sex researcher, used this approach in order to get people to talk about their sexual lives. During the early 1950s, when Kinsey was first doing his research, sex was a taboo subject that people did not discuss outside of highly intimate circles. Kinsey assumed that most people engaged in sexual activity, so he let the respondents know it was okay to talk about their sex lives by using leading questions. Instead of asking if they had ever done *x*, Kinsey asked how many times they did it, the assumption begging the question and thereby putting the respondents at ease and in a frame of mind to talk. In a general way, it is similar to the old detective movies where the detective tells the bad guy, "You might as well talk. Your partner told us that you did the dirty deed." The point is that the respondent is made to believe that the investigator knows the score and nothing the respondent says will shock him or her.

FORMAT

So much of how the respondent interprets the meaning or intent of questions depends on how the questionnaire is physically put together. There are no hard and fast rules for designing a format for a questionnaire; however, the following principles and strategies are worth considering in order to enhance communication between the researcher and respondents.

EASE ON IN

In normal everyday conversation, it is considered rude to start an encounter with a sensitive personal question, such as about how much money the person makes or how his or her marriage is doing.

The same is true of questionnaire design. It is best to start the questionnaire with relatively neutral, personally innocuous questions and then build into the more sensitive questions once some degree of rapport has been established. Commonly asked questions, such as ones about name, address, birthdate, the number of people in the family, and religious affiliations, are good introductory questions. Also, by getting background information early in the questionnaire, you will be able to say something about the characteristics of individuals who do not complete the questionnaire, should that be the case.

CLOSE ON A HIGH NOTE

Try to place yourself in the shoes of the respondents in order to figure out what the high notes might be, that is, topics that the respondents find easy and pleasant to answer. For example, younger people find it very difficult to discuss death and dying. It would be a mistake to have death and dying questions at the very end of a questionnaire used for young people. On the other hand, very elderly respondents have thought about death and dying a lot and yet have very little opportunity to discuss their view on the subject. For the elderly, closing with death and dying questions would be a high point. Whatever the reference point, make sure to end on a positive note. One general strategy for ending positively is to allow the respondent the opportunity to write or say anything that he or she considers important but was inadvertently left out of the questionnaire. "Is there anything that you would like to add to the questionnaire?"

____ Yes (please specify)

____ No

DON'T FENCE ME IN

As the song about the wide open spaces of the Old West told it, do not clutter up the questionnaire by trying to cram as many questions or lines as possible on a page. Waste paper if you must. It is better to have too little on a page than too much. Strive for as much white or open space as possible by placing just a few questions on a page with ample space between response categories and questions.

Always put just one question on a line and never abbreviate questions or response categories with a view to saving space. Spell out everything, and squander the space.

I can recall a questionnaire in which the researcher used "ER" for emergency room, "SD," "A," "D," and "SA" in place of "strongly disagree," "agree," and so on. The odds are good that most respondents read the abbreviations correctly, but you cannot afford the error associated with the respondents who misinterpreted things. Furthermore, spelling out all the words gives the impression of thoroughness and professionalism.

RESPONSE CATEGORY FORMAT

The following is a commonly used response category format:

1. Physicians are more interested in making money than they are in helping patients.
   ____ Strongly agree ____ Agree ____ Disagree ____ Strongly disagree
2. Physicians deserve their incomes.
   ____ Strongly agree ____ Agree ____ Disagree ____ Strongly disagree

There are at least two weaknesses with this format. For one, the response categories occupy more eye attention than the questions. It is a bit intimidating and conveys the impression of being more work to answer than it really is. Second, the open line for the respondents to check often produces results that are difficult for the researcher to interpret. I have seen responses which are large x's covering most of the response category. Is the respondent saying that the response is the one she is choosing or the one she is rejecting?

A cleaner format is to place the response categories vertically directly under the question and to provide brackets or parentheses for the respondents to fit their check marks into. For example, the above questions might look as follows:

1. Physicians are more interested in making money than they are in helping patients.
   [ ] Strongly agree
   [ ] Agree
   [ ] Disagree
   [ ] Strongly disagree
   [ ] No opinion

If you have several items, a scale of twelve items, for example, you are better off defining the response categories in an introduction and numbering them. Then the respondent can simply circle the appropriate number for each of the statements or items. The scale should be repeated on every page. The following is an example of this format:

"Below are some statements that you might agree or disagree with. Please read each statement and **circle** the response that most nearly represents how you feel about the statement. There is no right or wrong answer, only how you feel personally about the statement."

```
7 = Strongly agree
6 = Agree
5 = Somewhat agree
4 = Neutral
3 = Somewhat disagree
2 = Disagree
1 = Strongly disagree
```

a. My religion is more important to me now than it was ten years ago
    7 6 5 4 3 2 1

b. There are people in my church who would help me if I needed it over an extended period of time
    7 6 5 4 3 2 1

STATEMENTS

Another convenient format designed to keep response categories and questions close together and to economize on pages is the matrix. A typical use for the matrix is when you are asking the same demographic information of several people. Figure 5.1 is an example of this format taken from a real survey.

Variations on the matrix exist, such as the concentric circles used in Figure 5.2 (on page 107) to measure a respondent's social network.[2]

Once the questions which allow the researcher to fill in the circles have been asked, then the matrix format can be used to develop even more information about the network members such as the example in Figure 5-3 (on page 108).

CONTINGENCY QUESTIONS

A **contingency question** is by nature a dependent question. Whether it gets asked or not depends on the response to the question preceding it. The term *contingent* describes this symbiotic relationship between the questions. One is contingent upon the other, that is, you ask it only if the response to the question preceding the contingency question demands asking. The following is an example of a contingency question:

1. Are you currently employed?
   - [ ] Yes
   - [ ] No

   If yes: "What is your specific job title?"
   _____

---

[2]See Salloway, J. C., and Dillon, P. B. A comparison of family networks and friend networks in health care utilization. *Journal of comparative family studies*, 4, (Spring 1974), 140.

Household Composition

(*Interviewer:* If R. lives alone in household, skip to #11)

10. Could you tell me the names of the people who live here with you?

Name of person	Relation-ship to Respon-dent	Sex	Age	Educ.	Marital Status	Occup	New Since 1974

(*Interviewer:* Indicate with an asterisk (*) persons who were *not present* in 1974.)

11. Who is the "head" of this household? _____

    Relationship to respondent _____

12. Who was the "head" of the household twelve years ago? _____

    Relationship to respondent _____

13. Is there anyone who is *not* living with you now but *was* living with you twelve years ago?

Name of person	Relation-ship to Respon-dent	Deceased/Moved	Year Left	Reason for Leaving

Figure 5.1 ■ Demographic Matrix Example

"What is your specific job title?" is the contingency question, contingent upon the answer to "Are you currently employed?"

Sometimes, contingency questions are two or three questions deep, so to speak. In my interview schedule for the survey of the rural elderly, I designed a contingency question with three levels. The format for this question was as follows:

1. Do you belong to any church-related organizations?

   [ ] Yes ⌐

   [ ] No ↓

If yes:

a. Please list the name(s) of the organization(s):

   _____

   _____

   _____

   _____

b. How often do you attend meetings?

   [ ] Once a week or more

   [ ] Once every two weeks

   [ ] Once a month

   [ ] Once every six months

   [ ] Once a year

   [ ] Do not attend meetings

c. Are any of your friends members?

   [ ] Yes ⌐

   [ ] No ↓

   If yes: "What percentage of your friends
   are members?"

   _____ %

INSTRUCTIONS

The general rule of thumb is to overdo it on instructions. The questionnaire should have general instructions that introduce the questionnaire in terms of the rules for filling it out, for example, by whom, with pencil or pen, how to change an answer, and so on and then it should have specific instructions for each different section of the questionnaire and for each change in response formats. For example, when the respondent fills out the demographic information and moves to the section on attitude toward growing old, there should be instructions telling the respondent about this transition and what the rules are for answering the questions. If only one answer is what you want, then the respondents must be told this. Without instructions, the respondents do not know whether more than one answer is permissible, nor do they know whether or not to rank order their attitudes. If you want ranked attitudes, then you need to say so clearly in the instruc-

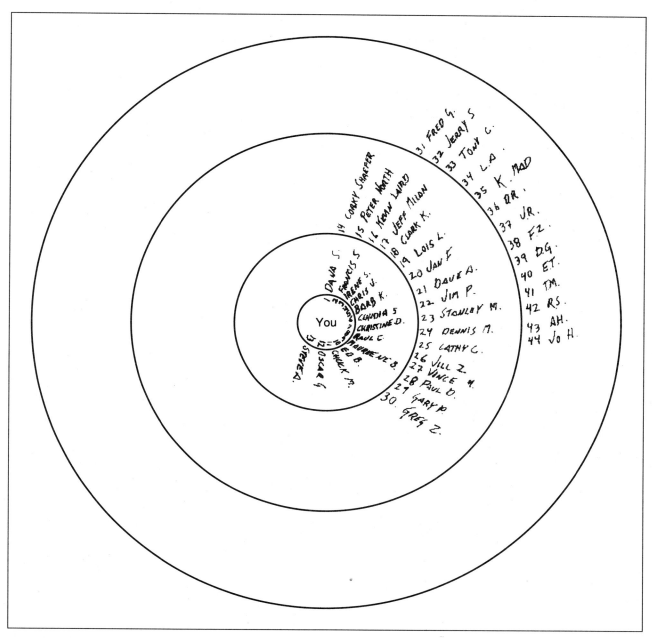

Figure 5.2 ▮ Personal Network

tions. Type the instructions in bold face and try to be consistent in terms of where you place the instructions throughout the questionnaire. If you put the first set on the upper left-hand side of the page, then put all the instructions in the same place throughout the questionnaire. With the more complicated matrix questions, be sure to tell the respondent that there is only one answer per row if you are operating on the one question-one answer format.

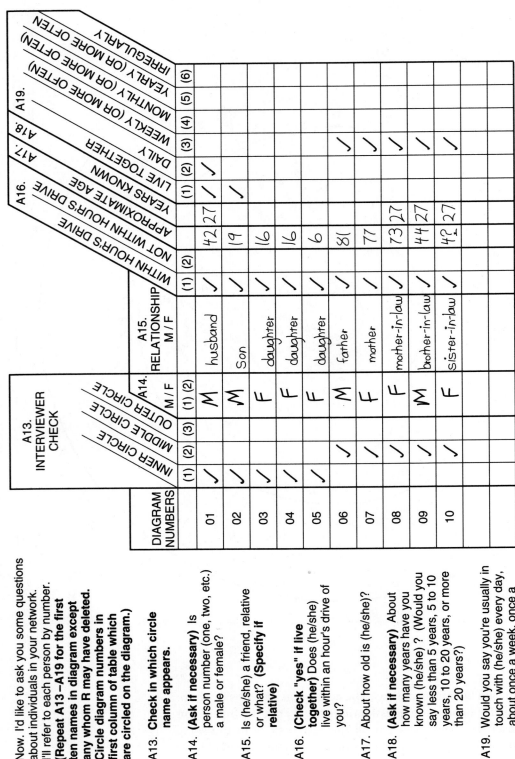

DIAGRAM NUMBERS	A13. INTERVIEWER CHECK — INNER CIRCLE (1)	MIDDLE CIRCLE (2)	OUTER CIRCLE (3)	A14. M/F	A15. RELATIONSHIP	A15 M/F (1)	(2)	A16. WITHIN HOUR'S DRIVE (1)	NOT WITHIN HOUR'S DRIVE (2)	A17. APPROXIMATE AGE	A18. YEARS KNOWN	LIVE TOGETHER (1)	DAILY (2)	WEEKLY (OR MORE OFTEN) (3)	MONTHLY (OR MORE OFTEN) (4)	YEARLY (OR MORE OFTEN) (5)	IRREGULARLY (6)
01	✓			M	husband	✓		✓		42	27	✓	✓				
02	✓			M	Son	✓		✓		19		✓	✓				
03	✓			F	daughter	✓		✓		16							
04	✓			F	daughter	✓		✓		16							
05	✓			F	daughter	✓		✓		6							
06		✓		M	father	✓		✓		81				✓			
07		✓		F	mother	✓		✓		77				✓			
08		✓		F	mother-in-law	✓		✓		73	27			✓			
09		✓		M	brother-in-law	✓		✓		44	27			✓			
10		✓		F	sister-in-law	✓		✓		42	27			✓			

Now. I'd like to ask you some questions about individuals in your network. I'll refer to each person by number. **(Repeat A13–A19 for the first ten names in diagram except any whom R may have deleted. Circle diagram numbers in first column of table which are circled on the diagram.)**

A13. **Check in which circle name appears.**

A14. **(Ask if necessary)** Is person number (one, two, etc.) a male or female?

A15. Is (he/she) a friend, relative or what? **(Specify if relative)**

A16. **(Check "yes" if live together)** Does (he/she) live within an hour's drive of you?

A17. About how old is (he/she)?

A18. **(Ask if necessary)** About how many years have you known (he/she) ? (Would you say less than 5 years, 5 to 10 years, 10 to 20 years, or more than 20 years?)

A19. Would you say you're usually in touch with (he/she) every day, about once a week, once a month, or once a year? **(Code "irregularly" if R can't give answer in terms of usual contacts.)**

A20–A21 omitted in this questionaire

Figure 5-3 ■ Personal Network Matrix

MAIL QUESTIONNAIRES

Follow-up contacts and clear instructions are the keys to achieving a decent return rate, say of 70%. Depending on how salient the research problem and questions are to the respondents, the return rate can vary from 20% to 80%, at best, but you can improve the basic rate by using some of the following methods.

Always contact those respondents for the second or third time by phone or letter (or both) who failed to return the questionnaires by the appointed date. If you can afford it, a phone call followed by a letter with a *new copy* of the questionnaire works well. The letter should reiterate the importance for the larger good of the respondent's participation as well as renew any promises that might have been made initially, such as confidentiality or sending the respondent a copy of the report. The new copy is just in case the respondent has lost the original.

Try to avoid mailing the questionnaires right before or after a holiday. Whether to use first class, stamp or no stamp, and envelope or no envelope are not critical decisions. More important is that the questionnaire have the official seal of the sponsoring organization prominently displayed. Also critical is that the questionnaire be typeset and printed in order to look as professional as possible. Personally, the booklet-type binding where the respondents or interviewers flip pages as they would a book is most appealing and functional. Invariably, some of the questionnaires with a staple in the upper left hand corner will shed a page or two. Given the hard use in store for a questionnaire, including possible widespread dissemination to colleagues should requests come in, it is best to spend the extra money and have the questionnaire bound in booklet form. A cover with the official seal, title of the study, date, the principal investigators, their affiliation, and the sponsoring agency, along with the grant number if there is one, is essential, too. These points are true for all types of questionnaires.

Regarding mailing strategy, my preference is to send the questionnaire without the envelope and have the return address with metered postage on the backside. This way, all the respondent has to do once it is complete is to fold, sample or tape, and drop in the mail. Another advantage of this approach is that the researcher does not waste postage. With metered returns, you only pay for what is returned in the mail.

∎ *Conclusions*

Constructing a questionnaire is part art and part science. The researcher needs a sharp eye for page layout and an even sharper sense for language. Clearly, writing cogent questions that tap what you want them to tap while making perfect sense to the respondents as well is an art. The science comes in with the methodological strategies learned through trial and error along with a liberal application of behavioral science principles.

A questionnaire is the operational map of your theory. Every question ought to have a conceptual origin, and the entire questionnaire should reflect the research problem and its solution.

Concepts are human creations in the sense that they are defined by people whose values and life experiences influence the definitional process. In the case of social science concepts, the training of the scientist is an added ingredient in the conceptual mixture. The point here is that there are many possible conceptual definitions for any given social science concept, a universe of potential definitions if you will. The social scientist samples from this universe, and the definition proffered therefore is neither the one "true" definition nor does it possess ultimate or absolute meaning. There are multiple meanings because there are multiple definitions possible. One definition is not better than another in some absolute sense, that is, according to some true standard, but it is good only insofar as it represents the concept's meaning relative to some theory or a tentative explanation, perhaps. For this reason, the operational definitions of the concepts are a sample from a universe of possible measurements. Thus, the questionnaire is merely one researcher's best guess as to how to operationalize the concepts being studied. Items or questions, then, are subject to measurement error and must be evaluated for reliability and validity.

The questionnaire is a patchwork quilt in the sense that many disparate items interrelate to form a coherent whole that should reflect the general purpose of the study and the theory. The existence of every question must be justified according to the role it plays in measuring a concept central to the study. There is no slack for idle questions whose function or role is unclear at the time of field work. The researcher who takes this approach usually ends up with a garbage can full of indeterminate and relatively useless material.

We discussed several methodological principles for enhancing the quality of the questionnaire, including the use of more than one question to measure a concept, providing the respondent with solid reference points in the questions, doing a pretest, and combining techniques by using a mixture of open-ended and closed answer questions. The wording of questions should be simple, with one idea or dimension per question. Usually, this means one-sentence questions. Avoidance of double negatives and leading questions was also stressed.

Hints for formatting the questionnaire were presented, including strategies for ordering questions, designing response categories, and setting up contingency questions. The importance of writing clear instructions for respondents and interviews was discussed, and the chapter closed with some hints for increasing the returns on mailed questionnaires.

GLOSSARY

closed answer questions   questions with defined, fixed choices in the response categories.

conceptualization/reconceptualization   the process of defining the concepts in abstract terms (conceptual definitions), then operationalizing the conceptual definitions (operational definitions) by designing a data-gathering instrument.

contingency question   a dependent question whose getting asked depends on the response to a question(s) preceding it.

exhaustive response categories categories that cover all the responses, that is, all the responses can be fit into at least one of the categories. All responses are classifiable.

leading question a question worded in such a way that suggests to the respondent that a certain response is preferred.

mutually exclusive response categories categories such that any given response will fit into one, and only one, category.

open-ended question questions without specific response categories. The researcher copies down the response verbatim on blank lines.

operational definition an item and rules for applying it in measurement.

pretest testing the questionnaire on a model sample before printing a final copy and starting the data gathering.

reference point the specific context for a question or statement in a questionnaire that grounds the item in time, space, and substance.

FOR FURTHER READING

Miller, Delbert C. (1977). *Handbook of research design and social measurement* (3rd ed., pp. 73-82). New York: David McKay.

Oppenheim, A. N. (1966). *Questionnaire design and attitude measurement*. New York: Basic Books.

Chapter Six

Sampling

■ *This chapter begins with the fundamental principles of sampling:
representativeness, the rule of homogeneity, randomness, sample size,
sampling error, confidence level, confidence interval, and the law of large
numbers. Terminology commonly used in discussing sampling is defined
using examples from the world of research. The crux of the chapter, however,
is the discussion of specific sample designs, when it is best to use them, and
their strengths and weaknesses.*

■ *Why Sample?*

We draw samples in order to spare the cost of measuring an entire population.
Suppose one's goal is to explain why German Jews immigrated to rural areas in
the United States between 1850 and 1880. If the researcher wants to be in a solid
position to generalize the findings to *all* German Jewish immigrants who settled
in the rural United States, then he or she can either: (1) measure all German Jewish immigrants (a population) or (2) measure a fraction or portion of German
Jewish immigrants (a sample). With the population, the researcher would have to
measure roughly 350,000 immigrants. On the other hand, the sample approach
would allow the researcher to set the number to be measured according to the
accuracy and precision desired coupled with the constraints of time and money.
Sampling is efficient and, at times, renders a seemingly impossible research
project possible. Sampling technology is a benevolent and exceedingly helpful
companion to the sociologist.

And yet, almost in spite of its importance, there are very few social scientists
who are expert in sampling. This is a problem, because sampling is one area of

methodology that is difficult and technical enough to require special dedication and effort to master. In fact, the early days of sample surveys produced some notorious failures in terms of false predictions. One of these classics was the 1936 *Literary Digest* survey that predicted that Alf Landon would win a landslide victory over Franklin Roosevelt. The *Digest* people used faulty sampling procedures (automobile registration records during the Great Depression, when only wealthy people owned automobiles) that caused the biased findings and erroneous prediction. For this reason, a very select few sampling experts serve as guides for the masses of social scientists needing advice. Most of us rely heavily upon these gurus, people such as Leslie Kish,[1] who devote their life work to designing and testing various sampling strategies. Because of their expertise and the tremendous effort put into sampling designs, we have a wide variety of interesting and effective sampling strategies available to help us do our research as precisely and as accurately as possible.

This chapter is a distillation of the work of some great sampling minds, but it also contains some of my own research experiences and adaptations to difficult sampling problems. The chapter starts with some terminology, then goes to the principles behind sampling. Various types of sampling designs are presented and illustrated through examples. The reasons for choosing one sampling design over another are discussed with the hope that the logic and thinking involved in choosing a sample design will become apparent to the reader.

■ *Some Basic Sampling Terminology*

SAMPLE ELEMENT

The persons, objects, or whatever the specific entity is that is sampled is called the **sample element**. Sampling has its own terminology, and this term has the same meaning as unit of analysis. The element is what is analyzed and as such can be identified with the answer to the question, "Data about what?" For example, my study of the conflict between doctors and the poor people served by comprehensive neighborhood health centers generated data on individuals and the neighborhood health centers as well. The research problem sought to answer the question, "What are the sociological factors associated with the genesis of conflict and the resolution of that conflict at neighborhood health centers for the poor?" The sample element was neighborhood health centers, and the interviews with physicians and neighborhood residents constituted data about the sample element. If you are studying attitudes toward war and your research problem states that the attitudes are of adult U.S. citizens who are eligible to vote, then the sample element is adult U.S. citizens who are eligible to vote. Another example is the twenty-year longitudinal (the same people interviewed repeatedly over the

---

[1]Kish, Leslie. (1957). Confidence intervals for clustered sampling. *ASR*, 154-165; see also Kish. (1965). *Survey sampling*. New York: John Wiley and Sons.

twenty-year period) study of the independently living rural elderly (Hessler et al., 1989). The sample was a complicated cluster design where we selected cultural areas first, then small towns, then houses, and finally one resident of the household aged sixty-five or older. In this case, the sample elements are individuals sixty-five years or older. The element is your ultimate and most significant source of the data. Again, the element is the same as the unit of analysis.

GENERALIZED POPULATION

The generalized **population** is the sum total of all elements that the sample elements supposedly represent. In the case of my rural elderly study, the population was the rural elderly defined by me as U.S. citizens sixty-five years or older living independently in towns with five thousand or fewer residents. The population must be defined by the researcher.

SAMPLING FRAME

The **sampling frame** is nothing more than a roster or list of all of the elements. There are situations where the researcher must create this list as he or she goes along selecting the **sample** and other situations in which such lists are already available from which to select the sample. For example, in a study I did of student power, the research population was the full-time undergraduate student body at the University of Pittsburgh. Since a list of all the full-time undergraduate students was available through the registrar's office, I was able to select my sample from that list, which became the sampling frame. On the other hand, such a list was not available for the research population of independently living rural elderly in Missouri. For that study, I was forced by the absence of a list to create the sampling frame through a process called enumeration. Here, I went door-to-door in each of the small towns selected and essentially created the sampling frame simultaneously with selecting the individuals who became members of the study.

It would have been more efficient and less costly if a list had been available, in which case it would have saved me from knocking on all the doors of people who were younger than sixty-five years of age. The absence of a list forced me to create one, which added another step to the sampling procedure.

Whether a list is available or not, the most important thing to keep in mind is to design a sampling frame that puts you as close as possible to the definition of the research population called for by your research problem. Once again, we see here the vital link between the definition of the research problem and the decisions made for sampling elements.

PARAMETER

Any fixed, usually unknown, value from the population is called a **parameter**. If 75% of all rural U.S. citizens sixty-five years of age or older are female, the value 75% is a parameter. The parameter is the "true" value, that is, the value you would get anytime all the units of analysis were observed or somehow measured.

STATISTIC

Any value generated from the sample is called a statistic. If I measure gender for my sample of rural elderly and come up with the finding that 78% of the members of the study are female, that value is a statistic. It will differ each time a different sample is drawn. A statistic is nothing more than an estimate (inferential statistics) of the parameter or true population value. The closer the estimate is, the more confidence you should have in the sampling procedures. The difference between the parameter and statistic is the sampling error.

■ *Principles of Sampling*

REPRESENTATIVENESS

Before I left to spend a year in Gothenberg, Sweden, I was told by a friend that all Swedes were alike, that is, perfectly homogeneous. Allegedly, all Swedes thought alike, held the same values, and even looked alike. If this was true, then I would need only to talk with one Swede in order to generalize the results to all Swedes. Because Swedes were alike in every respect, one Swede would be perfectly representative of the total population. No sampling problem here. Just pick any Swede and you would be in business.

   Of course, my friend was being foolish, and I did not believe for a moment that all Swedes were alike in every respect. But his point underscored a very important principle, namely the principle of **representativeness**. A sample must be representative of some larger group, called the population. This principle of representativeness guides much of sampling decision making. Representativeness means that what you know from the sample is the same as what you would know if you studied the entire population. In my case, representativeness meant that a few Swedes interviewed would yield the same results as interviewing the entire population of eight million.

THE RULE OF HOMOGENEITY

Homogeneity or the property of being alike in critically important ways goes hand-in-glove with the principle of representativeness. The more homogeneous the population is, or can be made to be through sampling strategies, the more representative the sample will be, all things being equal of course. The population need not be homogeneous in all respects for purposes of sampling. Rather, it should be homogeneous on those characteristics that are most relevant to the research problem. For example, in my study of the independent rural elderly, I was able to enhance the representativeness of the sample by selecting it from a population consisting only of elderly individuals, a population homogeneous in terms of age alone. By creating a homogeneous albeit artificial population from which I drew the sample, I improved the chances that the sample would be representative of all rural elderly. The chances would have been worse if I had drawn the sample from adults of varying ages.

The **rule of homogeneity** in sampling verifies the link between theory and method. It is theory and the nature of the research problem that guides the use of this rule. Without theory, there is no logical way to decide whether or not you need homogeneous population, nor is there a basis for deciding which characteristics the population should have in common. In fact, it is difficult to imagine a way to decide what the sample should be representative of without theory to guide that decision.

RANDOMIZATION

A sample is accurate (unbiased) if it represents the population from which it is drawn. Random selection means that the researcher uses chance alone to draw the sample. **Randomization** is the process of giving each element in the population an independent and equal chance. Each unit in the population must have an equal chance of being selected if the procedure is to qualify as random. For example, bingo numbers typically are selected by placing numbered balls of equal size and shape in a randomizer. Each time the randomizer is rolled, each ball has an independent and equal chance of being selected. If selected balls are returned to the randomizer after each selection, the odds of selection stay the same for each draw. The fact that the balls are the same size and are contained in a randomizer means that the selection of a ball is independent of the action of the other balls. If balls are removed after each selection, the odds will change, but the remaining balls still have an equal, albeit different, chance of being selected each draw.

Randomization is the key to being able to calculate how accurate your sample is. Tables of randomly generated numbers have been published to use in selecting elements for a sample. An example of these tables is found in Appendix B, and most main frame computers have a random number generating capacity.

Using random numbers to select the sample removes the problem of bias in selecting cases. Bias can occur in the absence of randomization either through self-selection, for example, only people with extreme health concerns volunteer for a particular medical experiment, or through some predisposition on the researcher's part to choose only those cases that seem at the time to support his or her theory. Randomizing the selection of the sample takes the researcher out of this danger zone and provides the added benefit of allowing for the estimation of error by invoking the laws of probability. Also, randomization enables the researcher to use parametric statistics, that is, statistics that are estimates of a population parameter, which is a significant advantage. More will be said about parameters and population later.

SAMPLING ERROR

One of the goals of sampling is to get as close to the true population value as possible, given time and money constraints. **Sampling error** is the difference between the results obtained with a sample and the true population value. Suppose, for example, you interviewed a sample of Chinatown residents and found that 60% of the sample used traditional Chinese medicine during the year. This is a statistic based on a sample of all the residents of Chinatown. Next, a check of the records of all the Chinese doctors in Boston showed that 83% of the residents actually used Chinese medicine. This second value is the true population value. If your measurement is relatively error-free, then the difference between the sample estimate (statistic), 60%, and the true value (parameter), 83%, is due to sampling error.

Probability theory provides us with a very important formula for judging how close any given statistic based on a sample comes to the true value in the population. The only requirement for estimating sampling error is that the researcher use a random sample design. The formula is:

$$s \;=\; \sqrt{\frac{P \times Q}{n}}$$

Where: P, Q = the population parameter for the dichotomous values of the dependent variable, for example, if 60% use Chinese medicine (P = .60) and 40% do not (Q = .40):

$$P \times Q = .6 \times .4 = .24 \qquad Q = 1 - P.$$

n   =   the number of cases in the sample or the sample size

s   =   the standard error

To complete the example:

$$s \;=\; \sqrt{\frac{.6 \times .4}{125}} \;=\; \sqrt{\frac{.24}{125}} \;=\; .04$$

Thus, the standard error in the case of a sample of 125 elements would be 4%. Now we need to introduce the concept of the sampling distribution.

SAMPLING DISTRIBUTION

The **sampling distribution** is based on a hypothetical case of drawing a very large number of samples. For example, instead of only one sample of Chinatown residents, one would draw dozens of samples. The laws of probability tell us that if you plotted the sample statistics, say the mean ($\bar{X}$) use of Chinese medicine, the means from all of the samples would form a normal bell-shaped curve. The sample statistics would distribute normally with the largest number of means ($\bar{X}$) falling within one standard deviation of the population mean (u). This is called the central limit theorem.

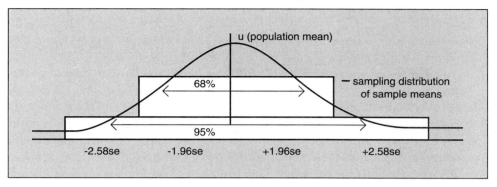

Figure 6-1 ■ Standard Error and the Normal Sampling Distribution Curve

The normal curve is divided up into areas whose boundaries are established by the standard error. Specifically, .3413% of the sample means should fall 1.96 standard errors on one side of the population mean (u) and .3413% should fall 1.96 standard errors on the other side of the u, for a total of a little over 68% of the sample means. Furthermore, .4773% of the sample means will fall 2.58 (1.96 + 1.96) standard errors on one side of u and .4773% on the other, for a total of over 95% of the sample means. Of the sample means, 99.9% will fall within three standard errors of the u. (See Figure 6-1.)

There is a simple application of this and the concept of confidence interval in sampling. The "interval" refers to the "spread" or range of values of the sample statistic that you are willing to have confidence in. In my Chinatown case, it might be 60%, plus or minus 4%, users of Chinese medicine. Here, I would be willing to stake my reputation as a sociologist that the sample estimate of 60% is within 4 percentage points of the population parameter (u). Going back to the standard error formula,

$$s = \sqrt{\frac{P \times Q}{n}}$$

if we want a confidence interval of which we can be 95% certain that it is an accurate representation of the population parameter, the standard error region is plus or minus 1.96. Thus:

$$\text{sample statistic} \quad \pm 1.96 \sqrt{\frac{se}{n}}$$

$$= .60 \pm 1.96 \sqrt{\frac{4}{125}} = 60 \pm .68$$

which means that 95% of the time, my sample statistic of 60% plus or minus .68 will be an accurate representation of the true population value. This is the **confidence interval.**

CONFIDENCE INTERVAL

Thus, the standard error is useful for setting the confidence interval around any results you might get using a sample of a given size.

You can see from the formula that the size of the standard error is a function of the quantity $P \times Q$ and of the size of the sample. Remember that P is a population parameter. Using the example of use of Chinese medicine, if you were able to interview every Chinatown resident and they told you the truth about whether or not they used Chinese medicine, the findings would be the true population parameter. If 50% used it, then 50% use would be a parameter. If all of the population used Chinese medicine (P was 1 or 100%) or none of the population did (P was 0), then the standard error would be zero. The standard error is largest when the parameter is 50%. In the example, you have the greatest error when the true value has a 50-50 split, which indicates a lot of heterogeneity and lots of room for variation in the use of Chinese doctors. Plugging in the formula, if P = .5, then $P \times Q$ = .25. Then again if P = .9 (90% using), $P \times Q$ = .09.

Standard error is affected as well by the size of the sample (n). The larger the sample size, the smaller the standard error. Using the formula and estimating conservatively that 50% use Chinese medicine and 50% do not, a sample of size 100 would yield a standard error of .05. If you wanted a smaller standard error, say .025, then we would need a sample of size 400. In the real world of research, we would not know the population parameter. If we did know it, we would have no need for drawing a sample in fact. Because we do not know the parameter, usually we use the sample statistic as our estimate. This means that you need some data before you can estimate the standard error of your sample. The simplest way would be to collect objective data on the use of Chinese medicine. Then you would use the actual results among the study sample as your estimate of the larger population parameter. In the absence of any data, you should take the conservative route and estimate the parameter (P) at 50%.

CONFIDENCE LEVEL

It is up to the researcher to decide just how confident he or she wants to be in claiming that the sample represents the true population parameter. For example, I can set the **confidence level** at .05, which means that 95% of the time I will be correct or safe in believing that the sample statistic falls within two standard errors of the true population parameter.

THE LAW OF LARGE NUMBERS

If one drew several samples and increased the size of each sample, one would observe the **law of large numbers** in action.[2] The key goal of sampling is to estimate

---

[2]This principle is in concert with the concept of standard error. You will recall that the standard error is reduced as n is increased.

the true population value (parameter) using a sample of the whole population. Usually, this estimate takes the form of a mean or average, such as the average age or income, of some population. The smallest sample would give you the least accurate estimate. As the sample size increases, the estimate becomes more accurate, that is, the average age or income, for example, would be closer to the true parameter. If the average annual income of a population of ten individuals is ten thousand dollars, a sample of two individuals might yield an average income (an estimate) considerably below or above the true average simply because the luck of the draw produced a sample with two individuals at the extreme end of the income range. A large sample, say of eight individuals, would get your estimate closer to the true value. Thus, the principle of large numbers states that the larger the sample, the closer the sample estimate is to the true parameter value.

■ *Sampling Designs*

Randomization is a principle of sampling that guides our decision making for all random sample designs. The reader will recall that each sample element should have a known, independent, and equal chance of being selected. With this point in mind, we turn our attention to some of the more widely used random sample designs (see Box 6-1)

SIMPLE RANDOM SAMPLE

A simple random sample involves assigning a unique number to every element in the sampling frame and then using a table of random numbers or a random number generator in the computer to select a specified number of the elements. If the number is selected at random, then the element with that number is selected as part of the sample. It is called simple random because there is only one step in the selection of the sample once the elements on the list have been numbered. Computers that have random number generating capacities may be used to select the sample elements. For example, if all phone owners constitute an adequate sampling frame for a particular research problem, you can use the random number feature to have a computer randomly select phone numbers that then can be dialed automatically (random digit dialing).

SYSTEMATIC RANDOM SAMPLES

Because it is cumbersome to produce a numbered list of all the elements in a sampling frame, researchers have devised systematic sampling. This method involves random selection just like the simple random approach, but instead of numbering the elements in the sampling frame, you pick every "kth" element for the sample. For example, if you have a long list of police officers employed by the Los Angeles Police Department and you need to sample from that list, it would be time-con-

Box 6-1

■ Sampling Chart

Type of sampling	Brief description	Advantages	Disadvantages
A. *Simple random*	Assign to each population member a unique number; select sample items by use of random numbers	**1.** Requires minimum knowledge of population in advance **2.** Free of possible classification errors **3.** Easy to analyze data and compute errors	**1.** Does not make use of knowledge of population which researcher may have **2.** Larger errors for same sample size than in stratified sampling
B. *Systematic*	Use natural ordering or order population; select random starting point between 1 and the nearest integer to the sampling ratio (N/n); select items at interval of nearest integer to sampling ratio	**1.** If population is ordered with respect to pertinent property, gives stratification effect, and hence reduces variability compared to A **2.** Simplicity of drawing sample; easy to check	**1.** If sampling interval is related to a periodic ordering of the population, increased variability may be introduced **2.** Estimates of error likely to be high where there is stratification effect
C. *Multistage random*	Use a form of random sampling in each of the sampling stages where there are at least two stages	**1.** Sampling lists, identification, and numbering required only for members of sampling units selected in sample **2.** If sampling units are geographically defined, cuts down field costs (i.e., travel)	**1.** Errors likely to be larger than in A or B for same sample size **2.** Errors increase as number of sampling units selected decreases
1. *With probability proportionate to size*	Select sampling units with probability proportionate to their size	**1.** Reduces variability	**1.** Lack of knowledge of size of each sampling unit before selection increases variability
D. *Stratified* **1.** *Proportionate*	Select from every sampling unit at other than last stage a random sample proportionate to size of sampling unit	**1.** Assures representativeness with respect to property which forms basis of classifying units; therefore yields less variability than A or C **2.** Decreases chance of failing to include members of population because of classification process **3.** Characteristics of each stratum can be estimated, and hence comparisons can be made	**1.** Requires accurate information on proportion of population in each stratum, otherwise increases error **2.** If stratified lists are not available, may be costly to prepare them; possibility of faulty classification and hence increase in variability
2. *Optimum allocation*	Same as 1 except sample is proportionate to variability within strata as well as their size	**1.** Less variability for same sample size than 1	**1.** Requires knowledge of variability of pertinent characteristic within strata.
3. *Disproportionate*	Same as 1 except that size of sample is not proportionate to size of sampling unit but is dictated by analytical considerations or convenience	**1.** More efficient than 1 for comparison of strata or where different errors are optimum for different strata	**1.** Less efficient than 1 for determining population characteristics; i.e., more variability for same sample size

Box 6-1 *continued*

■ *Sampling Chart*

Type of sampling	Brief description	Advantages	Disadvantages
E. Cluster	Select sampling units by some form of random sampling; ultimate units are groups; select these at random and take a complete count of each	1. If clusters are geographically defined, yields lowest field costs 2. Requires listing only individuals in selected clusters 3. Characteristics of clusters as well as those of population can be estimated 4. Can be used for subsequent samples, since clusters, not individuals, are selected, and substitution of individuals may be permissible	1. Larger errors for comparable size than other probability samples 2. Requires ability to assign each member of population uniquely to a cluster; inability to do so may result in duplication or omission of individuals
F. Stratified cluster	Select clusters at random from every sampling unit	1. Reduces variability of plain cluster sampling	1. Disadvantages of stratified sampling added to those of cluster sampling 2. Since cluster properties may change, advantage of stratification may be reduced and make sample unusable for later research
G. Repetitive: multiple or sequential	Two or more samples of any of the above types are taken, using results from earlier samples to design later ones, or determine if they are necessary	1. Provides estimates of population characteristics which facilitate efficient planning of succeeding sample, therefore reduces error of final estimate 2. In the long run reduces number of observations required	1. Complicates administration of fieldwork 2. More computation and analysis required than in nonrepetitive sampling 3. Sequential sampling can only be used where a very small sample can approximate representativeness and where the number of observations can be increased conveniently at any stage of the research
H. Judgment	Select a subgroup of the population which, in the basis of available information, can be judged to be representative of the total population; take a complete count or subsample of this group	1. Reduces cost of preparing sample and fieldwork, since ultimate units can be selected so that they are close together	1. Variability and bias of estimates cannot be measured or controlled 2. Requires strong assumptions or considerable knowledge of population and subgroup selected
I. Quota	Classify population by pertinent properties; determine desired proportion of sample from each class; fix quotas for each observer	1. Same as above 2. Introduces some stratification effect	1. Introduces bias of observers' classification of subjects and nonrandom selection within classes

Reprinted from Ackoff, Russell L. (1953). *The design of social research* (p. 124). Chicago: University of Chicago. By permission of the University of Chicago Press. Copyright 1953 by the University of Chicago.

suming to place a number after each police officer's name. With systematic sampling, you would consult the table of random numbers and randomly select a number (k). First, you need to calculate the sampling interval, which is the total number of elements in the population divided by the number of elements selected for the sample.

$$\text{Sampling interval} \quad = \quad \frac{\text{Population size}}{\text{Sample size}}$$

In the case of my study of the rural elderly, the total population of individuals living independently (based on the 1960 U.S. Census) was 60,000 and my desired sample size was 1,700 individuals. Thus, the sampling interval would be 35.3. In using the table of random numbers to systematically draw every kth element from the sampling frame, I would first select any random number between one and 35 in order to establish a starting point and the interval for selection. Assuming that I had such a sampling frame whereby all 60,000 independently living elderly were enumerated and assuming that my trip to the table of random numbers netted me number 28, I would go down the list to the twenty-eighth name, select it, and then proceed to draw every thirty-fifth name on the list until 1,700 names were selected.

The one danger with this method is called **periodicity**. This problem stems from some nonrandom order to the list that might affect the selection of the elements, in the case cited above, the names of police officers. For example, suppose that the list of police officers is organized by rank or by salary level. In either case, picking every seventh name from the list ordered in either of those ways could net you a biased sample. If the highest-paid officers or the highest-ranking officers were first, with decrements as you went down the list, then your sample would have too many highly paid officers of higher rank versus officers of lower rank and pay. Another example might be a study of clerics in which the list of clerics for each church is organized with the pastor's name first followed by the assistant pastor, other assistants, deacons, and secretarial staff. A sample of every seventh element might get you only deacons in the sample.

The safest method for ensuring that the order of the list will not bias the sample is to randomize the list prior to selecting the sample. Some sampling frames are amenable to this, but others, such as phone books or city directories, are way too large to randomize conveniently. The general rule of thumb is to randomize the sampling frame when it is convenient to do so. Remember, the key to random sampling is that each element in the sampling frame has an independent and equal chance of being selected. As long as that requirement is met, the difference between pure random and systematic random sampling is a matter of efficiency and convenience. Whichever one of the two designs is easiest, use it.

STRATIFIED RANDOM SAMPLING

Representativeness and the rule of homogeneity are two principles of sampling that guide the design of stratified samples. Ultimately, these two principles, along with the decision whether or not to stratify a sample, are rooted in theory. Strata are qualities or classes of the sample elements. If you are studying student power and your elements are students, appropriate strata might be year in school or grade point average (GPA). If you organized the population of students (the sampling frame) by year in school, you would have stratified the population.

Each class or stratum should be more homogeneous than the population as a whole, which harks back to the rule of homogeneity. The more homogeneous the population, the less sampling error. But the researcher needs to think about how representative the sample is of what usually is a heterogeneous or diverse population. The more representative the sample, the lower the sampling error, too. Stratified sampling is a means to achieve both homogeneity and representativeness.

Back to the example of my study of student power at the University of Pittsburgh during the turbulent 1960s. If I had used a simple random sampling design, I would have had to draw a much larger sample than the number I used if I were to have each year in school and GPA adequately represented. Instead of the simple random design, I stratified the population into year in school and GPA, then I selected the elements (students) randomly from each homogeneous stratum in proportion to the total number in that stratum. Because each stratum was homogeneous, a small number of elements could be drawn without increasing sampling error. If you know that all the elements in a particular stratum are college freshmen, then sampling from that stratum ought to get you closer to the parameter, for example, the willingness of freshmen to commit civil disobedience, than you would get without stratification. Also, you are more certain that your sample will represent the total population of students if you have sampled proportionately from the strata. That is, you are assured of getting the proper number of freshmen, sophomores, and so on, in proportion to their existence in the population. Sometimes it is better to sample a stratum or subpopulation disproportionally, that is, to oversample in order to make sure that there will be enough cases in certain categories for the analysis. This can be done by physically drawing more cases from the desired subgroups or by weighting the analysis. Computer programs exist that allow the researcher to count select subgroups twice or three times over the other categories. For example, women live longer than men. In my study of the rural elderly, the analysis of the respondents aged eighty-five and older bore this out, as only 10% were men. If I wanted to analyze the social network patterns for men and women, controlling for health status, I would have too few cases in certain categories to complete the analysis for men. Thus, I would be wise to oversample men initially, in which case I would have enough cases of men eighty-five years and older to run the analysis.

The key here is that you must have some rationale based on theory for stratifying the population. In other words, I have to have a theoretical reason for choosing GPA and year in school as the strata, as opposed to any number of other variables. I should stand ready to defend my choice on theoretical grounds if another researcher should criticize my choice and argue that I would have been better served by stratifying on gender. In this situation, I must be able to argue that year in school is more important than gender because sociological theory shows that commitment to the values and norms of an institution increases as one's tenure in the institution increases. Student power and the concomitant willingness to commit civil disobedience is partly a function of socialization into the norms and values surrounding social control at the university. This process of internalizing the norms and values is similar for men and women, therefore, stratifying by sex would have been less productive for the study of student power than year in school. That was the theoretical rationale for selecting year in school as the basis for stratifying the population. The decision was based on previous research and theory, which reinforces the point made earlier that research decisions are interconnected and that science advances through a process of communicating methodologies and research findings.

CLUSTER SAMPLE: SINGLE STAGE

Clusters are large sociological entities, such as small towns, universities, city blocks, churches of a particular denomination, and so forth. Clusters are sociologically relevant in that the elements within them ought to be more similar than elements compared across clusters. Cluster sampling is used when a list or preexisting sampling frame is unavailable and difficult to construct. In such situations, cluster sampling is more efficient than trying to construct a list and using simple random sampling. But you pay a price for this efficiency in the form of sampling error. Cluster samples have more error than simple random samples, all things being equal, because you introduce an extra step in the sampling procedure with the selection of clusters and then the selection of the sample elements. There are at least two steps in the cluster design versus one step with simple random sampling, and error is incurred at each step of any sample design. Thus, two steps produce more error than one step, if all other procedures are held equal.

Again, the rule of homogeneity and representativeness come into play in order to help the researcher decide how to draw a single stage cluster sample. The problem is in deciding how many clusters to draw. Assuming that your desired sample size is known, the number of elements drawn from each cluster is a function of the number of clusters you decide to use. Your choice ranges between few clusters and more elements from each cluster and lots of clusters with fewer elements from each cluster. Since clusters are or should be naturally homogeneous entities and since there ought to be diversity between clusters, you can employ the two principles to help you decide between more clusters with fewer elements from each cluster or fewer clusters with more elements drawn from each cluster.

Representativeness demands that you tap the diversity among the population elements, thus, under this principle, you would want to choose more clusters than less clusters, since the diversity between clusters is greater than the diversity within clusters. One cluster would represent poorly the diversity of the population elements, and a great number of clusters would better represent that diversity. Similarly, since clusters are naturally more homogeneous than the population of elements at large, and since error is reduced with homogeneity among the elements, you would want to select a larger number of clusters with a fewer number of elements from each cluster.

For example, if you wanted to study the opinions of U.S. physicians concerning the possibility of having national health insurance, you could define each state medical society as a cluster consisting of the names of all physicians practicing medicine in the state. From a list of the clusters (state medical societies), you could select a subset or sample of the clusters at random. Then you would randomly select a certain number of elements from each of the sampled clusters. Theoretically, the physicians practicing in Mississippi should be more alike in their attitudes toward national health insurance than physicians working in California, and you would expect significant differences between the physicians in those two states. If you are trying to represent the diversity of physician opinion across the country, it would not represent all physicians' attitudes, assuming for example that you need a sample of two thousand physicians, to select Mississippi as the only cluster and then to randomly draw two thousand physicians. It would make more sense methodologically to randomly select one cluster from each of the cultural regions of the country, for example, the North, South, West, Southeaster, New England, and so on, and then to randomly select the appropriate number of physicians from each cluster in order to achieve a sample of two thousand.

MULTIPLE-STAGE CLUSTER

Like the name suggests, the multiple-stage form of cluster sampling has more than one set of clusters, and samples of the different clusters are drawn one after the other, hence, the "multiple stage" aspect. For example, my study of the rural elderly was a multiple-stage cluster sample. Remembering that clusters must be sociologically justified, we defined the following natural clusters: cultural regions of the state, small towns, and blocks within the towns.

You probably recognize that these clusters range from huge organizations, that is, a cultural region that takes in dozens of counties and perhaps a hundred small towns, to blocks consisting of a dozen or so households. As you select clusters within clusters, the units decrease in magnitude until you arrive at the smallest unit, the sample elements, which in my case were individuals.

My sampling procedure went as follows: First the state's four cultural regions were identified through socioeconomic analysis of census data and other rural sociological studies done over the years. Because we needed to represent the entire state, we selected all four of the regional clusters. We knew that our sample elements were to be rural elderly individuals, and we knew that we needed seventeen hundred of these individuals in order to achieve the .05 level of confidence. We decided to go for a larger number of towns with fewer individuals from each town, which led to the decision to select sixty-four towns from which to draw the individual respondents to be interviewed. We wanted the number of towns selected form each cluster to be proportional to the total number of small towns in each of the cultural regions. This is called cluster sample proportional to size (PPS) in that the town clusters had a greater or lesser chance of being selected, depending on the size of the cluster that the particular town was in. For example, the Ozark cultural region had fewer small towns in it than did the northeast region, thus fewer towns were selected from the Ozark region than from the northeast. The ten towns selected from the Ozark region were in proportion to the total number of towns in the region, as was the thirty or so towns selected from the northeast region.

Once the sixty-four towns were selected, we designed a procedure for randomly selecting twenty-seven individuals from each town. By selecting an equal number of individuals from each town, we equalized the chances of individuals or the sample elements being selected since older persons residing in larger regions or towns had a lower chance of being selected than individuals from smaller clusters. The criteria for inclusion in the study were that individuals had to be living independently and be sixty-five years of age or older. Given this definition of the sample elements, we wrote a three-page set of procedures for the interviewers to follow. These procedures were pretested using several small towns not in the study. Based on the pretest, we ironed out the wrinkles and sent the twenty interviewers out to draw the sample of seventeen hundred elderly individuals and then to do the interviews.

The procedure for randomly selecting the sample elements was fairly simple. The interviewer listed all the blocks on what was called a dwelling unit (DU) segment form. Each block was assigned a unique number, and the interviewer went to the table of random numbers and selected one block. The interviewer went to the northeast corner and proceeded south, knocking on every household door. If someone answered, the interviewer explained the purpose of the study and then conducted a census of the household. If a person or persons were living there and if they fit the criteria for inclusion in the study, the interviewer filled out the DU form, which contained the household address and potential respondent or respondents' names, and then told the person that he or she would return for an interview once the sample was drawn for the town. The interviewer continued with this enumeration, using systematic compass directions to go from block to block.

When the designated number of households containing at least one person sixty-five years of age or older was complete (thirty-seven households, ten more than required as backups in case of refusals), the interviewers returned to select the respondent, ask permission, and conduct the interview. If more than one person resided in a given household, the interviewer picked one of the individuals using a die. We had planned on interviewing only one person from each household in order to gain more coverage, thereby improving the representativeness of the sample. Thus, we ended up with seventeen hundred households and seventeen hundred individuals as the ultimate unit of analysis. Theoretically, each household containing a person(s) sixty-five years of age or older had the same chance of selection. This is an important requirement for ensuring representativeness.

A more conventional way to proceed with PPS sampling would have been to count all the households on each block and then draw the sample of households at random. This would have worked, had we not needed to obtain a sample consisting solely of individuals sixty-five years of age or older. Using the more conventional approach, we would have had to overdraw the sample by a rather large number in order to end up with the required number of elderly. This would have kept our interviewers in the field twice to three times as long, and our costs, both in time and money, would have been much greater.

To calculate the odds of a household in our study being selected, you first need to know how many blocks there are in the small town. For example, one of the towns had 103 blocks and we sampled 25. In this instance, the chance of any given block being selected was 25/103, or .24. If, for example, the number of blocks was 203 and you sampled 25, the chances of a household being selected would be lower at .12.

From this simple point, things get a bit more complicated. Earl Babbie (1986) is of great help in outlining the procedure for calculating: (1) the probability of a cluster being selected; (2) the probability of an element within a cluster being selected; and (3) the overall probability of an element being selected. Let's assume that in my study of the rural elderly, I had decided to select twenty-five blocks from each town for a total of sixteen hundred blocks from the sixty-four small towns. Also, we decided to sample twenty-seven individuals from each of the sixty-four towns, which would give us the desired seventeen hundred respondents plus twenty-eight extra interviews to cover ourselves. What are the chances of a block cluster being selected? What are the chances of an element within a cluster being selected?

Theoretically, the chance of an element from a large cluster being selected should be equal to the chance of an individual from a small cluster being selected. This is how it might work given the case of my research problem. (1) The chance of a cluster being selected is equal to (a) the number of clusters to be selected times (b) the clusters proportional share of the total population of elements. Remember that I had set out to select sixteen hundred blocks, and I will select twenty-seven blocks in each town. This is unrealistic, given the peculiar problem of selecting only elderly respondents, but for the sake of demonstrating how you calculate the probabilities, let's say that I will select one respondent or household on each of the blocks chosen. If Houston, Missouri, has twenty-five households on a given block and if there are two thousand households in Houston, the probability of the block being selected is equal to:

(1). $27 \text{ blocks to be chosen} \times \dfrac{25}{2,000} = .3$

Now to the second question, that is, the probability of an element within a cluster being selected. Having selected that block, each household or element has a probability of being selected within a cluster equal to the number you set out to select within each cluster (one, in our case) divided by the number of elements making up that particular cluster (for example, the number of households on the particular block). Assuming we are to select one respondent (household) from each block, a block with twenty-five households would mean that each household has a probability of being selected equal to:

(2). $\dfrac{1 \text{ to be selected}}{25 \text{ households on the block}} = .04$

Finally, the overall chance of a single element being selected, in our case, the odds of an elderly person living in Houston, can be calculated by multiplying (1) times (2). In this case, the overall probability is $.3 \times .04 = .01$.

Taking another cluster (block) with only ten households on it, the chance of that block being selected is:

$$27 \times \frac{10}{1500} = .19$$

The chance of any given household on that block being selected is:

$$\frac{1}{10} \quad \begin{array}{l}\text{(to be selected on each block)} \\ \text{(households on that block)}\end{array} = .1$$

Again, the odds of an element from that cluster being selected is $.19 \times .1 = .01$, the same as the chance of an element being selected in the larger cluster. Each element has an equal chance of being selected regardless of the different sizes of the clusters form which the elements are drawn. This is a distinct advantage with PPS multiple-stage cluster sample designs.

■ *Nonprobability Sample Designs*

Certain research problems and situations require that the researcher use nonrandom sampling designs. Because the sample designs below do not use randomization in the selection of the sample elements, it is impossible to determine sampling error and to estimate confidence intervals around your sample statistics. You have bias but are unable to measure it. This is a serious disadvantage that the researcher must weigh against the obvious convenience and efficiency of nonrandom sample designs.

QUOTA SAMPLING

In the early days of public opinion polling, George Gallup, Elmo Roper, and Archibald Crossley developed and used successfully the quota sampling procedure. The basic assumptions underlying this procedure are the same as the probability sample designs, especially the desire to (1) have the sample drawn from all corners of the population and (2) to have the key characteristics of the population represented proportionately in the sample.

The first step is to "stratify" the population into mutually exclusive and exhaustive subgroups. Census data and other sources can be used for this purpose. Depending on the research problem and the adequacy of these secondary sources of data, you might group the population geographically, racially, along age and gender lines, and so forth. You determine the number to be drawn from each subgroup based on their proportion to the total population size. Then field workers are given the strata and the number to be interviewed or given a questionnaire from each strata. How the individuals are chosen is left up to the field worker. For example, as a field worker, you might be given a list of census tracts in a particular city. In each census tract, you would be required to select fifteen white males between the ages of eighteen and sixty-five, then black males in the same age range, and so forth.

PURPOSIVE SAMPLING

Some research situations require that the researcher really focus in on a small geographic area or limited population. In short, you have a strong purpose for "pinpoint" selection.

Exit polling is a procedure where people leaving the voting place are interviewed about who they voted for and some demographic background. This information can be used to target a similar group in the next election for predicting the election's outcome. You would "purposively" select certain types of people given the exit poll results. Or, if you know how all the precincts voted, you can target those precincts that most nearly reflected the city wide vote or even national vote. Then you could "purposively" select those precincts for preelection interviews the next go-around.

SNOWBALL SAMPLING

Snowball sampling is called "reputational" sampling by some, and it involves purposively selecting the starting point, then asking the starting point to recommend other suitable respondents. For example, I am studying "decision elites" in Southern California and I happen to know that Otis Chandler, the publisher of the *Los Angeles Times*, is a very powerful and influential decision maker. I would start my interviewing with him, then ask him for a list of names of people who are like him and who would be "good" subjects for my study. Those individuals would recommend others, and so on, until the circle is completed.

■ *Conclusions*

The most important lesson to keep at the front of one's thinking regarding the choice of a sample design is to use a probability or random sample design if at all possible. The number one goal of sampling is to set your confidence limits and to be able to say with confidence that the statistics derived form the sample fall within a known predetermined margin of error. Because I set my confidence limits at .05 for my study of the rural Missouri elderly, on any given finding, I am 95% certain that the statistic, for example, health status, falls within five percentage points plus or minus of the true value, that is, the parameter. How would I know whether or not this is correct? I would have to interview every elderly person in the entire state of Missouri in order to get the true health status value. Thankfully, I have random sampling to do the work for me.

It is crucial to know the major principles of sampling because these principles guide your choice of which sampling design to use, along with considerations of efficiency. Representativeness, the law of large numbers, the rule of homogeneity, randomization, and the link between stratification of a population and theory should be reviewed before embarking on the design of a sampling procedure. Lastly, it is important to know in advance what your analysis plan is in order to be sure to end up with the proper number of certain characteristics in your final sample. For example, if my analysis called for splitting the respondents between Catholics and Baptists, I had better stratify my sample design along membership in the Catholic and Baptist churches.

Moving from simple random to the more complex, multistage designs, we gain in efficiency and perhaps even representativeness, but error is higher. With any sampling design, representativeness can be improved by increasing the sample size, but this comes at a price. As researchers, we make decisions not in terms of right and wrong, but on the basis of the best compromise given our resources and the research problem.

Finally, we are able to see in sampling design and theory the strong interdependence between theory and research as well as how strongly decisions made at one stage of the research process affect decisions made in later stages. The choice of a sampling design is based in part on efficiency needs and also on the research problem, theory, and the analysis plan.

GLOSSARY

confidence interval   The range of the mean value of a sample statistic that the researcher, with a specified degree of confidence, believes the true population mean falls within; for example, "I am 99% certain that the mean IQ score is one hundred, plus or minus four points."

confidence level   the odds, set by the researcher, that any given sample statistic represents the true population parameter.

law of large numbers   the larger the sample size, the more representative is the sample.

parameter   any value on a variable from a population.

periodicity   a bias in systematic sampling designs stemming from some nonrandom inherent order to the sampling frame.

population   the sum total of all the elements that the sample elements supposedly represent.

randomization   any procedure for selecting sample elements in which every element has an independent, equal, and known chance of being selected.

representativeness   the state of a sample that yields the same information (statistics) that you would get had you measured the entire population (parameters).

rule of homogeneity   the more homogeneous or alike the population is, the more likely it is that a sample drawn from it will be representative.

sample   a representative part of a larger whole.

sample element   the entity that is sampled and measured. The same as the unit of analysis.

sampling distribution   a theoretical distribution of many samples in which the distribution of the sample means would form a normal curve.

sampling error   the difference between the sample value (statistic) and the population value (parameter).

sampling frame   a list of the population elements from which the sample elements are drawn.

FOR FURTHER READING

Kish, Leslie. (1965). *Survey sampling*. New York: John Wiley and Sons.

Stephan, Frederick F., and McCarthy, Philip J. (1963). *Sampling opinions*. New York: John Wiley and Sons.

Chapter Seven

INTERVIEWING

■ *An analysis of conversation serves as the launching point for a discussion of the principles underlying the sociological interview. This discussion focuses on the barriers to and facilitators of communication, with special attention paid to "taking the role of the other," or empathy. Types of interviews (clinical, data-gathering, structural, etc.) and their social settings are discussed. Methodological strategies for enhancing communication are presented. These include planning the first verbal contact and the opening question, the order of the topics covered, confrontation, facilitation, support, reflection, and summarization. Problems associated with the background of the interviewer and respondent are discussed, which leads to points on training interviewers and methods for evaluating the quality of the interview.*

Interviewing is the direct face-to-face or indirect over-the-phone method of gathering information one-on-one. The everyday interaction that is closest to the research interview but not quite capturing its scientific power is the conversation. Because the conversation is a close cousin, it is common for newly emerging sociological researchers to treat interviewing as a facet of methodology that is easy to master. After all, the thinking goes, with so much everyday practice, interviewing should be a snap.

The very fact that I am spending considerable effort on this chapter should be clue enough that interviewing is difficult to learn and even more difficult to put into sociological practice. In all of my research experience, including supervising medical student interviews over an eighteen-year period, the number of good interviewers I have observed is between fifty and sixty. Without question in my mind, a good interviewer is a rare species.

In this chapter, I first discuss philosophy of science issues and basic sociological assumptions underlying interviewing. Next, I have classified the various types of interviewing in an effort to define what a scientific interview is. Then I spend considerable time on specific techniques of interviewing and lace all of this with examples from actual research interviews. Finally, I conclude matters with some guidelines for determining which interviewing styles and techniques are best used under which conditions, including the problem interviewer, the problem respondent, and interviewer training strategies.

■ *Philosophy*

The interview is one of several means of observing social action or subjectively meaningful behavior. It is especially valuable for certain research problems and almost worthless for certain others. In and of itself, interviewing is not more valuable than the dozen or so other data-gathering techniques, such as questionnaires, direct observation, and so forth. However, having said this, we must recognize the fact that interviewing is the most sociological of all the techniques because it involves intense interaction between the researcher and the subject. Live and direct words and sentiments are exchanged during the course of an interview, and the meanings behind those words and sentiments are, it is hoped, captured accurately in the course of gathering the data. This circumstance is not only unlike any other data-gathering technique, but it is uniquely sociological because it involves a one-on-one relationship between the researcher and each subject in which rapport and trust must be achieved if research is to be conducted. None of the other data-gathering techniques requires such intense interpersonal relations as the interview does. When you use it, you are applying basic sociological principles, such as the interdependence of interaction and sentiment, exchange relationships, and the internalization of norms and values, as a means of securing your data.

The uniqueness of the interview sociologically helps us understand why methodologists argue that interviewing transcends normal conversation and requires special knowledge and training in order to do it at all well. Not only do you have to design a valid and reliable data-gathering instrument, but you also need interactive skills that will compliment and even enhance the validity and reliability of the data. A sound interview schedule is one half of the puzzle, the interview itself, the other. Make no mistake about it. If you go into an interview situation with the philosophy that your normal conversational skills will carry the day, you stand a very good chance of conducting a very poor interview. What, then, are the philosophical tenets to keep in mind as you approach the task of conducting an interview?

■ *Forget Everything You Have Learned about Everyday Conversation*

TALK AS LITTLE AS NECESSARY

Everyday conversation has norms associated with it that, from a superficial analysis, seem to be perfectly appropriate for the data-gathering interview. Most of these norms or rules of conversation are detrimental to the interview if followed rigorously. For example, you are required by the norms of conversation to reciprocate by carrying your share of the burden of keeping the conversation going. The burden is on the individual engaged in conversation to talk as much as the other person. Silence may be golden, but it can be the kiss of death if one uses it instead of reciprocating by taking turns talking. You should not dominate the conversation by talking incessantly and thereby not allowing others to talk. But on the other hand, you need to respond in kind each time someone makes a point. A good conversation, that is, one that follows the norms, is one in which all the conversationalists say roughly the same amount or talk around the same amount of time. An interview that looked like this would be highly suspect, and any interviewer who talked as much as the respondent would be out of a job if it continued. Since interview data come from respondents and not interviewers, the good interviewer talks as little as necessary to get the respondent to talk as much as possible. The good interviewer strives to minimize his or her talking.

MAINTAIN CONTROL

The rules of everyday conversation specify that control over what is said and who says it is shared more or less equally among the conversants. Not so for the interview, where tight control is a central goal of the interviewer. The interviewer must take complete charge of the interaction, including such things as where people sit, when the interview begins and ends, what topics are covered, when they are covered, and so on. Losing control of the interview is almost always a methodological disaster that terminates useful data gathering. One striking example from the world of medical interviewing is worth presenting here. I was training first-year medical students in the art and science of conducting a data-gathering interview, a very important methodological skill for physicians to possess. The interviews were with real hospital patients, and the students were trained to conduct a social history-type interview. There were no hard and fast questions to be asked, only topic areas to be covered. Thus, the student was instructed to ask open-ended questions about how the patient decided to come to the hospital, the process of becoming aware that something was wrong with his or her health, the family situation, work, and so forth. The student would do well if he or she asked such questions as, "Tell me, Mrs. S., what is your family situation like at the moment?"

and not so well if he or she asked, "Is your family large?", a question that could be answered yes or no. Armed with the topics and general philosophical principles, the students would conduct an hour-long interview that they were instructed to tape-record. Later, I would listen to the tape with each student, make suggestions, and evaluate his or her interviewing skills. At one such review session, the student arrived at my office in a state of near panic. As I rose from my chair to greet him, the student blurted out that his patient refused to talk with him. I decided to listen to the small amount of tape that he had recorded, and this is what I heard: "Good morning, Mr. W. I am _____ , a first-year medical student, and I will be doing an interview with you about your medical problem, your family situation, and some other social background things. Before we start, do you have any questions?" "Well . . . I am going to die, aren't I?" "I don't know any thing about your case, Mr. W., because I am only a first-year student and don't know enough about medicine yet to tell you anything. In the first two years of medical school, we learn about diseases but not very much about how they affect patients. Tell me, what was it that brought you to the hospital?" At that point, the patient turned his back to the student and said nothing. The student tried several more questions on various of the topics to be covered, but the patient was silent. The student commented that it seemed that the patient did not want to talk, and he excused himself. My diagnosis was completely different from the student's. The student thought that the patient was angry because the student did not know the answer to his question. My thought was that the student had lost control of the interview when he asked the patient if he had any questions and then allowed the patient to turn the tables by becoming the interviewer. Think about the situation from the patient's perspective. He expected the student to ask the questions, then the student opened the door for him to ask questions, and when he asked, the student refused to answer. In fact, by answering in a situation such as this, the interview becomes hopelessly biased. You are damned if you do and damned if you don't. The key is to never allow the tables to be turned where the respondent, in this case, the patient, gains control over the interview. The student should have waited until the interview was over before asking the patient if he had any questions. More to the point of the loss of control, when the patient asked the question, the student should have turned the table right back on the patient. His response should have been, "What do you think is going to happen, Mr. W.?" If he had asked this question in lieu of the response he actually gave, the respondent would have opened up about his fear of dying alone and how frustrated he was that none of his doctors was willing to talk with him about his feelings toward his impending death. I know this is what he would have said to the student because I went back to the patient's room and reconstructed the interview up to the point where the student lost control. At that juncture, I asked the patient what he thought, and the result was exactly as I described. By not allowing the tables to be turned and maintaining control, I ensured that the patient's views were primary and heard out. What I thought about his illness was completely irrelevant to the goal of gathering data about the patient's pathway to the hospital and his attitudes and values concerning his illness. As it turned out, I learned a great amount about the patient and was able to start the ball rolling to help him cope with his feelings.

TAKING THE ROLE OF THE OTHER

Symbolic interactionism (W. I. Thomas) is responsible for alerting those interested in the methodology of interviewing to the power of taking the role of the other, that is, trying to see the situation through the other's eyes. This concept has great relevance for observational methodology, as we have seen, but it is particularly relevant for interviewing.

In order to effectively establish rapport, maintain control, and do all of the myriad other things necessary to conduct a successful interview, understanding the respondent's perspective is critically important. For example, you introduce yourself and the study and the respondent lashes out at sociological research, saying it is trivial and worthless. You need to understand the respondent's perspective and this is a good time to start. Rather than trying to forge ahead with the interview and forsaking the respondent's perspective, you need to call a temporary halt to the plan and spend some time learning about where the respondent is coming from. The most effective way of accomplishing that in this hypothetical case is to confront the respondent, gently, with the observation that "You seem to be angry." Then you remain silent until the respondent has had sufficient time to think about your challenge. Or, if the respondent begins to ask you questions, this is a direct challenge to your control. It should be met with "I am much more interested in hearing what you have to say about these questions. I will be glad to answer any questions you might have after I have had the chance to hear you out."

Your turning the tables back in this fashion should stimulate the respondent to share with you his or her perspective on research. Perhaps he or she had a negative interview experience in the past, or maybe the respondent is angry about something completely unrelated to the study or the interview. You need to find the handle, in this case, the respondent's perspective, and then you may be able to continue the interview under full control.

EXCHANGE

Maintaining control does not mean dominating the respondent or flaunting your power. A power relationship means that the individual in power takes while the powerless one gives. It is a one-sided relationship in this sense: one person is doing all the giving and the other, all the taking. Control exercised by the interviewer should be done in the context of giving something back to the respondent. Returning to the concept of "taking the role of the other," the interviewer can anticipate the respondent asking, "What's in it for me to do this interview?" The answer to this question rests with the basic philosophical principle of giving. This principle is commonly expressed in Western culture with the adage "Give and you shall receive." The gift is a symbol of giving, a marker of the exchange relationship. It is an exchange relationship between the giver and receiver because the act of giving obligates the recipient to give something in return and so on as the relationship grows. Thus, it is with interviewing that you must delve into the philosophical realm and question what gifts you are prepared to give and what gifts you are prepared to receive. This is not a methodological issue but rather a deeper philosophical one because the type of gift you select will color or affect the very essence of the relationship you will be able to establish with the respondent. For example, if you pay the respondent for the time spent doing the interview, the relationship is fundamentally a materialistic one. You will receive the interview in exchange, but there now exists the possibility that the respondent will give you what he or she thinks the payment was worth. Should you want to go beyond the interview and delve deeper into the respondent's thinking or experiences, that might be viewed by the respondent as going beyond what was paid for and a breach of contract. On the other hand, if you invite the respondent to be a part of your research by giving the respondent the right to communicate with you about the study or to receive summaries of the findings, you have created a spiritual bond in the sense that the gift is intellectual in nature. In this case, the respondent should share your interest in seeing the study achieve excellence and should do whatever it takes to provide you with the data you seek.

CONFIDENTIALITY

Fundamental to the interview is the belief, ideally on the part of both the interviewer and the respondent, that the interview will improve the quality of life in some fashion. Certainly the belief that what was said in the interview would ultimately harm the respondent would make it extremely difficult, if not completely impossible, to do the interview. Philosophically, the interviewer must value the safety of the respondent and believe in the positive impact that the data will have on the respondent and the larger society. The researcher must not divulge *any information* about a respondent to anyone, including colleagues, spouses, and other family members.

Confidentiality is a state of trust that exists between the respondent and the interviewer. Both parties trust in the efficacy of the interview and believe each other to be committed to idea of doing some good with the data derived from the interview. There are varying degrees of this trust, but the more of it, the better the interview will go. It is easier to dismiss a request to allow an interviewer to take an hour of your time asking questions about which soap you use and why you use it than it is to be interviewed about socially relevant issues, such as health care, abortion, poverty, drug use, and so on. The more you and the respondent share the belief that the subject matter of the interview is important beyond the two of you, the more likely that the interview will yield valid and reliable data.

RAPPORT

The so-called bottom-line philosophical issue underlying interviewing is the necessity for the interviewer and respondent to share meanings. Mutual agreement about meanings is the core of what methodologists have labeled **rapport**, that is, the state of a social relationship characterized by mutual feelings of being in harmony. This means that the interviewer and respondent are able to decide, to their mutual agreement, what it is that they would feel or do if they were in the other's shoes. Max Weber (1964) recognized this as an essential subjective characteristic of science, which he called *verstehen*, or understanding.

You may have experienced this with a very close friend where the two of you understand each other's likes and dislikes so well that you never have to bring the subject up or worry about some action occurring that would violate those expectations. Usually in situations such as this, disagreements are relatively minor and are settled quickly and without rancor. There exists a mutual understanding that goes beyond words. You have rapport with each other.

Rapport is the final result, the outcome of taking the role of the other, confidentiality, exchange, and control over the interview. If all the other principles of interviewing are taken care of properly, if the methodologically correct philosophy is in place, then rapport is a necessary outcome of the interaction surrounding the interview.

What are some of the signs or indicators that you have established rapport? Perhaps it is easier to consider the signs of poor or nonexistent rapport first, as much of the interaction we engage in is weak on rapport. All of us have interacted with someone who was highly insensitive to our needs. When I was employed as a clerk in a supermarket trying to pay my way through college, I worked briefly for an assistant manager who repeatedly scheduled those of us who were college students for back-to-back night and day shifts. Because we were part-time employees, the union was unable to control the number of hours we received and the type of shift. In any case, this manager should have noticed our complaining or absenteeism as signs that we were unhappy with his schedules, but he never did. Our grumbling was detected by the supervisor, who eventually intervened by moving the assistant manager out of the store and into the central office, where he did paper, not people work.

People who forget a loved one's birthday or back out of a dinner engagement may be weak in the rapport department, too. Public displays of what we call rudeness is another sign of rapport deficit. I work and live in a college town and consequently encounter hundreds of university students daily. Occasionally, a student will call me at home after 10 P.M. to talk about a test or grade, a conversation that easily could have been carried out during the normal work day. Then there are the times that students have walked out of my class after fifteen or so minutes or, better yet, have called me shortly before class and asked if I think they would miss something important, should they cut class on that day. One student came to me complaining about the grade I had assigned his paper. I had given him an F, and he was angry because he was sure that his paper was about the same quality as that of his fraternity brother, who also was in the class. The frat brother had received a D.

All of these observations are examples of serious deficiency in taking the role of the other and hence in establishing rapport.

On the positive side, there are signs that indicate rapport was established. First, you can be pretty sure that things have gone well with rapport if the respondent does not want to end the interview. Many a time I have put my pen down and tucked the interview schedule away in my briefcase only to have the respondent open up along some new, unexplored lines. In some ways, it was as if the interview began once I formally ended it. Another sure sign is post-interview contact. In the study of the rural elderly, one of the interviewers, a medical student, received a birthday card from one of the respondents months after she had done the interview. Another medical student talked fondly about a ninety-nine-year-old woman who promised him that he would get an invitation to her hundredth birthday. She never made it to one hundred, but her daughter sent a note to the medical student telling him how much her mother enjoyed the interview experience and how much she had been looking forward to seeing the student at her party. Similarly, I have received several notices from sons and daughters of former respondents informing me of their parents' deaths. I take all this to mean that the respondents involved enjoyed their contacts with the interviewers. Another sign of good rapport is the absence of problems in the data obtained from the interview. Lots of missing values or "Don't knows" may signal poor rapport; complete and full data is a sign that rapport was established.

The ability to establish rapport is partly innate and partly acquired. Fortunately for those of us who wish to improve as interviewers, it is a skill that can be improved upon with proper training. The following are some of the factors that in my experience work to the advantage of the researcher seeking to maximize rapport.

COMPLETENESS OF INFORMATION

The completeness and accuracy of information that the interviewer and respondent have about each other going into the interview is a very important predictor of rapport. For example, I was assigned the job of observing and interviewing a Mexican-American and Yaqui Indian health board at a new neighborhood health center in the Southwest. The center was designed to serve the poor by providing comprehensive health services and health-related jobs for the community. The research problem was a general one of discovering how the citizen health boards got organized and what the nature of their struggle with the medical establishment was. The methodology involved some direct observation of meetings, center conflicts, and other action involving the board members and medical providers. Also, we conducted focused interviews with board members and medical providers. This was very difficult due to the large gap in social background and life experiences between the researchers and the board members. It was not so great a problem with the physician and other providers, because the researchers were faculty members at a prestigious medical school and shared lots of professional experiences with the providers.

In order to increase my understanding of the life situation facing the board members, I enrolled in a intensive Spanish language course. I had grown up in Los Angeles speaking street Spanish, so the language came back fairly well. Also, I read literature about the Chicano movement and watched films depicting the struggle of Mexican-Americans for justice. Finally, I spent the first month of the field work at the center just hanging around and working in a local Chicano-owned candle factory. During this time, I read a couple of histories of the community and the Yaqui people. In this way, I improved my knowledge base, and that really worked to improve rapport. I can recall being able to break the ice by mentioning some local lore or event, and often the respondents demonstrated their confidence in my knowledge by mentioning fairly idiosyncratic or esoteric things without stopping to explain them to me. Most important, I was able to conduct the interviews in Spanish occasionally when necessary, and culturally specific concepts and ways of thinking were clear to me. This is difficult to illustrate, but one example stands out in my mind. It occurred at a meeting between the board members and the center director, a physician who was the head of the family and community medicine department at the local medical school. The medical school was providing the medical services at the time, and the medical school's control over the way services were organized at the center was under attack by the board members. Throughout the debate, there were veiled comments by the board members about center doctors not "knowing how it is," but the director did not follow up on these comments. Knowing what I had learned about the folk medical practices and how incredibly widespread and important they were to the people, I surmised that the board members were telling the director to hire doctors who appreciated and would work with the folk medical practitioners. Later, I found out that this was in fact the case, but had I not been aware of the cultural nuances, I too would have missed this very important bone of contention. The board members were too guarded, perhaps out of embarrassment, to lay the issue out on the table.

PAST EXPERIENCE

During the many years I taught interviewing to medical students, it never ceased to amaze me how nervous large numbers of the students got prior to doing their interviews with hospital patients. Not only were they nervous, but often the quality of the interviews was also fairly poor. I was never able to substantiate the folk wisdom among the faculty as to why the students had so much trouble with interviewing, but the word was that medical students spent so much time studying as undergraduates and then as medical students that they were deficient in human relations skills. Sitting in a library all day and half the night is not conducive to building social skills because such academic dedication limits the individual's experience with situations and people. The chances of being a good interviewer are greatest with individuals who have had a wide variety of experiences and who have interacted with people from all walks of life. In short, interactive skills are improved with practice, such as having to negotiate with people whose values and expectations are very different from your own. Taking the role of the other well requires that you understand the social and cultural context of the individual as well as have a track record in role taking.

In my case, I grew up in a blue-collar community with several different ethnic groups. Being around working-class people all my growing-up years made it very easy for me to establish rapport with and to interview working-class respondents. My problem arose with upper-class respondents because I had such limited experience with their life-styles and values. Wealthy respondents made me feel nervous and a bit intimidated, I must admit. The same has been true with ethnic experience in my research. I had lots of contact with Mexican-American children as a child myself, and this facilitated the interviewing I did for the neighborhood health center study in the Southwest. Another colleague was Chinese, and he did very well with the Native-American and Mexican-American centers. However, he did less well with the black respondents, whereas the native New Yorker on our research team was perfectly at home in the East Coast black centers. We were most effective at centers where our past experiences caused the current events and people to seem familiar.

Sometimes the past experiences are too subtle for the uninitiated to observe or to understand, yet they are powerful nonetheless. For example, I put a very small tattoo on my left hand in the fashion of the old *pachucos* from East Los Angeles, where I grew up. All kids who aspired to be anything except nerds put these little dots on their hands with India ink and a pin so they could be like the gang boys. Interestingly, when I first introduced myself to one of the neighborhood leaders at the Southwest research site, he noticed the mark and launched a conversation that led to my staying at his house in the heart of the Mexican-American community. A lasting friendship developed between our families.

Life experiences and the research problem may correspond nicely, as in the case of a former colleague who had undergone a kidney transplant several years before doing research on kidney disease. This colleague capitalized on his long struggle with the disease. He knew firsthand what it was like to learn that you had an illness that was terminal without dialysis or transplantation. He went through the pain and uncertainty of dialysis and the transplant. Thus, he was finely tuned in when he conducted interviews with kidney transplant patients and their families. As an interviewer, he gained the respondents' trust in large measure because he was "one of them," a victim just like they were, a person who would not be likely to pity or patronize other transplant patients. Once he shared the fact of his own transplant operation with the respondents, the barriers fell in the respondents' rush to find out how successful his operation was along with other experiences that might be applied to their case. A sort of bonding occurred around shared experiences. People felt that they were talking the same language of the kidney patient. E. Digby Baltzell gained rapport with Philadelphia social elite in good measure because he was one of them. Howard Becker was able to do his study of marijuana use and jazz musicians partly because he is a fine jazz pianist, and Clifton Bryant parlayed his years of traveling with his father's circus into some fascinating studies of the carnival life. Baltzell would have had his problems with the carnival workers, as would Bryant with the Philadelphia gentlemen.

KNOW THYSELF

Anticipate some of the things that can go awry in the interview and play out in your mind how you would react. For example, think of an interview situation where the respondent is from a culture that you know absolutely nothing about. You do not recognize phrases, and the body language is equally unfathomable. What do you do? Or imagine a respondent who breaks out crying in the first five minutes of the interview. Would you offer consolation and lay your hand on the person's shoulder, or would you remain silent while awaiting the end of the cry-ing? How would you react to a respondent who jumped up and angrily insisted that you were doing the work of the devil. All but one of these situations have happened to me during interviews, and usually I was unprepared, because I had not rehearsed them in my mind. The devil one involved a research assistant for my study of the rural elderly, and it was the most difficult one for me. I must con-fess that the research assistant and I handled it poorly. The assistant was doing an interview with an elderly woman in her home. The husband was moving about in the back bedroom during the better part of the interview. When the interviewer was approaching the finish, the husband emerged and more or less invited himself to sit in. The interviewer ignored him at first but then realized that his presence was a biasing factor, since none of the other interviews had more than the respon-dent and the interviewer present. Furthermore, the interviewer felt obligated to keep his promise to the respondent that the interview would be kept strictly con-fidential. Thus, he asked the husband to leave the room until the interview was finished. The husband complied but returned almost immediately and began to shout at the interviewer that he was doing the work of the devil. The wife did not say a word once this tirade started, and the husband, although old and seemingly frail, began to advance on the interviewer. At this point, the interviewer started to move away from the man, all the while exclaiming that he was a member of the university research team. The husband became even more agitated, so the inter-viewer shouted at him to leave. The husband picked up a flower pot and started to wind up when the interviewer grabbed his stuff and bolted out the front door. He could hear the husband shouting all the way to his car, which was parked across the street from the house. The interviewer left and called me with a description of the blow up. I should have called the local police and explained the situation. This might have led to someone checking on the couple to see if the wife was safe. In-stead, I did nothing beyond sending out the standard thank you letter. I have re-gretted my inaction to this day. Mental preparation for situations such as this increases the odds that the interviewer will react quickly and effectively to abnor-mal behaviors, settings, and events.

CURIOSITY

Good interviewers are like good detectives who seem to have been born with an overactive inquisitiveness gland. The curious interviewer never takes the spoken word at face value. Instead, he or she looks beneath the surface to what sociolo-gists call deep meanings, not so much to question the truthfulness of what the respondent is saying but rather to get at the core values and beliefs that form the foundation of what is said. Regardless of the extent to which the interview is structured, curiosity plays a role in building empathy and hence the quality of the interview. Whether to ask a structured question again versus accepting the re-sponse to the first query depends in part on how thoroughly the interviewer scru-tinizes the response and relates it to other answers earlier in the interview. For example, the interviewer considers each response relative to other responses and questions and consistency of the answers. Or the interviewer may relate the observable setting to the substance of the respondent's answers and thereby detect an underlying problem with the interview. If the respondent's living room is full of photographs of many different people, and yet the respondent has very little to say by way of responding to the questions on social networks, the curious interviewer would pursue this apparent discrepancy. Likewise in unstructured or semistructured interviews, curiosity will help the interviewer recognize leads to be probed. The additional impetus and attentiveness that curiosity adds to the interviewer's presentation of self should lead to greater empathy.

■ *Types of Interviews: Purpose*

Interviewing is a tool serving the purpose of its architect. Reasons for conducting interviews can be grouped into two broad categories that form two general types of interviews: (1) the data-gathering interview and (2) the therapeutic or clinical interview. Certainly all data-gathering interviews have an element of therapy, and likewise, the therapeutic interview gathers data. But in the main, the therapeutic interview concentrates on helping the interviewee, with the data considered incidental, and any psychological benefits that the respondent in a data-gathering interview receives are considered a fringe benefit. In short, the data-gathering interviewer will not allow therapy to enter the interview situation formally.

In sociology, the data-gathering interview is the methodological tool of choice because sociology is in the business of explaining the social world, not treating individuals. Clinical psychology, social work, and psychiatry utilize the therapeutic interview because their goals center around providing direct help to individuals. From the perspective of someone interested in conducting a therapeutic interview, the data-gathering interview seems almost heartless. Once I was demonstrating the techniques of the data-gathering interview to a class of first-year medical students. I was on the stage and was showing a videotape of an interview I had done with a low-income elderly lady.

The interview took place in her tiny apartment, which was crammed full of her possessions gathered over a lifetime. During the course of the interview, it became apparent that this woman was frightened of her neighbors possibly entering her apartment and stealing things or harming her. Also, she was concerned that her health was poor and that she did not know a physician anymore since her family doctor of many years retired and left the state. Finally, she expressed a strong need to get outside once in a while and to go to her church. All during the interview, I would probe for more information and even offer support at times with "It must be rough" or "I understand." However, I did not shift into a therapeutic interview and held my course of collecting information about her situation and thinking. I had invited a physician to the class and had asked him to offer comments on my interview. He jumped me for being "a cold fish" and for "not picking up on the serious needs" of the respondent. His attack was so pointed and fierce that many of the students were shocked to the extent that they came up after class and offered me their support. I tried to defend my interviewing approach on the basis of the distinction but to no avail as far as the physician was concerned. He had mixed up therapy and data gathering in his thinking, and I dare say that empirical research involving interviewing would not be possible for him if he had to do the interviews. An action orientation is fine and appropriate in sociology, but it does not mix with data gathering, especially with the interview. There are several important ethical questions that arise from this distinction that we will discuss later.

■ *Types of Interviews: Structure*

THE STANDARDIZED INTERVIEW

Standardization is a concept that should be familiar to all of us who have survived elementary and secondary educations. In those systems, it is a method for creating sameness, for making it possible to compare students and to classify students in come fashion that is understood the same way by everyone involved and applied equally to those classified. For example, letter grades are derived the same way for all students in the school and therefore carry the same meaning, regardless of the particular students involved.

With interviewing, standardization applies to the questions and the answers. Questions and answers are standardized when some effort is made to ask the same questions and to record answers in the same fashion for all the respondents. There is a range of standardization, to be sure, and any given interview method could incorporate more than one type or degree of standardization. The most highly **standardized interview** has questions worded exactly as they are to be asked. Also, the order of the questions is fixed and the same for each interview. Finally, each response must be placed in one and only one predetermined response category. For example, a structured interview question and response might look like the following taken from my study of the rural elderly:

1. People my age are set in their ways.
   Strongly agree   ____
   Agree   ____
   Undecided   ____
   Disagree   ____
   Strongly disagree ____

The question is asked exactly as worded for every individual interviewed and the response categories are equally fixed. The same stimuli are presented to every respondent so that the researcher can attribute any differences found among the respondents to the independent variables and not to the differences in question wording, order, or response categories. Another advantage to having a standardized interview is that standardization forces the researcher to be explicit and clear about what the key variables are and how they are to be measured.

SEMISTRUCTURED

There is a happy medium between the highly structured interview and one with barely enough structure to determine who the interviewer is. In fact, one finds a mixture of structures within any given interview-based study. For example, the **semistructured interview** might have specific topic areas that need to be covered but the exact wording of the questions or the order in which the questions are asked is left up to the discretion of the interviewer. The structure stems from the particular topics to be covered, but it is minimal structure. The interviews I did with the rural elderly were a mixture of structured and semistructured. The less structured questions were asked the same way for all the respondents, but the responses were left open-ended, that is, there was simply a line or two on which the interviewer recorded the respondent's answer verbatim. Even less structure was found in the **oral history interviews** I did with twenty of the rural elderly respondents. I had several topics, such as education, child rearing, marriage, and health care, that I was free to ask about in any way I deemed appropriate. Just as long as the topic was covered to my satisfaction, the wording and order of the questions was not an issue. No two respondents experienced exactly the same interview, but I learned about the one-room school experiences of all the respondents. The data were not standardized in a strict sense, but the research problem called for deep meaning and interpretation. Thus, the semistructured interview data were perfect for the problem of understanding historical events, such as the Depression or women's suffrage, from the perspectives of elderly individuals who experienced the events firsthand. For the other research problem having to do with sociological factors associated with longevity, the structured interview yielded the type of standardized data that was needed in order to explore those factors statistically. The degree of structure in the interview depends primarily on the nature of the research problem.

■ *Interviewing Techniques*

SILENCE

In loquacious cultures, silence can be a most powerful incentive to talk. The norms of conversation vary tremendously from culture to culture, and thus, generalizations concerning the role of silence in interviewing are difficult to sustain. Nevertheless, silence normally means that there is an opportunity for someone to speak up. In a two-person conversation, silence usually is a sign that one person is finished speaking and that the other person may now speak. This is more or less the norm for U.S. society.

Silence is an effective interviewing technique when used sparingly and in the right situation. It indicates to the respondent that you the interviewer want to hear more about what was just said. Talk is the comfort zone, and silence is unnerving to people. Being silent even for five seconds can cause some discomfort, and it is doubtful that you could sustain silence in a group of four for more than twenty seconds before someone would blurt out something to break the quiet. Using silence in the interview is very tricky because there is a very fine line between effectiveness and dysfunction. One or two seconds too long and the technique can backfire, causing a loss of rapport. Used too much, the interviewer will seem cold and distant and will make the respondent very uncomfortable, sort of like you feel when someone stares at you.

Silence works well with elderly respondents. Many of the respondents in my study had lived alone for years and were used to long periods of silence. More important, they talked more slowly than younger people and took a bit more time to formulate answers to my questions. Silence on my part conveyed to the respondents that they had the time they needed to answer the questions. My use of silence during the course of the interviews sent the message to the respondents that I had the time and patience to hear them out, however long that might take.

SUPPORT

One of the great fears that most people share is to be the lone champion of some obviously unpopular and hopelessly deviant idea. This fear is so strong, in fact, that even powerful, well-educated, and experienced individuals will go along with a group decision in spite of their firm belief that the group is wrong. The classic example of this "group think" is the Cuban missile crisis during President John Kennedy's administration, when members of the Cabinet acted on what they thought the others were thinking, rather than following their individual best judgments (Allison, 1971). In situations where your ideas are on the line, you look for company out of fear of being odd person out.

Given this very human tendency, it is very important to let the respondent know during the interview that you are not going to pass judgment on his or her ideas. Quite the contrary, you need to convince the respondent that you are following what is said and that you understand the feelings expressed. Be careful not to overdo this technique, but be sure to use it. A simple nod of the head, a forward lean, and eye contact can do wonders for conveying **support**. Occasionally, you might say "Yes" or "I understand." At times, the interview can become very emotional, and then more direct support is called for. Once a respondent began to cry as he began to answer the questions about his health status. I stopped asking and placed my hand on his arm, saying, "It must be difficult for you. I understand." It was a genuine expression on my part. Anytime you offer support, it should come from the heart. In the case of this man, he opened up about his fears of leaving his wife in the lurch, should his health continue to decline. It turned out that his wife was a brittle diabetic whose eyesight was going downhill fast. Once he had gotten these feelings off his chest, he calmed back down and said that he wanted to complete the interview.

Keep in mind that support does not mean that you should agree with the ideas expressed by the respondent, for to do that would severely bias the interview. Support means to show an appreciation for what the respondent is saying or feeling, not that you express agreement with it. For the most part, my interviewing experience has taught me that most respondents are not looking for approval from the interviewer but certainly seem to appreciate genuine gestures of understanding and reassurance.

FACILITATION

Mannerisms, words, or gestures that encourage the respondent to communicate are techniques of **facilitation**. One of the most effective facilitative technique is to simply repeat the last word or words that the respondent said. For example, the respondent might have said, "I am applying to the health services management program after quitting medical school because health services management is more humane educationally." A facilitating response would be "More humane?", which should encourage the respondent to talk more about the inhumane medical school environment. Similar to support, body language plays an important role in facilitating communication with a respondent. A nod of the head, hand movements, leaning forward in your chair, and good eye contact all can contribute. Verbal cues include "I see," "And . . ?", "You were saying. . . ?", and the old standard "Uh huh."

SUMMARIZATION

There is no question in my mind that the most effective technique for increasing communication while at the same time checking the quality of interview data is **summarization**. I use this technique in every interview I do, regardless of the type or length of the interview.

The technique is really very simple. Periodically during the interview, you stop and summarize what you think the respondent has told you. For example, I might have just finished asking about the personal background and health status of the respondent. The health status information might contain actions that the respondent took when he or she was sick. Because this historical information is difficult to remember and because of the amount of information gathered at this point in the interview, I would stop asking questions and say, "Now I want to take a moment to go back over the things you have told me to be sure that I have gotten it right." I would summarize what the respondent told me and then ask, "Is this correct? Did I leave anything out, or is there more that you might want to add?"

A couple of things can happen as a result of this technique. You might strike pay dirt and get the respondent to open up more about the health problems and background data. If this happens, it is probably due to the respondent having the opportunity to reflect on what was said, thereby getting new insight or thoughts on the matter. Or you might have misunderstood the respondent the first time through and recorded incorrect information. Similarly, the respondent might have misinterpreted your questions, which would lead to misinformation, too. Finally, things may work out fine, and you are safe in moving on to the next set of questions.

CONFRONTATION

Confrontation is the most difficult technique in terms of deciding when and in getting up the courage to use it. It is the act of presenting to the respondent your judgment that something is amiss with the interview. This can be either the respondent's attitude or demeanor or what the respondent has said.

It is useful under the following conditions. Take a case where the respondent is in treatment for alcoholism and the interviewer is trying to get a social history of the events and decisions leading up to the decision to seek treatment. The interview begins with an open-ended question, "Tell me, Mrs. _____ , what brought you to the hospital?" The respondent launches into a lengthy and seemingly polished analysis of why she is an alcoholic and how grateful she is to have reached this level of understanding and control over her problem. She concludes by affirming repeatedly her commitment to never drink alcohol again. She says she is cured. With the social history of the respondent's problem in mind, you ask her to describe or recount how the alcohol problem got started. In the course of this description, you learn that she had been hospitalized three times prior to the current hospitalization. Now you begin to question her opening statement. Why the sudden insight? Is the cure really that simple? Also, your scientific knowledge about alcoholism tells you that treatment is a lifelong process and that the medical experts do not talk about cures, only lifelong recovery. At this point you should draw the hypothesis that the respondent is giving you a rehearsed party line, something she has developed over countless interviews and sessions with treatment agents. It is a line that she thinks you want to hear, a spiel that will expedite her passage through the treatment program. There appears to be a level of denial that might interfere with her recovery in the long run. This situation calls for a direct confrontation with the respondent. Remember that you are gathering data, not doing therapy, but you are in a bind because the data may be spurious in this case. How does one confront another person without alienating the person or ruining rapport?

There are no easy answers, but we can draw upon years of interviewing experience to provide some useful suggestions. You might summarize what the respondent has said for starters. Then you could say, "Is it really that easy, Mrs. _____ ?" If this does not produce a different response, then you might confront her with: (1) the scientific knowledge concerning cure versus control or (2) her previous hospitalizations, indicating the failure of past cures. You would then ask her to tell you what causes her to be so certain this time around. At this point, you have exhausted the technique. If the respondent persists with her story, you will have to go with it as accurate data.

Another excellent use for confrontation is when the interviewer meets up with a "reluctant" or even hostile respondent. This is very likely to happen if you are conducting interviews with people who are in the midst of personal crises, particularly individuals who are trying to cope with life-threatening illness. Passing through crises, as Fred Davis so elegantly described in his book, *Passage Through Crisis* (1963), causes people to become tentative and uncertain as to their competence. This might be manifested by the respondent saying such things as "Oh, I don't think I can discuss that" or "I'm not the person to ask. I just don't know."

Confrontation in situations where the respondent's attitude or demeanor seems to be a problem might take the following forms: "You seem to be uncertain, Mr. _____" or "You seem sad, Mr. _____." If the respondent opens up at this point, you might reassure him by saying, "That must be tough. I understand how you feel."

Sometimes this type of confrontation will lead the respondent to return the confrontation. It might go something like this: "You seem to be angry, Mr. _____." "You're right. Wouldn't you be angry if that happened to you?" At this point, the tables are about to be turned, and the interviewer could become the respondent. How do you handle this? By reflecting on the word *angry*. Simply repeat the word and be silent. It should produce the effect intended originally when you confronted him with his apparent anger. Should it not work, you will be in a bit of a pickle. You might try a slightly different tack and ask, "Why did it make you angry?" Should this fail, you need to go back to square one and try to build the rapport necessary to get the interview beyond this impasse. Clearly you will not be able to conduct a meaningful interview with an angry or depressed respondent, so you either need to take the time to get the respondent to open up about his or her feelings or back out of the interview as gracefully as possible. In my experience, once the respondent has gotten the feelings out in the open, the interview can be conducted effectively.

PROBES

Semistructured interview questions often contain, in parentheses, hints to the interviewer or what to ask should the initial response prove inadequate. These are **probes**. Referring back to the open-ended question, "Tell me about your family (e.g., number of members, feelings toward one another, hardships, successes, traditions)," the interviewer knows to probe on the number of members, feelings, and so on, should these issues remain uncovered in the respondent's initial answer.

■ *Special Circumstances*

THE ELDERLY

One of the most interesting interviewing challenges for me was posed by the twenty-year longitudinal study of the rural elderly. The respondents were living in small towns scattered all over the state of Missouri. The respondents were living in their own homes, and it had been twelve years since the last interview. During those years, over 450 of the respondents had died, and the survivors had grown quite old. When I returned in 1987, the "youngest" respondent was eighty-six; and the vast majority were in their mid- to late nineties. This called for some special interviewing techniques.

I spent much more time building rapport with the elderly than I normally do with younger respondents. This was difficult to do at first because I was operating under the assumption that the respondents had very little energy and would tire very quickly. Thus, I felt pressured to get to the heart of the interview quickly and to not "waste" time on nondata-gathering conversation. It is difficult to convey in writing just how valuable each and every respondent's participation in the study was. Twenty years of data on the aging process was hanging in the balance, and I could not accept the possibility of a respondent refusing to be interviewed, or worse, finding it too difficult to continue the interview because it was too long. Very quickly, my stereotypical thinking about the elderly changed in light of the early interviewing experiences. The respondents did not get tired of the interview but rather seemed to relish the opportunity to tell their stores. It became apparent that the respondents were not used to having a younger person listen to what they had to say and to care enough about it to write things down. Also, I had assumed that rapport would not be an issue since this was the third interview. This was not true. The elderly respondents had vague memories, at best, of the last interview twelve years prior. In several cases, the respondents had been victimized by unethical salespeople who sold them useless burial or cancer insurance.

So, I began to spend more time just talking with people. I would comment on a photograph hanging on the wall or start talking about what I had learned thus far from talking with other respondents. The most useful rapport-building situation was to sit with the respondent and look through old photographs for a few minutes. Another good situation was when we could talk about some person in the town we knew in common. These were great ice breakers and gave me the opportunity to set the tone for the interview—slow paced with lots of time for the respondent to answer. Before I adopted this approach, the rush to get through the interview was communicated to the respondent and the quality of the data suffered. As a final note on rapport, being relatively young facilitated communication, primarily because the younger interviewers reminded the respondents of their grandchildren and because the respondents had very little opportunity to interact with younger people, which made it interesting for them.

One problem I encountered was that the elderly respondents had difficulty hearing. I was able to overcome this by facing the respondent and speaking slowly with somewhat exaggerated lip movements. This enabled the respondents to read my lips, as the famous presidential aphorism has it. I never shouted, and in cases where I was sure that the respondent could read, I gave her or him a large-print version of the interview schedule to follow along with. This, too, facilitated communication, not only in the hearing department but also by giving the respondents a sense of being an active partner in the interview.

There were several instances where the respondents were bedfast from strokes. In every case, a family member or members were taking care of the respondent and living with the person around the clock. In one instance, the grandson and granddaughter-in-law (I will call her Jane here) took turns living with the respondent. I happened to arrive at the home when Jane was there. I explained the study to her and told her that I would appreciate it if she would fill out what she could of the interview schedule. I offered to leave the schedule with her along with a self-addressed envelope. Much to my surprise, Jane suggested that she and I interview her grandmother. I was reluctant, given what I had observed of her condition, especially the respondent's paralysis and difficulty speaking. Nevertheless, Jane and I conducted the interview. Jane completed all the factual background information and then helped ask her grandmother the attitudinal questions. I could barely discern her responses, but Jane seemed to have no trouble. It was incredibly slow going and I became nervous about the well-being of the respondent. I breathed a great sigh of relief when we asked the last question, but Jane assured me, as we were walking out to the car, that the interview was really good for her grandmother. She felt that the intellectual stimulation was just what her grandmother needed and that it was the most animated and responsive she had been for a long time.

On a final note, I took my ten- and fourteen-year-old daughters on several of the interviewing trips mainly because they seemed to enjoy meeting the respondents and listening to their stories. Having them along helped me establish rapport, no question, but there was an unanticipated payoff related to the respondents' difficulties hearing me. I discovered that the pitch of one of my daughter's voice was audible to a respondent when I had all but given up hope that I could make myself understood. My daughter conducted the entire interview with relative ease. This experience convinced me that it would be worth the expense and effort to have male/female teams of interviewers in cases where the respondents have hearing problems. Of course, it is difficult, if not impossible, to tell in advance what the hearing status might be. In my experience with eighty-seven- to one-hundred-year-old individuals, it is safe to assume that some degree of hearing impairment will exist and that a mixed voice pitch interviewing team would be helpful.

LANGUAGE

At times, cultural circumstances place an interviewer in a setting where the interviewer is unfamiliar with words and phrases. Pretesting should catch this, but, at times, it does not. I was interviewing in the Ozark Mountain region of Missouri where I heard the expressions "down in the back" and "feeling puny" used to describe back pain and general malaise, respectively. At other times, inner-city residents had me baffled with such words and phrases as *short* (automobile), "burn coal" (blacks having sex with blacks), *jive* (lying), and so forth. The only thing to do is to ask the respondent to translate terms and idioms that you are unfamiliar with.

PROBLEM RESPONDENTS

The problem respondent is a fiction of the interview situation. When it comes down to it, the problem stems from a lack of fit between the personality of the respondent and the requirements of the interview. A person is a problem relative to some standard. Thus, to label a respondent as a problem in no way casts negative judgment on his or her character. All this label is designed to accomplish is to alert the methodologists to the personality characteristics of the respondent that, in the context of the interview situation, might make it difficult to gather the desired data.

We discussed earlier in this chapter the angry or hostile respondent and how effective confrontation can be in those situations. More commonly, the interviewer often will encounter respondents who appear to be resistant simply because they lack self-confidence and view the interview as a "test" of their knowledge or intellectual ability. Placed in the interview setting with a professional interviewer hanging on his or her every word, the respondent might experience a form of stage fright and clam up. A common symptom of this reaction is the tentative answer, such as "I'm not sure" or "I don't know." This should be particularly obvious to the interviewer when the "don't know" answers begin to happen on attitudinal and other nonfactual or informational questions. When this happens, the interviewer should stop the questioning and deal with it. One way I have found effective is to reiterate the point I usually make at the start of the interview that there are no right or wrong answers, that the respondent is not being "tested" in any way. Sometimes I will say, "It is not necessary to know all about the things I am going to ask you. In fact, I just want to get your opinions and ideas about x, y, and z. There are no right or wrong answers, just your ideas, which are very important to me."

Sometimes a respondent thinks more slowly and deliberately than the interviewer has allowed for. If the respondent has the impression that the interview must proceed at a quick pace, he or she might use "don't know" as a device to speed up her answers. To test this possibility, the interviewer might repeat the question and say, "Well, take a moment to think about it."

Perhaps the most common problem is the respondent who talks too much about subjects that are irrelevant to the interview at hand. The respondent has stories he or she wants to tell the interviewer, and nothing as minor as a question will get in the way of telling those stories. Most commonly, the respondent will start out on the answer to the question but then take a detour. The interviewer has no recourse but to interrupt the respondent and get the interview back on the correct path. This sounds easy, but it can be stressful for the interviewer. After all, interrupting someone is never a pleasant thing to do.

There are ways to do this gracefully. The interviewer should act quickly, that is, should establish the pattern of interrupting and exerting more control over the interview as soon as possible. Hold up your palm, the universal body language for "stop," and either use the last comment made by the respondent or use the question to get the respondent to pick up back where he or she had departed the course. One possibility is to break in with "That is a very interesting point, Mr. Jones, which leads us back to your description of your last hospitalization. You were saying that. . . ." This should get the interview back on course for a while, but eventually, the interviewer will have to interrupt again. The main thing to keep in mind is that interrupting a respondent hurts the interviewer more than the respondent. The respondent is probably quite used to being interrupted and considers it a normal part of conversation.

THE PROBLEM INTERVIEWER

Again, problems with the interviewer usually exist only relative to the particular interview context in which one is working. The following are some basic issues that occur frequently when several interviewers are involved in gathering data.

Interviewers can be reticent or too diffident, similar to one of the problems found with respondents. When this occurs, it is usually followed by more than average refusals. Whenever one interviewer turns in more refusals than the others, it is time to explore the possibility that he or she is the problem. Usually, if caught early enough, the interviewer can be trained to overcome the problem.

A case like this occurred during the early stages of the interviewing on my rural elderly study. One interviewer called (I asked all ten interviewers to call at the end of the first week of field work) and reported a high refusal rate relative to the other interviewers. I asked him to return to home base, where I spent several hours with him, first to determine exactly what went on in the refusals and then to try to rectify the problem. In his case, he was approaching the respondents with a somewhat apologetic attitude, saying, "This is a fairly long interview and it can be tiring, so if you would like, I can do some of it now and come back later for the rest." Generally, while he believed in the worth of the study and certainly wanted to do a good job, he lacked confidence in himself. His lack of self-confidence showed through to the respondents, and they turned him away.

Another problem is the talkative interviewer. The basic principle of interviewing is to have as little of the interviewer as possible and as much of the respondent as possible. The interviewer who talks too much can overshadow the respondent to the extent that the quality of the data suffers. Respondents need to know that the interview is for them to air their views, that they are center stage, and that the interviewer is merely a facilitator whose sole purpose is to bring out the best in the respondent. The more the interviewer talks, the less the respondent does. The respondent can be intimidated by a too talkative interviewer, and, in the worst case, the interviewer who cannot stop talking may bias the answers by conveying his or her opinions or values to the respondent.

STRATEGIES BEYOND INTERVIEWING TECHNIQUES

Some tricks of the trade exist for improving the chances that interviewers will perform at the level you intend. You should emphasize the following during the training sessions for the interviewers: (1) Expect to be successful. Pound it into the minds of the interviewers that they are well trained and on top of their profession, that they need to believe that they will succeed. Situations defined as real are real in their consequences. (2) Develop and maintain a strong interest in the research problem. This interest will be obvious to the respondents. (3) Be convinced as to the theoretical and applied value of the research. If the interviewer believes in the value of the study, the respondent might become a believer, too. (4) Never agree or disagree with a respondent's expressed point of view. In the context of the interview where you and the respondent are relative strangers to each other, any disagreement will be interpreted as disapproval of the respondent as a person. Any agreement will bias the following answers. (5) Know your values and beliefs. Be secure enough in them to not feel threatened personally by opposing views. Practice keeping your lid on when someone is expressing values that you despise. (6) Train the interviewers to never suggest an answer or never to put words in the respondent's mouth.

Training for interviewers often concentrates on mastering the interview schedule to the exclusion of interviewing techniques and personal qualities. If a solid pretest of the field work is conducted, the researcher should have a fairly clear and concrete picture of the interactive problems, both actual and potential, that the interviewers might face. How to handle these problems, along with the common ones which can be expected to crop up, should be incorporated into the training of the interviewers.

■ Conclusions

Interviewing is live sociology because the researcher and respondent are interacting, sharing feelings, thoughts, and meanings. Interviewing is uniquely sociological, of all the data-gathering techniques, because the researcher-respondent relationship is intense, face-to-face, and built upon rapport and mutual trust.

Interviewing shares lots in common with normal conversation. However, it is a scientific tool that requires techniques and skills that are not part of everyday conversation and thus must be learned specially. These special skills include learning to talk as little as possible, maintaining control of the interview, taking the role of the other and establishing rapport, ensuring confidentiality, and rehearsing mentally the interview, and anticipating possible problems before actually conducting the interview.

The types of interviews were discussed. Structured interviews provide standardization of questions and responses so that comparisons across respondents are enhanced. The semistructured interview provides specific topic areas to be covered but leaves the way the questions are worded and the number of questions up to the interviewer. Oral history interviews are examples of semistructured interviews.

The specific interviewing techniques discussed were silence, support, facilitation, summarization, confrontation, and probes. The chapter concluded with an example of special respondents, the very elderly, and the special interviewing techniques required, such as varying the pitch of one's voice, careful enunciation, frontal positioning so the respondent can read your lips, and attention to special or unfamiliar terminology. Problem respondents and problem interviewers were discussed with an emphasis on strategies for overcoming those problems.

GLOSSARY

confidentiality   a state of trust in the relationship between researcher and respondent that the researcher will not divulge any personal information about the respondent.

confrontation   the act of presenting to the respondent your judgment that something is wrong with what the respondent has said or how the respondent is behaving.

facilitation   a technique of interviewing, sometimes called reflection, where the interviewer actively encourages the respondent to talk more about a particular subject. Often, simply repeating a word or saying, "Tell me more" will do the trick.

oral history interviews   a semistructured technique in which the interviewer probes deeply into the respondent's memories of past events.

probes   these are hints to the interviewer as to what to ask should the initial response prove inadequate.

rapport   a state of interpersonal relations characterized by mutual respect, trust, shared meaning, and harmony.

semistructured interview   usually involves precisely worded questions with open-ended response categories. Or the interviewer may be given topics to be covered and then left to his or her devices as to how to cover them.

standardized interview   the questions and response categories are asked exactly as worded for all respondents.

summarization   one of the most effective interviewing techniques, the interviewer pauses during the interview to "play back" what he or she thinks the respondent has said. "Now I want to take a minute to go over some of the things you have told me to be sure I have it right."

support   an interviewing technique in which the interviewer conveys to the respondent that he or she is listening and empathizes with the respondent, for example, "It must have been difficult" or "I understand."

FOR FURTHER READING

Bartis, Peter. (1983). *Folklife and fieldwork: A layman's introduction to field techniques.* Washington, D.C.: American Folklife Center.

Gorden, Raymond L. (1987). *Interviewing: Strategy, techniques and tactics.* Homewood Ill.: Dorsey Press.

Mishler, Elliot G. (1986). *Research interviewing: Context and narrative.* Cambridge: Harvard University Press.

Part Three

RESEARCH DESIGNS FOR COLLECTING DATA

Chapter Eight

The Experiment, Survey, and Case Study Designs

▌ *Mill's method of agreement and method of difference are presented, along with the issues of causality and proof. Time and control of extraneous factors and the independent variable are discussed using the Solomon Four-group experimental design. Other quasi-experimental designs, such as the Latin square and factorial, are described. Stouffer's excellent paper, "Some Observations of Study Design," in which he uses the experimental design as the ideal against which all other research designs are approximations, is utilized. The panel design is stressed because it enables researchers to explain social change and to determine causal relationships among variables. The three survey designs are illustrated through examples of survey research and compared in terms of their advantages and disadvantages. The strengths and weaknesses of the case study design are discussed in terms of depth of meaning, subjectivity, and joining historical, observational, and interviewing techniques.*

I have stressed throughout this book that research methodology is a decision-making process. Each decision made is affected by and in turn influences every other decision. It is a system of decisions, all of which are interrelated. Of course, the one decision that drives all the rest is the definition of the research problem. If the problem is defined as an exploration into the nature of competitive sports, that is, the researcher really does not have a clear idea of what the problem is or where the research is going but rather is in the business of discovering the world of competitive sports, then the research design would probably involve some elements of participation/observation research. There are other research problems that call for experimental, survey, and case study designs. This chapter explores those designs. Historical sociology with its attendant secondary document analysis, content analysis, and oral history methods are not discussed in this chapter but are presented as suggested student projects in the companion student project manual.

Certainly, the term **research design** includes all of the decisions that go into a research project. However, there is a more technical use of the term that methodologists use and that this chapter adopts. This use is restricted to the following research designs, which this chapter covers: experimental, survey, and case study. Research design in this chapter means a special way that the data gathering is planned and carried out. For example, the problem might have been defined in such a way that a large representative sample of U.S. people is necessary, for example, "What are the factors associated with the U.S. public's attitude toward the war with Iraq?" This is a descriptive task involving a cross-section of the U.S. public at one point in time. The fact that the problem statement does not ask about changes in the attitude means that a "one-shot" or cross-section design is appropriate. Also, the fact that a representative sample of U.S. opinion is called for demands a large number of cases. Similarly, if the problem were worded "Is personal involvement more powerful in changing attitudes toward war than noninvolvement?", this requires that the researcher manipulate or control in some fashion the independent variable involvement. The problem is to design a study in which some individuals are involved or become involved, while others are not involved. Most probably, this would take the form of an experiment.

And so it goes with the research problem constraining and steering the researcher toward particular research designs. Recall that the research problem is the *dependent* variable and the explanation variables are the *independent* variables. The variance in the dependent variable, for example, some people are sick, others are healthy, is what the independent variables are brought in to "explain." This chapter begins with a discussion of some of the methodological principles of research design that can help the researcher decide which designs to consider using. Then, I will define each of the above research designs in terms of their features and performance. Examples of each of the designs will be presented, along with their strengths and weaknesses.

■ *Principles of Research Design*

EPISTEMOLOGY

"Know when you know" is as good a starting principle for design as any. **Epistemology** is the branch of philosophy that dissects the nature of knowledge. When you say that you know something, what exactly do you mean? What evidence do you rely upon to back up your assertion that you know something? Are what you know objective facts in the sense that they exist "out there" independently of your knowing them? Do you simply come along and know this order, which has always existed regardless of people's knowing it? Or does your knowing something involve a creation of that something in the sense that it does not exist independently of your knowing it? Some sociologists argue, as you may recall from

Chapter 1, that social reality is objective, existing outside of the researcher's knowing about it. This view accepts the model of the researcher discovering the objective social order through research. On the other side, are those who contend that social reality is produced through research, that is, it is a subjective creation of research designs and analyses. When you study Yaqui Indians and identify the religious symbolism behind the Pascua ceremony, you have "created" the social reality of this cultural symbolism. It would not exist outside of your knowing it (subjective analysis). The questions above are tough to answer, to be sure, and epistemology is the discipline to be used to sort out the answers.

The problem with coming up with answers that all social scientists could accept and do scientific research under is that there are several equally legitimate epistemologies spread throughout the members of the scientific community. Like any community, there are fundamental differences among the members about what reality is and how one can best know it. Thus, the first principle is that there are multiple equally legitimate epistemologies held by the members of the social scientific community. The definition of social science knowledge is varied and problematic because it will depend on the particular epistemological stance of the researcher. Extending this principle, what a given researcher defines as scientifically acceptable evidence and proof also depends on his or her epistemology.

SCIENTIFIC KNOWLEDGE: DESCRIPTION, INFERENCE, AND PROOF

The above principle means that whatever is said about the nature of scientific knowledge cannot be generalized to the entire scientific community of scholars. Nevertheless, there is a general principle that seems to be acceptable to a majority of methodologists. This is that the level of scientific knowledge sought, be it descriptive, inferential, or proof positive, serves as the basis for choosing a research design. Proof positive, an impossibility, can be sought best with experimental, structured observational, and longitudinal survey designs. Here you are close to being able to say X caused Y in all or most cases under study. If your goal is to describe some phenomenon, perhaps even with a view to understanding how it works, case study design may be your ticket. Finally, a **description** of a sample of a population or an **inference** that a set of variables are significant in producing some desired effect may be best served with a one-shot survey design.

THE CONDITIONS OF PROOF: CAUSE AND EFFECT

John Stuart Mill developed two principles of **proof** that are relevant for all research designs. These are: the method of agreement and the method of difference. The **method of agreement** says that if all or most of the instances of the dependent variable have only one circumstance in common, that circumstance is the cause of the dependent variable. For example, you are studying instances of bribery where professional athletes deliberately throw games or sporting events for extra money. You discover that most of the instances differ from one another in every respect save one thing. The 1919 Black Sox scandal, numerous horse races,

Boston College along with other college basketball programs, and so forth all differ from one another in terms of the type of sport involved, the kinds of people doing the bribing, the historical era in which the bribery occurred, and a host of other differences. However, all of the instances of sport bribery have one thing in common. In all the cases, the athletes who accepted the bribes were aware of the fact that they were earning millions for the owners or people in control while receiving relatively little in return. The athletes had class consciousness about their deprivation relative to the owners. If this were true, then class consciousness among the athletes would be the cause of the bribery scandals.

The **method of difference** is the opposite side of the coin. It says that if instances of the dependent variable have every circumstance in common except one, the one circumstance in which alone the instances differ is the cause of the dependent variable. Together, these two principles form the core of research design because they contain the requirements for proving that one variable causes another. In the language of research, you try to explain as much of the variance in the dependent variable as possible. Of course, social scientists are not able just yet to prove that a variable causes another, but we are getting close. Until we succeed, it is useful to "talk" cause and effect, at times, in order to set lofty goals and to strive for this level of proof. The above two principles set the tone for design in terms of forcing the researcher to consider the control of extraneous variables and, I will add, the control of time. All of the research designs we will discuss in this chapter deal with varying degrees of success with the control of time and the control of extraneous variables.

Remember that "cause" is used in a less than strict sense when it is applied to social scientific research and theory. Patrick Suppes (1970) wrote a classic paper on causal thinking in the social sciences in which he argued that it is impossible to prove with absolute certainty that one variable causes another. The reason for this is found in the complexity of social reality. It is impossible for the social scientist to control all, or even most extraneous variables, but, in order to prove beyond a doubt that A causes B, all extraneous variables have to be accounted for. Because such control escapes us in the social sciences, Suppes offered the idea of probable cause. This puts us in the position of the odds maker, giving out the chances or odds that A causes B. We use such terminology as "in all likelihood, A produces B" or "with 95% confidence, we believe that A causes B." Thus, when we use the concept "cause" or say that we have "proven" that A causes B, it is in the spirit of probable cause and probable proof.

CONTROL OF TIME

In order to prove that X caused Y, the researcher must be able to show that X came before Y in time. If, for example, I am trying to prove that overt materialism in families causes adolescent delinquency, I must establish the fact that materialism occurs first, then delinquency follows. Following the scientific approach of trying to prove oneself wrong, in this case, I would try to prove through empirical analysis that delinquent children cause families to become more materialistic. In other words, I would try to prove the opposite and hopefully by failing to do so would then gain support of the original contention that materialism is the cause of delinquency.

Table 8-1 ■ Analysis of the Relationship between Participation and Longevity for Healthy versus Sick Individuals

		Formal Participation in 1966			
		High		Low	
Health Status in 1966		Healthy	Sick	Healthy	Sick
Longevity 1966-1987	Yes	N	N	n	n
	No	n	n	N	N

In this example, the control of time occurs by designing the research in such a way that you know which variable came first. Research designs which allow the researcher to study variables over time (experiment, panel, trend) are called **longitudinal designs.** You will see in a moment how each of the research designs helps to a greater or lesser extent in achieving this goal.

CONTROL OF EXTRANEOUS VARIABLES

In the pure sense of the word, no variable is really extraneous. If there is a social system out there, then all things we can call variables are interconnected or interrelated. But we are unable, because of our relatively puny science, to study entire systems at once. Thus, we take a small segment for study. The easiest way to think of this is to envision a chain of causes and effects. Each cause has an effect but also is an effect for some prior cause:

Cause → Effect → Cause → Effect → Cause → Effect → Cause

Somewhere along this chain of cause and effect, a particular research problem is carved out. Theory and research help us sort out which of the pre- and post-variables we should consider. All other variables then become extraneous to the particular research problem we are working on. One goal of research design is to control those extraneous factors. By doing so, we are in a position to argue that the cause is X and not something occurring before X in time that we failed to consider. Taking my study of the rural elderly as an example, suppose that I had established that a strong relationship existed between participation in formal organizations and longevity. I want to prove that participation causes elderly people to live longer. If I had neglected to measure or control health, I would be vulnerable to the very reasonable charge that I was wrong because it was health that caused participation, which then caused longevity indirectly at best. People whose health was poor would be unlikely to participate, and thus it was health that affected how long a person lived, rather than participation. If I had not controlled health, I would be defenseless in addressing this point. By measuring health, I would be able to "control for health" by analyzing the relationship between participation and longevity for healthy versus sick individuals. This analysis might look like the example in Table 8-1.

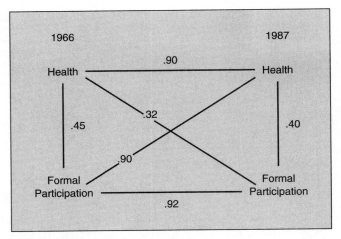

Figure 8-1 ■ Cross-lagged Correlation

The capital *N* represents a large number of cases whereas the lower case *n* represents a small number of cases.

As strange as this appears, the table says that individuals who participate in formal organizations live longer regardless of health status. Put another way, knowing the health status of the respondents in 1966 would not help you predict how long those individuals would live. Formal participation is a better predictor regardless of health status. Prediction is a powerful component of explanation. You may be able to explain how a particular group interacts and stays together (cohesiveness) and, in this sense, you understand the group and have "explained" it. If you are able to *predict* the cohesiveness of a group, then you have moved your explanation of the group forward a notch or two.

In order to understand what the time sequence is between health status and formal participation, you need to have measured the two variables in at least at two points in time. Another way to decide which variable is the more powerful predictor of longevity is to determine the causal sequence between the two variables. Whichever variable comes before the other in time causes the other and therefore is the more powerful predictor. We can use a causal analysis to help us decide whether or not health status is relevant tot he prediction of longevity. One technique for doing this is called cross-lagged correlation. Figure 8-1 is an example of this approach.

Figure 8-1 shows the correlations between the two variables, first in 1966 and then in 1987 (.45 and .40 respectively). Then the correlations between health in 1966 and health in 1987 and formal participation over the two time periods are calculated (.90 and .92, respectively). Finally, the cross-lagged correlations are run between health in 1966 and formal participation in 1987 (.32) and formal participation in 1966 and health in 1987 (.90). The higher correlation coefficient tells you that formal participation causes health, rather than the other way around. That is, changes in formal participation will produce changes in health. Health status is a function of formal participation, rather than the other way around. Individuals who participated in 1966 will have good health in 1987, whereas the nonparticipants should have health problems in 1987. Formal participation overrides health problems in that neither poor nor good health in 1966 affected participation in 1987. In short, you do not have to worry about health status when studying the effect of formal participation on longevity.

Remember that we only *infer* causality, never fully prove it. In the analysis, the one overriding criterion for inferring cause and effect relationships is theory. We need a logically coherent, empirically tested, theoretical framework to guide our causal thinking.

SAM STOUFFER ON DESIGN

The late Sam Stouffer set the record straight on research design. During World War II and later as a professor of sociology at Columbia University, he more or less wrote the book on survey research methodology. One of his contributions was a paper (1950) explaining the major research designs. Stouffer made the point that the **experimental design** was the queen of all the designs in that the others were simply approximations, having parts of the experiment but not all of its pieces. Stouffer viewed the designs as shown in Figure 8-2.

The experiment has what it takes, namely a before and after time sequence along with a **control group** and the researcher actually introducing the independent variable, to get very close to proving that X caused Y. The survey designs have one or more of the experiment's parts missing. For example, the panel has the two points in time but lacks the researcher control of the independent variable as well as a genuine control group. The one-shot survey has only one point in time, lacks a real control group, and does not allow the researcher to introduce the independent variable. The case study has no control group and no researcher control over the independent variable. In fact, the case study design does not use variables as such but rather places the researcher squarely in the realm of qualitative data.

Stouffer viewed the experiment as the model with all other designs being compromises or approximations to it. In each case, what you give up in rigor is gained in meaning or quality of understanding. Terribly precise measurement with rigid control over extraneous factors is scientifically rigorous, from a positivist perspective, but dangerously sterile in terms of understanding from a Symbolic Interactionist perspective. It is impossible to have it both ways unless you have the time and money to mix designs within one study, that is, use a combination of case study and survey designs. In any case, it should be clear given the earlier chapters on measurement, qualitative data, and scientific explanation that highly structured data precludes the ability to shift gears in the middle of data gathering in order to pursue something that just arose. You cannot dig too deeply through probing follow-up questions and other in-depth interviewing techniques if you are doing a survey of hundreds of individuals using fixed-choice questions. There is just too much structure and too little time to probe.

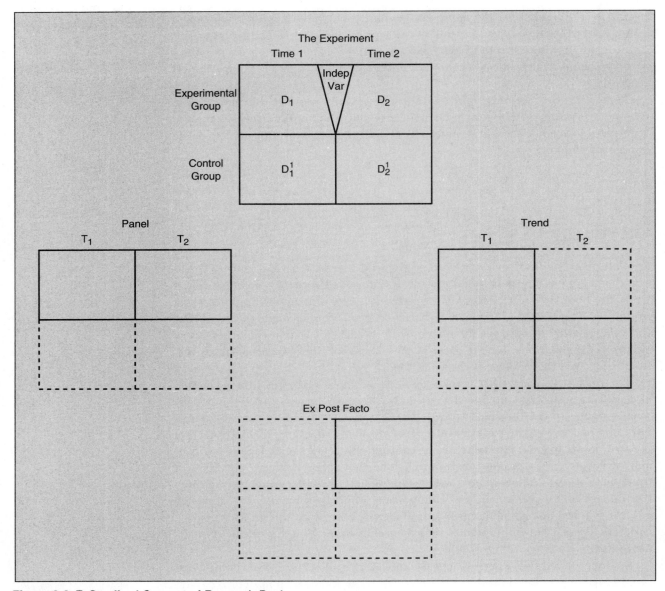

Figure 8-2 ▌ Stouffers' Concept of Research Designs

THE SOLOMON FOUR-GROUP EXPERIMENTAL DESIGN

The **Solomon four-group design** is the same as the classic experiment portrayed by Stouffer with the exception of having two extra control groups. The Solomon design is the Cadillac of the experimental designs. Figure 8-3 presents the design.

The O stands for observation or measurement of the dependent variable. In other words, when you see the O, it means "measure" the dependent variable. The X stands for the independent variable, indicating that the researcher introduces the independent variable (the treatment) to the **experimental groups**. The

R Group 1	O_1	X	O_2
R Group 2	O_3		O_4
R Group 3		X	O_5
R Group 4			O_6

Figure 8-3 ■ Solomon Four-Group Experimental Design

subscripts 1, 2, 3, and so on stand for the time sequence, for example, time 1, time 2, and so on. The *R* stands for random assignment of subjects to one of the four groups.

Remember, the distinguishing characteristic of the experiment is that the researcher introduces the independent variable or the **treatment**. For example, the research question might be, "Does watching violence on television lead to a predisposition to commit violence?" The dependent variable is predisposition to commit violence, which is an attitude variable. The independent variable or "cause" is watching television violence. This becomes the treatment in the sense that the researcher introduces television violence to the experimental group and withholds it from the control groups. The key to deciding whether or not the research design is an experiment is this control and introduction by the researcher of the independent variable.

INTERNAL AND EXTERNAL VALIDITY

Internal validity exists when you are able to answer yes or no to the question, "Did the experimental treatment make a difference?" Another way to ask the same question is, "Is the main effect (the treatment effect) valid?" **External validity** has to do with the environmental conditions affecting the experiment. Can the experimental effect be generalized to settings and individuals outside of the experimental situation? External validity has everything to do with this generalizability issue.

INTERNAL VALIDITY PROBLEMS

History Effect.   You would have a validity problem with history if events occurring between the first and second measurement of the dependent variable affected the dependent variable at the second point in time. This is the **history effect**. For example, at time 1, the researcher measures willingness to commit violence in the experimental subjects. Again, at time 2, the researcher remeasures the same variable in the same subjects. Ideally, any changes that occur in the dependent variable, for example, the subjects who saw the TV violence were much more willing to commit violence at time 2 than they were at time 1, is due to the particular event of watching TV violence between time 1 and time 2. If, for some unlucky reason a major war had broken out between time 1 and time 2, then the change in willingness to commit violence could be due to that event. This is a history problem caused by historical events.

Maturation Effect.   If the time period between time 1 and time 2 is very long[1], say two years, then you can rest assured that the subject will change not only as a result of the treatment but also because they have "matured." This is the *maturation effect*. The passage of time produces changes in the subjects regardless of the experimental treatment. These changes in the subjects that occur as a result of the passage of time is the maturation problem of validity.

Testing Effect.   Asking individuals the same questions repeatedly over time might sensitize people to the issues covered in the questions. By the very act of asking the questions, the research could alter the natural responses of people in the study. For example, if you were interviewed about retirement issues and you knew that the interview was to be repeated a few months later, you might read up on the subject or pay particular attention to articles and news reports on it, thereby becoming much more retirement literate than would have been the case. This is known as the **testing effect**.

Instrumentation.   Minor changes in the data-gathering procedures might produce unwanted changes in the dependent variable. If the study gathered the data through face-to-face interviews, changes in the interviewers themselves could pose nasty internal validity problems if those changes actually interfered with the measurement of the dependent variable. Thus, if a respondent was interviewed by a young male interviewer at time 1 and a middle-aged female interviewer the next time around and his responses to a marital fidelity scale changed because of the female interviewer, there is a serious validity problem that must be reckoned with—an **instrumentation** problem.

Statistical Regression.   **Statistical regression** says that extreme scores at the outset of the study will tend to regress toward the mean at time 2, independently of the independent variable's effect. For example, if you are studying attitudes toward civil disobedience and you have a mean (average) score of 50, extreme scores (1 and 100) will move toward 50 over time.

Experimental and Control Group Mortality.   Attrition or loss of subjects will occur between time 1 and time 2 of any experiment. The longer the time interval, the greater the mortality. If the loss of respondents is random, then there is not much of a validity problem to worry about, as long as the total number stays high enough to permit you to do the analysis planned. On the other hand, if the younger subjects tend to drop out or any other similar systematic bias in the drop outs, then it is a validity problem to be dealt with either by oversampling initially

---

[1]The length of time is relative. It depends on the variable under investigation and the rate of change concerning that variable.

Box 8-1

■ *The Zimbardo Experiment*

Can a person be brainwashed, that is, conned into going against his or her values and beliefs by placing the individual in an institutional situation? Is the "definition of the situation" in a total institution stronger than one's established self-identity?

Phillip Zimbardo and his colleagues (1973) set up an experiment at Stanford University to try to answer the above question. They set out to test the relative strength of the social self. Can one set up a situation powerful enough to change established self-concepts? Is one able to "de-individualize" people, that is, to create a situation in which their established identities are no longer appropriate and new, "foreign" identities emerge?   In order to test this idea, the researchers designed a laboratory experiment. They created a mock but realistic prison in the basement of a building on the Standford campus. Student subjects were recruited with an ad in the campus and local newspapers asking for people to participate in a study of "prison life." The researchers were careful to screen candidates such that they were able to hire at fifteen dollars a day twenty-one male college students all of whom were in good physical and emotional health, had respect for the law, and who were middle class. Next, the subjects were randomly assigned to be guards and prisoners.

The prison setting was quite realistic, and the subjects knew that the situation was experimental and not real. The guards were issued uniforms, handcuffs, nightsticks, whistles, and one-way sunglasses. The prisoners were stripped of their normal clothes and identification papers and were required to wear a uniform. The researches left it up to the subjects to create the rules and patterns of prison life.

Incredibly, the guards and prisoners shed their normal identities and roles. Guards became power-hungry brutes who abused the prisoners more or less constantly. The prisoners, in turn, became submissive and obedient. Within hours, the researchers who were observing everything knew that they were too successful in changing identities through a prison situation. One-by-one, the prisoners had to be removed from the experiment because of physical health problems, extreme depression, or fear. The researchers called a halt to the experiment long before the scheduled termination date.

Clearly, the profound behavioral changes in the guards and prisoners could not have been due to personality quirks or other personal characteristics because the subjects were matched on key characteristics and they were randomly assigned to the two groups. The changes must have been caused by the prison situation as such. As Zimbardo and his colleagues concluded:

> Rather, the subjects' abnormal social and personal reactions are best seen as products of their transaction with an environment that supported the behavior that would be pathological in other settings, but was 'appropriate' in this prison. Had we observed comparable reactions in a real prison, the psychiatrist undoubtedly would have been able to attribute any prisoner's behavior to character defects or personality maladjustment, while critics of the prison system would have been quick to label the guards as 'psychopathic.' This tendency to locate the source of behavior disorders inside a particular person or group underestimates the power of situational forces (p. 41).

for categories of subjects you think might drop out or by determining what the characteristics were of the dropouts and weighting the responses of similar subjects who remained with the study to make up for the loss of subjects.

EXTERNAL VALIDITY

Artificiality. External validity represents the ability to generalize the findings of research beyond the boundaries of the research design. In the case of the experiment, the setting should be as unobtrusive and as natural as possible. If you are studying the interaction patterns of individuals suddenly thrust together in a bomb shelter, then the experimental setting should be as close to a real bomb shelter as possible. The goal is to generalize beyond the specific experimental situation, which means that the researcher needs to take pains to make the laboratory setting as much like the real world as possible. In the example of the bomb shelter experiment, a real study in which I participated for pay during my days as an impoverished graduate student, the researchers built a real bomb shelter in a warehouse and equipped it with all of the gadgets found in a real shelter. However, most laboratory settings are far from replicas of real life and consequently suffer from the **artificiality** problem. You simply cannot generalize from a unique research setting to anything beyond that setting.

Referring back to the Solomon four-group design, the independent variable had an effect on the dependent variable if:

$$O2 = O5 \neq O4 = O6$$

That is to say that the value of the dependent variable at the second observation of the dependent variable (02) is the same as the value of the dependent variable at O5, while the observations on the dependent variable for the control groups (04 and 06) have different values. If the independent variable has the hypothesized effect, then the values obtained on the dependent variable for the groups that received the treatment (independent variable) should change between the time prior to the treatment and the time after the treatment, whereas the values of the dependent variable for the control groups that did not receive the treatment did not change and therefore were different. If you were investigating the effect of pornographic movies on subjects' level of cynicism toward members of the opposite sex, then you would randomly assign subjects to either the experimental or control groups. The experimental and control groups would be measured at time 1(01) on the dependent variable, cynicism. The experimental and control groups should have similar scores on the cynicism scale at time 1. The experimental group would watch porno movies, while the control group would watch a documentary on exploring the oceans. If porno movies make individuals more cynical, then the experimental group's scores should change after watching the porno movies and they should end up scoring higher on cynicism than the control group members.

There is no history problem in the experiment if 01 = 03 = 06, nor is maturation an issue if 03 = 04 = 06. Also, the instrument and testing effects would not be a problem if 04 = 06 and 02 = 05.

METHODOLOGICAL WEAKNESSES OF THE EXPERIMENT

Every advantage has a rival disadvantage. The high degree of control that the experiment affords over the independent variable, time, and extraneous variables has a price. The negative side of the experiment is two-fold. First, the issue of artificiality is a difficult one to solve. The laboratory is not like the real world where individuals are not subject to the researcher introducing the treatment in a carefully contrived setting. Much of social life cannot be controlled and manipulated experimentally. Second, by controlling what the researcher decides are extraneous variables, he or she takes those variables out of the analysis. Once the variable is controlled, it is no longer possible to analyze it along with the other variables because it is no longer a variable. For example, if you control for personal background characteristics of the subject by matching experimental and control groups on sex, education, race, and age, there is no longer any variation in those factors, hence they are technically no longer variables. If all the subjects are males, you cannot analyze the effect of gender on the dependent variable and so on for all the controlled variables. This level of control is fine for proving that the independent variable alone produced the desired effect in the dependent variable, but it presupposes that you have controlled the most salient variables and that you have not left any important ones out of the picture. Of course, given the complexity of the subject matter of the social sciences, control by matching for all or even most of the most relevant variables is impossible. With the experiment, the researcher ends up with great control on a few variables, while the vast universe of other potential candidates for the "extraneous" label remain untouched. Given this control problem, it is safer in terms of proof if you measure tons of variables and then analyze their effect on the relationship between the independent and dependent variables. This is statistical control.

Also, the regression effect, the sensitization of the experimental subjects, and the dropout problem are all methodological weaknesses that plague the experiment.

■ *Other Types of Experimental Designs*

THE FACTORIAL DESIGN

The **factorial design** is a type of experimental design where several treatment effects or independent variables are introduced simultaneously. Figure 8-4 presents the factorial model. *A* represents one treatment and *B* a variation of that treatment, while 1 is a different treatment yet, and 2 is another variation of it. One example of the factorial design comes from my experience teaching medical students. I designed a factorial experiment in order to test the hypothesis that a combination of teaching techniques (treatments or independent variables) was most effective in producing positive change in the students' knowledge and attitudes toward human sexuality. Medical students eventually become doctors, many of whom will be called upon to treat their patients' sexual concerns and problems.

Experimental Groups	T_1			T_2	
I	O_1	XA-1		O_2	A = Treatment
II	O_3	XA-2		O_4	B = Treatment
III	O_5	XB-1		O_6	1 = Treatment
IV	O_7	XB-2		O_8	2 = Treatment

Figure 8-4 ■ Factorial Design

Negative attitudes toward homosexuality or even one's own sexuality have been shown to be detrimental for the doctor-patient relationship. Also, negative attitudes and lack of knowledge about human sexual functions are known to be interrelated in the sense that negative attitudes and ignorance reinforce each other. Given these findings, we designed and conducted several sex vality workshops for first-year medical students. These workshops used several methods to try and impart information as well as change attitudes, including films and faculty presentations. The workshops were voluntary and three fourths of the 110 students participated. The opportunity was ripe to conduct an experiment to test the effectiveness of various teaching methods; and so I designed the following factorial experiment.

The research problem was to produce positive change in medical students' sexual knowledge and attitudes (the dependent variable) through a combination of teaching techniques (the independent variables or treatment effects). More specifically, four techniques were used in combination. A was pornographic films with heterosexual and homosexual themes, B was a film that presented graphic sex but strictly heterosexual and in a clinical medical context. The other treatment was the faculty lecture. A lecture that was conducted in a strictly instrumental fashion, that is, it covered only the medical "facts," was 1. Absolutely no mention of any ethical or humanistic points were allowed. The variation of this treatment (2) was a strictly humanistic lecture, where no facts were covered, but instead human concerns and ethical issues were presented.

The twenty-five or so students who did not attend the workshop were to serve as the control group. They would be measured for sexual knowledge and attitudes (SKAT) twice but would not receive any of the treatments. I expected no change in their sexual knowledge and attitudes. The rest of the students participating were randomly assigned to one of the four treatments. Each student would be exposed to only one combination of treatments, that is, any given student might see the porno film and hear the humanistic lecture, while another might see the porno film and hear the instrumental talk. Among all of the experimental groups, I expected positive change in their SKAT scores. However, the hypothesis was that the greatest change would occur in the group watching the pornographic films and hearing the humanistic lecture (A-2). Unfortunately, the experiment was never conducted, so I was unable to test my hypothesis. Nevertheless, it serves as a good example of a factorial design.

Experimental Groups	T_1	T_2	T_3	T_4	T_5	T_6	T_7
I	O_1	A	B	C	D	E	O_2
II	O_3	B	C	D	E	A	O_4
III	O_5	C	D	E	A	B	O_6
IV	O_7	D	E	A	B	C	O_8
V	O_9	E	A	B	C	D	O_{10}

Figure 8-5 ■ Latin Squares Design

The key advantage of the factorial design is its use of multiple independent variables, which recognizes the complexity of social reality. On the other hand, factorial designs suffer from all of the disadvantages that plague the Solomon designs, including the fact that each experimental subject is exposed to only one combination of treatment effects. The Latin squares design addresses this latter problem.

LATIN SQUARES DESIGN

In this **Latin squares design** (see Figure 8-5), you expose all experimental subjects to all of the treatment effects (A, B, C, D, E). Introducing the treatments must be done in such a way that no treatment appears more than once either in a row or a column, thereby ensuring that the subjects experience all of the independent variables but only one time.

Latin squares is defined as a design "in which each treatment appears once and only once in each row and increased only once in each column. It is important to remember that in Latin squares, the numbers of rows, columns, and treatments must be equal" (Namboodiri, Carter, and Blalock, 1975). N. Krishnan Namboordiri, Lewis Carter, and Hubert Blalock, Jr. provide a useful example of the design (p. 332). The problem is to compare three different programs designed to get people to use family planning techniques. These are: A = the clinical approach that provides family planning services through clinics; B = the clinical approach plus comprehensive health services; and C = clinical, comprehensive health and adult education. Also, the researcher wants to include "sociocultural milieu," which is an index of economic development (low, middle, high), and subculture, "which includes ethnic, racial, language groups" (three subcultures). The Latin squares design would look like the following:

	Subculture		
Sociocultural milieu	1	2	3
Low	A	B	C
Middle	B	C	A
High	C	A	B

Each treatment (A, B, or C) is applied only once in each sociocultural milieu and only once to each of the three subcultures.

This design has the same problems as the Solomon with the addition of the unanticipated effect that the order in which the treatments are experienced might have on the dependent variable and the practical difficulties posed by having to introduce all of the independent variables to all of the subjects. Obviously, it would take a huge commitment of time and money to apply the Latin squares to anything but a small number of subjects. Actually, all of the various forms of the experiment have this problem of small numbers of subjects. On the positive side, the Latin squares ensures that all of the subjects receive all of the treatments.

THE NATURAL EXPERIMENT

Any of the above mentioned types of experimental design can be conducted outside of the laboratory in the natural setting. This is extremely difficult to pull off in that the researcher must be able to introduce the treatment(s) in one natural setting, withhold it in another, and gain the cooperation of people to have their everyday lives disrupted in a rather massive fashion. Another disadvantage is the loss of control over extraneous factors contained in the diverse contexts of the subjects. The only advantage of the **natural experiment** is that it is not as artificial as the laboratory, hence the researcher is better able to generalize the results to the larger social world.

A classic natural experiment was conducted by Elain Cumming and John Cumming. Their book (1957) describes their attempt and ultimate failure to change community residents' attitudes toward mental illness by introducing an education program. The dependent variable was attitude toward mental illness, the independent variable was education, and the experiment was conducted in a natural community setting. Because the subjects were on their home ground while the researchers were "guests," the subjects were in a position to throw the researchers out, which they did upon tiring of the experiment. This would not have happened in the laboratory, where the researcher is in control and the subjects are "guests" by prior agreement. It is precisely this absence of control over the setting that is both the chief strength and weakness of the natural experiment.

SURVEY DESIGNS: STRENGTHS AND WEAKNESSES

Before discussing the specific survey designs, some general comments about their strengths and weaknesses are in order. The late Edward Suchman, one of the founding fathers of survey research and one of my professors, argued that survey designs and the case study design were infinitely more powerful and useful than experimental designs because of what he saw as a beautiful fit between survey research, case study, and present-day industrialized mass society. He told us graduate students that case studies were necessary to test the waters and to do the groundwork necessary to define research problems adequately. Survey research was best suited for the study and analysis of industrial society's problems, which require the study and analysis of massive amounts of data. For example, we could not generalize about Americans at work, aging among the rural elderly in the United States, or U.S. voting patterns using experimental designs. Mass society contains research problems that are massive in scale. Such problems demand large numbers of cases, which survey designs are built to deliver. But in order to get a good start on research of such massive dimensions, small-scale qualitative exploratory research is needed. For this purpose, the case study is well suited.

There are several other important advantages of **survey designs**. Survey designs force the researcher to formalize on paper for all to see certain phases of the research process that other designs are likely to skip over. This formalization includes the sampling plan, the data-gathering instrument plan, and the analysis plan. Because of the sheer magnitude of the numbers involved in survey research, the user of survey designs simply must document and make formal the following key research decisions.

SAMPLE

In order to take full advantage of the techniques for checking reliability and for assessing the extent to which the survey is representative of some larger population, you must draw a random sample. Without a random sample of some type, explanation based on large numbers is highly suspect, if not entirely erroneous. Survey designs, with their large numbers and emphasis on broad representativeness, should use some form of the random sample. Thus, one almost always finds a random-type sample associated with survey research. In this sense, the decisions about who gets studied and how they are chosen are made explicitly. This is an improvement over the experiment and case study, where the method for obtaining respondents or subjects is usually not stated and not a random sample.

DATA-GATHERING INSTRUMENT

Because of the large numbers of respondents coupled with the internal control issues, especially standardization of the data gathering instrument, the survey researcher needs to formalize this stage of the research. Once the data-gathering instrument is written and standardized (formalized), other researchers are able to replicate your study and to criticize the operational measures of your concepts. In short, other researchers are able to challenge the reliability and validity of your measures.

ANALYSIS PLAN

Again, due to the tremendous pressure exerted by massive amounts of data and costly data collection procedures, survey design demands a specific and clearly spelled out analysis plan. Without a clear plan, the survey researcher would probably end up having gathered the wrong data for the emerging analysis plans. Had these plans or needs been stated in writing at the outset of the study, the researcher would have been in a position to ensure that the data gathering phase would cover the ground necessary to pull off the analysis. Similarly, the survey researcher without a clear plan would become buried in a morass of data due to the problem of sorting out what is relevant from the irrelevant in the absence of a plan as to what manipulations and questions the data will be put to.

DISADVANTAGES

Survey research is very costly in time and resources. The current cost per interview is in excess of one hundred dollars. A random sample designed to be representative of the United States costs approximately fifty thousand dollars to design. Computer work and data storage are exacting tasks with high price tags as well. In short, surveys are expensive.

Control over the independent variable and extraneous variables is not as precise and powerful as in the experiment, and this is a weakness of surveys as far as explanation is concerned. In surveys, the researcher cannot control the environment, nor is there any real control over events external to the research that may in fact alter the outcome of the research. You cannot hold the external environment constant when it is an entire community or the United States.

Perhaps the single most difficult (to address) weakness of surveys is the "words versus deeds" problem (Deutscher, 1973). Can or will people really say what they feel, and will there be a correspondence between how people say they feel and what they do? Part of this problem stems from the extent to which the researcher's questions measure what he or she really intended them to measure. Does the respondent see the same meaning in the question as you the researcher, and does the respondent act or behave in a manner consistent with his or her attitudes gleaned from an interview or questionnaire? This words-versus-deeds problem is a serious criticism of survey research, for if people are unwilling to tell the truth or if the "truth" does not match with what people actually do, then the validity of survey data must be called into question. Irwin Deutscher's book, *What We Say, What We Do*, recounts the classic LaPiere field experiment in which racially mixed couples were sent to motels and restaurants several months after the staff and owners of those establishments had been surveyed with a questionnaire asking them how they felt about racially mixed couples and if they would allow such couples to be served in their establishments. The answers (words) were highly negative, with few reporting a willingness to serve the couples. The observer teams, on the other hand, found just the opposite behavior, with almost all of the proprietors actually serving them (deeds). Based on this and other similar studies, Deutscher concluded that survey data is invalid. We have to conclude that the evidence is not in yet on this point but that the criticism merits our careful attention.

THE PANEL DESIGN

Bruce Biddle, Ricky Slavings, and Don Anderson (1985) present a compelling case that the panel is the most powerful survey design. With a panel, you follow the same individuals over at least two points in time. There is neither a control group nor control of extraneous variables through matching or manipulating the research environment. In short, the panel is conducted in the real world, outside of the controlled laboratory situation. Any control that the researcher has comes through careful theorizing and knowledge of prior research. Thus it is that the researcher learns which variables to measure, thereby allowing for statistical control in the analysis stage. Rather than trying to match the subjects on education, age, or income, the researcher would try to sample a mixture or variety and then control those variables statitstically. For example, you might study the relationship between the key independent variable and the dependent variable "controlling for education," which essentially is the elaboration model discussed in Chapter 11.

Some theories of society are relatively static. Studies of society based on such theories take "snapshots" at a single point in time, a cross-section. **Panel design** is predicated on theories that view the social system as dynamic and that seek to explain change. By introducing the time factor into the research design, the panel design itself becomes dynamic with time as the axis along which changes take place. In essence, the panel is a whole series of snapshots over time.

■ *Panel Analysis*

ADVANTAGES OF THE PANEL

Biddle et al. (1985) argue that the panel is the only real alternative to the experiment, which they view as flawed due to its artificiality. Certainly, the panel is the most powerful survey design in that it allows the researcher to make judgments about causal sequences among variables. Because the panel follows the same individuals over time, the researcher has a clear idea not only about change but about who changed. Thus, the panel is a good design for assessing social change and for explaining that change in terms of providing knowledge about who changed. If you know the background characteristics and the other social factors about individuals at time 1, then you are able to measure how much change occurred in those factors between time 1 and time 2 and to explain that change using time 1 characteristics. Using my panel study of the rural elderly as an example, I interviewed the respondents three different times over a twenty-year time frame. Thus, I was able to measure the changes that occurred in each individual's life during those years, and I was in a position to explain the changes as well. One group of individuals experienced rapid deterioration of their health, while another group stayed relatively healthy between the first two time periods. I studied the social patterns that I had measured at the first interview and was able to explain the changes in health through a variable called social participation. Those individuals who had changed from good to poor health were participating less in organizations and were generally more isolated socially than were the people whose health remained relatively good. I would not have been able to study and explain the change in health had I not used a panel design. One advantage, then, is the ability to study and to explain social change.

The panel design also bypasses the problem of relying on respondent memory to piece together the dynamics of change. If you are interviewing only once, any change or preconditions to that change that you may need to measure must be got through the respondent's collective memories. This can be dangerously inaccurate.

Because the researcher collects data repeatedly at various points in time, the panel gives the user the advantage of a growing body of information. The more you interview an individual, the more you learn about his or her background and way of thinking. Inaccuracies that are bound to occur will probably sort themselves out the longer you carry on the field work. Consequently, panel data is more reliable than data gathered using any of the other survey designs. This means, among other things, that the researcher can get by with a smaller number of cases than he or she might using other survey designs.

DISADVANTAGES OF THE PANEL DESIGN

Several important problems are associated with using the panel design. For one thing, members of the panel are more likely to tire of the exercise and to call it quits than are people who are interviewed or given a questionnaire only once. Familiarity can breed contempt, even in research situations.

Also, there is the problem of articulateness. Not all people in the panel will be equally articulate, nor will all members develop the same level of articulateness over the course of the study. Some groups of people become increasingly talkative and knowledgeable over repeated contact with the researcher, while others become less so. Responses can become skewed or biased due to this factor of improved responsiveness on the parts of some and deterioration by others.

Mortality, figuratively and literally, is a problem for panel studies. In my case with the rural elderly, it was relatively easy to keep track of the people in my study because the elderly rural people did not move much. However, it was expensive to touch base again with these respondents after a number of years. Letters were written, lots of professional time was expended, long-distance phone calls were made, and automobile trips were taken in order to track down the locations of those respondents still living. Even with the stability of the rural elderly, there were many cases that mystified me and exhausted all of the resources devoted to tracking them down. For example, in 1966, we compiled a list for each of the sixty small towns in the study containing the names and addresses of the respondents. Also, the interview schedules had the names and addresses along with the computer data files. Finally, I kept on file all of the letters that were sent to each of the postmasters in the sixty-four towns asking them to verify the list of the respondents and their addresses. There were cases where the lists all contained the name and address of a particular respondent, say Mrs. Ola Jones on 14

Oak Street. I had the interview schedule with the name and address along with the data on Mrs. Jones. Incredibly, the list I sent to the postmaster prior to the second wave of interviews, eight years after the first round, came back with the messages of deaths, moves, and "addressee unknown" for Mrs. Jones. I would check all the other sources, such as the county court, tax records, funeral home lists of burials, and even cemetery lists, all to no avail. Finally, I would send an interviewer to the town, and he or she would locate the correct address but the person living there was not the respondent. Furthermore, the resident would not have known the respondent, nor would any of the neighbors ever have heard of the respondent. Elderly people in the town, the ministers who had lived there for years, and other people who ought to know everyone would draw a blank on the respondent. It was as if the respondent had never lived there. In the twenty-five or so such cases, I was not able to locate a single one of the missing respondents.

In urban areas, especially with younger respondents, the mortality factor is significant, and the expense of keeping a panel together for any length of time is very great. The Alameda County study of the urban elderly (Kaplan, 1988) employs a full-time social scientist whose sole responsibility is to keep track of the panel members. This panel study has been underway since 1966. Also, younger people in the lower socioeconomic strata are the most difficult to keep tabs on. Unfortunately, it is the urban young from the lower-income brackets whose attitudes are the most labile. If a panel study loses this group in greater than random fashion, then the researcher could be left with a more conservative, older group, and the data would reflect this bias.

Critical set is the problem or bias due to repeated attention paid the respondent by the researcher. Repeated interviewing may cause the respondent to develop an interest in the subject that he or she would not have developed had there not been a study. His or her attitudes might not be representative of others who were not in the study but to whom the researcher is seeking to generalize. These losses and biases may be dealt with by weighting the responses of the remaining panelists in such a way as to compensate for the lost members' views. This is one reasonably effective method for dealing with panel mortality.

A final problem, perhaps more of a theoretical issue, is the choice of times when one gathers data. How much time should elapse between interviews or questionnaire administrations? In my study of the rural elderly, I waited eight years between the first and second waves of the interviews and then twelve years between the second and final waves. There was no magic to these numbers. The general principle was to allow as much time as possible in that aging is a slow developmental process that takes a lifetime to unfold to completion. Eight and twelve years are purely arbitrary time periods, but they make more sense than one or two years, given the nature of the research problem. The research problem will dictate to a certain extent what the time frame should be. The resources available to the researcher, such as time, staff, and money, will play a role in deciding as well. For example, if the research team is stable, has the funding, and plans to be together for several years, then a longer time frame with more frequent data-gathering episodes makes perfect sense. On the other hand, if the researcher needs to get the study out and published because he or she is going up

Table 8-2 ■ Panel Table

		Time 2 R	Time 2 D	
Time 1	R	57	0 T	57
	D	0 T	3	3
		57	3	

for tenure, then a short time frame is in order. Expediency is a compelling deciding factor. In any case, the choice of the time frame is mainly arbitrary and therefore difficult to justify on scientific substantive grounds.

In order to understand precisely how the panel design works, I have concocted a simple contingency table called the turnover table. It is called a turnover table because measuring change or **turnover** is the primary mission of the panel design, just as it is in the experiment, which the panel approximates more closely than the other nonexperimental designs. Table 8-2 presents the essential features of the panel.

The left side of the table represents interviews at time 1 with individuals who were asked to indicate their political preference, either Republican or Democrat. The top of the table represents time 2, where the same individuals were reinterviewed about their political preferences. Again, the choices were Republican or Democrat. The right side of the table contains the "marginal frequencies" for the time 1 interviews. The bottom of the table is the time 2 marginals. In specific terms, there were fifty-seven individuals who intended to vote Republican at time 1 and three who said that they intended to vote Democratic. Then at time 2, the same marginals occurred. The *T* stands for turnover, that is, change from intentions at time 1 to time 2. The cells of the table with T in them are the cells where you would see turnover, should there be any. The T cells contain individuals who were Republicans at time 1 and then changed to Democrats at time 2 or Democrats at time 1 who changed to Republicans at time 2.

If the total numbers are the same, turnover tables may be compared by simply comparing the totals in the T cells. For example, if you were studying two panels from two different cities and the total number of individuals in city A was one hundred and in city B, one hundred, then the turnover tables might look like Tables 8-3 and 8-4.

Comparing turnover for the two cities, you can say that turnover was greater for city A (T = 80) than for city B (T = 20). Unfortunately, you seldom end up with the same total for different panels, which means that the simple comparison of the raw turnover values would not be reasonable. Thus, you would need to use an index of turnover, which is standardized for different size samples. One such index called the turnover index is expressed in Table 8-5 on page 184.

One nice thing about this index other than it being very simple to calculate is the fact that it is a derivative of the Phi coefficient (ø), which is a type of corre-

Table 8-3 ■ City A   Turnover Table

		Time 2 R	Time 2 D	
	R	10	30	40
Time 1	D	50	10	60
		60	40	100

T = 80

Table 8-4 ■ City B   Turnover Table

		Time 2 R	Time 2 D	
	R	50	10	60
Time 1	D	10	30	40
		60	40	100

T = 20

lation coefficient for contingency tables. Phi has values from -1 to $+1$, which are the same values derived from the turnover index.

By way of illustrating this index, I have placed arbitrary numbers in parentheses in the index. P1 is the proportion of that marginal relative to the total, for example, P1 = 100/200 = .50. Q1 is a function of P1, that is, the two values must equal 1. If P1 is .60, then Q1 must be .40, and so on. In our example, Q1 also is .50. Tb is the proportion of that cell frequency relative to the total. In this case, it is 20/200 or .10. Plugging in the values, we get:

$$T = .10/.25 = .40$$

Using this index, it is possible to measure turnover for contingency tables with varying totals and still compare the turnover.

THE LAZARSFELD SOLUTION: A SIXTEEN-CELL TABLE

Paul Lazarsfeld has provided us with an ingenious method for analyzing the change in two variables and deciding which one is the cause and which the effect. The technique requires that you have panel data and that each variable is treated as a dichotomy, that is, as having just two values. Thus, the sixteen-cell approach uses two dichotomous variables from a panel design set up in a contingency table

Table 8-5 ■ Turnover Index

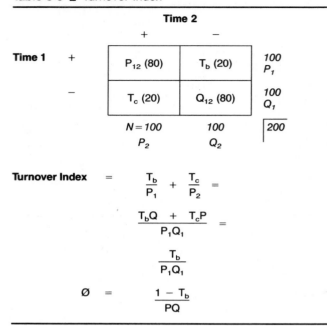

$$\text{Turnover Index} \quad = \quad \frac{T_b}{P_1} \quad + \quad \frac{T_c}{P_2} \quad =$$

$$\frac{T_b Q \quad + \quad T_c P}{P_1 Q_1} \quad =$$

$$\frac{T_b}{P_1 Q_1}$$

$$\emptyset \quad = \quad \frac{1 - T_b}{PQ}$$

format. Table 8-6 is a modern example from Lazarsfeld's own work that illustrates this approach.

In this example, a panel of prospective voters was asked at two points in time how they intended to vote and whether or not they liked George Bush. Only the time 1 data are presented here. The problem is to determine which of the two variables, either vote intention or opinion about Bush, is the cause and which is the effect. Does preference for Bush cause vote intention or vice versa? Table 8-7, a sixteen-cell table, provides a solution to this problem.

The numbers in parentheses are labels designating each cell. Since a cell is made up of a row and a column, the designations are based on the particular row and column making up the cell: (11) is row 1, column 1; (31) is row 3, column 1; and so forth. The numbers in each cell are the frequences. The left hand margin contains the four combinations of the two variables at time 1, while the top of the table represents the four combinations of the two variables at time 2. Thus, cell (11) has sixty-eight individuals in it who were Democrats against Bush at time 1 and who remained Democrats against Bush at time 2. Cell (44) is made up of Republicans who were for Bush at time 1 and who remained for him at time 2. Cell (34) are Republicans who changed from opposing Bush at time 1 to favoring him at time 2. And so it goes for each of the sixteen cells.

What does this tell us about the causal sequence question concerning the two variables? The answer is quite a bit, once you recognize the key assumptions about causal sequence and know which cells to study for the answer.

The assumptions behind the assertion that variable A causes variable B are: (1) The situations "out of adjustment" logically, for example, Republicans who

Table 8-6 ■ Opinion vs. Vote Intention: The Lazarfeld Solution to the Question of Cause/effect

		Opinion of George Bush		
Vote Intention		*Dislike Bush*	*Like Bush*	
Time 1	*Democrat*	72	24	96
	Republican	35	135	170
		107	159	266

Table 8-7 ■ Lasarsfeld Sixteen-Cell Table

		Time 2				
		Democrat against	*Democrat for*	*Republican against*	*Republican for*	**Total**
	Democrat against	(11) 68	(12) 2	(13) 1	(14) 2	23
	Democrat for	(21) 11	(22) 12	(23) 0	(24) 2	25
Time 1	Republican against	(31) 1	(32) 0	(33) 21	(34) 11	33
	Republican for	(41) 2	(42) 1	(43) 3	(44) 129	135
	Total	82	15	25	144	266

dislike Bush and Democrats who like him will change toward "adjustment" at time 2. The more powerful variable, the "cause" if you will, will pull the other variable to adjust to it, and the adjusted situations will remain stable. Lazarsfeld used a vitamin-health example to illustrate this point. If vitamins cause good health, rather than the other way around, situations out of adjustment will adjust in favor of the vitamin variable. For example, if vitamins cause and preserve health, then people taking vitamins and enjoying good health (AB) at time 1 will remain so at time 2. Similarly, people who do not take vitamins and who are in poor health at time 2 ($\neq A \neq B$) will remain in that state at time 2. Maladjusted situations at time 1, for example, people who do not take vitamins and who are in good health ($\neq AB$) and individuals who take vitamins but are in poor health ($A \neq B$) will adjust in favor of vitamins. $\neq AB$ at time 1 will become $\neq A \neq B$ at time 2, that is, people who did not take vitamins at time 1 but were in good health will have poor health at time 2. Also, $A \neq B$ will change to AB at time 2, that is, people who took their vitamins but were in poor health at time 1 will experience an adjustment to good health at time 2, providing they continue to take their vitamins, of course. (2) A produces B and preserves B. (3) If you have A and not B ($\neq B$), then $\neq B$ will change to B. Since A is more powerful than B, B will adjust to A over time. (4) Not A ($\neq A$) and B at time 1 will become $\neq A \neq B$ at time 2. (5) AB and $\neq A \neq B$ will remain stable, that is, will not change. People who take their vitamins and who are in good health will remain as such at time 2, while the folks who do not take vitamins and who are in poor health will stay that way at time 2. In short,

Table 8-8 ■ Trend Table

		Time 2		
		R	D	
Time 1	R			57
	D			3
		57	3	

"maladjusted" health statuses adjust to vitamin status, rather than vice versa. Vitamins is the more powerful of the two variables. In a sense, vitamins cause good health.

The maladjusted individuals at time 1 are found in the following cells of the sixteen-cell table above: 21 and 41. If health adjusted to vitamins, that is, if opinion of Bush adjusted to vote intention, then Democrats for Bush would become Democrats against at time 2 and Republicans against at time 1 would shift to Republicans for Bush at time 2. Democrats for Bush at time 1 would not change to Republicans for Bush at time 2, nor would Republicans against Bush at time 1 change their vote intention to Democratic at time 2. Democrats against Bush at time 1 would stay that way at time 2, as would Republicans for Bush. Thus cells 11, 21, 34, and 44 would be larger than 22, 24, 31, and 33. Lazarsfeld supplies a convenient statistic that assesses the various cell frequencies and determines the significance of one variable's power over the other.

TREND DESIGN

The **trend design** is a cheap substitute for the panel. The big difference in the two designs is that unlike the panel, the trend does not follow the same people over time. With a trend design, you would gather data on one group at time 1 and then obtain the same data at time 2 from a completely different group of people.

Because the people are not the same over the time periods, the researcher using the trend design is unable to say anything about who changed. All you know about, referring to the contingency table (Table 8-2) presented earlier in the discussion of the panel, is the marginal change, or the time 1 and time 2 marginals. You know nothing about the cell frequencies because different people were interviewed or given questionnaires at the two points in time. Table 8-8 illustrates the trend design.

Since we are dealing with different people over the two time periods, we cannot fill in the cells of the table. Thus, all we know is that fifty-seven people intended to vote Republican and three Democratic at time 1 and time 2 had the same distribution of voter intention. We might conclude on the basis of this trend data that there was no change or turnover in vote intention between time 1 and time 2. However, because we are unable to fill in the cells of the table, that is, we

Box 8-2

■ *Panel Design: Granberg and Holmberg Study of U.S. and Swedish Voters*

The research question pursued by Donald Granberg and Sören Holmberg was, "Once an intention is formed, what happens on the road from intention to behavior?" What is the relationship between what people say they intend to do and what they actually end up doing? If the research question is to follow the process by which intentions become behaviors, then the panel design is the only research design capable of doing the trick because "becoming" requires that the researcher study intentions over some time period.

Their research used panel data that had been gathered as part of election studies in the United States between 1952 and 1988 and in Sweden between 1968 and 1988. In addition to methodological differences between the two panel studies in terms of sampling and the data-gathering methods, there were substantive differences between the two studies that reflected cultural differences between the two countries. Specifically, the U.S. election surveys focused on political party preference and the candidate that the respondent intended to vote for in the coming election. In the Swedish study, the respondents were asked about political party preference, just as their U.S. counterparts were asked. But, given the fact that Swedes vote for a party rather than a candidate, the two studies parted ways a bit, with the Swedish portion asking which party the respondent voted for while the U.S. panels asked about the candidate of choice.

In each panel study, a representative sample of adults was interviewed during the eight-week campaign period before the election and then after the election. In each preelection survey, the respondents were asked. "Generally speaking, do you usually think of yourself as a Republican, a Democrat, an independent, or what?" The people also were asked if they voted in the prior election and who they voted for. The intention question asked in the preelection interview was, "Who do you think you will vote for in the election for president?" The Swedish panel used different questions in order to accommodate the cultural differences, such as different types of political parties and voting for a party rather than for a particular candidate.

The table (8-2-1) illustrates how a panel analysis of the data was set up by the researchers. The table is an analysis of the proposition that people who intend to behave, that is, vote, in a way suggested by their self-identity are more likely to do what they intend than are people who intend to behave in ways at odds with their self-identity. Intention and behavior are nearly the same in both countries (97% in both) when prior behavior and self-identity are congruent. Where they are at odds, the percentage of intention-behavior consistency drops to 78% in the United States and 63% in Sweden. This is an example of what you can do with panel data.

Box Table 8-2-1 ■ Panel Design: Granberg and Holmberg Study of U.S. and Swedish Voters

Percentage of Intention-Behavior Consistency as a Function of the Compatibility of Prior Voting Behavior. Current Party Identification, and Intention

Sweden

		Party Identification and Intention		
		Same	*Different*	*Effect of Party Preference*
Prior Vote and Intention	*Same*	97_a	86_b	11
	Different	85_b	63_b	22
	Effect of Prior Vote	12	23	

United States

		Party Identification and Intention		
		Same	*Different*	*Effect of Party Preference*
Prior Vote and Intention	*Same*	97_a	89_b	8
	Different	89_b	78_c	11
	Effect of Prior Vote	8	11	

Note: Entries are the percentages of people for whom intended vote and self-reported vote are the same. Thus, for instance, in the upper table, among those who intended to vote for a party that was the same as they voted for previously but was different from their current party identification, 86 percent had an intention and a behavior that were the same, and 14 percent had an intention and a behavior that were different. Within each of these effects tables, percentages without a subscript in common are significantly different ($p<.01$), on the basis of a test for the significance of the difference between proportions. The Swedish data are based on the combined results of six elections, the U.S. data on the combined results of eight elections. For Sweden, the Ns for the upper left, upper right, lower left, and lower right cells are 4184, 43, 413, and 73. For the United States, the corresponding Ns are 5092, 476, 560, and 506.

Table 8-9 ■ Disadvantage of Trend Data:
                 No Turnover Masked

		Time 2		
		R	D	
Time 1	R	57	0	57
	D	0	3	3
		57	3	

Table 8-10 ■ Disadvantage of Trend Data:
                  Turnover Masked

		Time 2		
		R	D	
Time 1	R	54	3	57
	D	3	0	3
		57	3	

are unable to know anything about who changed, we are essentially making an inference about change and hoping that we are correct. If the cells of the table were like Table 8-9, then our conclusion based on the marginal totals from the trend design would have been correct.

But if the data were as in Table 8-10 with relatively large turnover, then we would have made a huge mistake in concluding that there was no change. Without panel data, there is no way of knowing if we are right or wrong. This is the main weakness of the trend design.

STRENGTHS OF THE TREND DESIGN

The trend design is much more economical than the panel for monitoring change over long periods of time due to the problem of sample mortality. A classic example of a successful trend study is Stouffer's *Communism, Conformity, and Civil Liberties*, conducted in 1954, and Lazarsfeld and Wagner Thelen's study of McCarthyism a decade later (*The Academic Mind*). Lazarsfeld and Thelen simply used Stouffer's questions in their study of college faculty, thus, the two studies taken together constitute a trend design. Both are trend studies of U.S. society's level of tolerance, that is, the attitude of support for beliefs or practices considered deviant by the larger society. Both research teams focused on communism, which was considered quite deviant back in the 1950s and '60s. Today, speaking out in favor of white supremacy or gay rights might qualify.

Three questions designed to measure tolerance were asked: (1) Would you allow a communist to speak on the radio (TV)? (2) Would you allow a communist to teach in a public high school? (3) Would you allow a communist to own a large newspaper? With these same questions asked over the ten-year period, the trend study sought to measure change in the U.S. public's level of tolerance.

ADVANTAGES OF TREND DESIGN

In addition to the advantage enjoyed by the panel design, namely the ability to study change, the trend offers the advantage of being relatively less expensive than the panel. In this sense, the trend design is best suited for studying social change over long periods of time if one needs to economize to the maximum within the framework of prospective designs.

DISADVANTAGES OF TREND DESIGN

Because the trend design does not allow the researcher to know anything about who changed, users of the trend design are not able to explain change with the same clarity and level of confidence as panel users. As we saw in Table 8-8 above, the trend design can mask significant change. Usually, major changes in the marginal totals between two time periods indicates significant change, and the researcher using the trend design can be reasonably confident that the change is real. Still, there will always be that nagging doubt that can only be assuaged with the panel design.

Gathering data from different people at each point in time does not increase the researcher's knowledge about the respondents in the same fashion as the panel because the trend does not provide the researcher with additive data on the same respondents over time. In the social sciences, where meaning and in-depth understanding is so difficult to come by, this is a distinct disadvantage of the trend design compared with the panel.

Because the trend design does not yield as much information about respondents as the panel, the total sample size must be larger for the trend in order to achieve statistical power comparable to the panel. For example, if you require a 5% confidence level, you might be able to get away with a sample of two hundred with a panel, whereas a trend design would require four hundred for the same level of confidence. Again, the dialectic of advantage/disadvantage is at work here, and every gain has its price. In this case, the economy you gain with the trend is offset in part by larger sample sizes.

EX POST FACTO OR ONE-SHOT DESIGN

Ex post facto (Latin for "after the fact") **design**, with only one point in time where the data is gathered, is so called because the researcher must rely on the collective memories of the respondents in order to reconstruct the relationship in time between the independent and dependent variables. In short, time 1 has to be pieced together by asking the respondents to recall what was going on then. For this reason, this is called **retrospective design**. For example, if you wanted to study the impact that the Medicare legislation (government-funded health care insurance for the elderly) had on physician attitudes toward socialized medicine or at least toward Medicare, ideally you would do a before-and-after study using the trend or panel design. At time 1, before Medicare was passed and implemented, you would measure physician attitudes toward it. Then, after a year or two under Medicare, you would obtain a time 2 measure on the same attitude dimension. If costs and time prohibited you from using one of the prospective designs, you would have to use the one-shot design. Here, you would go into the field after Medicare had been around for one or two years and measure physician attitudes toward it. In order to piece together the time 1 attitudes, you would ask the physician respondents to recall what they were thinking one or two years earlier before Medicare existed. In this example, "after the fact" refers to the point that the study is unable to have a time 1 sampling. Instead, it must recreate time 1 through the memories of the respondents after the fact.

ADVANTAGES

Of course, this is the most economical of all the survey designs. There is no control group to contend with and only one data-gathering session. Money and time saved by avoiding having to keep track of respondents or by doing repeated interviews can be put into having more questions or items in the study and doing more extensive analysis of the data.

DISADVANTAGES

A larger sample size is required for the ex post facto design because of the memory issue along with the absence of increasing knowledge that comes with repeated questioning of people. But the major problem resides in the design's reliance upon memory or, in some cases, historical documents in order to settle the issue of the independent variable coming before the dependent variable in time, one of the requirements for proof that we discussed earlier. Surveys of people's health are often conducted in the ex post facto fashion. You might have had the opportunity to be questioned by a health survey team or questioned by a physician in the course of a physical examination. If so, you will have noticed that health status was measured by first establishing a time frame, say the last six months. The questions might be worded such as "In the last six months, have you had . . . (1) pain in the joints? (2) trouble breathing?," and so forth. The contingency is "If 'yes,' does it now bother you very much, some, or not at all?" The point here is that the past is reconstructed in the memory of the patient in order to get a perspective on the development and change of health problems. The alternative would be too costly and time-consuming for health researchers to pursue. Furthermore, the emphasis on most health surveys is broad scope, which

Box 8-3

■ Survey Research Design Flaws Lead to Public Policy Flaws: The Women's Health Study

Richard Kronmal, Carolyn Whitney, and Stephen Mumford (1991) recently reanalyzed the survey interview data from the Women's Health Survey (WHS). The WHS was conducted between 1976 and 1978 at sixteen hospitals in nine cities in the United States. In 1981, the findings were published by R. T. Burkman. He concluded that intrauterine devices (IUDs) increased the risk of women users contracting pelvic inflammatory disease (PID). This conclusion led to the discontinuance of the Dalkon Shield and the bankruptcy of its manufacturer, the A. H. Robins Company. Kronmal and his colleagues discovered that the original survey was seriously flawed methodologically. Their reanalysis found that the original WHS should have concluded that IUDs do not increase the risk of PID. What went wrong?

The original WHS was a one-shot survey that used a control group and a "case" group that was exposed to the independent variable (epidemiologists call this the case control design). The survey subjects were recruited from the population of patients in sixteen hospitals in nine U.S. cities during the period 1976 to 1978. Women eighteen to forty-four years of age who sought treatment for PID at the hospitals were screened for inclusion in the study. Out of 2,761 women screened, 1,447 were accepted into the study. These women were interviewed using a standardized interview schedule. The control group was selected from the population of women admitted to the same hospitals during the research period. The quota was three controls for each two subjects with PID. The control women were not matched with the PID subjects, but they had to meet specific criteria, such as being fertile, sexually active, not recently pregnant, and within the age range. From 7,199 candidates were derived 3,453 individuals for the control group.

Several serious design mistakes were made that led to erroneous findings. In general, Burkman violated several principles of survey design, the most telling of which were bias in the selection of the subjects for inclusion in the study and treating correlations or associations between variables as cause and effect. Kronmal and his colleagues presented the following survey design standards that were violated.

Select the Subjects before the Field Work and Analysis

In the absence of following this standard of selecting the subjects before the field work, it would be very easy for a researcher to do a preliminary analysis of the data and then to drop subjects in such a way to enhance the findings. The best way to avoid this selective dropping of subjects is to finalize the selection before data are collected or analyzed. Unfortunately, Burkman eliminated 52% of the PID subjects and 25% of the controls after an initial analysis in which they had been included. For example, use of the pill and barrier methods of contraception "protect" the user against PID. Burkman dropped those who did not use contraceptives from the control group in favor of pill and barrier users.

This decision was made after he took a look at the potential control group members. He would have been better off using women who did not use contraceptives as the control group because this would have eliminated the "protection" factor. If you are going to provide the acid test for the hypothesis that the IUD causes PID, then you do not want your control group of non-IUD users protected for PID by some factor other than not using the IUD. Burkman stacked the decks for providing that the IUD causes PID.

Clearly Define the Independent Variable and Its Role in "Causing" the Dependent Variable

If you are going to make the case that you were unable to prove yourself wrong and therefore that your hypothesis was true, you need to define, precisely, what "exposure" to the independent variable is. In the case of the WHS, the independent variable is use of the IUD, which allegedly causes PID. Again, similar to the first standard, this definition should be done well in advance of the data analysis. This is to prevent some crafty researcher from changing the definition in such a way that data are produced that support the hypothesis.

The WHS apparently had poor to nonexistent definitions as to what IUD use was. In one case, it was IUD use one week prior to hospitalization, and later, after data analysis, it was changed to three or more months. You can see how findings could be manipulated by changing the definition of exposure to the independent variable. If the three-or-more months women had a greater prevalence of PID, then it would be a simple matter for the researcher to change the definition to exclude anyone who had used an IUD 2.11 months or less prior to hospitalization. This is stacking the decks.

Blind Data Collection

Unbiased data collection is a goal or standard of research. If prior to doing the interview, the interviewer knows who has PID and who does not, who is using an IUD and who is not, this is a serious source of bias in the data collection itself. The interviewer could influence the answers by asking the questions in a biased fashion. The best protection against this, short of training the interviewers, is to make sure that the person collecting the data is blind as to who is a control subject and whose is not.

Anamnestic Equivalence

This is a fancy way of saying that you need to minimize the difference between the control subjects and the case subjects in the subjects' abilities or willingness to remember key details. The WHS asked about sexual history. One can see that the incentive for being detailed and accurate about sex practices might differ considerably between the PID respondents and the control group members who did not have PID. If sexual history was related to the choice of contraceptive method, as Kronmal indicated it might be, then the computation of risk factor associated with the use of the IUD would be affected. This is the confounding effect of selective memory.

Avoidance of Constrained Cases and Constrained Controls

Kronmal et al. defined this standard as one of random selection. Any procedures for selecting the case and control groups other than random selection

Box 8-3 *continued*

are problematic and may create bias. They cite the example from the WHS where women were declared ineligible for the control group if they had one or more illnesses that might affect their use of contraceptives. The same selection procedure was not used in selecting the case group. Nonrandom selection procedures applied to one group and not the other introduce systematic bias. The subjects eliminated from the analysis might have been overexposed or underexposed to the independent variable in a systematic fashion. Thus, their elimination could raise or lower the values on the dependent variable artificially.

Clear and Unambiguous Definition of the Dependent Variable

The Burkman study suffered from the absence of a single definition of PID. This problem reflects the inability of medical science to define PID and its symptoms clearly. In the words of Kronmal et al., "A clinical diagnosis of PID is frequently wrong. When a series of cases clinically diagnosed with PID were examined surgically in Sweden, one-third of the clinically diagnosed cases were determined to be wrong false positives. The difficulty in making an accurate diagnosis increases the likelihood that diagnostic bias may be present related to the presence of an IUD." The authors go on to point out that one-third to three-fourths of all PID cases are symptom-free, meaning that people who are classified as not having the disease really have it. Obviously, control group members might have had the disease and been misclassified as symptom-free, and this would have inflated the relationship between IUD use and PID.

Equal Opportunity to Become a Research Case

Kronmal et al. point out that this principle is designed to ensure that exposure to the independent variable is independent from measuring the dependent variable. In the WHS case, this principle was violated with serious consequences. The WHS should have screened women for PID prior to hospitalization because, once in the hospital, the women who were using IUDs were more intensely screened for PID than the nonusers. The reason for this disparity in the intensity of hospitalization screening is the knowledge that medical personnel had about the risk of using IUDs in contracting PID. A physician would put more effort into trying to diagnose the existence of PID for women using IUDs as opposed to women not using them.

Equal Demographic Susceptibility

This principle states that the case group and the control group should be matched or as alike as possible on the demographic factors that might be associated with PID. Kronmal and his colleagues criticized the WHS for inadequately matching the two groups particularly on sexual history, socioeconomic status, and race. For example, they pointed out that blacks made up 35% of the case group but only 25% of the control group. Perhaps black women were more likely to have had the IUD prescribed and the white women the pill, given the cost factor. Also, Kronmal suggested that white women were more likely than blacks to obtain early treatment for PID, thereby reducing the hospitalization rate for whites. Matching the two groups on race would be a step in the right direction.

Avoidance of Berkson's Bias

Women who were both using an IUD and had PID were more likely to end up in the hospital than people who were not. Conversely, women who were admitted for diseases other than PID would be less likely to use an IUD, given their precarious health, because certain health problems contraindicate the use of an IUD. This is Berkson's bias.

The authors conclude that the above violations of survey standards, flaws in both design and data analysis, render the conclusion that IUDs cause PID close to null and void. Certainly, the demise of the use of the IUD and the A. H. Robins Company in the United States probably should not have occurred on the basis of the original design and analysis.

means a large sample representative of a large segment of the population. Most important, health status changes in such an unpredictable fashion that it is difficult to set time periods for reinterviewing. It makes more sense to do the occasional one-shot survey under these conditions. Nevertheless, the reliance on memory is a serious weakness. Several studies have first asked people to describe from memory the health problems they have experienced during some limited time period. Then the respondents are examined physically by a physician, and the results from the one-shot memory report and the physical examination were correlated. Interestingly, there were disparities between the data derived from the two approaches, suggesting that people's memories about health matters are faulty relative to physical measures or that people interpret health differently than physicians. Regardless, if the self-fulfiling prophecy theory of W.I. Thomas has any validity, situations in which individuals define themselves as sick ought to have consequences in terms of those individuals behaving as if they are sick. If they think they are sick, they are sick, regardless what the blood tests indicate.

CASE STUDY DESIGN

One of the most maligned designs is the **case study**, in which the sample size is one or close to it. Usually, the case study involves a time frame that it shares with the panel, trend, and experimental designs. The emphasis is on detailed, deep data. No stone is left unturned as the researcher explores every possible avenue in a concerted effort to penetrate below the surface of things. Case study is best used to generate research questions and to help the social scientist formulate concepts and theory. The case study is useless for testing hypotheses, but it is indispensable for in-depth viewing of social life.

If the scientific community agrees on the appropriate research questions and explanations concerning, say, the urban Irish family, then survey designs are called for with large enough numbers of cases to enable the testing of hypotheses.

However, if very little is known or agreed upon, then a case study would help to formulate the questions and concepts. Alexander Humphreys' *The Dunn Family* is a classic example of a case study of one urban Irish family in Dublin. Through that study, he uncovered the concepts that form the core of modernization theory, and we readers gained great insight into the values and norms of the working-class urban Irish.

Perhaps the most important case study ever done in sociology was *The Polish Peasant*, by W.I. Thomas and Florian Znaniecki. This case study of a Polish-American immigrant family led to the creation of some of the core concepts in the social sciences: closed system, the definition of the situation, the interdependence of individuals, social life, inner mental life, culture, and the mandate that the central subject matter of sociology is attitudes and values that are determined by structures and definitions of the situation. In addition to this phenomenal gift of theory, *The Polish Peasant* established a methodological breakthrough of major proportions. Through their use of personal letters written between Polish-American immigrants and their families back in Poland, Thomas and Znaniecki pioneered the use of personal documents as a legitimate tool for observing spontaneous first-person accounts that reveal innermost personal intimate attitudes and values. Their case study demonstrated that a small "sample," historical methods, personal documents that provided great depth of meaning, and qualitative analysis work well together. Furthermore, they demonstrated the power of the case study for generating classifications and hypotheses.

DISADVANTAGES

The case study is a subjective design in the sense that the case chosen for study and the personal documents selected, if any, are usually based on the personal preference or special interest of the researcher. This is in sharp contrast to the survey designs where the cases are large in number and are usually chosen by random impersonal sampling procedures. The subjective nature of case studies has come under fire by positivistic social scientists. The result has been a stigmatization of case study design as less than worthy for serious research. Bernard Phillips (1971) had the following excellent point to make about Thomas and Znaniecki's subjectivity and the inherent subjective bias in all case study design:

> Many sociologists felt this method provided an excellent opportunity to convey a thorough account of all phases of life, and, in particular, man's inner mental life. A number of quantitative or statistically oriented sociologists attacked the method on the grounds that the citation of examples does not constitute scientific proof and that the method is highly subjective, especially because the investigator can select life histories to suit his own purpose.
>
> This controversy within sociology has been resolved to some extent, with most sociologists agreeing that both case studies and statistics can contribute to the scientific process (p. 99).

Thus, while the subjectivity of the case study is seen as a weakness by some, others see the opportunity to "triangulate" case study observational and historical documents with survey statistics, all in the same study.

Case studies are labor-intensive and require a great time commitment by the researcher. Many social scientists do research in conjunction with teaching and service roles to their universities and professions. Digging into a case study with the endless searching through archives for personal documents and other documentation may not be possible to fit into a full-time academic job.

■ *Conclusions*

One point to keep in mind as you reflect on this chapter is the natural fit between certain kinds of data-gathering techniques and types of research designs. Questionnaires and structured interviews go well with the survey designs. Structured observation fits nicely with the experimental designs, although structured interviewing and questionnaires will work nicely, too. Unstructured or semistructured data-gathering techniques, such as observation/participant observation, focused interviews, personal documents, even photography, are better suited for the case study design than any of the survey designs.

Also, it should be apparent at this point that the decision to use a specific research design is constrained by the epistemological assumptions and beliefs of the researcher along with the nature of the research problem and the status of scientific research and theory about that problem. If, for example, a particular research problem is in its infancy and one can barely find any literature on it, then a case study or participant observation design might be in order. Once concepts are developed and a clearer picture of the relevant research questions emerges, then the researcher is wise to move onto more statistical quantitative analyses that require survey designs. And so all of the decisions are connected in research.

Sociological research can help relieve the pressure that many researchers feel from the need to publish or perish and from pressing social problems. Often, the time-consuming designs, such as panel, trend, or case study, are passed over in favor of such designs as the ex-post facto with its high-yield, quick and dirty data. The case study requires lots of patience and the will to put tenure and the social problems on the back burner for awhile. In the long run, if the case study is successful, new and better concepts and theory will be available to be applied to the resolution of the social problems via large scale surveys, should that be the most appropriate means to the goal of eradicating the problems.

Finally, it is always wise to mix designs in any one study. If you have the resources in time and money, you can mix designs in order to gain methodological advantages and avoid disadvantages. A one-shot survey could be accompanied by a case study, which would add quality to the quantitative data. Where one design falls to some weakness, the other picks up the slack.

GLOSSARY

artificiality   an external validity problem caused by an obtrusive and/or unnatural experimental setting or environment.

case study design   a longitudinal design that focuses on a single unit of analysis, be it an organization, family gang, or a few individuals from a particular occupational group (e.g., jazz musicians) for example. The case study usually uses qualitative measurement techniques and secondary data sources.

control group   individuals in an experiment who are assigned by random procedures to not receive the treatment or independent variable.

description   the simplest form of scientific knowledge, involving a listing of the dimensions of the key variables in your study.

epistemology   a branch of philosophy that considers the nature of knowledge, the process of knowing, and the verification of knowledge.

experimental design   research design in which the researcher controls the introduction of the independent variable to a randomly assigned experimental group while withholding it from the control group.

experimental group   individuals in an experiment who are assigned by random procedures to receive the treatment or independent variable.

ex post facto design   a retrospective survey design with measurement at any one point in time.

external validity   a condition of proof that exists when the environmental conditions external to the experimental design are such that the researcher can rule them out as causes of the effect on the dependent variable.

factorial design   an experimental design where different experimental groups are exposed to different treatments.

history effect   an internal validity problem concerning events that occur between the first measurement of the dependent variable and the second measurement and affect the dependent variable at the second measurement.

inference   a conclusion based on reasoned logic.

instrumentation   an internal validity problem caused by minor changes in the data gathering procedures that, in turn, cause changes in the measurement of the dependent variable.

internal validity   a condition of proof that exists when the internal structure and conduct of the experiment design is such that the researcher can prove that the treatment (independent variable) caused the dependent variable.

Latin Squares design   a type of experimental design in which the experimental group is exposed to several treatments.

longitudinal design   a research design where the key variables are measured at least twice during the research time period. This is also called "prospective" design because it allows the researcher to look forward in the sense of studying and even predicting the dependent variable over time.

maturation effect   an internal validity problem where the subjects change over the course of the experiment in spite of the independent variable (treatment effect).

method of agreement   John Stuart Mill's principle of experimental design that says that if all of the cases in a study have only one circumstance in common, then that circumstance is the cause of the dependent variable.

method of difference   Mill's principle of experimental design that says that if all of the cases in a study have every circumstance in common except one, the one circumstance in which all cases differ is the cause of the dependent variable. The method of agreement and method of difference both are needed to prove causality.

natural experiment   an experimental design that utilizes a natural setting where the researcher does not control the external environment.

panel design   a longitudinal survey design in which the same individuals are measured at least two different times in order to analyze turnover or social change.

proof   a conclusion based on empirical evidence and a compelling research design.

research design   the strategy for gathering the best evidence within reason and economy for attempting to disprove your theory.

retrospective design   called retrospective because the "before" or time 1 feature of the panel, trend, and experimental design is missing, therefore, the researcher asks the respondent to reconstruct time one through his or her memory.

Solomon four-group experiment design   an experimental design with two experimental groups and two control groups.

statistical regression   an internal validity problem caused by extreme scores on the dependent variable regressing toward the mean score.

survey designs   research designs that rely on sampling, involve the natural social setting, use large numbers of cases, and statistical control of extraneous variables. They include the ex post facto, panel, and trend designs.

testing effect   an internal validity problem stemming from repeated testing (measurement of dependent variables) that makes the respondent "test-wise."

treatment   the independent variable in the experimental design.

trend design   a longitudinal survey design in which one group of respondents is studied at the first point in time and a different group of respondents is studied at the second point in time. There are different respondents over at least two points in time.

turnover   a term used with the panel design to describe the change of the respondents or key variables, for example, individuals who say that they intend to vote for proposition one at the first interview but say they intend to vote against it at the second interview.

FOR FURTHER READING

Goetz, Judith P., and Margaret D. LeCompte. (1984). *Ethnography and qualitative design in educational research*. Orlando, Fl.: Academic Press.

Goffman, Erving. (1961). *Asylums*. New York: Doubleday Anchor.

Moustakas, Clark E. (1990). *Heuristic research: Design, methodology, and applications*. Newbury Park, Calif.: Sage Publications.

Stouffer, Samuel A., et al. (1949). *The American soldier: Adjustment during army life*, vol. IV, *measurement and prediction*. Princeton, N.J.: Princeton University Press.

Yin, Robert K. (1984). *Case study research: Design and methods*. Beverly Hills, Calif.: Sage Publications.

Chapter Nine

OBSERVATIONAL RESEARCH

▋ *Using my own observational studies of faith healers, neighborhood health centers for the poor, and my twenty-year study of the rural elderly, strategies and tactics for conducting observational research are covered. Observational research designs are defined and the nature of sociological inquiry under this approach is discussed with special emphasis on the principles and processes of theory building through observational research. The naturalistic paradigm (Lincoln and Guba, 1985) is presented as the philosophical foundation for observational research. Problems in gaining entry to the field are presented and strategies and principles are offered as solutions. Quality control, reactivity, researcher sentiments, internal consistency, and field notes are discussed. Various analysis strategies are covered. The chapter concludes with a discussion of the ethical dilemma of censoring findings versus protecting the integrity and public image of those observed.*

This chapter may be the most fun for the reader because observational methodology is a scientific refinement of one of our most basic powers, the ability to observe the comings and goings around us. Through training in observational methodology and the discipline to adhere to its precepts, the powers grow to such an extent that the practitioner usually is astonished at how little of substance he or she really observed in the course of everyday life observations. I can recall the first observational methodology course I took in graduate school where this realization of how much I was missing in the course of causal observations of my environment was brought to my mortified attention. The professor, Morris Berkowitz, invited seven of us students into his office in order to discuss his expectations for the course. We spent forty-five minutes discussing this and that, then he handed each of us an envelope and told us to go to the graduate student lounge to work on its contents. Each envelope contained a unique set of questions about the physical environment of Berkowitz's office, such as "How many chairs were there?", "How many ash trays were there?", "What was Berkowitz wearing?", "How many windows were there?", and "What color was the floor?" We collaborated like mad and quickly developed a serious lack of confidence in the answers. Arguments broke out with all seven of us proffering seven different answers to some of the questions. I can recall that we never fully agreed on any one question. We felt foolish for being so weak in an area that we had so much practice performing, and that was the point of it all. Berkowitz knew we would not believe him if he had told us that we needed to train and discipline our powers of observation, so he showed us just how weak our abilities were. It convinced me that there was a lot more to observation than merely looking around to see what is happening. I hope that you too will be convinced.

This chapter covers several areas: the nature of observational research; gaining access to the field; data-collecting techniques; quality control; analysis of observational data; and ethical problems. I will bring in my own observational research experiences from the studies of faith healers, neighborhood health centers for the poor, and the twenty-year longitudinal study of the rural elderly. I hope this will fire your sociological imagination and tempt you to try your hand at observational research. At the very least, these examples will give you a behind-the-scenes view of observational research that should add some substance to the methodological framework of techniques and rules. These experiences are fairly common to observational research generally.

■ *The Nature of Observational Research*

All sociological research through which the researcher gathers primary data is observational in the most fundamental sense of the term. No matter what tools the researcher uses, be they face-to-face interviews or questionnaires, the purpose of applying tools is to observe social reality. However, there is a huge difference between this type of observation and observational research. **Observational research** is a form or special type of observation, but the key to the difference lies in the phrase "see the world through the eyes of the other." With interview schedules or questionnaires, the researcher imposes a framework, a particular way of seeing the world that may be more in the eyes of the researcher than the eyes of those studied. The fact of the matter is that these data-gathering instruments constitute a layer between what the research subjects and the researcher may be seeing. Observational research is designed to avoid this layer of social reality. Here, the researcher tries to take on a role that will place him or her as close to the thinking and behaviors of those under study as possible. This means that you must try to capture the social reality in all its rich detail without the narrowing, researcher-created "artificial" categorization associated with questionnaires and interview schedules. You can think of this problem in the following way. The researcher defines a concept and constructs a series of fixed-answer questions to measure it. Once measured, the researcher transforms the answers into numbers and then categorizes the numbers. In the final stage of this process, the researcher is working with data that is quantified and at least three steps removed from the qualitative meanings associated with the research subjects. Observational research tries to cut down on the number of steps between the researcher and the "true" meaning of the data. Before I discuss the roles unique to observational research, a few words are necessary on a couple of features unique to observational research.

PROPOSITIONS

When you are working within the observational research design, you would not state a proposition and test it. Rather, you would have some preliminary propositions that you would refine and reformulate throughout the observational research. In this sense, you might think of propositions in observational research as emerging. Observational research helps you build theory, not test it. During the course of observational research, propositions are formulated and linked together so that by the end of the study you have a theory.

RESEARCHER JUDGMENT

Another unique characteristic of observational research is the fact that there are no statistical rules or norms that the researcher can use to help him or her decide which findings are true and which ones are false. Much more so than other more quantitative designs, observational research forces the researcher to make judgment calls. Anselm Strauss et al. (1964) put it nicely when they wrote:

> The fieldworker usually does not enter the field with specific hypotheses and a predetermined research design. To be sure, he does have general problems in mind, as well as a theoretical framework that directs him to certain events in the field. The trained sociologist or anthropologist is equipped to make discriminations rather quickly between what may be theoretically important or unimportant. The initial phase of fieldwork is a period of general observation: Specific problems and foci have not yet been determined. The fieldworker is guided mainly by sensitivities to data derived both from his professional background and from general notions about the nature of his research problem. As he surveys the field initially, he is continually "testing"— either implicitly or explicitly—the relevance of a large number of hypotheses, hunches, and guesses. Many preconceptions fall by the wayside during this initial period, as the observer struggles to ascertain the meaning of events and to place them in some initial order.

One can think of observational research as a continuum of research roles, from pure observer on one end to pure participant on the other. In the middle, we have the participant observer doing both roles equally. The pure observer does not exist, nor does the pure participant. These are ideal types, useful fictions that help us understand the broad spectrum of roles open to the observational researcher.

The pure observer would remain a complete stranger to the research subjects involved in the study. He or she would simply watch the action and record it without so much as saying a word or communicating a gesture. There would be no role in the research setting for the pure observer. He or she would have no status, no responsibilities, no rights or expectations. Ideally, the pure observer would melt into the woodwork and be perfectly unobtrusive. He or she would function as a perfectly objective recording instrument, eliciting no emotions or sentiments of those observed and feeling nothing in return.

One danger with the observer role is that the researcher will be identified as an outsider by the subjects. Invariably, because the researcher is human and subject to all the same stresses that the subjects experience, he or she will feel various emotions relative to the subjects and their situation. Unfortunately, there is no place for the researcher to go with these emotions. As an outsider, the researcher is estranged from the subjects at best and may even be viewed with suspicion and veiled hostility by the subjects of the observation. Certainly, there is little or no opportunity for the researcher to gain the confidence of the subjects if all the researcher has done is observe. Consequently, the researcher cannot grapple with rising emotions by sharing feelings with the subjects and perhaps thereby clarifying those feelings. If the feelings are kept bottled up, even the researcher who has those feelings may not be aware of them enough to control them. It is best from the standpoint of objectivity to recognize one's emotions and to prevent them from biasing scientific decisions. Under the burden of the pure observer, it is easy to lose sight of this point.

The pure participant, on the other hand, would do little or no recording because he or she would be too busy playing a role in the research setting. This would be a real role, one that would be recognized by the subjects as legitimate and functional. Under this condition, the researcher and subjects would interact and engage in the sharing of feelings. Understanding of each others' emotional needs would be enhanced, and there would be greater opportunity for everyone involved in the research to better control emotions through mutual understanding.

A MIDDLE GROUND

Neither of these two extremes is very productive if the goal is to get some research accomplished. And yet each role has strong points. The participant gets closer to the perspectives of the subjects because he or she essentially is a research subject, too. The danger here is that the researcher will lose sight of the research objectives by becoming strongly committed to his other role. The observer, on the other side of the coin, runs the risk of never getting close enough to the life-styles and values of the subjects to understand their perspectives. By not taking some role, the researcher could become marginal to what is going on, an outsider.

This is one reason why some balance between the extremes is necessary to successfully carry out observational research. While the two extreme roles are available and constitute part of observational research, the roles of participant observer or observer participant are much more likely to yield methodologically solid research findings.

PARTICIPANT OBSERVER

As a participant observer, the researcher puts more emphasis on playing a role in the research setting but not at the expense of observing and recording. The participation is designed mainly to place the researcher closer to the action and to allow the researcher the opportunity to see life from the perspectives of the subjects. If you were to add up the energy spent on the research, this approach would place you at a slight deficiency in terms of observation and recording. There is only so much time in a day, and effort spent participating is effort taken away from observing. Action research, where the goal is to produce constructive social change, often finds the researcher doing a bit more participating than observing.

During a qualitative study of neighborhood health centers for the poor (Hessler and Beavert, 1982), we encountered highly militant Black and Chicano residents who were gatekeepers of the health centers. In one memorable situation in the Southwest, I had to "pay my dues" before I was allowed to follow the head Chicano leader around to meetings and to interview him. For two weeks, on and off, I worked in his candle factory making candles for no pay. Also during this time, I spent a lot of time just hanging around his house. This was natural because the candle factory was a family operation, and I worked with most of the members of his family. This led to fairly comfortable interaction off the job, during leisure hours. All the while that I worked in the candle factory, I was participating but doing very little observational research in the sense of recording my observations and conversations. For one thing, I had not been granted "permission" yet to do the interviewing that was central to the study. Thus, it would have been very risky to show any signs of doing research before the official go ahead. Of course, I was able to record some fairly sketchy field notes during the few times I was alone for any extended period, but for all intents and purposes, I was a full-time participant and a very part-time researcher during this testing period.

Although I was not getting much research done, this period was valuable in the long run, not only because it enabled me to do the research eventually but also because I became much more perceptive and in tune with the issues and culture of that particular neighborhood health center. At one point during the testing stage, I was sitting around the leader's house when he was called to the phone. It was his brother calling in a great panic about being cursed by his recently deceased wife. The leader took his wife, his second son (who was around fourteen at the time), and me across the city to a neighborhood right on the edge of the open desert. As we arrived, it was dark and three white coyotes ran in front of the car and disappeared into the night. The cursed brother was panic stricken and seemed oblivious to everyone and everything going on around him except his brother. I noticed that there were several other people there, besides us, but I never learned who they were. In any case, I watched as a woman uncovered the evidence of the curse. It was a pillow that the victim slept on. There were hundreds of spider eggs in among the feathers of the pillow, along with a tiny wax figure of a male. A recent photograph of the victim had been cut out to fit the wax figurine, and several pins had been thrust through both the photo and the figurine. The woman took holy water from the local Catholic church and sprinkled it on all of the contents of the pillow, which was torn open and lying on the kitchen floor. Then she threw small amounts of the water on all the people gathered in the house before she went outside and sprinkled the victim's car. None of this seemed to assuage the victim, and I learned on the way home that he would have to go the next day to Mexico to have a *curandera*, a good witch so to speak, take the curse upon herself and hence off him. This procedure was going to cost the victim plenty of money, but he had no choice, apparently, if he wanted to resume his life where it left off before discovering the hex. While this situation had little to do directly with the research problem of citizen control of neighborhood health centers, it was a valuable experience in terms of understanding with some depth the culture of the Chicano people in that area. Later on in the study, when my interviews with the people were turning up a strong commitment to having physicians and nurses at the center who respected the folk medical practices of the people, I understood better empirically the cultural basis for this view.

OBSERVER PARTICIPANT

The same discussion holds for the observer participant, except that the emphasis is on observing, rather than participating. More research gets accomplished, but it may be at the expense of the depth of understanding and the quality of the data generated through participation. The less time you spend interacting with the subjects, the more difficult it is to see the world through their eyes.

Often, qualitative research projects will take place over a rather long time period, and the roles of the researcher may bounce back and forth between observer participant and participant observer. Or the observer role may constitute 90% of the research activity, while the participant role makes up the small remainder.

Qualitative research, where observation takes up the bulk of the research activity, is very appropriate when the research problem involves studying behavior in public places. For example, Peter New and I used to take the Boston and Maine train home together after work at Tufts New England Medical School. Peter, in his unswerving dedication to the impossible task of making me into a qualitative researcher, would sit next to me while waiting for the train at Boston's North Station and challenge me to classify correctly the occupations of our fellow travelers. I was a participant in a small sense of having the role of waiting for the train, which I shared with most of the other people in the station. But I did not interact directly with the others in the sense of speaking with them or even establishing eye contact and nodding to them. I would make my guesses, Peter would ask me what my indicators were, and then he would proffer his guess and go over to the person observed to ask them what they did for work. He was never rebuffed, and my record was dismal compared to his. I think Peter had more experience observing and participating than I had, which may have accounted for his record. Then again, he may have had the gift of the artist, too.

THE NATURALISTIC PARADIGM

A final point concerning the nature of observational research comes from the philosophy of science and has to do with the basic assumptions behind observational methodology. Two questions from epistemology (the philosophy of knowledge) form the basis for a researcher deciding what type of research design to use, or even how the research problem should be defined. The two questions also force the researcher to evaluate the adequacy of his or her design decisions. The two questions are: (1) What can we know? and (2) What is the best way(s) for knowing it? Is what you can know "objective" reality out there in some formal and ordered fashion just waiting for the researcher to discover it? Or is reality more nebulous and subjective, a construction of the researchers and even of the respondents, perhaps? Every reader of this book should try to formulate answers to these basic questions because the "objective" reality answer will lead you away from the qualitative approach. Qualitative methodology is more in tune with "subjective" reality, that is human mental constructs. The answer forms the foundation for the basic paradigm you as a researcher subscribe to. The **naturalistic paradigm** (Lincoln and Guba, 1985) comprises one set of answers that place the researcher using this paradigm squarely in the fold of observational research. Of course, statistics can be used productively with observational methods, but much of the positivistic basic assumptions are treated as meaningless.

■ *Gaining Access to the Field*

In late 1969, I was involved in a study of militant Black and Chicano neighborhood health centers (Hessler and Beavert, 1982). I and my colleagues at Tufts worked long and hard to secure entry to the centers, which were controlled in some cases by medical schools and in other cases by local citizen boards. The issues affecting the very survival of the centers were volatile, and there existed throughout the land a siege type of mentality, a palpable "We the people of the ghetto versus the establishment." This translated poorly for our cause of **gaining entry** because we were obvious members of the established academic order and, as such, could not be trusted, on the face of it.

"WHAT'S IN IT FOR US?": RESEARCH DUPLICATES EVERYDAY LIFE

The first question asked by the centers was "What is in it for us to participate with your study?" Or, put another way, "Can you help us, or will you get in the way at best and even hurt us at worst?" Much of our research planning was spent discussing answers to this question, which really meant discussing our values. This was a case of human beings figuring out what ought to happen in order to have a quality life. Perhaps it is true of all sociological research, but it was certainly true that this study was inherently subjective from the start. Our problem in this regard was to control the subjective biases as much as possible.

At the same time, we recalled the exchange methodology (Hessler and New, 1972) that served us so well in guiding us to the methodological principle that sociological research is part of everyday life. This principle calls attention to the need for researchers negotiating difficult fieldwork entry to concentrate on the social relationships behind researcher-respondent interaction. William Shaffir, Robert Stebbins, and Allan Turowetz, in their introduction to their excellent book on the sociological foundation of fieldwork (1980), wrote:

> To be sure, field researchers share with other scientists the goal of collecting valid, impartial data about some natural phenomenon. In addition, however, they gain satisfaction—perhaps better stated as a sense of accomplishment—from successfully managing the social side of their projects, which are more problematic than any other form of inquiry (p. 5). . . . While descriptions and analysis of the various dimensions of the field research experience have recently become more plentiful, it is unfortunate that the social aspects both underlying and shaping this experience have not received more critical attention (p. 7).

Howard Becker agrees. As he wrote more than twenty years ago, "As every researcher knows, there is more to doing research than is dreamt of in philosophies of science, and texts in methodology offer answers to only a fraction of the problems one encounters" (1965, p. 602). Thus armed, we sought entry with a desire to apply this principle to the everyday needs of the respondents. What was in it for the respondents to allow us to do the research?

In order to gain access to the neighborhood health centers, first we had to negotiate with our funding agency, which was the U.S. Public Health Service, the now defunct Office of Economic Opportunity (OEO), and the local powers in charge of the neighborhood health centers selected for study. The government-level negotiations were not as simple as I thought they would be when I began them. The OEO wanted us to stay out of centers where there had been lots of conflict between the doctors and the neighborhood consumer boards over who would control the centers. My best guess to this day is that the OEO was very worried about its congressional relationships and also concerned about its liberal constituents. As such it wanted us to study "showcase" centers, where things were running relatively peacefully, rather than calling political and public attention to the medical war zone.

At first, we sought permission to study twelve of the most conflict-ridden centers, but the OEO fought us on this plan. Eventually, we compromised our research design and offered to split things in half, selecting six troubled centers and six relatively quiet ones. Actually, this turned out to be a good decision methodologically for a couple of reasons. First, it enabled us to approach the more peaceful centers first and to negotiate entry without the additional pressures associated with shouting matches, medical workers' strikes against doctors, and extreme hostility toward any research. This meant that we could gain entry to a more peaceful center and use that accomplishment in our pitch to a more conflictual center. We promised confidentiality, so we were not at liberty to tell one center what the names of the other centers were. However, we were able to tell a center administrator that we had gained entry and were underway at two other centers. This information helped establish our credibility with the more militant gatekeepers. More importantly, we were able to start gathering data, which enabled us to revise our methodology before we got too far into the study to change things.

KEEPING TABS ON ENTRY: THE FIELD JOURNAL

We kept detailed **field journals** in which we recorded all of the entry experiences. At one point, my colleague, Peter New, and I were trying to gain permission from the center administrator to interview and observe a class of health center workers called "neighborhood health workers." These employees were local residents who would have met the poverty guidelines for service at the center had they not been employed at the time of our study. These workers represented the outcome of the neighborhood health center strategy for breaking the cycle of poverty by creating jobs and other employment opportunities for local residents. The theory of new jobs at the centers was predicated on the career ladder concept in which the neighborhood health workers would be trained by the centers, work there for a while, and then move on to better related jobs in the larger health care system. Our request for access to these workers was denied, so we discussed the options beyond just giving up on interviewing the workers. Peter reminded me that we could go to the board, which was made up of neighborhood residents who were eligible for services at the center. Surely, he thought, they would be sympathetic with our request to talk with their neighbors. I thought that it would be better to engage in what Peter at one time had called "creative bumbling." This is behavior that goes against the normal rules of conduct but that is not illegal or unethical. For example, you may know that a certain area of the baseball park is off limits, so you act as if you had never heard of such limits and proceed to enter with all the confidence and aplomb of someone who belongs. The security person or the usher is clued in to spot hesitant or otherwise suspicious-looking people, and the false confidence stands a good chance of tricking the gatekeeper. Peter agreed.

We wrote up the field notes to the point of this decision, and then we reentered the center and walked straight into the office area where the neighborhood health workers were based. I told the secretary that we were there to talk with some of the workers and that we would wait for her to find a couple of workers who were free at the time. No questions were asked, and within a few minutes we were engaged in conversation with the workers. Things went very well and we had several very good interviews completed when the center administrator barged into the office I was using and demanded to know who had given me permission to interview the worker sitting there in front of me. I told him that I had decided on my own and was using the center office rather than talking with the worker at her home. The administrator was outraged and shouted that I was going to have to leave the premises. I assured him that the worker had nothing to do with the problem other than having agreed to be interviewed, but before I could finish what I had started to say, two of the administrator's assistants physically forced me from the office and out the door, where I was joined in seconds by Peter New exiting in the same fashion.

We sat on the wall in the warm Los Angeles sun and scribbled the events into our respective field work journals. Peter's notes were more detailed than mine, so he titled them "On Being Forcibly Removed from X" and distributed the copies to our colleagues who were working at other centers all across the country. These observations were valuable for our colleagues, but they also were the key to our negotiating reentry to the center. Based on the notes and our ability to discuss the events accurately and objectively, we decided to go to the center board with the situation and request that we be allowed to resume the research.

It was in the context of this request that I had to deal with the question of what was in it for the board to go out on a limb for us. The board president seemed to be in favor of the research from the first contact we had back at the beginning of the study, when we first asked permission to study the center. But I did not have the opportunity prior to the board meeting to meet with her and to get a sense of how she felt about our creative bumbling. So in the absence of any indication one way or the other, I went to the board meeting prepared to bare my soul in the sense of stating my values and personal objectives for the study.

This was good preparation, it turned out, as I was asked by one elderly man on the board what I planned to do with the results of the study. I went through the usual things about publishing papers and writing a report for the funding agency, adding that we had promised a copy of these papers and any reports for the board. He nodded approvingly, then he asked me how these papers and report might help the community and the center. At that point, I realized that it was time to take a stand on my values and personal goals.

At this point, Howard Becker's challenge ("Whose Side Are We on?") became a reality as I struggled with the problem of my values. Should I take a stand and tell the citizen board members that I supported total citizen control of the centers, thereby placing myself squarely on their side and in conflict with the physicians, medical schools, and even possibly the governmental granting agencies, or should I try to escape the question by retreating into the world of scientific objectivity and value neutrality? Would I "**go native**" and so thoroughly "take the role of the other" that I would be unable to analyze the field notes? As I turned these thoughts over, I recalled a piece of advice from Rosalie Wax (1971). She put years of field experience into her book, which had become one of our most important directional aids during the course of our study. In her book, she reflected on the trials and tribulations of negotiating entry in Native American reservation communities. No matter what she said, the community gatekeepers dismissed her words. The key to gaining entry for her was what she did, her actions, not what she said. The Native Americans had excellent reason to distrust any white person, and so did the black citizen board members. Reflecting on what Wax had written about her experience, I decided to keep my values out of it and to direct my comments at what I had accomplished for other community groups as a result of various research projects in the past. I mentioned the Boston Chinatown study, which I had just completed, and how the findings had enabled the Chinese American Civic Association to negotiate a series of concessions from the neighboring medical providers. This greatly improved the problem of access to medical care of the average Chinese resident. Also, I mentioned another center (not by name) that I was currently working on. At this center, I had been able to serve as a liaison between the medical school, the funding agency, and the neighborhood board. I successfully retrieved data for the board, put the members in touch with the emerging association of neighborhood health center boards, helped various members obtain tape recorders, provided transportation to meetings around the city, and even did some English-language tutoring. Once again, I went over the general purpose of our study and speculated on how I might be able to help the board directly and the community indirectly during the course of the study.

I was granted permission to continue the study and to talk with anyone working at the center. Based on the comments of the board members during this meeting, it is clear to me that I was granted a "pardon" first and foremost because the board members viewed the administrator's action as stepping over the line of his authority. After all, the members reasoned, it was the board members who had granted us permission to do the study in the first place, not the center administrator, and if anyone terminated us, it would be the board. Later observations confirmed the fact that the board members were very sensitive to their former status as "advisors" to the medical school. As you are aware, you can take or leave someone's advice if there is no power or control behind the advisor. The other reason for the pardon was the expectation by the board members that the study would result in a justification or vindication of board control of centers. I think that they saw us as being objective researchers who were committed to the study enough to appeal our ouster. Also, they had confidence in the way their center was organized and in the legitimacy of the board's role, so any writing we might do on the board was viewed as positive publicity that might enhance their center's status relative to others. All of the board members were keenly aware of the scarcity of resources and the competition between centers for those resources. Our research would highlight the center and the board, thereby giving them a competitive edge, perhaps.

The next few months were very productive for Peter New and me at the center. We completed lots of interviews, observed at countless meetings, and poured over written documents with our abstract forms in hand. The only repercussion of our being reinstated was a notable cooling toward us of the administrator, but it did not go beyond that. We interviewed him almost at will, and the files in his office were opened to us as well. Perhaps he was fearful of the board and its wrath should he give us a hard time, or perhaps he realized that we were proceeding with the study and that the only way he would be able to influence what we observed and recorded about center administration was by cooperating and talking with us, sort of his chance to make sure his position was represented. This was uncomfortable for me personally at first, but eventually I realized that my wanting to be liked by the administrator was irrelevant to the research goals. Being disliked came with the territory of choosing sides, and if his feeling toward us interfered with our ability to gather data in an objective fashion, it did so certainly less so than would have been the case had we remained banished souls. To sum up what we learned about research entry from this study, conflict was so high and suspicions so great that we were forced to deviate from the standard methodological techniques for gaining entry. A rigid adherence to the conventional cannons of scientific technique, cannons that demand that the researcher keep the everyday needs of the respondents out of the entry process, would have doomed the study. We departed from the standard procedures and brought the lives of the respondents and the research together, thereby making it very difficult to avoid taking sides and to remain objective enough to cover all perspectives. It seems upon reflection that we had established a type of attitude toward research relations that placed discovery of new knowledge and the very real needs of the respondents above rigid adherence to standard methodological techniques of science. We designed a method called exchange methodology, which helped us uncover and control the complex social relations that form around the interaction between researcher and the everyday lives of the respondents.

ANOTHER DIFFICULT ENTRY PROBLEM: THE CASE OF THE TWENTY-YEAR LONGITUDINAL STUDY OF THE RURAL ELDERLY

A very difficult entry problem emerged when I tried to contact respondents and gain their permission to be interviewed for the third time in a twenty-year period in my study of the rural elderly. Under more ordinary circumstances, there would not have been much of a problem because these respondents had been in the study for such a long period of time and they had agreed on two previous occasions to allow me to interview them. This time, unfortunately, it was different. The youngest respondent was eighty-seven years of age, and most of the members of this unique panel were in their nineties. In the neighborhood health center study, the heat of battle over control of the centers was fierce and researchers were suspect. On the other hand, the study had immediate utility for the respondents, who saw the potential knowledge gained as power in their struggle to wrest control of the neighborhood health centers from the medical establishment. In spite of the hostilities and suspicions, the research had something to offer in exchange for us being allowed to do the observational study. The respondents were future-oriented and commited to community control over the institutions that affected their lives.

In contrast, the elderly respondents were not fighting the system, and advanced age rendered somewhat moot the appeal that the neighborhood health centers study had in terms of the findings having beneficial impact in the near future. It was not possible in this situation to use the exchange methodology, which worked so well in the centers study.

■ *Some New Principles of Research Entry*

In stark contrast to the health center scene, the small midwestern rural towns in my study had not been sites of civil rights conflict since the Civil War. Furthermore, the elderly respondents' views of the benefits that my study held for future development and social change is summed up nicely by the comment made by one woman in my study. When promised a report on the findings of the study, she replied: "Don't make it too long. I am ninety-seven you know." She was telling me that time was short for her, and consequently she had adopted an ethos of living life day by day. The future for her was now, in the moment, and the concept of research having an impact on the future was not terribly meaningful for her. And so it was for the other respondents in my study.

To make matters even more difficult, most of the respondents had very brittle health. They tired easily and had difficulty hearing and seeing. Several were bedfast and most moved about their homes slowly and with considerable difficulty. The advanced age and precarious health were compounded by the socioeconomic poverty experienced by most of the respondents. Thus, it was that we were faced with previous entry strategies that would not work. We turned anew to the question "What is in it for us?" and the entry principle of research duplicating the respondents' everyday lives. In this vein, we decided to fit the entry strategy with the norms of sociability of the respondents and meet with the respondents face-to-face in order to ask their permission to do the interviews. But I get ahead of myself here. First, let me take you through the entry procedure in a more comprehensive fashion. This includes the steps and decisions taken from the initial attempts to locate the respondents after a twelve-year hiatus since the last interview.

CONSCRIPT LOCALS AS MEMBERS OF THE RESEARCH TEAM

In 1974 and again in 1986-1987, we asked the postmasters of the sixty-four towns in the study to "join" the research by reviewing a list of the respondents and their last known addresses and then sending us their judgments concerning the correctness of our list. If a respondent had died, the postmaster would inform us, at times even indicating what year the death had occurred. For those individuals who moved, the postmaster would give us a forwarding address if one existed. Unfortunately, there were respondents whom the postmasters knew nothing about save the fact that they no longer lived at the last known address we had.

Thus, our first contact with the study towns was with the postmasters, all of whom were local residents. Because we had sent them a detailed description of the study and the rationale for doing it, the postmasters were informed about the research and could pass on this information to others who might be interested. And others were interested, indeed. The postmasters served the dual role of helping us locate the respondents or verifying correct addresses and of being the first line of defense against our problem of being strangers to the townsfolk. Strangers in small towns stick out, and one way or another, the rumor mill identifies and labels the strangers. It was imperative that we controlled the labeling process as much as possible in order to avoid false and damaging rumors about who we were and what we wanted. The postmasters "introduced" us even before we arrived in person. They helped us take the first step in letting the townsfolk know about us.

AVOID THE TELEPHONE AND LETTERS

There was considerable pressure from the granting agency and from the immediate availability of good interviewers to get into the field quickly and start the interviewing. But the most compelling reason for our haste was the advanced age of the respondents and the possibility that sickness or death would foil our plan to reinterview them. Consequently, we did not test different entry strategies on non-study individuals before we entered the field for real. We started the interviewing, spent one week in various towns scattered all over the state, and then reconvened back at the university for a session about how things went. We had sent letters of introduction explaining the study and the respondents' past cooperation. This letter was followed up with a phone call a few days before going to the town to do the field work. Each interviewer carried a letter of introduction printed on university letterhead.

When we reconvened after the first week, I realized that the interviewers had several refusals. This situation was very frightening to me because I could see twenty years of data and the enormous potential of this unique study going down the tubes, not because the respondents had died, but because they refused to be interviewed. Upon further discussion, a pattern to the refusals emerged. Most of them took place over the phone with only one occurring at the door. On the other hand, each of us had instances where we were unable to reach the respondent by phone so we simply showed up at the door, knocked, and did introductions right there on the spot. This extemporaneous approach was praised by the interviewers as feeling right to them and for its ability to gain entry. What was the problem with the approach of phoning ahead and making an appointment? It was only toward the end of the year and the wrapping up of the field work that the answer became apparent. Telephone appointments and formal introductory letters were foreign to the everyday lives of the respondents. So was being interviewed, but there was no reason to make matters worse by introducing additional foreign matter. The letter and the phone call caused respondents to worry about not being able physically on the appointed day to do the interview, since most of them were frail and had good days and bad ones. The letter led some of the respondents to talk about it with a significant other, some of whom expressed concern to the respondent about being able physically to do the interview or who said negative things about the university per se. Finally, most of the respondents were unused to talking on the phone because they had difficulty hearing, so they avoided the phone as much as possible. Using it was viewed as a burden, and this negative attitude carried over into the study.

FACE-TO-FACE NEGOTIATED ENTRY

The respondents were of a generation that valued neighborliness and hospitality, even toward strangers. It was simply against the rules to turn away or not at least to hear out a young interviewer who had traveled many miles just to interview the respondent. Once the conversation began, the social relationship began, too, and the respondent could begin to sense that the interviewer was really committed to the study and that the interviewer held the respondent's knowledge and past cooperation in high esteem. Also, the personality of the interviewer had time to emerge and be appreciated by the respondent. Of course, the same processes were happening to the interviewer, which reinforced his or her commitment to the study and to the task at hand. Once you got to liking the respondent, there was no way you were going to take "no" without a fight.

The interaction on the doorstep was more natural and meaningful to the respondents, who had spent their entire lives working within the oral tradition with agreements and other decisions made in the physical presence of the other. Talking things out in person was more meaningful to the respondents than seeing the study goals written out on paper and hearing some disembodied impersonal voice on the phone. Eye contact, a smile, the youth of the interviewer, the sincerity, all could be taken in by the respondent in just a few short moments. The chemistry of personal contact and exposure to each other's personalities broke the ice and formed the first steps toward entry.

Once the ice was broken and the interview got underway, the majority of the respondents thoroughly enjoyed the change of pace afforded by the interview. They talked about their lives in ways untold while at the same time contributing to our research project. Once the first couple of questions were completed, the respondents' fears of getting too tired or of not knowing "the right answers" melted away. The key to this happening was getting into a face-to-face situation and initiating the exchange process without the baggage imposed by the telephone and mail. It was a case of deeds being stronger than words.

FIELD HELP WITH ENTRY: FUNERAL HOMES, RESTAURANTS, AND SENIOR CITIZENS' CENTERS

Please do not get the impression that the entry strategy in this or in any similar field work was carefully and meticulously planned, tested, and then implemented. On the contrary, we were flying very much by the seats of our pants, innovating all the while as the particular situations demanded. Serendipity, that is, the unanticipated lucky strike, played a larger-than-life role and complemented the more rational and predictable methodological decisions. The pretest and debriefing session with the field workers taught us to show up at respondents' doors unannounced, but it was happenstance, intuition, and reflection on what was unfolding that produced the final highly successful version of our entry strategy. We added restaurants, senior citizens' centers, and funeral homes to our bag of methodological tools.

The first thing we did when arriving at a research site, in this case, a small town, was to stop at a local restaurant. Being strangers to the town, we found it advantageous to explain to the waitress or owner who we were and what we were doing there. At times, the waitress would ask even before we had a chance to tell our tale. A local patron would overhear what we had said and would express an interest in the research. Once a conversation about the study was underway, it was easy to show the list of respondents and addresses to one of the locals. Usually, this led to directions to respondents' homes, advice as to how to proceed with contacts prior to seeking out the respondent, or information about the status of respondents who had moved or died. Several times, waitresses or patrons looked up phone numbers and even called respondents on our behalf. These people functioned as **informants** by helping us gain entry.

In one of these instances, I arrived at a restaurant with my fourteen-year-old daughter a little after 8:00 P.M. We had the name and address of a ninety-three-year-old respondent whom the postmaster had indicated lived in town. We told the waitress what we were doing and who we were looking for. A man, his wife, and their teenage daughter sitting at the table right behind us overheard the conversation, and the man expressed an interest in the study. I turned and talked with them for several minutes, upon which the man offered to call the respondent for me. At the time, I thought he was wrong but did not comment when the man said that he had sold a truck to the respondent a couple of months ago. I thought that the respondent would have been too old to drive a truck. But the respondent had such an unusual name, the only one of its kind in the local phone book, that I thought again that perhaps the respondent had purchased a truck from the patron. The call was made and the patron engaged the respondent in a conversation about the truck. After a couple of minutes, the patron gave the phone over to me. I introduced myself and determined that indeed it was the correct person. However, the fact that the patron, a person who may have been well-known in the town but whom the respondent did not know, had talked to him about the truck sale made the respondent suspicious that we were trying to sell him something. It took me several minutes of fast talking to explain the sequence of events leading up to the phone call. The fact that I was speaking from the restaurant seemed to help matters as the respondent knew the waitress and the owner. I was able to do the interview the next morning with the help of my daughter.

Funeral homes emerged as an important facilitator for entry to the interviewing. We initially began to contact funeral homes because we had run into a dead end with trying to get the state bureaucracy to give us dates of death for the deceased respondents. Just by chance, I happened to go into a funeral home to speak with an employee who was referred to me as someone who knew the missing respondent I was about to give up on. One thing led to another, and the employee offered to go through her book and look up all the respondent names that the postmaster had indicated were deceased. In a matter of a few minutes, she had dates of death on all but a few of the deceased respondents. From that moment on, we never failed to touch base with the funeral homes. In only a few cases, the funeral parlors were not owned by respected and prominent members of the community. In most instances, the owners or employees were able to give us valuable information and, at times, even were able to convince recalcitrant respondents to consent to the interview.

Similarly, the senior citizens' centers, while not in every town, usually were run by individuals who were lifelong residents of the area and who seemed to be very well connected with the elderly of the community. They seemed to have the respect and trust of their constituents. At several centers, the respondents were active members of the centers' programs, which afforded us yet another means to obtain entry.

Basically, the people at the funeral homes, restaurants, and senior centers served two important entry functions: (1) they provided the interviewer with an opportunity to establish an identity and to place that identity into the local rumor mill in a relatively controlled fashion; and (2) they became advocates and helped locate respondents and information about them.

INTERVIEWING

Entry to the research does not end with the interview. Entry is a process that continues throughout the research project. Gaining entry to the home was no guarantee that an interview would be completed. As the reader can empathize, I was under great pressure to complete each and every interview. Out of 1,700 persons interviewed in 1966 and 560 interviewed in 1974, I was down to 128 individuals who represented twenty years of unique and valuable data on the aging process. The study was unique in its design, and as such, it had the potential to make a substantial contribution to the sociology of aging. Each respondent was too old to take any chances on being able to do the interview at some later date. Time was my enemy, and the ultimate failure as far as I was concerned was to locate the respondent only to be denied an interview. Unfortunately, this happened twice very early in the field work. Fortunately, I learned from the experience and altered traditional interviewing techniques to fit the special circumstances posed by such elderly respondents.

In 1966 and 1974, the interviewers were middle-aged women who worked for the university extension division. They were experienced at making contact with community residents and presenting programs to them. At the time, we thought that this would be least threatening to the respondents, many of whom were women living alone. We thought that middle-aged interviewers would present a mature image.

In the course of preliminary field work, I used college junior and senior sociology majors to do interviews with very old residents of two small towns not in the study. The students, all of whom were very young, expressed highly positive sentiments about their contacts with the elderly respondents. The more the students discussed their experiences with the interview, the more it became apparent that the rapport between the students and the respondents was excellent. Some of the students, when asked by me why they had such warm feelings toward the respondents, replied that the respondents reminded them of their grandparents. The relationship in our society between grandparent and grandchild generally is one of unconditional love and mutual respect, free from the tensions associated with the discipline-plagued parent-child relationship. Perhaps the middle-aged interviewers reminded the elderly respondents of their own children. Maybe the interviewers related to the respondents as they would to their own parents. Or perhaps the respondents thought of the young student interviewers as they would their grandchildren. It would be excellent methodologically to conduct studies to determine precisely what the impact of the interviewer's age is on the rapport of the interview, but at this point, we do not have enough research to enable us to answer the question in the case of the rural elderly study. Also, it seemed to me that the rural elderly respondents did not have much opportunity in the course of their everyday lives to talk with young people. They had very little contact with young people, the data showed that, so having a young interviewer show up and propose to talk for a couple of hours may have been a treat for the respondents. Thus, I decided to have young interviewers for the final wave of interviews with the very oldest respondents.

The rapport that seemed to emerge between the very old respondents and the very young interviewers came through strongly on the several field trips on which I dragged one or more of my children ages fourteen, ten, and eighteen. There was no question that introducing them to the respondents as my children who were interested in learning about all the experiences that had intervened since the last

interview in 1974 facilitated completing the interviews. The respondents were reluctant to turn interested young people away at the door. Besides, it was an exciting interlude and a change of pace.

Interestingly, my children taught me something about the methodology of doing interviews with frail, elderly respondents. Usually, my children would sit back
and take in the surroundings while listening with one ear. They would fill out a
back-up interview schedule as I went along through the interview, and at the same
time, they would make notes about the various items in the room, the photographs, and so forth. Also, they were in a very good position to observe the reactions of the respondent to the questions. Having another pair of eyes and ears
added to the quality of the data. But there were times when their help went beyond this level and as such opened my eyes to some real methodological problems
with doing field work with the elderly.

In one case, I and my fourteen-year-old daughter located a ninety-three-year-
old female respondent's home and knocked on the front door. There was no answer, so we went back to the cafe where we had just had breakfast and asked the
waitress what she thought of the situation. She said that it was probably too difficult for the respondent to get to the door, but if we could go shortly after noon,
then the cleaning person would be there and she would let us in. So we bid our
time by talking with an elderly neighbor who was the grandmother of a former
student of mine. It was fortunate that I remembered that this student, a well-
known runner, had come from the town we were in at the time. The grandmother
told us several stories about the respondent and her seeming eccentricities, especially her insisting that she could walk to church, setting out one Sunday, and
becoming confused and lost right in front of the grandmother's house. The grandmother then had to call one of the respondent's children who lived several miles
from the town and try to hold the respondent in her front yard until help arrived.

At the appointed hour, my daughter and I knocked, only this time we went to
the back door at the suggestion of the grandmother. The cleaning lady, a neighbor
in her mid-thirties, let us in, and I gave her the spiel. She asked us if we could wait
an hour as she had just drawn the respondent's bath. We went back to the restaurant and waited. When we went back, the neighbor decided to leave us alone with
the respondent, who was perfectly willing to be interviewed. It seemed to me at
the time that she was more than a cleaning lady in that she asked how long the
interview would take so she could return before we left. She obviously did not
want to leave the respondent alone after we left. It was nice to know that she
trusted us to take care of the respondent during the two hours that it took to do
the interview. However, much to my dismay, whereas the cleaning lady had no
difficulty making herself heard to the respondent, it became readily apparent that
the respondent was hearing every third or forth word which I spoke, if that. I
would ask a question, draw a blank, try again louder, and then the respondent
would start to talk about a topic unrelated to the question. After several bumbling
question-and-answer episodes, my daughter repeated a question. The respondent
heard it the first time and answered appropriately. She asked another question
with the same success. Because my daughter had the interview schedule in front
of her and had been through it so many times, I decided to let her conduct the
interview, which she did successfully. Apparently, the pitch of my voice was out of

the range of the respondent's compromised hearing, but the higher pitch of my daughter's voice hit the proper chords. Thus, I learned not to assume that hearing loss means that the interviewer needs to shout more loudly. In fact, shouting never, in my experience with the elderly, paid off with a quality interview. Rather, it is important to try different pitches in voice and to speak facing the respondent so he or she can read your lips.

GETTING TIRED

When respondents showed signs of fatigue or said they were tired, we stopped interviewing. Our plan in those situations was to resume interviewing sometime either later that day or the next day. Sometimes, we were able to do some work tracking down missing respondents or establishing dates of death for respondents whom we knew had died sometime between 1974 and 1986. In all cases of interrupted interviews, when we returned to complete the interview, we spent a considerable amount of time reviewing with the respondent what had been said. This is called "summarization technique" in interviewing.

In several cases, respondents were in very poor physical shape. Usually, there was a younger member of the respondent's family present to try to help us. This made field work both easy and hard. On the one hand, when the respondent inevitably tired, the family member would take over and answer with the respondent nodding or otherwise just looking on. This enabled us to come away with a complete interview. A disadvantage of this arrangement was that we might have been getting the perspective of the family member and not the respondent's.

We tried to anticipate this situation by asking all of the demographic questions of the family member and saving the attitudinal and opinion questions for the respondent, hoping that he or she would have the strength to do it. This worked very well. In one case, the respondent was bedfast and barely able to move, having suffered a paralyzing stroke. Her mind was intact but she appeared, at first glance, to be too sick to interview. She was living in her own small home just off the main street of a tiny town in the Ozark region of the state. Her granddaughter-in-law, around twenty-five years old, was there when we arrived around 3:00 in the afternoon. After seeing the condition of the respondent, I had pretty much decided to forget trying to do the interview. That was until the young woman urged me to do the interview. Her point was that intellectual stimulation would be good for the respondent and that she had the strength to do it. Since she spent all day with the respondent and her husband, the respondent's grandson, slept there every evening, I had no reason to doubt her. In fact, I greatly admired her dedication, given what I had learned about her role in the care of this infirm elderly lady who wanted above all to remain in her home until she died.

Thus it was with a mixture of confidence and trepidation that I and my fourteen-year-old daughter started the interview. We asked the young woman all of the demographic questions very slowly and deliberately, making sure that the respondent heard and understood them. At one point, the respondent interrupted the young woman and corrected a date. The respondent seemed to barely have the energy for the attitudinal questions. Here the young woman reasked them and helped us understand the respondent's answers, which at times were barely audible. I kept a close watch and asked the young woman repeatedly if we should stop. She replied that it had been a long time since she had seen her grandmother-in-law talk so much and with such enthusiasm. Of course, I would have had no way of knowing this since I did not share her long-term perspective on the respondent's everyday life patterns. However, I could tell that the young woman tried very hard to convey how the respondent felt about the issues posed by the attitudinal questions. I can recall asking the respondent about her attitudes toward death. These questions had a Likert-type response category of strongly agree, agree, neutral, disagree, strongly disagree. The respondent could only nod yes or no at this point. I came to the question "Death leads to something better than this life on earth." The respondent nodded yes, and the young woman interjected that the respondent was highly committed to her religious beliefs about the afterlife and on numerous occasions had reflected on how much she was looking forward to leaving this world for the next.

On the minus side, there was the case of a ninety-year-old respondent living in her own home with her retired sixty-five-year-old daughter. The home was larger and more luxurious than most of the respondent's homes I had visited. The daughter met me and my fourteen-year-old daughter at the door and was obviously reluctant to let us in. Here was one situation where the presence of my daughter made all the difference as I was able to convince her to just let us talk with her mother as we had traveled over 125 miles to learn something from her. She looked me over very suspiciously, then switched her gaze to my daughter, who was smiling expectantly. She let us in.

The respondent was mobile but completely house-bound and dependent upon the daughter. But she was completely intact mentally and even remembered the previous 1974 interview.

From the very first question, I could see the daughter trying to sway the respondent's thinking and even trying to take control of the interview. The daughter could see that the respondent wanted to do the interview and that it would have been difficult to get rid of us before its completion, so she was going to disrupt it as best she could. I asked the respondent if it would be possible for us to do the interview in private, but she declined. So the interview went from a bad start to a worse middle with the daughter literally answering for the respondent, despite my efforts to turn the table back to the respondent. Finally, the daughter got some factual answer wrong and the respondent corrected her. The daughter held her ground, and the respondent won out with more facts that the daughter could not deny. This was the turning point that saved the interview. The daughter, I learned later, had retired from a menial job and was a loner in the community. Her memory was not as acute as her mother's, that was for certain. From that point on, the respondent did the answering with a much chastened daughter piping up rarely.

Even though the daughter would have had difficulty evicting us, she could have tried it, which would have made it difficult, if not impossible, to complete the interview. Most important, we did not want to risk the respondent's fragile health or stimulate any conflict between her and her daughter. Fortunately, the respondent took the bull by the horns and did not become too fatigued in the process.

PUBLIC PLACES

Much of the field work, including several interviews, was conducted in public places, such as senior citizens' centers, libraries, funeral homes, restaurants, and county courthouses. One ninety-three-year-old woman, a practicing attorney, preferred to do the interview in her downtown law office during her normal forty-hour work week. Other interviews were conducted at senior citizens' centers, at times because respondents feared being alone with the interviewer but also because respondents spent a great deal of time at the center and were comfortable there. One day, I arrived at a most dilapidated house, which I knew the respondent had been renting. She peered at me and my fourteen-year-old daughter through a torn newspaper that was covering the glass on the front door. We talked through the closed door, and it seemed that she was unwilling to do the interview. My daughter knew from our visit earlier to the funeral home that the respondent spent most of the day at the senior citizens' center, so she asked her if it would be possible to do the interview at the center the next day. To my great delight, the respondent agreed immediately. It turned out that she was embarrassed about the clutter and general condition of her house, which explained why she did not want us to enter to do the interview. The center, while somewhat noisy, was a perfect solution to this problem, and we completed the interview successfully. In fact, because the respondent spent so much time at the center, we were able to observe firsthand her social network and the role that it played in her everyday life.

■ *Quality Control*

The quality of your observational data hinges on three important situations facing the field worker: (1) reactivity; (2) researcher sentiment toward the research subjects; and (3) focusing the many different observations to see if they validate or support one another.

REACTIVITY

Reactivity is a complex process that involves the effect that the researcher has upon the subjects as a consequence of observing, interviewing, and other research activities. Your very presence in the research setting changes that setting. If you had not entered the field and had not conducted observations, would the life and events that you recorded have been any different? Did your presence change the field in any way? If the answer is yes, then reactivity exists. The subjects have reacted to your presence, and this reaction makes the entire research situation different from what it might have been without your presence.

There is no methodological magic bullet to prevent reactivity. The best we can do is to try to minimize it. Fortunately, there is a technique that I call "touching base" that helps us assess the extent to which reactivity has affected the quality of our observations. However, there is no way that I am aware of at this writing that allows us to understand reactivity or the impact we have had on the setting itself. More will be said about touching base later.

RESEARCHER SENTIMENTS

I made the point earlier when discussing the problem of gaining entry into difficult field work settings that the exchange methodology was a powerful and successful approach. However, using it places the researcher in the precarious position of having to choose sides if the research setting is rife with interpersonal conflict and power struggles. That is one way that the researcher's sentiments or feelings toward the subjects enter the research equation. But there is a natural tendency for a researcher engaged in field work involving intense face-to-face interaction with people to begin to root for certain people and to look less favorably on others. It is part and parcel of being human, which, after all, researchers are. Sentiments of liking lead to increased interaction, which in turn increases the sentiments of liking. The end result is that during the long haul of field work, the researcher may begin to spend more and more time with some subjects and less time with others. Unless recognized, this perfectly natural tendency will impinge upon the quality of your observational data. One strategy that I have adopted during my own field work is something I call "get uncomfortable." Here, you force yourself to interact with people you may dislike and to observe in settings and situations that are distasteful to you personally. It is part of trying to stay reasonably objective, on the one hand, and of trying to keep the scope of the observations as broad as possible.

TOUCHING BASE

Returning to the problem of reactivity, we are faced with an inexorable force against which we can obtain only symptomatic relief. This is because we are unable to know enough about the research setting prior to our entry to describe or to analyze the impact we might have had on it because of our presence. But we can check our data in terms of the effect that any reactivity might have had on its quality. In essence, we are checking to see how valid our observations are. Recalling the principle of measurement, "Valid for what?", field observations ought to reflect social reality as seen through the eyes of the subjects. Thus, the symptoms of invalidity of observations or, in this case, of reactivity would be field observations and interpretations of those observations that the subjects would disagree with. Touching base involves sitting down with the subjects most directly involved with the particular observations being validated and discussing with them the essential features and interpretations contained in the observations. It is very important that confidentiality be maintained, so you should never report on what particular people said or did. Rather, you simply stick to general observational points, present them to the subjects, and see if the points make sense to them.

When I was observing the development of a comprehensive health center for the poor in a Chicano and Mexican-Indian community in a large southwestern city, I was fortunate to have met a very influential Chicano leader who must have seen some utility in taking me under his wing. I worked a bit at his candle factory, did some editing for him, and gave him one of my tape recorders. I lived for a brief time in his house along with his five children, wife, grandchild, daughter-in-law, and mother-in-law. The cultural nuances were very difficult for me to observe and record because I was a complete stranger to the community and because the Spanish spoken was a different dialect than the Spanish I had grown up with in Los Angeles. Touching base involved me getting some field notes together, making copies of them at the university across town, and blocking out names. I would sit with my informant and go over my more general recordings with him. Then I would ask him if I had observed the particular event or confrontation between a neighborhood resident and the medical director correctly. I even checked my interpretations, which I had bracketed in the field notes. After several sessions, my informant began to get the hang of what I was trying to do with my study, and I began to get a feel for the quality and accuracy of my observations.

FOCUSING DIFFERENT OBSERVATIONS

Say, for example, that you have been in the field for two weeks and that you have compiled dozens of lengthy field notes. These notes include observational reports and interviews. Suppose that one leader told you that the center director had offered him a job at the center and the same bit of information cropped up in several other interviews with other community residents. This should tell you that this particular piece of information is widespread but not necessarily that it actually happened. You have partial corroboration when your observations turn up repetitive information from widely scattered sources. It would be better to get your hands on documents, such as official memos or minutes of meetings where the job offer was discussed and recorded. If this was your good fortune and focusing different methods hit pay dirt, you would enjoy greater confidence in the quality of your observational data in terms of capturing the multiple realities accurately.

INTERNAL CONSISTENCY

All of the dates and other particular pieces of information should be consistent throughout the field notes. The notes should be edited for this type of consistency. If the chronology of events changes during the course of writing a long field note, you need to catch them and make the proper corrections. The spelling of proper names, sequences of events, and social networks, such as kin relations and friendship groups, are particularly difficult for the researcher to keep straight. Periodic checking is very important in order to avoid perpetuating errors.

FIELD NOTES

Field notes are the guts of observational research. This tool helps you to produce the primary data set from which you will conduct your inquiry into the research problem. The field notes is the record, on paper, of the observations made in the course of the field work.

These notes should contain: (1) a narrative of your entry into the research setting and the ongoing business of building and maintaining rapport and relationships; (2) methodological decisions as well as the strengths and weaknesses of those decisions; and (3) the events and conversations observed. These include conversations overheard and interview-like conversations. You should distinguish between direct quotes and paraphrases by placing the direct quotes in quotation marks. All of these notes should be dated and written in chronological order. In the final accounting, you should end up with a set of field notes in chronological order, from the first to the last written. Make several copies of all notes and store them in different safe locations (see the HyperQual section in the instructor's manual).

The observations of events and conversations should be in the form of discrete sets, each of which reflects a particular discrete phenomenon. For example, when I observed a neighborhood health center staff meeting, I would take brief notes as unobtrusively as possible on a small note pad. Waiting no more than two hours after the meeting, I would retreat to some private quiet place and write up the meeting in as much detail as possible. If the meeting was one hour, it would usually take two to three hours to write it up. I would put my name and date in the upper left hand corner, the title of the particular note (in this case, it was "Neighborhood Health Center (Name) Board of Directors' Meeting"), the location of the meeting, and the time from start to finish. When I was finished, I stapled the pages together, and thus was born a discrete field note.

When there was a physical setting that was relevant to the interaction being observed, I would draw a diagram. Meetings held in the same room time and time again require only one diagram, but if seating plays an important role and it changes, then a new diagram is called for. My study of faith healers required detailed diagrams because so much of what happened in the actual healing sessions was choreographed by the healers and their rather large staffs. The front stage and back stage interactions could not have been described adequately by me without the detailed physical layouts. For example, one world-famous healer used a fifty-thousand-seat round auditorium. The stage from which the healing took place was in the center, and she had assistant healers roaming through the audience. These assistants would usher the petitioners along the myriad aisles that all funneled into the center stage area. Thus, people were converging from all directions, giving the impression of a mass movement of souls seeking healing. The "staging" of the healing sessions depended so much on the physical structures that it was absolutely necessary to include detailed drawings of those structures as an integral component of the field notes. Once drawn, however, it was not necessary to redraw it for every session. If things changed a bit, I would photocopy the drawing and indicate the changes in red ink, incorporating then the revised drawing in that particular day's field notes. Just once during the study, I was able to conduct a face-to-face interview with the world-famous faith healer. I had heard second-hand that she was a very charismatic person in a one-on-one situation, as I had observed her to be certainly in a mass audience setting. Also, I learned in advance that her office was an entire floor of one of the elite hotels in the city. I remembered Peter New's course, where we had to observe rooms and then recall the most minute details such as the number of ash trays and the types of flowers in the vases. Also, I anticipated having to concentrate extra hard on the physical layout since her charisma would undoubtedly be a distraction to me. Just as I expected, the interview with her was so compelling that I had great difficulty observing the surroundings. This was a problem because she had a world-wide mission operation and a television, radio, and publishing empire all administered from that suite of offices. In short, I was in the nerve center of the most successful faith healer ministry in the United States, possibly even the world, with a once-in-a-lifetime chance to observe its physical administrative structure. It would have been a major loss to have come away without a good drawing of the layout, including her private office. Fortunately, the hours of drilling that Peter New put me through paid off, and I was able to capture the setting with good detail. In fact, the observations and diagrams were so vivid and interesting years later that Andrew Twaddle and I included the faith healer study in our book, *A Sociology of Health*.

In addition to the observational "facts," that is, the objective recording of what went on, from time to time I would insert my interpretation or some idea or hypothesis I might have gotten as I was writing up the note. These researcher memos should be put in parentheses or brackets. If you use a computer word processing program, which I urge you to do, the researcher material could be in bold-face type or italics. Whatever system you develop, be sure to include those decisions as well in your field note narrative dealing with the everyday methodology of the study. Documenting these decisions will pay off in spades later on down the line when you are trying to write a description of the methodology along with the reasons for doing things the way they were done. Just recently, I published a paper discussing the methodological problems involved with the twenty-year longitudinal study of the rural aged that I am currently wrapping up. I would not have been able to analyze these problems and to design solutions to them had I neglected to keep field notes on all of the methodological decisions made during the course of the study.

The HyperQual and Ethnograph computer programs are very useful for organizing field notes into document and analytic files and for retrieving data along concentrated or key word lines. HyperQual has a drawing feature. These programs are discussed in the instructor's manual.

■ *Analyzing Qualitative Data*

Now the problem before you is to wade through the chronological pile of field notes and to solve the research problem. Sounds fairly simple, as well it might be if you are extremely creative and have the gift of the sociological imagination. Unfortunately, most of us slog along with more modest gifts, which makes the task of analysis quite difficult. But there are several methodological tricks of the trade that we can use to make life a bit easier in this, the most exciting yet toughest stage of observational research.

HAWKING IT

The old adage that has to do with trees getting in the way of seeing the forest is what "hawking it" is all about. The analyst, buried in reams of paper containing descriptions and diagrams of hundreds of discrete actions, needs to extricate himself or herself from all this detail and break away from the views and perspectives of those individuals studied. Being in the field for long periods of time can lead the researcher to assume the perspective or dominant views of the subjects being observed. Or the wealth of detail can cause the researcher to think microscopically, thereby getting lost in details. Getting up above the fray, like a hawk, is very useful as a first step toward gaining a perspective or framework that will produce a sound sociological analysis of the research problem. Being a high-flying hawk gets you away from the details and widens the field of perspective. Consider the Nasca drawings in Peru: on the ground, they appear as massive lines without any discernible pattern, but from the air, they form precise drawings of animals. How do you get into this hawk mode?

Here we have help from Alvin Gouldner (1979), who defies us to be perverse. Take the predominant perspective, such as in the case of the neighborhood health center to be citizen participation and control of health care decision making, and turn this dominant view of social reality into a research problem unto itself. Be perverse by refusing to accept the view. Challenge it, in fact. Take none of the assumptions or perspectives contained in the field notes for granted. Turn them into problems.

In the case of the neighborhood health center study, all of the participants accepted the basic medical model, which was the primary goal and organizing principle of the health centers. This model is predicated on the idea that germs invade human defenses and make people sick. These infected people must go to allopathic physicians who are solely in charge of all decisions concerning what are now called patients. The medical model treats disease with medicine and the patient, it is hoped, returns to normalcy. From the hawk's view, I could challenge this model. Perhaps people had germs, but was that a primary organizing mission? Unemployment, child abuse, substance abuse, and poverty, in fact, were more pressing models than the medical one.

Now we were in a position to begin to think creatively and to see the struggle in a way that none of the participants really understood. Rather than accepting the view that citizen board members and doctors were fighting over issues of administrative efficiency and effectiveness of medical care delivery, we saw the struggle as one of the medical model versus the socioeconomic development model of "health." The world we had captured in our field notes was only a medical world on the surface. From above the fray, the hawk eye saw a political and economic world in which health care for the poor was secondary, perhaps one of several possible tools for change. The physicians were preoccupied doing what they were trained to do, and the citizen board members were working within the framework that the government and medical profession had provided. The centers were providing medical services at a supersonic clip, but the root cause of the health problems, the poverty of the people, essentially was unaffected by all the activity spun off through the medical model.

John Lofland (1984) has some tricks up his sleeve to help the less imaginative of us take advantage of the hawk's vantage point. It is one thing to step away from the notes and to try and see their content in some new totality, but it is quite another thing to develop terms or concepts that lend order and new sociological insight. He suggests that we use the metaphor as a means of creating these new concepts. What is the neighborhood health center context like? The *Queen Mary* sitting in a swamp? Factories producing health? The black sheep of medicine? A bridge to nowhere? Popcorn (lots of noise and steam not much nutrition)? Similarly, we can subject the faith healers to the metaphor machine. Going to a faith healer is W.C. Fields looking for loopholes in the Bible or the Barnum and Bailey of organized religion. And so it goes. The metaphor can be a powerful tool of conceptualization and analysis.

On a more mundane level, analysis of qualitative field note data demands a decent filing system. You must be able to retrieve information grouped or organized along analytically useful lines. For example, suppose you are working on a section of the analysis that has to do with conflict between board members and physicians at the neighborhood health centers. All instances of this conflict should be brought up out of all the field notes. Somehow the notes need to be filed according to the important categories. The best way to do this is to put your notes on a computer using any word processing program that allows you to do word searches and to dredge up all text with a particular label. This enables you to sort and view your notes any number of ways that you have determined by tagging the text with labels. All instances of conflict would be highlighted, so to speak, through word tags at the beginning and end of the appropriate text. Particular types of field notes would have their unique identifying tag, and so forth. Thus, in place of a physical filing system in which you would have to cut and paste the notes many different times and ways, the computer enables you to do this electronically. Laptop computers make it possible to type field notes out in the thick of things, away from your PC or mainframe computer.

In any case, your filing system should result in (1) labeled field notes that are central to the analysis; (2) the methodological decisions, problems, and so on; and (3) your interpretations, metaphors, wild ideas, and so forth. You should be able to print all the notes pertaining to a particular day, week, site, individual, or issue with the stroke of a key.

The analysis, according to M. Glazer (1978), involves a balance and interaction between data and researcher ideas. Half the pages written should be data and the other half the researcher's interpretation of the data. Unbalanced analyses are either terribly difficult to make any sociological sense out of because there is too much description and too little interpretation, or they are boring due to an absence of detailed field data. In this latter case, the reader misses the delightful antics and direct quotes and may even be denied understanding as to what went on in the research setting. Organize the analysis using subheadings derived from the concepts, then intersperse your interpretations with observational data and direct quotes, "quotable quotes," as Peter New used to say. Again, I recommend touching base with the people studied (some, not all) and with colleagues as well. You should show them what you have written and get some reactions prior to revising your thoughts and rewriting the analysis.

■ *Ethical Problems*

Qualitative research is no more prone to ethical problems than is survey research, but the closeness that invariably develops between researcher and subjects creates a heightened awareness of ethical dilemmas common to all forms of sociological research. Here we will discuss one particularly nettlesome and persistent problem, that is, the publication of findings and the manner in which this is received by the people studied. The researcher gains the cooperation and trust of the people, does the study, publishes the results, and incurs the wrath of at least some of those who made the research possible. The people who are angry feel betrayed. The findings do not reflect how they perceive the situation. The findings may be highly critical or, as Everett Hughes has argued, the dispassionate, objective sociological view of social life may strike people living that life as inaccurate or cold. More likely, the sociologist's interpretations might air dirty laundry that the people involved would rather the rest of the world not see. Let's look at some examples of the dirty laundry issue, and then we will discuss the ethical problems associated with it.

In one case, I had established a strong exchange relationship with a group of community residents who participated as full colleagues in the research decision-making. One part of this intensive community study involved face-to-face interviews with a sample of the residents. The survey turned up considerable concern over illegal drug use on the part of teenagers. The community made the bulk of its living from tourism and a public image of law and order. The community residents on the research committee opposed any disclosure of the drug problem and in fact were angry that our study had uncovered it in the first place. The citizens had a strong vested interest in what Erving Goffman called "impression management." They wanted to preserve the public image of a crime-free community where families were strong and children obedient to their elders. The publication of the drug use portion of the study would have blown the whistle on the charade. But then whose charade was it anyway?

Another example comes from the observational study of Plainsville by Carl Withers (1945). The late Noel Gist, a valuable colleague and dear friend here at the University of Missouri, told me one day that Plainsville was his boyhood home where he lived until enlisting in the service for World War I. He told me that almost everyone in the town had been angry and hurt by Withers's book. At the time he was doing the field work, Withers was considered harmless enough, albeit a bit of an oddball, according to Noel. However, once *Plainsville USA* was published, the townsfolk did not like how they and their town were portrayed. No one

BOX 9-1

■ *Qualitative Research*
The Sociology of AIDS

People the world over value health, perhaps more than any other quality of life. To lose one's health is viewed by most people as a major catastrophe. In the United States, illness heralds the grim possibility of socioeconomic ruination, the loss of the capacity to produce, and ultimately the spectre of death itself. Few events in life hit people as hard as deteriorating health does. Hearing the diagnosis of any chronic degenerative health condition is likely to produce intense feelings of fear, abandonment, and hopelessness in the patient, much more so than facing a divorce or loss of a job. AIDS is modern society's most feared health problem.

Once the victim has contracted the AIDS virus, there is no stopping the inexorable stigmatization, physical suffering, and eventually death. The vast majority of the victims are between the ages of twenty and forty-five and in the prime of their lives. The emotional and social impact is powerful and pervasive.

Given such intense emotions, it is difficult, if not entirely impossible, for a healthy social scientist to understand the victims' perspectives using survey research methodology. What is needed, at least at the beginning stages of research on AIDS victims, are qualitative studies that attempt to "see the world through the eyes" of AIDS sufferers.

Joseph Conrad captured in words how losing something very important must feel. In *Heart of Darkness*, he wrote of the profound sense of loss that the captain experienced when death threatened to cut short all he had worked for: "You can't understand. How could you?—with solid pavement under your feet, surrounded by kind neighbors ready to cheer you or to fall on you, stepping delicately between the butcher and the policeman, in the holy terror of scandal and gallows and lunatic asylums—how can you imagine what particular region of the first ages a man's untrammeled feet may take him into by the way of solitude—utter solitude without a policeman—by the way of silence—utter silence, where no warning voice of a kind neighbor can be heard whispering of public opinion? These little things make all the great difference. When they are gone you must fall back upon your own innate strength, upon your own capacity for faithfulness" (p. 122).

Karolynn Siegel and Beatrice Krauss (1991) used participant observation and focused, unstructured interviews to study the impact of AIDS on a group of gay men. They obtained long narrative accounts from the men about the problems they encountered as they tried to grapple with impacts that AIDS had on their lives. A review of the literature on chronic illness turned up several interesting theories that attempt to explain and categorize the adaptation to loss of health. This literature led the authors to focus on the problems that the AIDS-infected men had in coping with their illnesses. No attempt was made to generalize to all AIDS-infected individuals, nor did the authors claim that the problems discussed by the gay men were all-inclusive.

The focused interviews were tape-recorded and transcribed. The literature review and participant observational data allowed the authors to develop

Box 9-1 *continued*

qualitative coding categories that were refined as the coding of the interview data progressed. The code categories, such as restoration of self-esteem, personal experience with AIDS, search for meaning, aggressive attempts to control the illness, feeling stigmatized, and vigilance about one's physical health, were inserted into the computerized text of the appropriate interviews by a coder. Another coder went through a subsample of the coded text and recoded to see if there was agreement between different coders. If the two coders agreed, then the coded text was considered reliable data. If they did not agree, a third coder decided the issue. The end result was the text of the focused interview bracketed or tagged with various codes indicating that the part of the text in question was related to that particular code or topic. A software program similar to HyperQual was used to tag, store, and retrieve the text for analysis. The following themes emerged: "dealing with a sense of urgency to attain life goals, deciding to what extent to invest in the future, deciding to whom to disclose their infected status, feelings of shame and contamination, the need to take control of their health, preoccupation with their body and health, treatment decision making, and maintaining emotional equilibrium." Remember that these themes emerged only after the authors carefully studied the text organized and associated with the codes.

The authors then collapsed conceptually the above eight themes into three general "challenges" facing all of the AIDS victims studied. These were: (1) "dealing with the possibility of a curtailed life span (dealing with a sense of urgency to attain life goals, deciding to what extent to invest in the future); (2) dealing with reactions to a stigmatizing illness (deciding whom to tell about their infective status, dealing with feelings of shame and contamination); and (3) developing strategies for maintaining physical and emotional health (the need to take control of their health, maintaining appropriate vigilance about their health, treatment decision making, maintaining emotional equilibrium)."

The analysis centered around each of these general themes. The authors' strategy for a qualitative analysis of this sort was to discuss each general theme using quotes to illustrate the key points. For example, they used the first theme as a subheading for one part of the analysis. The subheading, "Dealing with the Possibility of a Curtailed Life Span," was followed by its definition derived from the perspectives of the AIDS victims themselves. In this case, the definition involved a belief that the disease was unpredictable and that their status could change from "well" (asymptomatic) to dead in a matter of weeks. Also, the men believed that they needed to "pick up the pace" in pursuing life goals because the timetable was so unpredictable and the disease so progressive. The authors included the following quote to illustrate this dimension of victim response to AIDS: "It's [being HIV-antibody positive] probably made me feel a little rushed in ways about doing . . . or accomplishing certain things, because I feel like my time has been cut down now."

learned this any harder than Art Gallaher when he went back to Plainsville fifteen years after Withers's book was published only to find a still smoldering, hostile citizenry. In Gallaher's own words:

> Problems involved in the restudy of a small, literate, community differ from those found in more conventional anthropological research. The people of Plainsville, for example, quickly made known their knowledge of West (Withers) and the first published report. Many remembered him with personal liking, but nearly all resented his book. I am convinced, however, that despite widespread conversational familiarity with the report few people have read it through. Those who have read it claim that, while essentially true, it emphasizes negative features of their culture. Many erroneously believe that West deliberately spotlighted them with ridicule, that he poked fun at their backwardness, or that the book was written for money. The question Plainsvillers most frequently asked us was "Why?" Why had they been studied in the first place? Why had the first book ever been published? Why had we selected their community for research? We tried to answer their questions accurately, but I am afraid that we were unable to communicate in a meaningful way to everyone the values supporting our research and the significance of it. . . . Our greatest problem was to establish a research role which would not identify us with the original research design and with West. This was not easy. We found, for example, that some people "naturally" identified us with the first researcher or assumed that I had come to check his findings. A few thought that I was going to investigate "scandals" mentioned in the first report.

These two examples illustrate an ethical problem with two edges to it. On the one hand, you have the possibility of your findings, because of the rich detail of qualitative data, harming the subjects directly through damage to their reputations or indirectly through damage to the reputation of the community. On the other hand, any censorship of valid scientific findings, whether researcher or community imposed, violates one of the basic tenants of social science. The deliberate suppression of knowledge is contradictory to the principles of free scientific discovery and the right that society has to view and to utilize scientific research findings.

There are no good solutions to this dilemma. I have used the exchange methodology and allowed the community residents who participated in the research decision making to exercise censorship if that is their chosen course of action. In the first case I mentioned above, it was clear to me that I should not fight their request to me to not to publish the drug use findings. The community members of the research group made a very strong case of irreparable harm, and I did not think that the benefits derived from going public with the finding outweighed the harm. Thus, I applied the least harm principle in this case. Withers, on the other hand, apparently did not interact with the community residents in any serious way about the purpose of the study and what he planned to do with the results. Had he set up a research group consisting of interested residents, perhaps he would have cast the findings in a slightly different light, one that was less negative as defined by the community residents. Censorship might have been applied in his case, too, had he established an exchange relationship with the community. In either case, censorship is the alternative to damaged reputations and a tarnished public image as far as sociology is concerned. Is full disclosure really such an important scientific value that one should do it at all costs? I think not. You have to weigh the costs. In the case of observational research, most of the time we are there doing the research not because the community or organization has asked us to do it, but because we want to do it. We are there by the good graces of the community, whose members can refuse to have anything to do with us. If more and more sociologists behaved as Withers did, then perhaps people would refuse to give any of us the time of day, in spite of our very best intentions.

The easiest way to head off the ethical problem of harming respondents is to establish an exchange relationship, thereby anticipating many of the sensitive matters that might arise during the course of the research. Censorship, under this condition, is negotiable. If I am convinced that the particular finding or paragraph under attack is absolutely essential for the solution to the research question, then I would go to bat for it and argue my case. The burden would be upon me to show the subjects that the potential harm to them was outweighed by the gains through disclosure. If the relationship is solid and based on mutual respect and trust, I stand a good chance of either getting my way fully or of striking a compromise of some sort. If sociology has any value to people, we should be able to start by convincing the people that its use is worth the effort. If not, then a deal is a deal and you simply have to be prepared to live with censored data. Who is to say that scientific knowledge is more important than privacy? We as scientists may say this, but I doubt that the nonscience public would agree.

■ *Conclusions*

Understanding social reality in all its richness of detail and depth of meaning, seeing things "through the eyes of others," is the primary goal of observational research. Often, observational studies generate theory and hypotheses for further research.

There are many roles that an observational researcher may take, ranging from pure observer to pure participant. Some balance between the extremes was recommended in order to maximize the opportunities to establish rapport and to gain enough empathy to facilitate deep understanding.

Gaining entry to the field is a real test of the researcher's interactive skills. He or she must anticipate the question from the observed, "What's in it for us?" The solution to this question is the key to getting in or not. A field journal should be kept to record the decisions make and the other circumstances surrounding entry. Exchange methodology, conscripting locals, face-to-face interaction, and knowing the cultural signs and symptoms of field work trouble are methodological principles and techniques that assist the observational researcher.

The quality of the observational data is affected significantly by reactivity, that is, the process of researcher influencing the subjects, changing the natural setting. "Going native" is one extreme form of reactivity where the researcher becomes a committed member of the group she or he set out to study. Controlling your sentiments as much as possible and touching base with informants and colleagues concerning how you are doing, whether your observations are on target and whether they are valid really helps to improve the quality of the data. Also, one can search for internal consistency in the field notes, a procedure greatly enhanced by computer technologies, such as HyperQual and Ethnograph (see instructor's manual), and by keeping field notes that are thorough and systematic.

Analysis of qualitative data is a brain teaser. You must get above the details of the field observations, documentary data, and so on, in order to discover patterns. A computer-assisted filing systems is recommended.

This chapter concludes with a discussion of an ethical dilemma common in observational research settings. This is the problem of objective recording and reporting versus the sensibilities and perceptions of the subjects. The researcher might be tempted to censor certain findings and, in some cases, probably should avoid disclosing information. Buy there are occurrences where the subjects are sensitive about something and the researcher does not share that view. Exchange methodology is one strategy for heading this problem off before the end of the study, when it is too late to do much about it.

GLOSSARY

field journal   distinct from field notes, a diary the researcher keeps describing all of the research decisions made during the course of an observational (or quantitative) study.

field notes   the data from qualitative observational research, involving narrative text written by the researcher reflecting the observations.

gaining entry   the decision process and actions taken by a researcher in the course of launching a qualitative or quantitative study. Entry involves establishing your legitimacy as a researcher in the eyes of the research subjects.

going native   a situation that could develop in the course of observational research where the researcher loses sight of the research role and becomes a full-fledged member of the group he or she is studying.

informants   individuals in the observational research setting whom the researcher can call on for help in gaining entry, interpreting qualitative data, and plotting data-gathering strategies.

naturalistic paradigm   a philosophical metamethodological position of which observational research is a component. This paradigm views subjectivity as the true social reality and legitimate objective of social scientific research.

observational research   a style of research usually employed with the case study design. The researcher attempts to see the social world through the eyes of the research subjects by taking on a role (ranging from pure observer to participant observer to pure observer) that will place him or her as close to the thinking and behaviors of the research subjects as possible.

reactivity   similar to the Heisenberg Principle in physics, where the very act of measuring something, for example, the light in an electron microscope, changes the object you are measuring. In the social sciences, reactivity involves the effect that the researcher has on the research subjects and setting. Reactivity would exist if the subjects and/or setting changes because of the actions of the researcher.

FOR FURTHER READING

Lofland, John. (1971). *Analyzing social settings: A guide to qualitative observation and analysis*. Belmont, Calif.: Wadsworth Publishing.

Wax, Rosalie. (1971). *Doing fieldwork: Warnings and advice*. Chicago: University of Chicago Press.

Part Four

DESIGNS FOR
DATA ANALYSIS

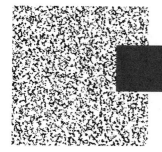

Chapter Ten

Coding and Data Management

■ *This chapter focuses on the principles of constructing a code book and the process of coding data. Common mistakes are discussed, and strategies for dealing with those mistakes are presented.*

This chapter is a practical guide through the thicket of data organization and data processing. The specific focus is on coding, which is the procedure for transforming data into forms that the computer is able to read and process. As simple as this appears, more research fails because of poor coding procedures and sloppy data organization than you or I would think possible.

This chapter first discusses some of the major principles of coding and data management. Next, some frequently made errors are presented. Finally, solutions to the mistakes are discussed.

Much of what you will read in this chapter is knowledge gained at the schools of trial and error and hard knocks. However, methodological principles of coding and data management that were taught to me by Ed Suchman, Peter New, David Ellison, Jiri Nehnevasja, and Alexander Humphries, S. J., are brought in to provide a systematic methodological framework.

■ *Principles of Coding and Data Management*

THE CODE BOOK

The code is a number system for quantitative data that denotes variables representing concepts. The book listing these codes and their respective variables is called a **code book**. Without question, write a code book! I emphasize this because modern computer programs have made it easy for the researcher to enter the data directly into the computer using an "internal" coding system.

237

The researcher might have dozens of interview schedules chock full of information gathered in the course of face-to-face interviews. The schedules contain many questions with response categories that represent the answers to the questions. The data at this level of the research process consist of lots of different words either preprinted with check marks made after them or written down by the interviewer.

Coding is the process of giving each response a unique number according to the "code" that tells the researcher which numbers go with which responses. For example, the concept gender, expressed by the words *male* and *female,* can be turned into a numbering system where the number 1 represents female and the number 2 indicates male. The code is the numbers 1 and 2. The code book is all of the codes for all the variables making up the data to be analyzed. In analysis, it is the numbers that are run through the computer, and the meanings of those numbers are contained in the code book.

Unfortunately there are data base programs that allow the researcher to load the codes into the computer without the use of a code book. This may seem to be more efficient, but it carries a price in the long run. Specifically, a code book is recommended because it allows the researcher to share the data with other researchers, plus it makes verifying the accuracy of the data entry easier. These fancy computer data bases allow the researcher to re-create the items or questions along with the response categories. The computer will then take the researcher through the questionnaire or interview schedule item by item. For example, question one would appear on the screen, and the researcher would type into the computer the appropriate code representing the answer that is being coded. The computer asks for the coded responses for each question, and the researcher reads the completed questionnaire and enters the appropriate codes.

This system makes it difficult to obtain a precise understanding of what the codes are. In the absence of a code book, the researcher must rely on a summary of the data base that only tells what the variable names are, where the variables are located, the size of the variable fields, and whether or not the variables are alphabetic or numeric. Also, code books can be duplicated and sent to other researchers along with a copy of the data. This facilitates collaboration and is an important part of the scientific enterprise. The data base is too vague to be of much use to other researchers in this sense.

One last reason for advocating the code book is that it is less cumbersome and more in tune with the safekeeping of the primary data, that is, the questionnaires or interview schedules, to check the coding from code sheets as opposed to the actual data forms. In other words, if I used the data base approach and as a result did not have a code book or the resultant code sheets, then I would have to pull out all the questionnaires in order to check the accuracy of the coding. The codes in the computer need to be checked against the original data source.

CODE BOOK FORMAT

The code book should have a little page that includes the name of the study, the key researchers responsible for the study, their affiliations, and the code book's publication date. Next, the identification number for the respondent should be given. If you have seventeen hundred respondents, then you will need four columns for this variable. The computer is organized by columns, with each column having ten spaces for a number. In other words, column one could have any number from zero to nine in it. Remember that the numbers that are placed in the columns are codes for specific data.

It is up to you the researcher to tell the computer what a file will look like, that is, what the complete data for a respondent will look like. It is best to set it up so that a file goes to the eightieth column and then continues on a new line. It might take several lines, each 80 columns long, to hold all the data for one respondent, but that is better than one line 320 columns long. The reason for this is that eighty-column lines make it easier to read your data on the computer screen because most screens will hold only eighty columns of data at one viewing. Remember to start each new line with the identification number of the respondent whose data is on the line above the new line. This will enable you to keep the right data with the right respondents.

The next thing that should appear in the code book is the first item (variable), then the second, and so on until the last item to be coded is reached. Each item has one or more unique columns on a unique line, which makes it possible to locate each and every variable stored in the computer. For this reason, we are able to describe a variable in terms of its location (the column number) and the "variable width" (the number of columns containing the variable: "variable width − 1"). If we started out using four columns for the identification number (one number in each column), then the next variable, if one column wide, would be located in column five and so on down the line. The following is a sample of what we have discussed so far about the composition of the code book.

Code Book for the Study of the Rural Elderly
University of Missouri-Columbia
Department of Sociology
Richard M. Hessler, Principal Investigator
August 1989

Columns 1–4: Respondent Identification Number (code exact number)

Column 5: Q. 1 "What is your current marital status?"

1 ____ Married
2 ____ Widowed
3 ____ Divorced
4 ____ Separated
5 ____ Never married
9 ____ No response

Notice that the 9 code represents a nonanswer, so to speak. This is missing data, that is, the code 9 is of little or no analytic use to the researcher beyond keeping track of the refusal rate for each question. It is wise to keep the 9 code reserved for no response for each variable, where no response is appropriate.

Some variables, like the identification number, will require more than one column to get the data coded. Here, the variable width is greater than one. As was the case for the identification number, where the four columns represent one variable, so might other variables be represented by more than one column. In other words, it is not a one column/one variable situation. Along this line, an important principle of coding is to code the data in the most "raw" form possible. If you have birthdate, then code the entire birthdate, rather than having a code number representing some age group. For example, if "age of the respondent" was the next question in the questionnaire, then the next item in the code book might look like the following:

Columns 6 – 11: Q. 2 "What is your birthdate?" (code exact birthdate month, day and year, e.g., 082541, which is Aug. 25, 1941; 999999 = No response).

A less desirable approach is to group age into categories and then to code the categories. This might look like the following:

Column 6: Q. 2 "What was your age on your last birthdate?" (code the grouped age)

1 _____ 20–29 yrs. old
2 _____ 30–39 yrs. old
3 _____ 40–49 yrs. old
4 _____ 50–59 yrs. old
5 _____ 60–69 yrs. old
6 _____ 70–79 yrs. old
7 _____ 80–89 yrs. old
8 _____ 90 and over
9 _____ No response

The general idea behind coding data in its most basic form is that you are able to turn raw data into grouped data but not the other way around. Once the data is coded as grouped data, you are stuck with those groupings. From the grouped ages above, I would only be able to get the mean code number statistically, e.g., 5 or 6. If the mean code was 5, that would tell me that the average group was 60 to 69 years of age but I would not be able to calculate the average or mean age of the respondents. However, if I had coded the exact age (using three columns for the exact age), the mean age would be no problem to obtain.

Remember that each new line of data must begin with the respondent identification number. Assume that the first line ends with column 80. The code book might look like this:

Column 80: Q. 36 "Death is peaceful"

1 _____ Strongly agree
2 _____ Agree
3 _____ Disagree
4 _____ Strongly disagree
8 _____ Don't know
9 _____ No response

Coder: Start a new line

Columns 1–4: Respondent identification number

CODING OPEN-ENDED QUESTIONS

Open-ended questions—where the responses are written out on a few blank lines—are difficult to quantify in the sense of turning the sentences into coded numbers. The trick is to write each response on an index card, then sort the responses according to whichever broad categories seem to emerge. Try to write fewer than nine code categories that would cover all of the responses (the categories are exhaustive) and where any given response could be placed in one and only one category (the categories are mutually exclusive).

In a study of cancer screening, I asked the people who had come to a cancer center to be checked over for any signs of cancer to describe their philosophies of life. The question read: "Tell me about the principles which govern your life, your philosophy of life."

As you can imagine, we had a difficult time figuring out the common themes in the answers by one hundred people. But there were several themes that allowed for the development of code categories. These categories were:

1 ____ Live life one day at a time
2 ____ Serve others
3 ____ Try to maximize your potential
4 ____ Compete to win
5 ____ Plan for the future
6 ____ Seek pleasure, avoid pain
7 ____ Serve God
9 ____ No response

Now it is a simple matter of reading each response for this item in the questionnaire and then deciding which of the above seven categories best fits the response. If there are several sentences representing a rather lengthy answer, then code the first sentence or idea. Here, the thinking is that the respondent will mention the most important idea first, then move on to the next most important, and so on down the line. Recall the two principles of measurement (Chapter 3 p. 58), mutual exclusivity and exhaustiveness: the same two principles apply to designing open-ended or qualitative code categories. Any given response should fit into at least one of the code categories (exhaustive), and it should fit only one of the categories (mutually exclusive).

Of course, you could use two columns for the item, in which case you would have ninety-nine code categories to play with. Given the fact that in my study there were only one hundred respondents, a two-column variable would enable me to assign a unique code to each and every response. I would end up with a two-column variable with ninety-nine categories, impressive in its scope but impossible to do anything with in the analysis. It is generally better to stay simple in the sense of seeking fewer code categories, rather than more. With ninety-nine categories, you will pay the price when you try to make sense out of the responses in the analysis.

On a final note concerning the code book: I strongly recommend that you write the first draft of the code book in pencil. Once the code book is complete, then sit down with a code sheet and code several questionnaires. Make the inevitable changes necessary in order for the coding to work smoothly before typing up the code book. Once typed, you might want to produce just enough copies for the coders, because there will be more changes once the coding starts in earnest.

MANAGING THE CODING

Coding usually is a team affair, especially if large numbers of cases need to be coded over a couple of hundred variables. No one coder has the stamina to code, say seventeen hundred cases within thirteen lines of data for each case. This is what the 1966 wave of interview data on my study of the rural elderly produced.

In this study, I had to hire and train a dozen coders with the goal of having them work forty hours per week doing nothing but coding all of the interview schedules. Several important methodological principles pertain to carrying off this difficult stage of the research. The rest of this section explores these principles.

CREATE A GROUP COMMITMENT TO THE STUDY: CODER SELECTION

Coding fundamentally requires sound judgment on the part of the coder. Coding is an interpretive act because the coder must identify with the respondent well enough to be sure of the meaning behind a given response, then interpret the appropriate code category before assigning a response to a category. There is no doubt in my mind that a good coding job starts with the coders being so familiar with the objectives of the study and the measurement goals of each question that interpretation is uniform and almost automatic. The best way I have found to reach this uniformity of interpretation is to build a real group with strong understanding and commitment to the study by the coders.

One does not build a group with just any old building materials. In order to have a viable group among the coders, I had to be very selective with the characteristics of the people I hired. I decided to select people with a service commitment to the rural elderly. I chose medical students and sociology graduate students who had come to me over the past couple of years requesting research experiences in gerontology. Some of these students had worked for me as interviewers on the study of the rural elderly. Interviewing experience on the study was excellent background for coding.

So, I started with coders who had an intellectual interest and commitment to the research, plus some of them even had interviewing experience, which made the study all the more familiar to them. All things being equal, there is no substitute for intellectual interest and commitment.

CODER TRAINING

I used that commitment first by having the coders read several key papers on the research problem we were working on, namely the precursors of mortality of the independently living rural elderly. This reading included the grant proposal that led to the funding of my study and contained the statement of the research problem along with a focused literature review. The first training session, then, involved a discussion of the substance of the research through a review of the reading material. I made sure that the coders were aware of the analysis we planned to conduct on the data. This first training session planted the seed in the minds of the coders that they were colleagues involved in intellectually challenging and important work. It gave them the clear idea that what they did in the coding really mattered and that they could not be too careful.

The second training session was devoted to going through the interview schedule item by item. Here, I defined what each item was intended to measure. For the interviewers, this was rehashing old ground, but they saw it through as a refresher course. One point I stressed was to take the key items involved in the main analysis plans and go over with the coders how these items would be used. For example, theory and other studies had shown me that social networks would play a prominent role in the mortality rate. Thus, I carefully went over all of the variables that comprised the social network concept and even produced a hypothetical analysis using those variables. The trainees were encouraged to ask questions about the substance of the items, the concepts that the items were designed to measure, and the analysis plans.

Before the third training session, I wrote a guide for the coders that stressed the importance of the task at hand and of working as a team. Then I laid out the ground rules for the coding work. These included the daily operating procedures, such as when work started and ended, the liberal policy concerning breaks (take often and/or as needed), retrieving and refiling interview schedules and code sheets, strictly adhering to the confidentiality promise I had made to the respondents, and so forth. The most important point in this document was one that forced the coders to act as a group.

■ *The Sociology of Coding*

COMMUNICATION AND DOCUMENTATION

Every three days during the first couple of weeks of coding, we held a meeting with all the coders to have an open discussion of our work. This was designed to be a forum for airing grievances over the work and to discuss substantive problems with the coding itself. Associated with this point, the coders were asked to communicate verbally with me and with one another any time a problem with the coding was encountered. For example, if coder A was unable to fit an open-ended response into one of the existing code categories, all of the coders would be informed of the problem along with me. A collective decision would be made on the spot, and I would write up the problem and the solution, which was added then to the code log, a document that all the coders received and had to read daily before starting to code. The log grew daily for the first couple of weeks as the problems with the code book emerged and were ironed out. Eventually, we perfected the code book by resolving all the coding problems. A final version of the code book was printed and used by the coders for the remainder of the coding. Many extra copies were run off in order to send them out to researchers who might want to use the data. The log became one of several documents that described the methodological decisions of the study. This was part of the paper trail, called documentation, which any good research project will have. It lets all other researchers know exactly what you did methodologically and why you did it.

MORALE

Morale was perhaps the next most important factor affecting the quality of the coding, given the backgrounds and intellectual interests of the people selected to code. I made sure that, as study director, I was present in the office at all times as long as coding was progressing. Also, I coded right along with the hired hands. This gave me insight into the quality of the code categories and the overall quality of the data. This conveyed to the other coders the impression that I was seriously committed to the coding and that I would not ask the coders to do something that I would not do.

PROFESSIONALISM

Another strategy for improving morale was to pay coders the going rate for interviewers. Give the coders a professional salary along with allowing them enough autonomy to make decisions, and they will respond as professionals. Situations defined as real are real in their consequences (W. I. Thomas and Florian Znaniecki, 1918). Expecting professional work is an important step to ensuring that professionalism exists. Having a sense of being a professional and being part of something important is a great morale booster.

PERSONAL RELATIONS

Frequent breaks and lots of one-on-one conversations with the coders are very important for maintaining morale. Personal problems will crop up, and the sensible project director will be there and have a close enough relationship with the coders to discuss those problems. The project director should really care about the coders as individuals, convey that caring to them, and consistently be available to handle problems as they arise. There is no substitute for genuine interest in the welfare of your staff. Loyalty paid is loyalty returned. Try to have social gatherings occasionally after work. You might think about budgeting enough money to cover gifts or social occasions as important symbols of the coders' importance. Be sure to write individual letters of recommendation for your coders once they have successfully completed the work. Remember, your data is only as good as your coders.

RELIABILITY OF CODING

If you are preparing a budget and plan for coding for the first time, the chances are pretty good that you will make the same mistake that I made in my first quantitative study. I budgeted only enough time and money to do the coding once. Once is enough, I thought. I know that I was perfectly happy to have finished the coding after eight weeks of nonstop work by ten coders. At the time, the thought of re-doing the coding never crossed my mind. Just be as careful as possible and trust that your coders do an accurate job. This was the easy way out, and I should not have taken it. I should have done the coding again, at least for a sample of the respondents and coders. The reliability of the coding, that is, the extent to which a second coder would get the same results as the first coder, cannot be taken for granted.

The way to ensure that the coding is reliable is to have the coders code behind each other. This should be done early in the coding and be repeated periodically enough so that you end up with at least 20 percent of the interviews or questionnaires recoded. For example, stop the regular coding after the first week. Start Monday by distributing once-coded questionnaires to different coders and have them coded. Mark the completed code sheets indicating they are recodes, and while the coders continue with the coding of virgin questionnaires, compare the duplicate code sheets. Note the discrepancies, then check the questionnaire to define the discrepancy and to resolve it. A mistake might have been made by one of the coders, or perhaps both of the coders were incorrect. The discrepancy can be due either to a misinterpretation or writing down the wrong number. The coder who made the mistake would get a mark for each mistake. The research director should keep track of the total number of errors, as well as the source of those errors. If one or more coders has a large percentage of the mistakes, the study director needs to get the coder aside and determine the reason for the problem. Perhaps the coder was unclear about a particular variable and what it meant, but it is also possible that the coder has a problem with concentration or judgment. In any case, the researcher must head off any systematic errors quickly before they become numerous.

If one coder tends to have more of the mistakes than the other coders, then it would be wise to check all or most of that coder's work. Similarly, a coder who seldom makes a mistake does not need to be checked as frequently as the coders who make more mistakes. Above all, keep careful records (documentation) of all the recoding. Study the record for any patterns, such as one or two coders contributing to the bulk of the mistakes or mistakes centering around particular items in the questionnaire. If one or two items consistently cause differences among the coders (intercoder reliability is low), there is fire there and something needs to be done quickly. Perhaps the coding categories are not mutually exclusive or exhaustive, or maybe the training missed the mark on that item of the questionnaire. Whatever the cause, you have a problem that the study director and all of the coders need to discuss.

DATA ENTRY

The coded data need to be entered into the computer. It is possible to code the data onto optical scan sheets and then feed them directly into the computer, but this is not as simple as it appears. Scanning is not error-free, nor is it easy to find the errors once they occur. It is more time-consuming and labor intensive to physically have a person or persons type the coded numbers into the computer, but it is worth the extra effort. Basically, **data entry** involves having a person sit down at a computer terminal and type in line after line of data, saving it as he or she goes along. Any number of individuals can do this task, which requires good typing skills along with a careful attitude and approach. One should not pay by the line but rather by the hour at a senior secretary level. Make sure that the terminal keyboard is at a comfortable height and that the chair offers good support and comfort. Much as been written recently about the hazards of spending long hours working on a computer keyboard, and this literature, much of it published in medical journals, should be reviewed before purchasing chairs and designing computer work stations.

DATA MANAGEMENT

Once the data are entered, it is time to check the reliability or accuracy of the entry process. This takes two people. One person reads the code sheet, and the other reads a computer printout of the **data set.** In other words, you would have two documents to compare. One is the computer output of the data as it has been entered into the computer. This should be lines of numbers, each one maximally eighty columns long. Each line on the computer output should have its counterpart on the code sheet somewhere. The lines of data in the computer should match the lines on the code sheet for each respondent. Thus, one person reads out loud while the other person compares. One person can read aloud for a while and then switch with the other person. Nor does it matter which data set is read aloud, as long as the two readers are on the same line and column. This requires that periodically the person reading aloud take stock of which line and column he or she is on and let the other reader know this. Mistakes are circled in red and later corrected on the computer. If the coding has been verified, then all mistakes at this level should be errors with entering the data. The data entry person might have seen a 6 when it was in fact an 8. The 6 was typed into the computer and was caught when 8 was read from the code sheet while 6 was found on the computer sheet. I suggest that you make a copy of the data files on the computer before you make any corrections to the computer data. Once all the corrections have been made and checked again, then you can delete the backup copies and make new backup copies.

BACKUP DATA AND STORAGE

Be sure to make photo-copies of the code sheets and all the documentation on the data processing. Regarding the computer data, the single biggest mistake you can make is to have only one copy of the data stored in the computer. The chances of losing the data off a hard disk in a large computer is remote, but it does happen. The best safeguard is to **back up** the data set by making at least two copies of it. One copy can be stored in the computer, but the other should be put on magnetic tape or disk. In fact, it is a good idea to have three copies, one in the computer, or on disk, and the other on a magnetic tape. The disk can be stored in a safe place, either in your office or home, but the magnetic tape should be kept at a computer center in conditions of controlled humidity and temperature. Also, split up the location of the copies of the code sheets, perhaps keeping one in the office and the other at home. The original or source data, namely the questionnaires or interview schedules, must be kept under lock and key in a place safe from the weather and fire. A fireproof box is a very good investment. I remember all too vividly the horrific Bel Aire fire in Los Angeles in 1961 in which scores of students at Mount St. Mary's College lost all of their research work, including one master's candidate who lost her entire thesis as well as the original data. Had she stored the data and thesis in two separate locations, or had she put the thesis and data in fireproof boxes, she might have avoided the disastrous loss of her work.

If the study has potential for other researchers using the data, then it is important to go the archive route. This entails contacting one of the social science data archives, such as the University of Michigan Consortium, and arranging for the electronic as well as mail transport of your data, code book, and other documentation. For a fee, other researchers then can get a copy of your data, code book, and documentation in order to do their own analyses. This is a valuable service scientifically, because other researchers working on the data allows cross-checking of the validity of the findings and improves the chances that the data will be fully exploited. Different researchers bring varying perspectives along with new ideas for analyzing the data. This is an effective pathway to the discovery of new theory. Finally, if your data set is anything but squeaky clean and error-free, you will hear about it from other users. Archival storage forces the researcher to clean as many of the errors out of the data as possible. While the researcher might get away with lots of coding errors if only he or she is analyzing it, public scrutiny through archive usage makes it impossible to "hide" sloppy coding and data processing generally. This is a real advantage from the perspective of one interested in building public confidence in the social sciences, and it meets the goal of public verification, one of the criteria of science that we discussed in Chapter 1.

How the data are stored in the computer can be a real headache if the following simple rules of thumb are not followed. First, there is no substitute for a clear plan of analysis. If you have a concrete plan as to which variables you will analyze and now that analysis will happen, then you have taken the first step in deciding what the computer files should look like physically. Generally, you want to be able to label all the variables with as little typing possible and you want the variables to be analyzed in one and the same data file. Because of this rule of thumb, it is advisable to have complete data sets and to not link different data sets. In other words, if I have a complete data set for the 1966 interviews done on the rural elderly respondents, I will want a different data set to contain the 1974 interviews. Even though there is considerable overlap of information, for example, birthdate, gender, Social Security number, and place of birth, it would be a mistake to leave these out of the second 1974 data set. In other words, if I made the mistake and left out birthdate, figuring that it was in the 1966 data set, I would have to call up the 1966 data set every time I wanted to run age against any of the variables in the 1974 data set. This is a very cumbersome method of data management. It is much simpler to recode all of the 1974 data or variables, including those variables that are duplicated in the earlier data set. Thus, I would code birthdate, and so on, assuming these were asked again in 1974. Even if they were not asked, which would also be a mistake (a missed opportunity to verify the reliability of the data), I would enter the variables knowing I would be using them in the analysis of the 1974 data set. In short, avoid linked data sets in favor of complete sets that can stand on their own.

■ *Conclusions*

Coding and data management challenge the researcher to be both a technician and a good social scientist. Just as in writing a short story, there are two worlds to master. One is the realm of technique, that is, the specific "how to" knowledge. Here, the techniques have been worked out by others, and all the researcher needs to do is select the right one. There is very little judgment involved once the technique is set in motion. On the other hand, there exists the nebulous world of "art" and the creative side of work. This is where social science principles come into the picture. There is much more to coding than simply following the best techniques for doing it. As we saw, quality coding is the result partly of the result partly of the researcher's creative talents in creating a group of coders with a consensus about what needs to be done and how to do it. The art is in using your best judgment as to how to motivate the coders to do the best coding job possible.

   Coding is inherently a matter of judgment. Thousands of times the coder will decide which of the categories is "the best one." Techniques go only so far. Ultimately, the coder will have to become an artist seeking to get the best fit for the data. Where one code category would work, another would be even better in the sense of best representing what the researcher intended. This creative artistic side of coding is best dealt with through group processes, rather than through coding techniques themselves. A sense by the coders as to what the study is about is as important to quality coding as a precisely written code book. Morale is as important as method.

GLOSSARY

backup   a must for any data analyst, this process involves making a copy of the data. Copies may be stored on diskettes, hard drives on PCs, and magnetic tape.

code book   a documentary tool of analysis that identifies the number system for quantitative data (code) and the variables that the numbers represent.

coding   the process of applying the code book to an interview schedule or questionnaire in order to translate the responses into numerical representatives.

data entry   the mechanical process of getting the numbers (code) into a computer file.

data set   usually the same as a file on the computer, involving all of the respondents and variables in numerical form, which constitutes a coherent analysis package, for example, respondents who died between the 1966 and 1974 interviews.

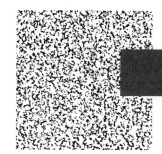

Chapter Eleven

DATA REDUCTION AND ANALYSIS

■ *This chapter begins with a review of the principles of measurement and analysis planning and then covers the methodological principles behind turning data into analyzable forms, coding of qualitative and quantitative data, and strategies for analyzing data. PC and mainframe computer use and interaction are discussed.*

Describing and explaining the social world are the two main strategies of analysis. This chapter covers both of these strategies from a practical "tricks of the trade" perspective. It begins with a discussion of the nature of social data and ways of "reducing" or transforming data into forms amenable to analysis. Next, the two basic forms of analysis, description and explanation, are defined. Descriptive analysis is broken down further into quantitative strategies and qualitative methods. On the explanation side, the chapter presents the issue of statistical versus substantive significance (Gold, 1969), the elaboration model, and how to set up contingency tables to meet the demands of sociological explanation.

■ *The Nature of Sociological Data*

I have vivid memories of my first sociology course in college. I remember feeling intimidated by the professor who had earned his Ph.D. at Harvard University working with Talcott Parsons. He made what to me in the early going of the course were obscure points couched in a language only slightly more comprehensible than Latin. However, one of the very first things he said to the class was bell clear. I can recall his exact words, which were "Data never speak for themselves." At the time, I had visions of data empowered with the ability to speak but some mysterious reason refusing to say what was on their minds. Along the lines of this false

251

impression, one of my colleagues not too long ago read me a review of his paper that had been submitted to a prestigious journal. This reviewer wrote "The data are crying out for logistic regression analysis." My colleague responded, "I have never heard data cry." I too have never heard data speak nor had I heard anyone speaking on their behalf. I guess it was my own lack of experience with data and what they did or did not do that led me to raise my hand for clarification. I will share with you the essence of my professor's response.

Data have no life outside of research. For something to be called data or fact, it must complement or fit into some system of research and explanation. All the comings and goings of the neighbors is not data unless someone has systematically recorded this activity for a specific research question. Merely pointing out that fifty-five people oppose abortion under any conditions is not data without some systematic way to understand who those people are and why they feel the way they do. In the absence of research, it is merely activity or numbers.

Data are creations of researchers. The raw materials are the everyday activities of human beings, but data are the end product of research into the why and how of those materials. By their very existence, data are spoken for. Contained within data are categories, even whole theories, representing carefully crafted methodical explanations.

QUANTITATIVE DATA

When a hospital organization or war protesters are measured and turned into numerals and numbers, the end product is called **quantitative data**. *Quantitative* means that some standard of measurement is applied uniformly or equally to all the cases under investigation. In the case of the protest movement, one might interview many individuals about their attitudes toward the government's peace initiatives. The answers would be standardized in some fashion and transformed into a code where numbers represent words. The following is an example. In response to the question "How satisfied are you with the government's efforts to end the war?", you could have the following answer categories:

1. Very satisfied

2. Somewhat satisfied

0. Neutral

4. Somewhat dissatisfied

5. Very dissatisfied

The numbers in front of the answer categories would be the codes used to represent the answers, and all questions with the same answer categories would be coded the same. Thus, a 5 always would represent "very dissatisfied," and so forth. These numbers are quantified data, that is, they are numerical representations of what are, in this example, attitudes. Discrete numbers represent categories that should not be added or subtracted, such as marital status, gender, or religious affiliation. Continuous data are numbers that stand for things that can be added or subtracted, such as income, age, height, and so forth. Another way to think about this distinction is as the difference between numerals, a conventional use of numbers to represent some category, and numbers that belong to mathematics.

Numbers can be used to describe the answers, at the simplest level, such as what percent of the respondents were neutral versus vehemently dissatisfied. Or more complex analyses could be performed where you would attempt to explain why men with college educations were more dissatisfied than their female counterparts. Statistics such as the percent agreeing with some response category or the difference in life satisfaction expressed by men and women are how quantitative data are used in sociological research. There will be more on this later.

QUALITATIVE DATA

Textual representations of interviews, observations, letters, and diaries are only a few of the many different types of **qualitative data**. The term *qualitative* means that the data are not reduced to numbers, added, or subtracted. In fact, there usually is no statistical analysis with qualitative data. Where statistical counting gives the researcher standardization and allows the analysis of large numbers of cases, qualitative data gives the researcher depth of understanding in terms of the inner workings of human organizations, the behind-the-scenes action that one can learn about only with time-consuming careful observations and interviewing away from the laboratory or fixed-choice interview schedules.

Trying to see everyday life through the eyes of other people, walking a mile in their shoes, taking the role of the other, are a few expressions describing a basic principle underlying qualitative data. That is, qualitative data provides a level of understanding more comprehensive and, perhaps, even more accurate than number-counting yields. Bronislaw Malinowski, one of the truly great qualitative methodologists of all time, wrote tellingly to anthropologists about the need to develop qualitative techniques. In his words:

> With this we are demanding a new line of anthropological fieldwork; the study by direct observation of the rules of custom as they function in actual life. Such study reveals that the commandments of law and custom are always organically connected and not isolated; that they only exist in the chain of social transaction in which they are but a link. I maintain that the staccato manner in which most accounts of tribal life are given is the result of imperfect information and that it is in fact incompatible with the general character of human life and the exigencies of social organization. A native tribe bound by a code of disconnected inorganic customs would fall to pieces under our very eyes (1926; pp. 125–126).

Malinowski is arguing that only through direct qualitative observation will we be able to grasp the complete picture of a social organization with all of its interconnected complicated parts. In short, he is saying that qualitative data gives the researcher a more complete and accurate picture. What you give up in terms of scope, you gain in understanding. Put another way, the more quantitative the measurement, the more superficial the knowledge.

■ *Purposes of Analysis*

The twin purposes of sociological **analysis** are to describe and explain. Although different in technique, both types of analysis share the same general purpose, which is to discover the inner workings of society. Description and explanation combined enable the researcher to find the social laws that help answer such questions as "How is society possible?", "Why do individuals who participate in formal organizations live longer than individuals who do not?", or "Why is winning the primary value of revenue-generating intercollegiate athletics?" Discovering the answers to these and other fundamental sociological questions is the challenge of sociology and is what drives researchers to put in the enormous effort it takes to gather data and analyze it.

DESCRIPTION

The following passage from Malinowski (1926) is an excellent example of what good descriptive analysis of qualitative data is about. No researcher has the time or the energy to describe everything observed or even recorded. For example, assume that you have observed a group of fans at a World Cup soccer match. The observation occurred over a four-hour period and you generated eight pages of field notes, single spaced. Giving someone the full text of the field notes as your descriptive analysis would violate the methodological rule that we began this chapter with, namely that data never speak for themselves. You are obligated to make some descriptive sense out of the field observations, even though the field notes contain reasonably pure descriptions. Thus, the researcher needs to focus on the description of the qualitative observations, highlighting certain actions, summarizing what the researcher believes to be key events and actions, cautioning against possible misunderstandings, and ignoring others. The following long quote from Malinowski illustrates this point nicely:

> Like all coral islanders, they spend a great deal of their time on the central lagoon. On a calm day it is alive with canoes carrying people or produce, or engaged in one of their manifold systems of fishing. A superficial acquaintance with these pursuits might leave one with an impression of arbitrary disorder, anarchy, complete lack of system. Patient and painstaking observations would soon reveal, however, not only that the natives have definite technical systems of catching fish and complex economic arrangements but also they have a close organization in their working teams and a fixed division of social functions. Thus within each canoe it would be found that there is one man who is its rightful owner, while the rest act as a crew. All these men, who as a rule belong to the same subclan, are bound to each other and to their fellow villagers by mutual obligations; when the whole community goes out fishing, the owner cannot refuse his canoe. He must go out himself or let someone else do it instead. The crew are equally under an obligation to him. For reasons which will presently become clear, each man must fill his place and stand by his task. Each man also receives his fair share in the distribution of the catch as an equivalent of his service. Thus the ownership and use of the canoe consist of a series of definite obligations and duties uniting a group of people into a working team (pp. 17–18).

Note that Malinowski's description goes beyond simply recounting everything that happened pertaining to fishing. He points out behaviors that occurred the most regularly, summarizes and categorizes interactions, such as ownership and teamwork, and even starts to draw some theoretical points together, anticipating the job ahead of explaining this complicated Pacific island society.

This brings us to another important principle of data reduction and analysis, which is that the distinction between description and explanation is somewhat nebulous. Since the researcher must choose and highlight certain features of the social landscape to be described, invariably there is some theory or rationale behind those choices, and the first steps toward explaining the observations are taken. In short, description involves some degree of explanation.

Again, we turn to Malinowski to learn how one moves from describing data to actually explaining things. Notice, in reading this passage, that Malinowski first uncovers key patterns of interaction through focused description, then he applies exchange theory to explain the patterns.

> To enter more deeply into the nature of these binding obligations, let us follow the fishermen to the shore. Let us see what happens with the division of the catch. In most cases only a small proportion of it remains with the villagers. As a rule we should find a number of people from some inland community waiting on the shore. They receive the bundles of fish from the fishermen and carry them home, often many miles away, running so as to arrive while it is still fresh. Here again we should find a system of mutual services and obligations based on a standing arrangement between two village communities. The inland village supplies the fishermen with vegetables; the coastal community repays with fish. This arrangement is primarily an economic one. It has also a ceremonial aspect, for the exchange has to be done according to an elaborate ritual. But there is also the legal side, a system of mutual obligations which forces the fisherman to repay whenever he has received a gift from his inland partner and vice versa. Neither partner can refuse, neither may stint in his return gift, neither should delay.
>
> What is the motive force behind these obligations? The coastal and inland villages respectively have to rely upon each other for the supply of food. On the coast the natives never have enough vegetable food, while inland the people are always in need of fish. . . . In all the facts described, the element or aspect of law, that is of effective social constraint, consists in the complex arrangements which make people keep to their obligations. Among them the most important is the manner in which many transactions are linked into chains of mutual services, every one of them having to be repaid at some later date (p. 22).

EXPLANATION

There are two basic approaches in analysis designed to explain some phenomenon. One is called analytic induction, where the researcher first pours over the data, pulling relationships and patterns out. With the patterns in hand, the researcher then turns to theory in order to explain those patterns. On the basis of the analysis of the data and the emerging regularities, one begins to build the explanation or theory. Concepts, categories, and propositions emerge out of the analysis.

In contrast, the deductive model involves the researcher first developing theory then testing it against the data. Given a particular research problem, the researcher would go to theory in order to find the most logical and empirically supported explanation for the problem. Once the theory is chosen, then the researcher derives hypotheses, which in turn are tested through data analysis. For example, I became interested in the sociological theory of social integration developed by Emile Durkheim. Durkheim actually developed this theory inductively by starting with observations of suicide rates for different countries and religious groups within those countries. To boil the theory down to its simplest terms, social integration keeps people healthy by providing them with a sense of purpose and norms or rules. Thus, a cohesive group shields its members from the vagaries of life by providing meaning, guidelines, and order. Durkheim argued that breakdowns of social cohesion lead to suicide, among other pathologies. I extended this theory by weaving into the concept of social cohesion the notion that membership and participation in formal organization is a form of social cohesion. I developed propositions and hypotheses, including one that stated, "Individuals who share membership and participate in formal organizations derive a sense of purpose and meaning to their lives. Furthermore, participating in the activities of the organization, particularly in roles which serve the needs of others, gives the individuals a sense of self-worth which, when combined with the other outcomes, provides the basis for a sense that life is worth living and that one must strive to carry on in spite of health problems and other personal adversities."

From this theory, I set about finding a way to test it empirically. I located a survey of retired rural elderly individuals, and I continued to follow them for over twenty years. I interviewed them about their health, family relations, friendship networks, and participation and membership in formal organizations, among lots of other things. I kept track of deaths and was able to determine what the background characteristics were, including formal participation, of those individuals who died versus those who survived. In this sense, I was able to test the theory by proceeding in a deductive way, from theory to data back to theory. I found support for the theory in that the survivors were individuals who were active members of formal organizations and who seemed to carry on in spite of rather serious health limitations. This was especially true of the oldest individuals who survived over the twenty-year study period. At their advanced ages, lots of chronic health problems plagued them, even slowing down their participation. But participate they did, which seemed to compensate for or offset the ravages of age. Also, I discovered that women lived longer than men and that gender was a more powerful predictor of longevity than formal participation was. This led me to turn back to theory and to add to the original set of propositions some others that related gender to social cohesion. In this way, the deductive approach came full circle from theory through data and back to theory.

■ *Descriptive Analysis: Quantitative*

Going back to the first basic task of analysis, namely to describe your data, you begin by setting up what is called marginal frequencies. Remember that most quantitative studies have too many variables for the researcher to describe each and every one. The researcher will need to decide which of the many variables in the study will be singled out for analysis, and this list will include the variables that the marginals are done on.

This task of selection is not as simple as it may seem at first glance. The research problem and theory can help you decide which variables to analyze. Also, common sense should help decide what the uninformed reader might need to know about the data. For example, the extent to which the findings of any study are generalizable beyond the respondents is a universal issue. Certainly, you would want to describe the sample in terms of the number of males and females, what their educational levels are, what their line of work is or was, and how much money they earn as a minimum basis for generalizing to the larger society. Also, the research problem can help to steer the researcher to particular variables. In my case with the study of the rural elderly, I needed to describe the types of participation along with the other background characteristics mentioned above.

A frequency distribution or **marginal frequency** is made up of the following things: (1) a title for the variable; (2) a set of labels for the values of the variable; and (3) numbers and their percent equivalents. If you want to be fancy, you can throw in a few more descriptors, such as means, modes, medians, and measures of dispersion such as standard deviation, but we will stay simple here and focus on numbers and percentages. Let's look at the following example from my study of the rural elderly. One of the important issues we were following was the extent to which health status changed as individuals grew older. There are several methods of measuring health open to us. We could have hired a physician to do physical examinations every time we interviewed the respondents. Another way to measure health would have been to have the respondents keep detailed health care diaries into which they would write descriptions of all the illness episodes, treatments, and so forth that might have befallen them in the course of the time interval between the interviews. Or we could have sought health records of one kind or another, such as hospital records, doctor office visits, and so forth. To do the latter, we would only have to have run a computer listing of the respondents' Medicare numbers. Finally, it was always possible to ask the respondents during the course of the interview how they view their health.

Of the above possibilities, the last one was the approach we chose. Medicare numbers are confidential and not available to researchers, doctor examinations are very expensive and require more cooperation from respondents than we could hope to have received. The diary is an excellent strategy, but the time periods between interviews were so long, seven and twelve years, that this was out of the question.

So we settled on asking the respondents directly, not a bad strategy when you consider W.I. Thomas and his concept of self-fulfilling prophecy. Thomas said that situations defined as real are real in their consequences. Thus, if an individual believes that he or she is sick, that person will behave as if he or she is sick. If the researcher is interested in the behavioral consequences of health and sickness, then getting it from the respondent's mouth may be the ticket.

To do this, we asked the respondents: "How has your health been generally. Would you say it has been . . . ?"

1. ____ Good

2. ____ Fair

3. ____ Poor

and "Compared to people your age, would you say that your health is . . .?"

1. ____ Better

2. ____ Worse

3. ____ About the same

I interviewed seventeen hundred individuals and asked each and every one of them these two questions, along with the two hundred or so other questions covered. For question one, the answers (responses) were distributed as follows:

Q. 1 Perceived health status
    Good = 250
    Fair = 486
    Poor = 964

Assuming that the study was done well and the data can be trusted, we would say with some considerable confidence that 964 people said that their health was poor, 250 claimed that their health was good, and 486 said it was only fair. So, what does this distribution mean? At this point, not very much, given the way we have presented it. A methodological principle is in order here.

COMPARE AND MEANING WILL COME

This admonition, borrowed in altered form from the movie, *The Field of Dreams,* a mythical journey to the past to watch "Shoeless Joe" Jackson and his Chicago White Sox teammates play baseball and throw away their careers, warns the researcher to never consider a number by itself because solo numbers are meaningless. Numbers are capable of meaning something when they are compared with one another or considered relative to each other. the number 486 from the question on perceived health means nothing by itself but starts to make some descriptive sense when you compare it with the other two numbers. The most powerful and yet simple way to do such comparing is to calculate percentages, which is a method for comparing numbers. Calculating percentages will net us a meaningful frequency table (Table 11-1) and a significant improvement over what we started with.

Now the number of individuals who view their health as good can be compared against those who see it as fair or poor by the simple technique of calculating percentages. All you need are the numbers and the total. Divide each category number by the total, for example, 250/1700 = 14.7%, and make sure that you round the percentages so they add up to 100%. A general rule is always to show the total, for example, 1,700 because you may choose to show only the percentages and not the numbers. That table would resemble Table 11-2.

Table 11-1 ■ Frequency Distribution of Rural Elderly Who
Perceive Their Health Status as Good, Fair,
or Poor

Perceived Health		Number	Per Cent
Good		250	14.7
Fair		486	28.6
Poor		964	56.7
	Totals	1,700	100

Table 11-2 ■ Percent of Rural Elderly Who Perceive Their
Health Status as Good, Fair, or Poor

Perceived Health	Percent
Good	14.7
Fair	28.6
Poor	56.7
	100
Total Rural Elderly	1,700

From this table, it is a simple matter to find the numbers of individuals who perceived their health as good, fair, or poor. Multiply each of the percentage figures by the total, 1,700 and you will have the category numbers. I have included the numbers in these descriptive tables for teaching purposes, but as a researcher, you should keep the descriptive tables as simple and uncluttered as possible. Unless there is some good reason for including all the numbers, the above type of table is preferable. If you need the numbers, they are easy enough to compute.

So, numbers can be seen as relative to one another and therefore meaningful, if we compute percentages using a common base. The common base in the example above is the total, seventeen hundred. This strategy for describing numerical results or quantitative data can be extended to situations where several different totals or bases are part of the data picture. For example, the rural elderly sample was drawn for sixty rural areas of the state. I wanted to describe how the rural elderly who lived in areas with high rates of mortality for people seventy years and older felt about their health versus elderly individuals from areas with lower mortality rates. Thinking like a true sociologist, I was on the track of a concept called relative deprivation. This concept says that there is no such thing as absolute deprivation, that is, people cannot feel deprived in some absolute sense. All feelings of being deprived must be relative to some standard. You do not feel that you have been cheated out of a job opportunity unless you have some sort of comparison case or cases to evaluate the circumstances surrounding your situation against, so the theory goes. The concept of relative deprivation was used to explain why African-Americans rioted in the 1960s. Poverty had always been a reality for African-Americans, but it wasn't until the media portrayed vividly the great wealth of other citizens on TV and in movies, magazines, newspapers, and so on that people

Table 11-3 ■ Perceived Health Status of the Rural Elderly Relative to Area Mortality Rates for People over 70 Years of Age

Perceived Health	High M Areas		Low M Areas	
	N	%	N	%
Good	200	20	117	16.7
Fair	250	25	150	21.4
Poor	550	55	433	61.9
Totals	1,000	100	700	100

in poverty realized just how badly off they were relative to the wealthy. The have-nots felt deprived relative to the haves.

Of course, it is sound methodologically to think of these things ahead of analysis time so that you are able to collect the correct or appropriate type of data. I anticipated this analysis and included another perceived health question that was much more relativistic than the general health question presented above. This more relative question asked, "Compared to other people your age, how would you say your health is?" Describing responses for areas with high versus low rates of mortality is presented in Table 11-3.

Even though the base for the high mortality areas (N = 1,000) is different from that of the low areas (N = 700), the numbers of individuals in the high mortality areas claiming good, fair, or poor health may be described and even compared with those individuals in the low areas, thanks to using percentages. We have standardized the two columns of data on perceived health by treating each number as a fraction of the total columns of data on perceived health by treating each number as a fraction of the total group, that is, the two hundred individuals in the high mortality areas who claim that their health is good is expressed as a fraction of one thousand and thereby standardized. Thus, it is easy to compare the percentages, either within the low and high areas or between the two areas. For example, we can describe the frequency distribution in the high areas by pointing out that 20 percent of those respondents living in the high mortality areas felt that their health was good versus 55 percent who perceived their health as being poor. A similar point could be made in describing the low mortality-area respondents.

A more interesting description is the one that compares the frequency distributions for the high and low mortality areas. Here, we observe that 55 percent of the high mortality-area people view their health as poor versus 61 percent of the individuals living in the low mortality areas. Does this support the relative deprivation notion? Well, the simple descriptive analysis presented above is inadequate to answer the question, but the description looks promising for relative deprivation and certainly should inspire the researcher to dig more deeply with more detailed and complex analysis.

There are a few more rules of thumb to keep in mind regarding percentages. One is to avoid computing percentages on categories that have less than ten cases in them. You can describe or report numbers that are smaller than ten. Another is to keep the number of decimal places to a minimum, preferably just one place. It is not necessary to report the percentage as 12.78. It is better to round off the .78 to .8 and report it as 12.8% (the rules is to round up above 5). Finally, do not compute percentages that add up to more than 100% and be sure to add all percentages to make sure they add up to 100%. If you end up short 0.1 or over 0.1, simply change either the lowest or highest percentage. If you are more than 0.1% off, recalculate the percentages and add them again.

Once these simple rules have been followed and you have the percentages before you, it is important to report the percentage figures relative to the base, which you must spell out clearly. For example, Table 11-2 above might be described as follows:

> Of the one thousand individuals residing in the high mortality areas (this defines the base, namely the total number living in the high mortality areas), 20% declared their health status to be good, 25% fair, and 55% said that their health was poor. In the low mortality areas, a lower percentage of the seven hundred respondents perceived their health as good or fair, while a higher percentage (61.9%) believed their health to be poor.

In this way, the base upon which the percentages were calculated is made clear to the reader.

MEASURES OF CENTRAL TENDENCY AND OF DISPERSION

A few simple statistical techniques are helpful in describing quantitative data. Whereas percentages are particularly useful for nominal data, for example, categories of good, fair, or poor in our example above, ordinal or interval data should be described using the mean, median, mode (measures of central tendency), and standard deviation (measure of dispersion). A **measure of central tendency** is nothing more than a method for describing the average or typical score, ACT (the mean ACT score is 28), age (the mean age for women is 78.5), or whatever the variable in question might be. **Measures of dispersion** give a picture of the full age of scores or ages in all their heterogeneity. Together, measures of central tendency and of dispersion give the analyst a fairly complete descriptive picture of ordinal or interval data.

■ *Qualitative Data*

Describing the results of research using qualitative data is a whole different ball game from quantitative data description. Here, the researcher is faced with the following issues: (1) a massive problem of classifying the words and sentences that make up the text of the data; (2) making sure that the coverage of the data is adequate, that is, that the central tendencies as well as the full range of the substance of the text is represented; and (3) ensuring that enough detail is included to maximize understanding.

CLASSIFICATION

Qualitative data, as you might recall, fundamentally is text. Within the pages of text, there might be descriptions of events or conversations observed, statements of values or judgments in the forms of letters or memos, historical analysis, and so forth. The range of possibilities is quite large, but regardless of the substance of the data, the problem of reducing the data in such a fashion that the researcher can summarize descriptions and draw sociologically relevant conclusions remains the same. Classifying the substance of the data is the key to producing descriptions and drawing conclusions from qualitative data.

Where does one begin? The answer is with sociological theory and the statement of the research problem. Remember that theory and the statement of the research problem emerge during the course of field work and reading the data. But it is the emerging theory and the research problem that dictate the direction and form of the classification process. The key principles of classification are: (1) Try and create an exhaustive category scheme, that is, one that takes care of all of the relevant data. An exhaustive scheme leaves no data unclassified because all possible variations of the data have been considered and are represented in the categories. (2) See to it that your scheme is exclusive. This means that any given bit of data should be classified into one and only one category. There should not be situations where data could be placed into two or more categories. (3) Make sure that the categories are derived from sociological theory. (4) Try to foresee the main points you will make in drawing conclusions, and design categories that enhance that effort and make it possible.

Let's look at a couple of examples. One very common type of qualitative data is the open-ended question. In our study of people who utilized a cancer screening program at a large state cancer center (Hessler, et al., 1990), we used a question that asked, "What does it mean to you when you say someone is healthy?" We provided three lines for the interviewer to write the exact response, word for word. After one hundred interviews, we had one hundred quotes on what healthy meant to the respondents. It was not possible to decide in advance of the interviews what categories were needed in order to classify the one hundred responses, so we read all one hundred quotes and then began to write out the categories. This creating the categories also was guided by the theory we were using and the analysis plans. The problem was to have just the right number of categories to meet the demands of the principles of classification while also satisfying our analysis and theory requirements. Certainly, one or two categories would not cut it, nor would one hundred categories.

The general rule of thumb is to stop creating categories when you are able to classify all the data accurately and exclusively. Have as few categories as you can get away with. Stay as simple as possible. In our case, we established eight categories, including "health is the absence of disease" and "health is optimal physical functioning." Given the eight categories each and every one of the one hundred quotes fit in one and only one category. There was no overlap (the categories were mutually exclusive), nor were there any quotes that could not be categorized (the categories were exhaustive).

Each of the eight categories is given a number, for example, category 1, 2, 3, and so on and the numbers can be coded and punched into the computer along with the quantitative data. In this sense, the qualitative data has been transformed into nominal quantitative data, and the researcher then is free to run frequency counts on the categories in order to describe the percentage of respondents who view health as the absence of disease versus those who see it as an optimal physical functioning and so forth.

The field note represents another form of qualitative data commonly used by social scientists. Quotes and observation can be used in analysis and in drawing conclusions but only if the researcher can locate the appropriate data, usually buried in the pages of field notes.

There are two techniques for classifying and otherwise keeping track of the relevant data. One is the age-old method of the cards, scissors, and glue. Relying on the analysis plans and theory, the researcher should have some idea of the direction that the analysis and write-up will take. The field work experience should help the researcher determine or solidify those plans.

For example, I studied neighborhood health centers in urban poverty areas scattered across the United States. In the course of attending hundreds of meetings and conducting hundreds of focused interviews at twelve centers over the course of eighteen months, I was faced with a mountain of field notes. Fortunately, I had developed some general categories, refined them over the first few months of field work, and had photocopied the field notes in order to have a copy that I could cut and paste.

The research problem was to describe and evaluate citizen participation on the center governing boards. Did having low-income community residents right up there on the boards sharing power with physicians and medical administrators affect, in any way, the health care product delivered by the centers? All of the centers were in the hearts of urban low-income areas, and conflict, including violent riots, was very much a part of the recent historical experience of the centers. Naturally, one of the broad categories I was interested in was conflict between the citizen board members and the professional power elite at the centers.

Thus, I tagged any observational or interview data that had anything to do with conflict by cutting out the relevant text and pasting it on a conflict card. I was able to refine things a bit more by further classifying conflict in terms of what the conflict was about (the issues) and who started it. So, I had dozens of file cards under the headings of "Citizen-Generated Conflict over Hiring Professionals," "Citizen-Generated Conflict over Control of the Center Budget," "Physician-Generated Conflict over Citizen Involvement in Quality of Medical Care Decisions," and numerous others. The text pasted on each card came from my written descriptions of meetings that I observed or transcripts of interviews, but it was only that limited portion of the text having to do with the particular category in question.

When I got to the section of the analysis having to do with conflict between providers and citizen board members over quality of care, I pulled all the appropriate file cards and pored over the data on those cards. These descriptions can be copied into the write-up, or they can be summarized and described in a more general fashion. Also, direct quotes can be included to illustrate or "flesh out" the bare bones of the analytic points being made. An example of the use of what Peter New called "quotable quotes" is where the researcher writes about a particular type of conflict and its resolution, lacing it with several quotes from doctors and citizen board members who had something interesting to say about the issue when the interviews were conducted.

Computer programs, such as HyperQual and Ethnograph (see the instructor's manual), are available that allow the researcher to use the personal computer in place of the physical card and text routine. Personally, I prefer the old method but have found the computer advantageous for gaining quick access to the data and for pulling text directly into the write-up of the analysis, rather than having to retype things. Another advantage of the computer approach is that categories can be changed and data moved around very easily, should that be necessary. In fact, the researcher might be reluctant to change categories to move text around if the task is as physically daunting as having to make up new cards, copy more field notes, and cut and paste some more. The computer actual may improve the chances that changes that are necessary will actually be made, thereby improving the quality of the data and the results.

■ Coverage of the Data

What data that gets into the cards or tagged by the computer is completely up to the researcher to decide. Moreover, the researcher decides what data to include in the analysis and write-up. What is to prevent the researcher from putting in only the data that supports his or her theory while ignoring data that goes in the opposite direction? There are methodological strategies that go a long way toward preventing researcher bias in the reduction and analysis of qualitative data. We explore these strategies next.

DOCUMENTATION

The wise researcher will keep careful written record of all the decisions made concerning data processing. Furthermore, an index to the data should be made that essentially outlines the categorized data. For example, an index might indicate that there were seven quotes from physicians in favor of citizen control over medical care decisions, twelve opposed, and so on. This **documentation** serves as a sort of map to the data. If no mention is made in the write-up about physicians in favor of citizen control, then it should be possible for someone to uncover this bias.

PUBLIC VERIFICATION

The researcher should make the data available, if it does not violate confidentiality, to other researchers. If carefully documented, it should be possible for someone to pick up the field notes, cards, and other data and to arrive at the same conclusions as the original researcher. It is unlikely that another researcher would go to the trouble of reanalyzing someone else's work, but public availability at least makes it possible for **public verification** to occur. It helps keep people intellectually honest if the potential for someone else looking over one's shoulder is there.

COLLEAGUESHIP

I think we can assume that most social scientists are genuinely intellectually honest and that bias in analyzing and reporting qualitative data mostly is inadvertent. Thus, a major strategy for ensuring that you gave the data a fair shake is to have a close colleague read the data and your analysis before publishing it. This is a good reason to conduct qualitative research with a colleague or two, just to have the benefit of two or three minds analyzing the same data. I honestly think I would have been in a state of panic over the probability of writing some biased analysis if I had not had really good colleagues during the neighborhood health center study. Many a time I showed my field notes and classified data to Peter New just to check on my thoroughness and accuracy. Often, Peter and I would attend the same meeting, which gave us the opportunity to check each other on what we recorded and did not record. But the main strategy for analytic integrity and adequate representation of the data was reading each others' data and analyses.

STRIVE TO PROVE YOURSELF WRONG

If you have a particular point or conclusion that you have worked hard to spell out, then it is relatively easy to make a list of potential data that would negate or falsify your conclusion. For example, I was convinced that the physicians tried to block the citizen board members from taking over control of the center because of professional ideology (the belief that the profession of medicine is all-seeing, and all-powerful in matters medical), rather than for reasons having to do with job security or future income. I had located lots of quotes and observations of conversations at meetings that supported this conclusion, such as doctors talking about consumers not having enough medical background to be able to administer a center or to decide which doctors to hire. As a bias check, I made a list of data that would contradict this conclusion, items such as doctors citing job security or income or instances where physicians affirmed belief in the competence of the average nonmedical citizen. Then I would search the data for such instances, trying to find enough to prove me wrong.

THE SUBJECTS' VIEW

Occasionally, it is possible to let a few of the research subjects critique the analysis and conclusions. This strategy works quite well if the researcher has established a solid exchange relationship with the subjects and if the data-gathering phase of the research is essentially over. Divulging the analysis and conclusions certainly intrudes into the normal thinking and actions of the subjects. It would be unwise to do anything that intrusive while field work was still being conducted because of the very real possibility that the researcher's actions will produce changes in the subjects that might not have occurred in the absence of those actions.

This procedure is quite simple to use, but it takes a strong sense of confidence to subject one's work to the critical scrutiny of the subjects of the research. Nevertheless, all one needs to do is show to an individual who was interviewed or observed as part of the study the analysis and conclusions and ask him or her to evaluate their accuracy. Remember to hide any identifying features of the data, such as names, dates, places, and so forth. The last thing you want is one subject going off and telling another how interesting his or her interview was. Also, it is wise to ask several subjects to do this evaluation in order to ensure that a fairly wide range of perspectives is presented. My general rule of thumb is to continue to recruit new subjects until their evaluations start to sound alike. At that point, cut it off and decide whether or not to revise your thinking.

I have used this procedure several times with major research projects. One of the more interesting and memorable occurrences involved the neighborhood health center study and a Mexican-American and Yaqui Indian community. The center board members fought tooth and nail for months against the white doctors and medical school administrators. All of the substantive issues, such as the right to pass judgment on the hiring of center professional staff were tinged with fears that the white folks would be insensitive to the ethnic needs of the local community residents served by the center. My field notes were full of observations of heated verbal exchanges, often in Spanish. When interviewed, the community board members often talked of medical practices and ideas that were quite foreign to me at the time. I checked and double-checked my cultural knowledge, but I still was a bit uncertain that I had it correct. When I had finished the field work portion of the study, I wrote up a preliminary analysis of that center along with some specific conclusions. I had befriended and lived on and off with one of the influential Mexican-American leaders in the community, so I approached him with the request that he read and critique my work. He was willing and even a little flattered, it seemed, but I was not prepared for the tough-minded criticism that he leveled at my analysis and conclusions. I was taken aback, partly because I really believed that after months of field work, I knew the score but also because my critic was a high school graduate and I, a Ph.D. with wounded pride. But at the same time, my knowledge of the local cultural dynamics increased, and fortunately, I had enough sense to take the critique seriously. The subsequent several other citizen critiques supported the initial one. I revised my interpretation and conclusions, ending up with a much more culturally sensitive and accurate report.

ENOUGH DETAIL

How much detail in the analysis is enough? How do you know when you have reached the limit as to how much detail the reader can absorb? I wish there were nice, tidy methodological principles I could offer as answers to these questions, but there are none. The art of research comes into play here much more than the science of research. Thus, we may turn to the world of art for some guidance.

The artist who paints a picture decides how much detail to incorporate. He or she bases the decision on the context of the painting, on past experience, and on the age-old gut feeling. The context includes the scene itself, the potential audience, and what the artist is trying to communicate. Experience involves lots of trials and errors and also successes. The message is whatever is on the artist's mind for the painting to say or be.

So, too, the social scientist must create the word picture. He or she has a dominant message to get across within the context of the particular study and the body of knowledge associated with the research. In the beginning, exploratory stages of research, great detail is helpful and even necessary in order to launch the next wave of studies. Less detail may be needed in research areas where extensive empirical knowledge exists. The artistry of the social scientist should improve with age and experience. The first qualitative report is so much more difficult to write than the fifteenth, simply because the researcher who has done it many times knows better how much detail to include for a given message. Finally, there is the most intangible quality of the above intangibles, which is the gut feeling. Whatever background characteristics or personality traits that researchers possess, the simple truth of the matter is that some researchers are better than others with the gut-feeling. A good example of this was the comparison of the health center write-ups by the five different social scientists on the project. All of us had Ph.D.s from top universities, along with similar years of experience. And yet there were wide disparities between us in terms of the effective use of details in our reports. I am convinced that we all got better over the two years of project experience, but the differences remained as testimony to the point that some had better guts for sensing when to add more detail and when to stop than others did.

My advice is to set a page limit for the analysis first, then outline the analysis in terms of the topics to be covered and the key points to be made. Now you will have some idea of the limit of pages of detail. Pick the most interesting (to you) details to include first and see if they do the job in terms of conveying the message. If so, then add a few more for good measure and quit. If not, bring in more details and see where the message stands. Perhaps you will need to cull out some of the details that you considered the most interesting in the first round because they do not fit well with the new additions. It is not at all unusual to go back to the drawing board several times with new ideas and lists of details to be included. Generally, if you are boring yourself with too much detail, you are boring your readers, too.

■ *Quantitative Data*

EXPLANATION

Explanation using qualitative data of the type generated in the neighborhood health center study is a very different process than explanation with quantitative measurement and data. With qualitative data, the researcher usually engages in a method that I call emergence. Here, the researcher writes up field notes, reads them, begins to define the research problem, generates more observations and notes, develops the problem further, and ultimately strives to explain the problem. The explanation and problem emerge from the data.

Explanation using quantitative data starts with the dependent or problem variable and its variance. The problem variable, be it health status, longevity, stress, or whatever, should vary in terms of its values measured. For example, health might have been defined conceptually as perceived optimal physical functioning. Perhaps the researcher measured it by asking the respondents if they had ever experienced any of a finite list of physical health problems and, if they had, whether those problems bother them now. The number of problems that bother the respondents can be summed and health status score derived for each individual. The health status scores will vary, with some individuals with really good health or low scores, others with high scores, and still others ranging between the extreme scores. This is what variance in the dependent variable is. The researcher seeks to explain why people's health status varies, that is, why some are healthy, some sick, and others in between. Without variance, there is nothing to explain, and thus the research analysis would end with simple description. If every person in the study was healthy and you had hoped to explain health status, you would be out of luck because there would be no unhealthy individuals to compare the healthy ones against. You cannot explain something unless that thing varies, for explanation fundamentally is based on establishing that certain factors are present when the dependent variable is "on," and not present when the dependent variable is "off." Guilt by association. So, no variance, no explanation.

Another piece of the explanation puzzle that must be in place is that the researcher have in the wings multiple variables designed to explain the dependent variable. It takes variables to explain a variable. Social behavior and society is too complex to have a single-variable explanation for any sociological problem. There is no one variable that will explain adequately health status, no "magic bullet." At its most basic level, relating one variable with another is called **cross tabulation**, that is, tabulating the results of two or more variables simultaneously.

The second principle means that the analyst will study the relationship between the dependent variable and the other explanatory variables called independent variables. You can think of the independent variables as the cause and the dependent variables as the effect, if cause-effect thinking helps sort out this point.

CROSS TABULATION

Analyzing two or more variables as they relate to each other is the task of cross tabulation. Let's take the simplest cross tabulation, namely the two-by-two table (called a contingency table). This table presents two variables (bivariate), each with two values (dichotomous variables) as they relate to each other. If health status is the dependent variable and it has scores ranging from zero (no health problems) to twenty (maximum health problems), we would transform or collapse the scores into just two values. These would be labeled "No Health Problems" and

Table 11-4 ■ Health by age

		Age		
		Young	*Elderly*	
Health	*Healthy*	100 (67)	50 (33)	*150*
	Sick	50 (33)	100 (67)	*150*
		150 *100%*	*150* *100%*	*Total = 300*

"Health Problems." You can see right off the bat how much information has been lost by collapsing the data like this. Individuals with only one health condition bothering them are put in the same analytic category as persons with twenty conditions. Nevertheless, for the sake of simplicity, we will proceed with the two-by-two table example. Since we are trying to explain why some people are healthy and others have health problems, we bring in age (continuous variable) as an independent variable. You can see how huge the table would look if all the ages of the respondents were strung out as categories of the independent variable. So, we need to collapse this variable and, because we are illustrating a two-by-two table, we dichotomize it into "Young" and "Elderly." Again, the problem of lost information should be obvious here. Now we are ready to build the table. Following the convention of placing the dependent variable on the left margin and the independent variable on the top, Table 11-4 emerges.

Note that the percentages are calculated with the subtotals of the values of the independent variable as the bases. Following this convention, you will then compare percentages across. Remember: percentage down, compare across. The reason for doing it this way lies in the fact that the independent variable is being analyzed in relation to the dependent variable as a possible "cause" of the dependent variable. It makes intuitive sense to be able to say, "Sixty-seven percent of the young respondents indicated that they were healthy versus 33% of the elderly respondents. Conversely, only 33% of the young respondents perceived themselves as sick, whereas 67% of the elderly respondents viewed themselves as sick." This way or organizing and analyzing contingency tables makes sense because you are investigating the relationship between age and health status, not between health status and age. It makes little or no sense to analyze health status as a factor affecting chronological age. For example, if the percentages were computed with the dependent variable as the base, you would end up saying, "Sixty-seven percent of the healthy respondents were young versus 33% of the sick."

Remember the point made earlier about no single independent variable being good enough to explain all or most of the variance in a dependent variable. Because of this fact of sociological life, it is very important to move the analysis beyond the univariate level to include two or even more variables (multivariate analysis). It is a simple matter, given the computer and the large number of fine multivariate statistical techniques, to analyze literally dozens of independent

Table 11-5 ■ Health by Age and Gender

Health		Gender				
		Male		Female		
		Young	Elderly	Young	Elderly	
	Healthy	50 (67)	25 (33)	38 (51)	37 (49)	
	Sick	25 (33)	50 (67)	37 (49)	38 (51)	
		75 100%	75 100%	75 100%	75 100%	Total = 300

variables simultaneously. These techniques, unlike the simple contingency table, will not let you see numbers with cross-tabulated variables. Instead, the researcher is given statistical values that are calculated from those numbers. The advantage of multivariate statistical techniques is that the researcher is able to analyze several variables at one time. The disadvantage is that you never really know exactly how variable A cross tabulates with variable B. The disadvantage with contingency analysis is that the researcher is limited to three, possibly four variables at one time. It is just too cumbersome and would require huge numbers of cases to have a contingency analysis that went beyond three or four variables. For example, if you split 1,000 respondents on the variable health, which has four values, along gender lines, each cell of the contingency table might contain 125 cases. Add another four-part variable, and the numbers in the cells get down into the thirties, and that is only three variables.

In any case, it is important to look at the multivariate contingency table in order to understand what is behind the statistical version with values in place of cells and numbers. Table 11-5 presents the same data as Table 11-4 with the addition of gender. Theory and empirical research suggests that men and women have very different "health careers," that the two genders are at different "risks" for health problems and, ultimately, death. Thus, we would expect that age would have a stronger relationship to health for men and that women might gain health benefits from involvement in social networks or other factors related to gender, rather than age.

Table 11-5 indicates that the relationship between age and health is strong for men but that there is no relationship between those variables for women. Again, read the percentages across, and it is clear that double the percentage of young men are healthy compared to elderly men, whereas almost equal percentages of young and elderly women are healthy.

If we had double the number of cases, we could add another variable in order to pursue the gender-health puzzle. It would make theoretical and empirical sense to add social networks to the equation. The contingency table would look like Table 11-6. Clearly, this table is difficult to read. The analysis has been set up to determine the extent to which health status is influenced by the three variables, namely social networks, gender, and age. Are socially isolated individuals

Table 11-6 ■ Health by Age, Gender, and Social Networks

		Social Networks								
		Small				Large				
		Male		Female		Male		Female		
		Young	Elderly	Young	Elderly	Young	Elderly	Young	Elderly	
Health	Healthy	30 (30)	25 (34)	20 (67)	10 (40)	23 (77)	15 (60)	100 (64)	90 (57)	
	Sick	70 (70)	50 (66)	10 (33)	15 (60)	7 (23)	10 (40)	57 (36)	68 (43)	
		100 100%	75 100%	30 100%	25 100%	30 100%	25 100%	157 100%	158 100%	Total = 600

(small networks) more likely to define themselves as sick in spite of age and gender differences, or does age influence the perception of health differently for men and women, regardless of social network activity? This type of analytic question is what the three-independent-variable contingency table is set up to answer. It should be presented in a simpler fashion, starting first with the most general analytic point you want to make and then adding more detailed points. For example, looking at Table 11-6 (the data have been contrived for this example), social networks might be considered as the main independent variable. Thus, we would want to break the table down to see the difference in men and women's social networks. Table 11-7 indicates that there is a huge difference in that men have much smaller networks than the women.

Breaking the data down again, we can look at the influence of age on size of social network. Table 11-8 shows that there is not much of a relationship here, with 41% of the young respondents having small networks versus 35% of the elderly. Conversely, 59% of the young had large networks, compared to 65% of the elderly. The older respondents were a bit more involved in social relationships than the young.

Finally, we need to look at the relationship between health status and social networks. Table 11-9 reflects the fact that social networks have the strongest relationship with health status. Only 37% of the individuals from small social networks indicated that they were healthy, compared to 62% of the individuals in the large networks. Likewise, 63% of the small network individuals said they were sick versus only 38% of those individuals in the large networks.

Table 11-6 contained all the relevant information, but it was difficult to read. When the data were broken down, we were able to see more clearly that social networks had the most powerful effect on health status. Women may have viewed

Table 11-7 ■ Percent Large Social Network for Males and Females

	Percent
Males	24
Females	85

Table 11-8 ■ Influence of Age on Size of Social Networks

		Age	
		Young	Elderly
Social Network	Small	130 (41)	100 (35)
	Large	187 (59)	183 (65)
		317 (100)	283 (100)

Table 11-9 ■ Health Status by Social Networks

		Social Networks		
		Small	Large	
Health Status	Healthy	85 (37)	228 (62)	
	Sick	145 (63)	142 (38)	
		230 (100)	370 (100)	Total = 600

themselves as healthier than the men in the study because women were much more active than the men in social networks.

■ *Elaboration Analysis*

The example presented above poses an interesting basic problem of analysis. When more than two variables are related to the dependent variable, the researcher needs a method for sorting out the findings. Is the first relationship between the main independent variable and the dependent variable worth anything? How does one decide, and what do you mean when you conclude that the relationship is "significant"? First, the issue of significance.

STATISTICAL VERSUS SUBSTANTIVE SIGNIFICANCE

Going back to the example from Table 11-9, we concluded that the relationship between social networks and health status was worth noting for its strength or "power." We could apply a statistical test of some sort, for example, chi square, and undoubtedly the test would register "significant" on the probability scale. In short, the statistic would tell us that our chances of being wrong in accepting the relationship as significant would be very slim, possibility only one in a thousand. The relationship is statistically significant.

But the mere fact that it is statistically significant does not mean that the relationship is true in the sense that one should change behavior as a consequence or design new programs to accommodate the findings. For example, long ago a statistician found a statistically significant relationship between the incidence of hay fever (the number of new cases over a specific time interval) and the price of wheat. As the price of wheat rose, so did the incidence of hay fever. Does one conclude as a scientist that hay fever and the price of wheat are related in a significant way? Or being really bold, would you argue that the price of wheat causes hay fever? Would you design programs to keep the price of wheat low in order to reduce or possibly eradicate the incidence of hay fever? Of course not, you reply. Such a finding flies in the face of our experience with everyday life and our knowledge of basic physiology. Clearly, we would do well to reject the initial finding in favor of launching a more extensive search for the cause of hay fever. Fortunately, the cause is well known in medical circles to be ragweed. But then why is the price of wheat in the picture? The answer is simple. The price of wheat is related to ragweed, principally, and it is ragweed that causes hay fever. The price of wheat is determined to a large extent by supply. When the supply of wheat is low, ragweed grows in the fields instead of wheat and in turn produces hay fever. When there is a lot of wheat, there is less room in the fields for ragweed, and consequently, hay fever declines.

THE ELABORATION MODEL

This example brings us to a major analysis strategy called the elaboration model, a powerful idea and technique developed by Paul Lazarsfeld back in the 1930s. The basic assumption behind this model is that no single independent variable is powerful enough to explain fully a dependent variable. This is a polite way of saying that one should distrust a two-variable relationship until such time as it has proven itself by standing up to the introduction of other independent variables, called test factors. You subject the original two-variable relationship to a series of tests by bringing in a series of third variables. If the original relationship remains unchanged under the duress of the additional variables, then our confidence in that relationship is justified.

First, some terminology is necessary before discussing the model. The original two-variable relationship between the independent and dependent variables is called the **zero order relationship**. Any new variable introduced into that zero order relationship is called, in the most general sense, **a test variable**. A first-order relationship involves three variables: the original independent variable, the test variable, and the dependent variable. If you introduce two test variables, the relationship is a second order, and so forth. There are three possible outcomes from elaborating the zero order relationship: (1) the zero order relationship is true; (2) the zero order relationship is spurious or false; and (3) the zero order relationship is qualified. The discussion of the **elaboration analysis** model covers these three possibilities.

TRUE

The zero order relationship is true if introducing test variables has no effect on it. For example, if we had a correlation coefficient statistic of .90 for the relationship between the price of wheat and the incidence of hay fever, it would be a **true relationship** if all the test variables we introduced did not change appreciably that statistic. Bringing ragweed into the analysis would not affect the zero order relationship, for example. The correlation would remain .90 or close to it for situations where ragweed was plentiful and scarce alike. In short, ragweed did not have any effect on the zero order relationship.

SPURIOUS

Two things need to be in place before one concludes that the zero order relationship was spurious or false. First, the test variable must exist or come before the independent variable in time. Second, the zero order relationship must be changed significantly when the test variable is in play, and you need to prove that the test variable produces the effects in both the independent and dependent variables. The first requirement can be represented as follows:

Test Factor → Independent Variable → Dependent Variable

Here, the test factor happens first, then the independent variable occurs, and finally the effect is seen in the dependent variable. An example would be a zero order relationship between education (independent variable) and health status (dependent variable). If gender were introduced and the zero order relationship fell apart, we would conclude that it was spurious because gender is in place before an individual developed educationally. Gender comes before educational status in time. Of course, the zero order relationship would have to be reduced significantly with the introduction of gender in order to conclude that the relationship between health and education was spurious. Our example of ragweed and the price of wheat is a case of **spurious relationship**. The growth of ragweed comes before the price of wheat in time and it has a direct effect on the incidence of hay fever, thus, the relationship between the price of wheat and hay fever is spurious.

QUALIFIED

If the zero order relationship is affected significantly by the test factor, but if the test factor occurs simultaneously with or after the independent variable in time (you are unable to prove that it happened before the independent variable), then you will qualify the zero order relationship with the proviso that the test variable is very important and that one should consider the two variables together as working to produce the effect in the dependent variable. Usually, the test variable will improve the relationship on one side and reduce it on the other. This is known as a **qualified relationship**. Referring to the social networks example (Tables 11-4 through 11-9), the zero order relationship between age and health status would be qualified if the test variable gender reduced the relationship for women and increased it for the men. In other words, the chi square or correlation statistic would become significantly stronger for the males, but the relationship between age and health would drop to insignificant levels for the women in the study. Age and gender occur simultaneously, so one cannot argue that one comes before the other in time. Because the zero order relationship is affected by gender, one needs to bring gender into the equation in terms of explaining variation in health status. In this example, the original relationship between age and health has been qualified.

■ *The Ecological Fallacy and Other Points on the Unit of Analysis*

Analysis can be a piece of cake or a tremendous trial, depending on whether or not the researcher follows a few simple precepts. First and foremost, keep the unit of analysis clear and segregated in the data files. Second, beware of the ecological fallacy and never mix units in the same analysis. Third, keep the analysis simple by limiting the number of variables to the bare minimum that theory and empirical findings tell you are the ones to include and by choosing the simplest statistical model with which to express the findings.

UNIT OF ANALYSIS

Recalling that the unit of analysis is the object of the research or analysis, it seems impossible but, believe me it happens, that researchers conduct the field work and analysis phases of the research without ever defining the unit of analysis. Clearly, it is wise to define the unit at the time you define the research problem. This can be done by simply stating what the unit is, for example, "The unit of analysis is individuals sixty-five years of age and older living independently in small towns in Missouri." Just because we talk of the unit of analysis, do not think that only one unit of analysis is allowed for any given study. Often, a study will have more than one unit, and when this is the case, it is necessary to keep separate data files for each unit of analysis. For example, my study of Boston's Chinatown had two units of analysis: (1) the individual and (2) the household. Thus, I created two separate data files, one for the individuals and the other for the households.

THE ECOLOGICAL FALLACY

The **ecological fallacy** occurs when the researcher analyzes two different units of analysis simultaneously. Using my Chinatown study as an example, I had collected lots of information on a sample of individuals who were Chinese and living in Chinatown. The data were collected through face-to-face interviews. Hence, the unit of analysis for the interview data was the individual respondent. Suppose that I had not been able to collect information about each individual respondent's health status and yet I wanted to analyze health status as part of the explanation of why the Chinese residents used Chinese medicine versus Western medicine. I could take government statistics on health status for the census tracts in Chinatown and use that statistic in my analysis. I would argue that the health status of Boston's Chinatown residents in my sample is as the census tract data suggested. This is unwise because the units of analysis are mixed, which means that there is no guarantee that the data from one unit have any relevance for the other unit. In the Chinatown case, the government health survey might have been conducted with white residents of Chinatown, or the subjects of the government study most probably were different individuals than my respondents. In any case, the odds are high that the two data sets are different enough in major ways to warrant separate analyses. That is why it is important to establish separate data files for each of the different units of analysis so that we are able to keep the units separate in analysis.

FISHING IN A SEA OF VARIABLES

Probability theory is both friend and foe. On the negative side, the odds are very good that if you have a large number of variables and a large number of cases, variables will be related to other variables significantly but simply because of chance or random occurrence. At the .01 level of confidence or significance, one bivariate relationship out of every 100 will be statistically significant by chance alone. At the .05 level, it is one out of 20. For this reason, it is better to pick the variables for analysis based on theory or other empirical work, rather than doing what is referred to as "fishing." Fishing is the process where the researcher picks a very powerful statistical procedure that has the capacity for loading a large number of variables in and then analyzing them all together and in various combinations until significant relationships are uncovered. As a colleague once described it, "You massage the data until it confesses."

In contrast, one should use the literature to pick carefully the variables that make sense theoretically and empirically. With a sample size of seventeen hundred and over two hundred variables, I chose only fifteen variables to analyze as predictors of mortality in my study of the rural elderly. Also, I chose a statistical procedure whose assumptions were met by the data and tried to use the simplest least complicated procedure that would do the job. Keep things simple!

■ *Conclusions*

Sociological data must be analyzed and interpreted by the researcher. Data never "speak by themselves." Quantitative and qualitative data share much in common with the great difference being that qualitative data unearths deep meanings and quantitative gives the research a wide scope of coverage. Quantitative can handle large numbers of cases because the efficiencies associated with numerical codes, and qualitative is for a small number of cases, even just one case.

Both forms of data must be analyzed with the goal of sociological explanation. Analysis may be descriptive or analytical (explaining variance). Typologies and classification are the tools for qualitative data and percentaging; cross tabulating and the elaboration model are for quantitative data. Throughout, the researcher must strive to prove himself or herself wrong.

The student is cautioned on being clear about the unit of analysis, avoiding the ecological fallacy, and not fishing for significant relationships in a sea of variables. Theory should guide the analysis of quantitative data.

GLOSSARY

analysis   the manipulation of data in order to describe and explain social reality.

cross tabulation   the physical representation in tabular form analysis of two or more variables in relation to each other. Such tables are called contingency tables.

documentation   a written narrative prepared by the researcher describing all of the research decisions made during the course of study.

ecological fallacy   may occur when a researcher mixes units of analysis (analyzes the relationship between a variable from one unit of analysis with a variable from a different unit of analysis) and draws a conclusion based on that analysis.

elaboration analysis   a procedure of data analysis where the researcher introduces additional variables into a two-variable relationship.

explanation   may be inductive or deductive in its logical form, but the goal is to achieve empirically validated theory about some aspect of social reality (a research problem).

marginal frequency   a technique of descriptive analysis that involves counting the numbers of cases as they distribute along the values for any given variable. Also known as frequency distribution.

measure of central tendency   statistics that help the researcher describe the average value or score on any given variable. These include the mean, median, and mode.

measure of dispersion   statistics that help the researcher describe the range of values or scores on any given variable. These include the range (highest value, lowest value) and standard deviation (measure of the dispersion of scores in a frequency distribution away from the mean score).

public verification   the potential in research for colleagues to gain access to the data and thereby replicate the analysis.

qualified relationship   a term used in elaboration analysis to characterize a zero order relationship that is affected by a test variable that occurs simultaneously in time with the independent variable.

qualitative data   information that has been measured but not coded into numerical form. Included are textual representations of interviews, written reports of direct observations, letters, diaries, field journals, and other such research documents.

quantitative data   information that has been measured by a standardized instrument and coded into numerical form.

spurious relationships   a term used in elaboration analysis characterizing a situation where the test variable affects the zero order relationship and where the test variable comes before the independent variable in time.

test variable   a term used in elaboration analysis to describe a second, third, and so forth variable introduced into the zero order relationship.

true relationship   a term used in elaboration analysis to characterize a zero-order relationship unaffected by test variables.

zero order relationship   a term used in elaboration analysis describing the basic two variable relationship between the independent and dependent variables.

FOR FURTHER READING

Lazarsfeld, Paul F., Pasanella, Ann K., and Rosenberg, Morris. (1972). *Continuities in the language of social research.* New York: Free Press.

Zeisel, Hans (1968). *Say it with figures.* New York: Harper and Row.

Chapter Twelve

THE WRITING OF GRANT PROPOSALS AND RESEARCH REPORTS

▌ *This chapter is a bit different from the others in that it is more practical and less grounded in methodological principles. I am aware that modern society, captured as it is by the electronic media, seems to have inoculated its denizens against the writing bug. People are rapidly losing the will and the ability to write. My students groan under the relatively paltry fifty or so pages of writing they have to do in my methodology course. I can see why as I convalesce from exposure to last semester's evidence of the dearth of fundamental writing skills, such as organization, vocabulary, precision, and so forth. Writing is an endangered species, no question about it. This is a very serious problem for the society in general and the research methodologist in particular. This chapter contains basic practical information designed to help the methodologist write grants and research reports with greater skill and effectiveness.*

The chapter begins with some basic techniques recommended for scientific writers. Next, the grant proposal process is outlined, along with strategies for organizing, writing, and securing a grant. Finally, the elements of the research report are presented, and hints for improving the written report are discussed. Portions of a successful grant proposal (it was funded by the National Institute on Aging) may be found in Appendix D.

Gone are the days when I, as a faculty member of a major research university, could count on my dean or department chairperson to supply my research financial needs. I can recall the late 1960s and early '70s when research support from the university was called "hard money" and was considered infinitely preferable to depending on outside or "soft" money.

Today, the world of research is very different. University support for research exists but in a much reduced form, usually as seed or start-up funds to initiate research projects. University-based research today, particularly longitudinal and other survey projects requiring a year or two of field work, will need outside sources of funding.

This means that the researcher must be adept at writing grant proposals and research reports, the two going hand in glove. Well-written grant proposals get funded, sometimes, and research reports must follow if the cycle is to continue. It is the kiss of death, in grant circles, to fail to write up or publish the findings from a funded study. You must write and communicate your findings because there is no hiding from a weak publication record. All grant proposals require a biographical sketch of the principal investigator, and the researcher's publishing history—or lack of it—is there in black and white for all to see. If you had a grant to study the rural elderly in 1987, you had better not apply for another in 1992 unless there are several publications listed from the 1987 study.

■ *Good Scientific Writing*

This section probably should be called "Good Writing," as opposed to "Good Scientific Writing." Mastery of the basic techniques of good writing enables one to write well in any discipline. A running buddy of mine, Joe Marks, is, when he is not running, the science news director and a professor in the College of Agriculture, University of Missouri. Much of the advice I am about to impart was given to me by Joe over the years. Joe wrote a little pamphlet, "Instant Writing Course," about how to write. Also, my son Peter has taken creative writing courses from Russell Banks and John McPhee at Princeton University, two masters of technique. So between my conversations with Joe and Peter, the pamphlet, and all of the rejection slips and reviewer comments I've received, I trust that I have put together advice that will be worth something to you.

■ *Thinking*

Everything written starts in thought. The nice thing about thinking is that there are no grammatical rules to follow to do it, nor do you have to stick to one topic during a thinking session. New thoughts replace old ones, flights of ideas take off, and you can go as fast as you like. But think before you write.

Thinking is conceiving and assembling ideas. Surely if you have been doing research, are contemplating applying for a research grant, or are under the gun to write up the results of some research, you have some ideas. Do some heavy-duty thinking about those ideas. Try to put some of them together in ways no one has done before, and above all, strive to generate new ideas.

Ideas come in strange packages. I have found that getting away from the sociological literature (assuming that one is familiar with the basic literature to begin with) helps my thinking. A sports story or a *National Geographic* article could be the ticket for generating new ideas. Take in the sights at some unfamiliar venue (for me, it may be a monster truck show or a professional wrestling bout). Inspiration requires a shift from security to insecurity. You should jar your mind a bit.

As you think, jot down ideas, connections, questions, and any other detritus even remotely affiliated with ideas. When I was a new graduate student in my first medical sociology course with Peter New at the University of Pittsburgh, Peter told me to observe faith healers. There was virtually no sociological literature on the topic, so I had no recourse but to think. I envisioned going as a patient and thought about what happened and why it was important. Ideas such as the hope bank, cunning unbeliever, enemy territory, the last heathen in Pittsburgh, and other banalities came to me. I wrote all of this apparent nonsense down, and much to my surprise, some ideas emerged to help me formulate a rough research plan.

■ *The Structure*

Good writing has a basic structure. Structure is what makes a piece of writing readable. Some key components of structure are headings, short sentences, short paragraphs, lots of paragraphs, simple words of precise meaning, active verbs, the heart of the matter up front in the first paragraph, and a hierarchy to the points made (with the most important one first, the next most important second, and so on), an introduction, and periodic summaries. Using simple words does not preclude using big words. In fact, big words often are simple words because their meaning is clear and the only other options are two or three smaller words, for example, *transfix* in place of "pierce through" or *transcend* as opposed to "rise above." Headings reflect organization and help keep the reader oriented. The introduction should let the reader know where you are taking him or her, and summaries are great for keeping your reader with you.

■ *Style*

Just as runners have many styles, so too should writers be allowed the freedom to develop their own styles. However, some elements of style lead reviewers such as Murray Wax to write (of one of my papers that he reviewed for a journal), "There are too many infelicities of style." Master the basics of sentence and paragraph structure. Review the rhetorical principles of coherence and unity and the methods of exposition, argument, description, and narration. There is no shortcut for this.

Once you have reviewed the rhetorical principles, then it is time to think about ways to polish your personal writing style.

USE THE ACTIVE VOICE

This may sound like a suggestion from Norman Vincent Peale, but it helps to think in positive, active verbs and to write accordingly. Avoid such words and phrases as "it was/is," "there were," or "became" when you can use action verbs instead. For example, I might write, "the elderly respondents became ill," which is fine. Assume that I am trying to connect their illnesses with going to nursing homes. I write, "The reason that the elderly respondents entered nursing homes is that they became ill." This is infelicitous. Better to write: "Illness forced the elderly respondents to enter nursing homes." In the same vein, substitute "Seventeen hundred elderly respondents were ill" for "There were seventeen hundred ill respondents"; "label each variable" for "each variable should be labeled"; and "probably" for "it is probable." Turn negatives into positives, such as by using "ignore" instead of "do not pay attention to"; "worthless" instead of "not worthwhile"; and "She thought that politics was unethical" instead of "She did not think that politics was ethical."

AVOID EMPTY PHRASES

Avoid what Joe Marks calls empty phrases. His list includes:

Empty	Full
so as to allow	to allow
make plans for	plan
in order to	to
disposed of on the market	sold
list a description of	describe
are suspected to having	might have
it is advisable to begin	begin
more uniformly shaped	alike
with the exception of	except
this is a subject that	this subject
owing to the fact that	since
in spite of the fact that	although
not worthwhile	worthless

Rather and *very* are two commonly used qualifiers that you also can do without (do not count the number of times I violate this injunction in this book). Avoid redundancies, too. "Most definitely" and "most unique" are two examples.

GOOD SENTENCES

If you write several sentences that have prepositional phrases, balance them with simple sentences. The mind tires quickly enough as it is without the added burden of lots of comma-loaded sentences with no relief in sight. The best strategy is to write a mixture of simple and complex sentences. Do not mix your tenses, for example, "Olla shopped and cooks the meal for her family." Write "Olla shopped and cooked . . ." or "Olla shops and cooks . . .". Make sure that the subject and the verb agree. "Which one of the following tables (*have* or *has*) a significant chi-square?" You can tell which of the two is correct by dropping the words between the subject and the verb. The sentence will then read, "Which one has . . . ". Finally, keep the construction parallel. Marks uses the following example: "We were told to write in ink, that we should use only one side of the paper, and we should endorse our papers properly." The correct version is: "We were told to write in ink, to use only one side of the paper, and to endorse our papers properly."

■ *The Grant Process*

THE RFP

Grants are competitive and creative endeavors. Research contracts are competitive, too, but they are much more constrained by agency requirements. Grants are born when a federal, state, or local agency decides to have some research done. The agency draws up a "Request for Proposal" (RFP), which usually is a one- or two-paragraph synopsis along with dozens of pages detailing what the agency wants researched and how it wants the proposal prepared. Agencies use these RFPs to solicit proposals from university and privately based researchers. Almost without exception, one needs to be affiliated with a public or private corporation or university to respond successfully to an RFP.

Federal RFPs are published in the *Federal Register* and are sent directly to university research offices and private research corporations deemed appropriate by the granting agency. The largest federal granting agency, the Department of Health and Human Services (DHHS), sent out the RFPs that are included in Appendix D. Note that the grant RFP is much less detailed and restricted than the contract RFP (which is 101 pages long) regarding what the agency wants done.

RFPs are prepared and administered by program officers, who are professionals educated in the physical and social sciences. Usually, the program officer's name is listed along with the agency phone number and address. You should send a query letter to the program officer describing what you plan to do. Ask for advice and counsel before you write and submit the proposal. Ask to see a copy of a successful proposal. Do this well in advance of the deadline.

AGENCY REVIEW

Once the grant has passed through the local institutional review process, involving IRB approval and budget review, it is sent to the agency. The grant goes through a central review preliminary screening, and defective grants are sent back to their investigators. If the granting agency wants no more than five pages for the research problem statement and you submitted six, your grant probably will end up in the defective pile. A missing section or signature, a missed deadline, or a research problem way off the granting agency's mark can lead to an early derailment of a grant proposal as well.

If your proposal passes this first round, it is sent to the appropriate program office within the agency. For example, if you are applying to the National Institute on Aging (program), the grant proposal is sent to the central clearinghouse of the National Institutes of Health (agency) first. The program staff assign a number to the grant that identifies the agency, program, date, and the number of times the proposal has been through the review process. This last identifier looks ominous. It probably is for those who expect success the first time around. My experience and that of my grant-writing colleagues is that getting funded more often takes two or three submissions, rather than one review process.

A program officer assumes responsibility for your grant and sends it out for review by your peers, usually four or five individuals who are active researchers in the area of the proposed research. These reviewers follow a set of evaluative criteria and assign numerical values to each of the areas in your grant. For example, the problem statement is assigned a number reflecting how well the reviewers thought it was stated; this is done for each part of the grant considered essential by the agency. Proposals that receive very low scores are rejected outright and sent back to the principal investigator with a pink sheet listing the score and a summary of the reviewers' comments. Take the reviewers' comments to heart, revise the proposal accordingly, and resubmit it for the next round. This is time-consuming, because reviews usually are done once every six months, or even once a year at some agencies.

A relatively small handful of proposals will pass to the next stage. Program officers, with the help of a few outside reviewers, meet and rank the proposals. With the program budget in mind, the staff will assign funding priorities to the proposals. Then, the top proposals that could be funded are selected. If there are lingering questions or firm suggestions for changes, a visit will be scheduled to the principal investigator. This is called the site visit. If you receive notification of a site visit, you are close to getting funded. The other proposals probably would receive notice that they "were approved without funding," a state of suspended animation, where the only recourse for getting the funds is to resubmit for the next round.

Sometimes the site visit is *pro forma*. The decision to fund has been made, and the visit is to negotiate some changes or to settle some relatively minor questions. But do not underestimate the importance of the site visit. Take charge of arrangements. Make sure that the facility for the meeting is close to the hotel where the site visit team is staying. Arrange for name tags and name plates for the table. The team members will have had breakfast, so you should have juice, coffee, and rolls and arrange for lunch to be served. The team members are required to pay their own way, so expect to be reimbursed for the lunches. Keep coffee and other beverages on hand throughout the day.

The meeting will take one day. The site visit team usually arrives the night before and leaves the evening after the meeting. The members of the team will meet on the evening before the official site visit and go over the agenda, which they set. A couple of weeks before the site visit, the principal investigator should have received the notification of the visit, the names of the members of the team, where they will be staying, and what issues they will discuss with the investigator. Be sure to address these issues in writing and make copies for each of the team members with a cover letter and envelope with his or her name on it. A fancy cover with the university seal or company logo is nice. Leave these copies at the hotel for the members to pick up when they arrive. This gives you time to do whatever homework might be necessary to address the questions effectively. Putting your answers in writing before the meeting helps avoid mistakes brought on by thinking on your feet, plus it speeds the meeting along. If things run smoothly, you should get the official notification within a week or two of the site visit that your grant is approved and funded.

■ *Strategies for Writing a Successful Proposal: The Research Plan*

SPECIFIC AIMS: DEFINITION OF THE RESEARCH PROBLEM

Granting agencies require that the research problem be stated at the beginning of the proposal. Get right to it. Save the introductory points for the "Significance" section later in the proposal. Follow the guidelines that were presented in Chapter 2 on defining the problem. Define the subproblems here, if there are any. Stick to one page or less. The dependent variable and major independent variables and the terms used in the statement of the problem and subproblem statements must be defined conceptually here.

HYPOTHESES

State the major hypothesis or hypotheses if the proposed study is of the hypothesis-testing variety. You can use the "If X, then Y" format or write simple declarative sentences; for example, "Longevity of the rural elderly is explained by social factors more so than physiobiological processes. More specifically, once one controls for the effects of age, gender, and health status, social networks will be the most influential predictor of longevity."

■ *The Significance of the Proposed Study*

THEORETICAL SIGNIFICANCE

The proposed study ought to be part of some theoretical tradition to which it will contribute. Ancient and modern theorists who are central to the tradition or school of theory should be cited by way of a brief explanation of how their work and the proposed study relate. This section of the proposal should communicate to the reviewers how the proposed research contributes to the particular discipline in question.

PRACTICAL SIGNIFICANCE

This section addresses what social and/or policy problems the proposed study will help to resolve. It should explain how the study will do this.

PRELIMINARY STUDIES

This is where you get a chance to display the work that you have done prior to the grant submission that has relevance to the proposal. It really helps the chances for getting funded to have a track record. In my National Institute on Aging (NIA) proposal, the previous two successful waves of interviews with the rural elderly panelists lent credibility to the proposed third wave of interviews. If you have a head of steam up, the chances are good that you will continue to move ahead with appropriate levels of funding. The reviewers weigh this factor heavily.

Of course, you have to start somewhere and build a track record of research and publication on the particular research problem in question, and reviewers know this, too. There are grants designed for new investigators who do not have established research identities in a particular field to give them this opportunity.

METHODOLOGY

Tell the reviewer in the first paragraph what the basic research design is. Include the unit of analysis, the number of cases, the method for selecting the cases, the analyses technique(s), and the design *per se*, be it an experiment, panel, or some combination. Think of this first paragraph as an abstract of the methodology.

Be sure to operationally define the key concepts and tell the reviewer how you will attempt to establish the validity and reliability of your measurements. Use established measures whenever appropriate.

Describe the procedures you plan to use to analyze the data. Any data reduction, such as abstracting newspaper accounts or coding raw interview data, must be described clearly and in detail. If you plan on coding, how will you do it? Will you use code sheets or punch the data directly onto the computer from the schedules? How many coders will you have, and how will they be trained and managed? What statistical techniques will you use, and what computer system will facilitate this? All of the methodological decisions surrounding the design of the study, the field work, and the analysis must be clearly stated.

LITERATURE REVIEW

Be selective by covering only the most salient recent studies, theoretical works, and reviews that support the proposed research. Use subheadings to organize the literature review around the key variables and hypotheses, if relevant. For example, the crux of my proposal to NIA was the relationship between social networks and mortality. Thus, I used a subheading "Social Networks and Mortality" for the key literature that deals with this relationship. The statement of the problem, hypotheses, and literature review should be interdependent.

OTHER MATERIALS

The copies of the proposal that get sent out for review contain the above bare bones of the proposed research. This streamlining produces quicker review turn-around time. The pressure to get the proposals reviewed by a body of one's professional colleagues has created the problem of too much to write and not enough pages allowed to write it. An old standby for getting things into the proposal that do not fit within the agency page limits is an appendix. Use appendices freely to present data tables, data-gathering instruments, descriptions or examples of statistical techniques, and so forth.

PREREVIEW REVIEW

Send a rough draft of the proposal out to colleagues who can give it a tough once-over. Take their criticisms seriously, and make changes accordingly before writing and submitting the final draft to the granting agency. Also, arrange to present your proposed research to a knowledgeable seminar group. The identification of problems in understanding the research problem or analysis and other criticism makes for a valuable, albeit painful learning experience. It helps overcome a subtle and relatively deadly mistake we all tend to make when writing about something familiar. We assume too much, taking for granted the nuances and assumptions of our research, which is tough on readers who do not share this knowledge. I have dozens of reviewers' comments on failed grant proposals and rejected publication submissions that told me that the reviewers stumbled over something I thought was clearly visible but obviously was not. Take nothing for granted. If in doubt, spell it out, even to the point of repeating yourself. Redundancy is not the worst sin in grant writing.

■ *The Research Report*

The research report is a much more detailed and lengthy document than the grant proposal. One, the report should have an extensive introduction along with acknowledgments. Two, the literature review should be more extensive and ought to include some history of the concepts and theory being used. Three, theoretical and methodological strengths and weaknesses are presented in detail. Four, the research report contains a full-blown analysis of the data. You must present findings that are tangential perhaps to the main research problem but that provide descriptive and analytic context for the readers. The report is more than a means of communicating key findings. It should have lots of data and findings to stimulate further research. Marginal frequencies, cross-tabulations, statistical tests, and other multivariate analyses all must be presented graphically, described, and discussed. Put most of the tables, charts, and figures in appendices. Save the key relationships and their graphics for the text. Finally, the research report has a conclusions section with appropriate recommendations for further research or application of the findings. The same principles of writing and organization discussed above in the grant writing section apply here.

■ *Conclusions*

A good scientific writer can name his or her own ticket for a career in research. Mastery over writing takes practice and basic writing techniques. Good writing starts with thinking. Ruminate on the problem that you are about to tackle. Think about angles or perspectives from which to write. Explore ideas that pop into your mind by playing out their consequences and relationships to other more established ideas. Think about how the objects of the evaluation might be thinking on the problem, think about the possible findings and their political consequences. Try to conceptualize the research problem so that you are shedding new light on things. Think until your thoughts start repeating themselves.

Use such writing techniques as summaries, relevant introductions, good sentences, and meaty phrases. Do not make room for words, phrases, and sentences that say little or nothing. You do not need filler in research publishing.

Grants and contracts are different. The grant is competitive, and the researcher has enough professional freedom to do the research and to write it up in a scientifically sound fashion. No one but the researcher decides what the conclusions are. The contract constrains the researcher, who is in danger of becoming a hired-hand evaluator.

Obtaining a grant is time-consuming, frustrating, and tedious. It takes concentration, sharp methodological skills, and, above all, tenacity. Perhaps the single greatest asset that a grant writer might strive to possess is doggedness. Success in grant writing comes with the ability to recognize and take advantage of reviewer advice, to resubmit the application, and to do this over and over again in the face of apparent failure. Big egos that are easily bruised do not do well in the competitive grant-writing game. Picking oneself off the floor and coming back for more is the behavior that gains the advantage. This doggedness conveys two important messages to reviewers. One, such determination is evidence of a high degree of interest in and commitment to the research. Enthusiasm is infectious. Two, revising the proposal in light of reviewer suggestions signifies open-mindedness and a willingness to learn, two excellent qualities for any researcher to possess.

Model your proposal after proposals that have been funded. Study the way the successful proposals address the RFP requirements, the way they are written and packaged. Communicate well in advance of the proposed deadline with the agency grant or contract specialist in charge of the RFP. Run your ideas by this individual and take his or her advice seriously. If you plan to cooperate with others on the proposal, make sure that the combined arrangements are workable and meet the agency requirements. Your act must be together before writing the proposal because you can rest assured that getting it together after the proposal has been submitted will show in the proposal. Submit your final draft of the proposal to colleagues and ask them to tear it apart. The copy submitted to the agency must be as nearly flawless as possible. Methodological weaknesses are inherent in all studies. *Flawless* does not mean without methodological problems. *Flawless* means alerting the reviewers to the problems, showing them that you are on top of the methodology and that you have made the best compromises possible.

Preliminary work or a track record in the area of the proposed research is a plus. It might be worth your while to spend a year doing preliminary research and presenting the results at seminars and professional meetings before going after big grant money. There are new-investigator grants for just this purpose. If you do not have much of a track record in the substance of the proposed research but you are a recognized methodologist, then you might consider collaborating with someone with a track record. The whole purpose of collaboration on grants is to take advantage of the wealth of talent within a university or profession and to put combinations of these strengths together for one project.

Finally, spend a lot of time and effort on the literature. This will help you take advantage of the methodological strengths and weaknesses of previous studies. Also, it will give you a strong sense of where your proposed study fits into the larger scheme of things in the discipline. Writing about the significance of the proposed research cannot be done effectively unless the researcher knows where the cutting edge of the research is relative to the proposed study. If the sociology of aging research is on the verge of solving a major social and theoretical problem and your proposed study is a vital link, you have the strongest possible case for getting high marks by the reviewers on significance. The point is that the literature review (and communicating with colleagues) puts the researcher in a position to design cutting-edge research.

GLOSSARY

request for proposal   (RFP) is an invitation to researchers to submit a proposal in accordance to stated requirements.

grant proposal   is a written request to do research within specific budgetary and methodological constraints spelled out by the researcher.

contract proposal   is a written request to do research within specific budgetary and methodological constraints spelled out by the agency paying for the research.

site visit   is a trip made by a team of reviewers to the home base of the proposed research to settle questions about the proposed research.

FOR FURTHER READING

Noland, Robert L. (1970). *Research and Report Writing in the Behavioral Sciences.* Springfield, Ill.: Thomas.

Reif-Lehrer, Liane. (1989). *Writing a Successful Grant Application,* 2d ed. Boston: Jones and Bartlett Publishers.

Strunk, Jr., K. W., and E. B. White. (1979). *The Elements of Style,* 3rd ed. New York: Macmillan Publishing Co., Inc.

Chapter Thirteen

EVALUATION RESEARCH:
A WINDOW TO POLICY RESEARCH

■ *This chapter starts with a definition of evaluation research and a discussion of its proper place on the social action-basic research policy continuum. Next, the societal and methodological principles underlying evaluation research are discussed. After this, the types of evaluation research approaches are presented and critiqued in terms of their relative strengths and weaknesses. Next, I present a section on how to do evaluation research, citing examples from Project Head Start, the "Coleman Report," and the "Sesame Street" evaluation. Because the "Sesame Street" evaluation was so well done and had such a profound impact on public policy, I have included a detailed examination of it in a separate box. Finally, I discuss the problems associated with getting evaluation research results into the proper social action systems.*

In a very real sense, the best in this book has been saved for the last. This chapter is not the best because of my doing but because of the subject matter. Evaluation research is a ticket for the social scientist to really make a difference in the society through the application of his or her discipline.

Another point that must be made is that evaluation research as a field within the larger discipline of research methodology is fraught with controversy. Evaluation is political and manifests legitimacy problems from within the ranks of social scientists. But a little controversy will not deter us from exploring evaluation research in this chapter.

■ *What is Evaluation Research?*

A clue to the definition of evaluation research is value, the root of the word *evaluation*. A value is something of worth or merit. To evaluate is to consider or to pass judgment on the worth or merit of something. Thus, in the broadest sense, evaluation research is research that passes judgment on the value of something. Because of this judgment aspect, evaluation research is very different from other forms of research that have been discussed throughout the other chapters of this book. Evaluation research is blatantly value-loaded. While it is methodologically incorrect to produce value judgments in the course of basic research, doing just that is a requirement of evaluation research. In basic research, you might analyze variables, discover interesting and significant relationships between the variables, and draw appropriate conclusions. You would discuss the reasons one maternal and child health program gave prenatal medical care to 50 percent of the pregnant women eligible to receive care at the program while the other program saw 75 percent of the eligible women. But you would not go any further with your write-up. On the other hand, an evaluation researcher would be obligated to pass judgment on both of the programs. He or she might place a higher value on the 75 percent program than the 50 percent one, or both programs might be declared unworthy for not hitting 100 percent of the eligible women, assuming that was the target performance level. So, not only is there research to do, but then the evaluator must take a position on the merit or worth of the object of the evaluation study.

Evaluation research is defined as research that compares objectives with accomplishments, then passes judgment on how well the objectives were met. It is important to keep in mind that the evaluation researcher goes forward hoping that (1) the assumptions are discernible; (2) objectives are stated (3) in measurable terms; (4) accomplishments are documented (5) in measurable terms; and (6) he or she knows what methodological tricks of the trade to pull out in order to compare the accomplishments with the objectives.

■ *The Research-Social Action Policy Continuum*

Because of its value judgment dimension, evaluation research is nested within the realm of applied social science. One way to understand evaluation research is to view it as existing on a policy continuum. If policy is viewed as the principles governing institutions and programs, we can define the process of formulating policy as containing basic research, applied research, evaluation research, and social action. Viewed as on a continuum, social action is one extreme of the policy process and basic research the other (see Figure 13-1). The social action people usually want only to get on with what they are sure works and what they feel is right, and that often is the action that they are engaged in. They have little, if any use, for research of any kind. Social action folks believe in what they are doing, or they would not be doing it. If you believe already, what use is research? I recall many

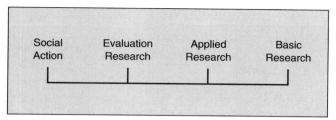

Figure 13-1 ∎ Evaluation/Social Action Continuum

instances during the course of a study of neighborhood health centers for the poor when social activists would comment to the effect that asking a bunch of questions about poverty and health care for the poor was not the way to create more opportunities and, ultimately, some wealth for low-income people.

At the other end of the continuum are the basic research people who may care deeply about the uses to which their research might be put but do not make this part of their research program. If I am interested in Max Weber's theory about charisma as it pertains to the charismatic Catholic movement, I will design a study of charismatic Catholics without considering the probability that I am the only soul in society who is interested in the research. Whether or not someone in a policy position uses my findings is immaterial to me.

There is quite a bit of tension between the basic research and social action camps. The basic research types point to history or eighteenth-century English literature as examples of legitimate academic endeavors that do not depend upon socially beneficial applications for their existence. Some even point to the fragmentation in social scientific data and theory and argue that social scientists are in no position to offer much of anything to the policy process. On the other side, the social action people argue that social scientific research should be funded, that is, supported by the society, only if the findings can be used to solve pressing social problems.

Somewhere between these two groups are the applied social scientists and the evaluation researchers. As shown in Figure 13-1, evaluation research is closer to social action, and applied research shades more toward basic research. However, whereas social action pays little or no attention to research, evaluation research can hardly afford to do that. Basic researchers pay little if any attention to the application of their findings. Evaluation researchers do not have that option either. Often the methodology of evaluation research is less complicated than that of basic research. If a program is being evaluated, the research problem is pretty well defined for the researcher by the program's objectives, and formulating theory and hypotheses are not necessary. But in other ways having to do with research entry and the dissemination of the findings, evaluation research can be much more difficult than basic research. Commonly, the evaluation researcher will have to interact with a suspicious or even hostile program administrator who views the research as a real threat to his or her job security. Suspicious administrators with a strong personal stake in the program might throw roadblocks in the way in the form of hiding relevant information or denying access to important

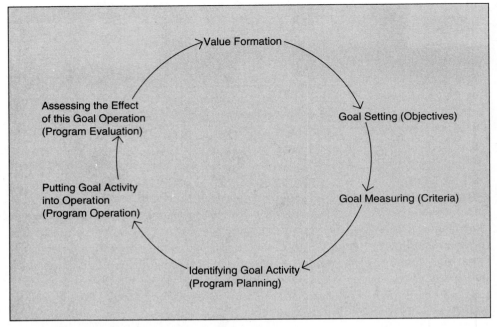

Figure 13-2 ■ Suchman's Evaluation/Policy Cycle

people and information. In some ways, one can think of doing evaluation research as walking a path down a steep and narrow canyon hemmed in on one side by the norms of methodologically sound research and on the other side by the political demands of judging important and visible human activities.

In a more precise fashion, evaluation research is scientific research methodology designed to compare accomplishments against objectives. In doing this, the evaluator passes judgment on the accomplishments, perhaps even on the objectives, in assessing the worth or value of what is under study. The key issues then are to know what *compare* means (research design issues), to be able to find objectives, and to measure those objectives by being able to measure the accomplishments. More will be presented on these points later.

■ *The Evaluation Research-Policy Cycle*

Suchman, in his excellent social action-sensitive book on evaluation research (1967), pointed out that evaluation research and public policy are inextricably intertwined and mutually dependent because values are inherent to programs and to evaluations of programs. Consequently, Suchman defined the evaluation process as a circular one, starting with values and ending with values (see Figure 13-2).

Suchman uses the example of cancer diagnostic programs. Value formulation is where the society defines the items of worth. Goals stem from values. One of the values associated with cancer detection is the value that living a long life is good. Next comes the objective of reducing deaths from cancer by 50 percent. You can see how this objective is highly compatible with and in fact derives from the value of living a long life. The next three steps, in reality, are not in the nice sequence that Suchman presents but involve a lot of interaction. The goal-measuring stage is necessary in order to evaluate some effort to reduce mortality, because before you are able to demonstrate success or failure regarding the 50 percent reduction, you must know what the current death rate is and have measured it. So, this second stage is crucial. If you are unable to achieve it, then the evaluation project should be scrapped and a new approach designed. The third stage involves conceiving a program that will achieve the objective. In this case, a cancer screening and detection program is designed at the third stage and implemented at the fourth stage. Usually, there is some revising and testing between the activities of these three stages before the fourth stage is realized. The fifth stage is the evaluation itself, the comparing of the objective with the program. Here, you would measure the reduction. Finally, the results of your evaluation, that is, your judgment of the program, leads you to reassess the original value of a long life.

Evaluation research includes the following areas of focus: (1) context—the setting or sociocultural environment, both internal and external, in which the object of the evaluation, for example, a social action program, functions; (2) content—the action produced by the program or whatever is being evaluated; (3) process—the functioning of the program, how it works; (4) output—the performance level of the program, a description of the number of times such and such happened; (5) outcome—how close the performance came to reaching the objective; and (6) benefit—whether achieving the objective lead to a better society or life. All of these steps are covered in evaluation research. Think of an evaluation of a bird trying to fly in order to gain clarity on these six points. The objective is to fly from point A to point B in thirty minutes. The context is the bird's level of health (internal) and the physical environment, both natural and human-made; the content is the bird's body parts designed to get it airborne; the process is the movement of the pectoral muscles, the movement of the wings and tail, and the position of the feathers; the output is the number of times the bird flaps its wings; the outcome is how well the bird flew, that is, how long the bird flew in what time frame; and the benefit is whether the flight did the bird any good.

Now we turn to the societal and methodological principles underlying evaluation research.

Principles of Evaluation Research

LEGITIMACY

Every institution, organization, even a social system such as an entire society must present an ongoing case to its constituency for justifying its existence. Legitimacy is a collective agreement by the persons affected by the organization or institution that the entity is worth protecting and nurturing. Legitimacy is a life or death matter, for no society or institution can survive long without it. The pressure to establish and maintain legitimacy drives the engine of evaluation research. Evaluation research is done to satisfy the demand for public accountability, for legitimacy. Evaluation research is not done to discover new knowledge, although that frequently happens in the course of evaluations. Nor is evaluation research conducted because there is a subgroup of research methodologists who love the action, so to speak, although most evaluation researchers I know love their work very much. No, evaluations are not done because program administrators are inherently curious about how their programs are doing. In fact, most administrators would love to be able to advertise only the successes and ignore the failures, a state that evaluation researchers would correct immediately. Rather, evaluation research is a universal requirement of societies where institutions depend on legitimacy for their continuance.

The greater the effort put into creating and maintaining institutions, organizations, and other patterned human action, the greater the demand for accountability and, hence, the greater pressure to assert legitimacy. Also, programs that have a minority constituency, that is, programs that are outside of the mainstream of the society, are under great pressure to achieve legitimacy. Finally, the more political clout, that is, power or influence, that a group has, the less likely it will be the subject of evaluation research.

According to these principles, President Lyndon Johnson's War on Poverty and other Great Society programs should have been evaluated to death, which indeed was the case. The U.S. Senate or the Department of Defense, on the other hand, should escape evaluation research efforts, which is also the case. The constituents for the War on Poverty were poor people with little political influence and virtually no political power. The Defense Department's constituency includes the power elite of the country. If you have the power to create hundreds of thousands of jobs and one hundred senators are able to take their due credit, you have enough power to stave off evaluation efforts. Legitimacy is still an issue, but the pressure to prove it is relieved for a time through political influence. The poor have no such luxury and are under constant pressure to show society that job training efforts, health care programs, and Aid to Dependent Children payments are efficiently managed and effectively implemented. The society has a strong image of welfare cheaters and lazy poor people who are breaking the federal treasury with the high costs of their programs. Almost no similar pressure is brought to bear on wealthy farmers in the West who enjoy huge water welfare programs or some of the largest defense contractors. Note how even the language reflects this bias. We "throw" money at welfare problems but "allocate" money for defense problems. Legitimacy demands are unequally distributed among the institutions and organizations of the society.

THE CHANGING NATURE OF SOCIAL PROBLEMS AND PUBLIC EXPECTATIONS

The social sciences have played a major role in the shift in perspective from viewing social problems, such as poverty, homelessness, unwed teenage mothers and fathers, unemployment, and health care-induced bankruptcy, as the responsibility of individuals to the view that society is responsible. As the blame shifted from the victim to the system, so did expectations held by citizens of the system. In short, expectations escalated so that citizens are demanding more productivity and more accountability of the society. In the health care institution, the expectations of citizens has shifted from health care as a privilege to health care as a basic human right. More and more people expect to receive health care regardless of their ability to pay. The expectation that the individual will assume the responsibility for insuring against catastrophic health care costs is shifting to the expectation that the society should assume this responsibility through some form of national health insurance with the risk shared by all citizens equally. Along with this shift in expectations is a change in theory about the cause of health problems. There has been a subtle but widespread change from viewing individuals as responsible personally for their health problems to the belief that social conditions cause the bulk of health problems. For example, the food industry is under fire for processing practices, e.g. nitrates, dyes, etc., that cause cancer and other forms of morbidity. The public is increasingly aware of the relationship between food additives, pesticides, herbicides, and cancer, and it is demanding accountability through evaluations of the industry. This pressure has risen so fast and so strong that the U.S. Food and Drug Administration has been caught off guard and has had great difficulty mounting enough evaluation studies to meet the pressure. Also, for the first time in the recent history of medicine, we are seeing serious efforts to evaluate the efficacy of high-tech medical procedures, such as cardiac catheterization, CAT scans, organ transplants, coronary bypass surgery, and so forth. There is more demand for evaluation in medicine than there is supply of trained evaluators to do the work. People expect more accountability, and evaluation research is poised to do the job.

SOCIAL CLASS AND VALUES

Societal values and the distribution of social class, power, and status affect how individuals judge the impacts of programs and institutions. For example, a job training program might produce a rapid increase in employment among poor blacks but a lesser increase among poor whites. If the society values affirmative action for its minority-group members, then the program ought to get high marks. However, if the evaluators' class position has distanced them socially from minorities, then the evaluators might not support the program so vigorously. Or if the folks paying for the evaluation are under political pressure from unions and similarly powerful groups to protect the status quo, then the evaluators could see their conclusions ignored or even changed by the funding agency.

OBJECTIVES AND THE BASIC ASSUMPTIONS UNDERLYING THEM

Program objectives need to be simple in scope, linear in progression, and clearly stated in measurable terms. Almost never is this the case. Furthermore, objectives carry hidden baggage in the form of basic assumptions about the people, the problems, and the context within which the program operates.

Organizations and programs have an unerring tendency to grow from simple to complex, pulling their objectives along with them. It is not too difficult, for example, to design an evaluation of a space program that has as its objective to put a person into orbit. Indeed, that was the objective of the early space programs in the United States and the Soviet Union. Over a relatively short period of time, however, the programs added exploration of space, extended living in weightless environment, manufacturing in space, strategic defense, biological experimentation, and space station design as objectives. On another front, the neighborhood health center program began with a fairly simple set of goals having to do with making primary medial care available to poor people living within the geographic areas served by the centers. Once the center planners and workers discovered that the health problems they were seeing in the centers were due more to living conditions than to germs, the centers shifted gears and added such objectives as environmental sanitation, job training, and local economic development designed to break the cycle of poverty. In both of these examples, some of the objectives contradict others. The primary health problems caused by poverty theoretically should be reduced by programs that eliminate or reduce poverty. Thus, the objective to treat all of the health problems presented at the center directly contradicts the objective to eliminate poverty. Similarly, the space program's objective to put a person in orbit contradicts its objective to have unmanned space probes or strategic defense initiatives. The more objectives there are, the more difficult it becomes to define them all in measurable terms.

The basic assumptions behind objectives are exceedingly difficult to uncover and even more difficult to take into consideration when designing the evaluation itself. For example, Project Head Start was designed to provide low-income preschool children with the opportunity to experience learning styles and academic content well in advance of their entering the first grade. The objectives were written and more or less said this. However, when one considers the basic assumptions underlying these objectives, things get a bit murky because no one involved with the program wrote the assumptions down nor thought about them very much. The program planners and designers assumed that preschool children were better off with Head Start in any form, regardless of the objectives, than they would have been had no program been offered. The Head Start designers must have assumed as well that intelligence, certainly IQ, is not predetermined or set at birth by genes but is influenced by social and economic environmental conditions. Indeed, if IQ were set at birth, Head Start would be an exercise in frustration. Also, the Head Start planners must have viewed the targeted children as deficient educationally, rather than as simply different academically. The objectives were predicated on the assumption that there is something missing in the social and economic backgrounds of the children for which the program is designed to compensate. Compensation, not enrichment, was behind the objectives, although this was not spelled out in black and white. Similarly, during the course of an evaluation I did on the extent to which the neighborhood health center program for the poor was successful in giving control over center operations to local people served by the center, I became aware of a hidden assumption held by many of the government administrative and policy people that the public funds for the health center program would be cut and that many of the 350 or so centers would go out of existence within eight years. The more cynical of the policymakers assumed that the centers were a temporary fix designed to placate or pacify the residents of ghetto areas torn by riots a few years before the center program was established. Of course, the citizens served by the centers were not privy to these assumptions, and they went about their business, for the most part, as if the centers were going to serve their communities indefinitely.

The key point here is to recognize that there are always going to be assumptions behind objectives and that some of the assumptions will be valid, while others will not. The invalid assumptions usually produce very unreliable assumptions, that is, assumptions that change all the time, which ultimately results in unreliable objectives. In such a situation, it is impossible to design a valid evaluation study because you cannot pin down the stated objectives if they are moving targets. Just as soon as you find one objective wanting, a new objective will pop up to accommodate the finding.

METHODOLOGICAL CONTROL

Comparing program accomplishments against stated objectives takes careful methodological design work. The very best methodological control is required if one is to have the kind of confidence it takes to pass judgment on a program or institution. And yet control over research decision making is always more of a problem for evaluation researchers than for basic researchers. Interestingly, the more at stake in terms of political power or funding, the more likely it will be that the evaluation researcher will have control problems with the research decisions. Administrators will want to call the research plays, if you are in a program evaluation setting. A fairly typical problem for the evaluator is having to follow company or organization procedures through all phases of the research decision making. In this case, one can expect innumerable problems with issues of research quality stemming from researcher control. Not too long ago, I was caught in a mild version of this bind. The state facility being evaluated also was the source of the research funds. Decisions to hire research staff had to go through the normal agency personnel system. This meant less researcher control over who was hired, and in one case, I was forced to work with existing personnel, rather than hire the people I wanted. Also, a rather outmoded computer-based data reduction system was forced on me with the reason, "It is ours, it is there, you might as well use it." I had free rein on the other more important methodological decisions, so the loss of control was not a serious quality problem. But with a bit more interference, the evaluation could have been compromised beyond salvaging it.

Since evaluation research depends upon the best scientific methodology possible to produce results that are of sufficient quality to say yes, no, or maybe to some important human activity, anything that makes it difficult or impossible for the evaluator to achieve the highest methodological standards is a real threat to the evaluation and to the people directly affected by the activity. The evaluation research on "Sesame Street," described in Box 13.1, illustrates the above points.

Box 13.1

■ The Evaluation of "Sesame Street"

Evaluation research places the researcher in the middle of the public policy arena with all of its political intrigue. The following case analysis considers the classic evaluation study of the television program "Sesame Street" (Strategies for Success in Compensatory Education, 1969). This evaluation contains most of the key principles of evaluation research and conveys the power of sociological research to influence the setting of policy through evaluation.

A group of evaluation researchers set out to judge whether or not "Sesame Street" met its objectives. First, the evaluators had to locate the objectives for "Sesame Street." This is often a very difficult step because programs do not always set forth their objectives. Or if they do, the objectives may be stated in unmeasurable terms. Thus, the first principle of evaluation research: Objectives must be stated in measurable terms. For example, one could state the objective for the space program as "to explore space." This is an objective, but it is not stated in measurable terms. How does one know when space has been explored successfully? A better way to state it would be "to land a person on the moon by June 14, 1969." The objectives for "Sesame Street" were stated clearly and in measurable terms before the program was aired. It was a nonclassroom experiment in compensatory education, twenty-six weeks long, costing $8 million dollars in 1969, designed to teach low-income children ages three to five eight things: body parts, letters, forms, numbers, relational terms, sorting skills, classification skills, and problem solving. The unit of analysis was individual children, and the evaluation problem centered on their learning experiences.

Often, the basic assumptions underlying objectives are unstated and remain hidden from the researcher. "Sesame Street" was an exception. The program designers went public with their view that the target group was deficient in educational skills, rather than merely different from the middle-class mainstream of society. Furthermore, the designers believed that cultural and ethnic heritage was valuable and worth preserving. Finally, there was the explicit assumption that racial cooperation and harmony were valuable. These assumptions got translated into special program effects, for example, racial harmony promoted by various "Sesame Street" characters of all different shapes, sizes, and colors playing with each other and cooperating as friends.   The accomplishments must be measured and documented in the same fashion as the objectives. The next step of comparing the accomplishments against the objectives requires minimally that the researcher measure the key dependent variable before the program begins and again after the program has had a chance to take effect. The dependent variable in the case of "Sesame Street" was learning in the eight areas. The evaluators conducted a survey before the show began and then after one year of broadcasting. They asked 203 questions focusing on the eight skill areas of a sample of 943 children living in four cities and one rural area.

The findings were truly impressive. The variance in the dependent variable, that is, the differences among the children in the amount of learning in the eight areas, was best explained by the amount of time spent watching "Sesame Street." Those children who watched the most learned the most, regardless of socioeconomic status, age, gender, IQ, and geographic area. Skills on which "Sesame Street" spent the most air time were the skills best learned; children watching at home without supervision learned as much as children watching under teacher supervision in a classroom. The question of benefit to the individuals and the society is the next-to-last step in the evaluation research process. There was little doubt that "Sesame Street" benefited the target children and even the middle-class children who watched.

The final step involves the insertion of the evaluation findings into the political and public policy arena. No matter what the evaluators conclude, some vested interest groups will benefit and some will not. There is bound to be some controversy and struggle. Depending on your political views, compensatory education for socioeconomically disadvantaged children is either good or bad, valuable or worthless. People opposed to the concept will attack the evaluation on theoretical and methodological grounds. The detractors of the "Sesame Street" evaluation argued that the theory and assumptions were incorrect, that children do not experience educational "deficits," but rather simply have different abilities. Others criticized the study conclusions by arguing that "Sesame Street" improved childrens' self-esteem and motivation, not skill levels. According to these critics, children did better on the skills because they were more highly motivated and felt better about themselves, not because they learned the skills. Other critics attacked the fact that the evaluators had not used an experimental design with random assignment to experimental and control groups. Of course, it would have been impossible to conduct the evaluation in the real-world setting using a classic experimental, design, but that methodological point did not dissuade the critics.

The point is that the evaluation demonstrated, with some degree of doubt due to compromises on the research design, that "Sesame Street" did what it set out to do—it benefited children in poverty and consequently the larger society. If early educational deficits caused by poverty can be overcome, then the opportunities for children in poverty should improve generally along with the chances of obtaining a high school and even a college education, thereby reducing welfare, crime, and so on. In short, "Sesame Street" could be viewed as an essential tool for breaking the cycle of poverty. Social policies that foster the continuation of "Sesame Street" and even promote its growth could be expected as a result of the positive findings.

This is exciting territory for a social scientist. In spite of the attacks and funding cuts, "Sesame Street" rode those compelling evaluation findings through the hard times. Today, the show is shown in eighty countries, reaching millions of children. The characters are syndicated and are fifth on the list of the best-selling toys, just ahead of the Disney products. Needless to say, "Sesame Street" is financially secure and going strong.

THE RELATIONSHIP BETWEEN EVALUATION, APPLIED, AND BASIC RESEARCH

The mutual dependence of basic and applied research is well documented in the physical sciences and less so in the social sciences. Medicine is an applied science that depends on the basic sciences of anatomy, physiology, and biochemistry. Without these basic sciences, medicine would be a trial-and-error pseudo-science. In turn, the basic sciences would not exist without the purely and inherently coherent disciplines of mathematics and logic. Evaluation research stimulates basic research in many ways. Methodological inventions have emerged from evaluation studies, including the Guttman scale procedure, the keeping of personal daily records, natural experimental designs, and community function indices, to name just a few. Also, evaluation research has raised the level of methodological discussion about validity, reliability, and the basic-versus-applied research controversy. In light of the rather impressive substantive and methodological contributions of evaluation research, few methodologists in the social sciences today give much attention to the applied-versus-basic issue.

To sum up, evaluation research is defined as research that compares objectives with accomplishments. The need to establish legitimacy is the main reason for the popularity enjoyed by evaluation research today. Basic assumptions underlying objectives must be uncovered, a task made even more difficult by the politically sensitive nature of evaluation research findings and the tendency for the evaluator to lose some control of the evaluation research decision process. Evaluation research can be defined operationally relative to the other forms of research and to social action. While social action and research are inherently incompatible, evaluation research is closer to social action than it is to basic research. Evaluators strive for the best of basic research, that is, carefully designed valid and reliable research, and the best of applied research where research findings ought to really make some impact or difference in the society. The Suchman notion of the value-social action-evaluation-value cycle was discussed, along with the foci of evaluation research, namely, the context, content, process, output, outcome, and benefit.

■ *Types of Evaluation Research Approaches*

COST-BENEFIT ANALYSIS

Weighing the benefits derived from a program against the costs of that program is a simple idea in theory, but in practice doing such a cost-benefit analysis is a real challenge. I have heard physicians easily discuss the costs of kidney transplants but get bogged down on the benefits side while trying to place a value on human life.

Thomas Glennan, Jr., has written an excellent discussion of cost-benefit analysis (1972). He used the Johnson administration's War on Poverty to illustrate gaps in planning knowledge and the need to use this evaluative technique. The War on Poverty had detailed and accurate records about how much money was spent, and, in the case of the job programs, output was fairly easy to measure, for example, new jobs and increases in income. Unfortunately, none of the program evaluations was good enough to be used in the planning process. They were so flawed methodologically that they were useless. But cost-benefit evaluation can play a very important role in deciding the fate of existing programs and to give the nod to new program ideas. The point Glennan makes is, "Let's do it right." So, what is cost-benefit evaluation? How does one know a good one from a flawed one?

EFFICIENCY

Getting the maximum output for the dollars spent with as little wasted effort as possible is one operational definition of efficiency. Efficiency is the core concept of cost-benefit analysis in that the substantive goal of such an analysis is to judge program efficiency. To do this, to work within the confines of efficiency, you must be able to design an evaluation that allows you to measure increments or systematic changes in program output. For example, you must measure the efficiency of a group of runners at six-minute-per-mile pace by measuring heart rate, fluid expenditure, body temperature, and lactic acid levels in the blood. Then one subgroup eats Power Bars while the other fasts, and they then run at the same pace. Under these conditions, you would be looking for incremental change in efficiency.

So, in cost-benefit analysis, the program output is measured in a way that allows the evaluator to describe increments (and decrements). If you have measured costs in a standardized fashion, usually in terms of units of money or time, the program with the greatest increment in output for a given cost is the most efficient program. Glennan's schematic (Figure 13-3) is instructive.

Here you are evaluating program X. The benefits are on the left, and they range from 0 to something above B'. The costs are on the bottom, and they range from 0 to something above C'. The figure portrays the marginal relationship between costs and benefits, a cost-benefit ratio, for increments of cost. In this example, the curved line represents the benefit-cost ratio for the program. The marginal cost-benefit ratio for program X operating at benefit B and cost C is calculated by dividing 0B by 0C. This gives you the slope of the line between 0 and A, that is, the marginal cost-benefit ratio. If an increment of cost is added, you need to measure the corresponding benefit and recalculate the new slope, or marginal cost-benefit ratio. Figure 13-4 portrays this concept for two programs, X and Y. The increment in cost (perhaps this would be one hundred more nurses) is C C' ($100. ____ $200. for example) and the increment in benefits for program X is B ____ B' while the increment in benefits for program Y is b ____ b'. The slope (cost-benefit ratio) for program Y is calculated by dividing bb' by CC,' and the ratio for program X by dividing BB' by CC'. In this case, at cost level C, program X achieved higher benefits (B) than program Y (b). But you can see how looking at the average cost like this without taking incremental changes into account can be very misleading. When incremental (marginal) costs and benefits are considered, which means designing such consideration into the evaluation, one is able to see

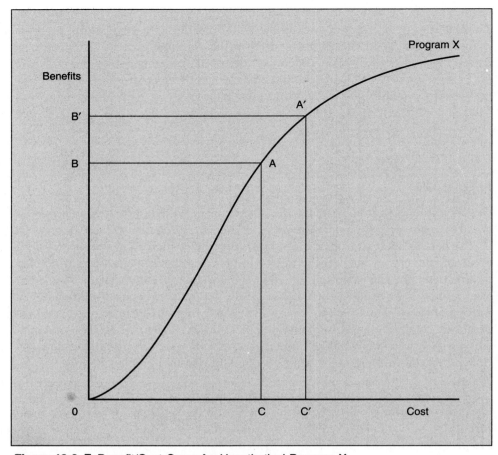

Figure 13-3 ■ Benefit/Cost Curve for Hypothetical Program X

that bb′ divided by CC′ is greater than BB′ divided by CC′. This suggests that the marginal cost-benefit ratio is greater for program Y and that any additional resources should be given to that program and withheld from the other one.

SOCIETAL VALUES, SOCIAL CLASS, AND THE PROBLEM OF CALCULATING BENEFITS

Earlier in this chapter, I discussed the principle of societal values and social class as a determinant of the conduct and uses of evaluation research. Calculating benefits, and even costs to a large extent, is affected by these social forces that operate well beyond the control of evaluators.

Economists are good at figuring out how much bang one gets for a dollar spent. Let's assume that $1 million will generate one thousand blue-collar jobs if the money is spent on public works projects. The same $1 million spent on building military machinery generates twenty jobs. People with a vested class-linked interest in maintaining the gap between the wealthy and the wage earners in the

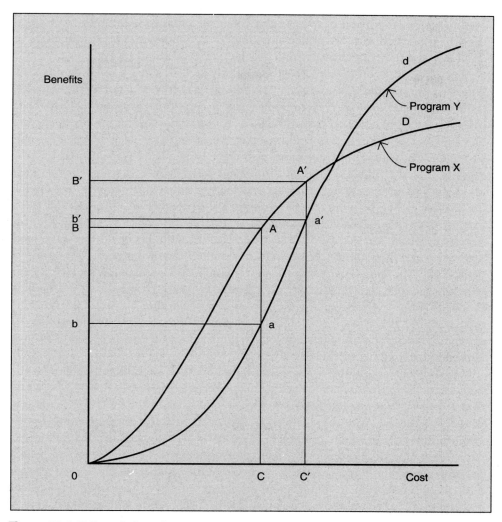

Figure 13-4 ■ Benefit/Cost Curves for Hypothetical Programs X and Y.

society probably would opt for the defense spending as being more beneficial for the society. Then again, individuals from a class position that values a more eq- uitable distribution of wealth in the society might decide that the money should be spent on roads, bridges, and railroads. Obviously, both camps are able to make a good case for benefits, one presenting the defense of the country from external threats and the other presenting the need for defense against the threat of internal decay. Both groups would agree that the benefit of having one thousand tax-pay- ing workers is greater than having twenty workers.

To a large extent, how we calculate benefits depends on what social class we are in. Calculating costs is also constrained by class position. Assuming that the $1 million is tax money, the cost to the working class and the poor will be much greater than the costs to the rich if the money is spent on defense. This is due in part to the fact that members of the working class in the United States spend a much greater proportion of their yearly incomes on taxes than do the rich. Also, the jobs generated with the public spending would employ more working-class individuals and the poor than the defense spending would.

The class and power position of the elderly in U.S. society offers another example of the cost-benefit calculus. The following statistic is reasonably close to the average figure from several national surveys. In the last year of life, individuals living in the United States spend roughly 50 percent of all the money spent in a lifetime on medical care. For the most part, these individuals are sixty-five years and older. Because of this enormous cost crunch, Medicare was enacted by Congress to ease the financial burden of medical care. People sixty-five years of age and older, along with kidney dialysis and kidney transplant patients, are eligible for Medicare. The benefits of this program are evidenced in every person sixty-five and over who has been sick enough to see a doctor or go to a hospital. Another benefit might be the net increase in elderly adults who, because they have medical care when they need it, are healthier and more functional than they would be without it. The care enables them to remain in the consumer society longer, which helps ease the transfer payment problem. Also, the increased entitlement produces more work for the medical professions, another stimulus to the economy. Finally, there are the nebulous quality-of-life factors, including the increased capacity for the elderly to enjoy their lives as a consequence of prompt and effective medical intervention.

On the cost side, there is the dollar figure for the program, which can be calculated for any given month or year. Another cost is the unnecessary procedures that are performed on elderly patients whose presence in the system is made possible by Medicare. Also, there is a cost associated with the displacement of other potential patients who are not able to gain entry to the medical care system because they cannot afford it or because the services are tied up by lots of elderly patients. If the lion's share of the finite health care dollar is allocated to Medicare, cuts in other medical care entitlement programs will have to be made. Finally, the quality-of-life area can become a deficit and a cost, both to the individual and to the society. For example, an independently living elderly person suffers kidney failure and, because of Medicare, is able to get into a kidney dialysis program. Once in the program, the person's health deteriorates further, and she has to go into a nursing home. Nursing home care is not covered under Medicare, and she does not have supplemental insurance. Thus, the only option is for the patient to do what is euphemistically called "spend down," or go broke, in plain English. What are the costs of this to the individual and society?

Individual societies are characterized by complex, even confused value systems. cost-benefit analysis works best as an evaluative tool when values underlying the evaluation problem are consistent and coherent. It is extremely difficult to conduct a methodologically and substantively sound cost-benefit evaluation within the context of confused values. For example, an evaluation study of accident prevention programs might calculate the benefits in terms of the number of accidents prevented in various modes of travel, farming, mining, and the home. The costs might reflect widely disparate values placed on the different accident sectors. For example, home accident prevention might have cost twelve hundred dollars per accident prevented, while air travel might have cost $1 million per accident prevented. Are the lives of air travelers valued more than the lives of people at home or agricultural workers? The data would suggest a tentative yes. In any case, such disparities make it difficult to interpret any cost-benefit findings.

NEEDS ASSESSMENT

Another type of evaluation research is needs assessment, where you judge the gap between what the program or other object of an evaluation actually is and what, by some calculations by the evaluator, it ought to be. A simple example is, "The rural health center patients are receiving primary medical care upon demand, but what they really need is a nutrition program and clean drinking water." A social worker said this during a meeting of the staff of a rural health center in Mississippi and members of the county served by the center. They were evaluating the first year of the center's existence. Actually, the social worker was reiterating the center's goals as written in the original grant proposal. The goals compared against the actual output led to the worker's judgment of the gap, which was expressed in the form of a needs assessment. Needs are really gaps between what is and what ought to be.

Several years ago, I participated in a needs assessment for the Missouri Department of Health. This experience illustrates the key steps and concepts of this type of evaluation research. The department head wanted to identify gaps in the services provided to the people of the state. We began by defining the service area, or the geographic area under the jurisdiction of the health department. Next, we defined the target population. This included all individuals who were considered eligible for services under the department's objectives. Then we designed the heart of the needs assessment—the analysis of the demand for services. This would uncover any gaps by identifying needs not met by the program. Unmet needs really are a type of demand for services.

The crux of the needs assessment is the methodology for identifying demand. There are many ways to do this. Face-to-face interviews with a random sample of the target population is very costly but quite effective. Another approach, one that we took, is to use existing data and compare the relevant characteristics of the target population against some national standard.

We broke the target population down into five-year age groupings for males and females and used the latest U.S. census data for the state to arrive at the numbers of individuals in each of the age categories. Next, national health survey data was used to identify the average encounters with medical care per year for each of the age and sex categories. By multiplying the service area population by the national average of encounters, a total encounters figure for the state was calculated. Figure 13-5 illustrates how this might look.

From here, it is a simple matter to zero in on any particular health service that the state offers. For example, if 25 percent of all U.S. medical encounters are for psychiatric treatment, then multiply .25 by the state total (87,700 in our incomplete example above), which will yield the demand for psychiatric services in the state (21,925 per year). At this point, you are in a position to search for gaps in

Age and Sex Groups	1990 Census for State	×	Average U.S. Encounters per Year	=	Total Encounters for State
17–22 M	7,500		4.2		31,500
17–22 F	6,000		3.5		21,000
23–28 M	6,500		3.0		19,500
23–28 F	6,800		4.5		30,600
Etc.					87,700

Figure 13-5 ■ Example of Service Demand Calculation

Psychiatric Specialty	FTE	×	Average U.S. Encounters per Year	=	Total Service Encounters per Year
Child	.5		10,000		5,000
Adult	1.5		20,000		30,000
Adolescent	.1		20,000		2,000
			50,000		37,000

Figure 13-6 ■ Example of Service Area Supply Calculation

existing services, but to do this, you need one more piece of information concerning the supply or current output in the service area. You must know the number of full-time equivalent (FTE) medical care practitioners in the service area plus the number of encounters per year in the service area for that type of practitioner. In our example, we were looking at psychiatrists, thus we used licensure and other state medical society records to locate each practicing psychiatrist in the service area. The encounter data would come from the same national health survey that provided information on the national average of encounters per year. Figure 13-6 represents a hypothetical case of measuring service area supply.

One FTE could be one psychiatrist or four quarter-time psychiatrists. There are child psychiatrists, adult psychiatrists, and adolescent psychiatrists, each with their own national data on cases seen per year, so this figures into the calculation. The national average of encounters per year is the same data from Figure 13-4, only specific for psychiatrists. In this hypothetical example, the gaps in service area supply are in child and adolescent psychiatric encounters, with an overall deficit of twenty-three thousand per year.

Let us turn now to some basic strategies for designing evaluation research.

■ *How to Design Evaluation Research*

DEFINITION OF THE EVALUATION PROBLEM

Like all other forms of research, evaluation research begins with the definition of the evaluation problem. Unlike other types of research, however, evaluation problems focus usually on total programs, rather than on specific variables and hypotheses. Basic researchers study why it might be the case that the more of A, the more of B. Basic researchers define research problems that should be, by design, nonevaluative in form. If the research problem is the incidence of heart disease in twenty- to twenty-nine year-old females, the hypotheses that state a relationship between lack of exercise or ingestion of saturated fat are stated in a value-neutral fashion, for example, the more saturated fats a woman ingests, the higher the incidence of heart disease. No judgment is made about the desirability or benefits of the independent variables in the hypotheses.

Evaluation problem statements are a bit different. The problem or dependent variable is the behavior or state of affairs that some program seeks to affect. In the case of heart disease, the evaluation problem or dependent variable would be the incidence of heart disease. But the problem would be defined with a slight twist, that being the planned increment or change in the problem area. The independent variable usually is some programmatic effort deliberately and within solid value terms (heart disease is bad and any reduction in the incidence is good or valued) set in motion to change the dependent variable in some planned way. If the plan or objective is to reduce heart disease by 25 percent in two years, then the evaluation problem would ask whether or not the specific program designed to do the job actually succeeded. Since research problems in basic social science research should grant that social reality is complex and that no one independent variable will determine or cause a dependent variable, the wise evaluator will state the problem in conditional terms. You would not, for example, state that program X (the independent variable) causes or fails to cause the desired changes in heart disease. Rather, you would focus on program X but consider the preconditions and intervening variables that might contribute to the desired effect. The intervening variables are essential in order to do the elaboration analysis needed to improve the odds that you were correct in whatever judgment you reached. How confident are you that program X is associated with the desired effect? Define the problem to include intervening variables, and you will gain in confidence.

Suchman (1967) felt that the classic Roethlisberger and Dickson evaluation of various management strategies to increase worker production demonstrated the importance of defining the evaluation problem to include intervening variables. Their study considered interest and visible concern by management as an intervening variable. The evaluation problem was to judge the effect that various planned management strategies, such as improved lighting, more rest periods, different working hours, and so forth, had on worker productivity. Specifically, did those actions, along with the fact that management showed an interest in the workers simply by doing the research, increase worker productivity? The results were fascinating. Worker productivity (the dependent variable) went up, regardless of the management strategies introduced. Productivity increased with bright lights and with dim lights, with no breaks and with extended breaks, and so forth. Fortunately, the evaluators considered the impact of the research itself as an intervening variable, coming between the independent variable (the management strategies) and the effect (increased worker productivity). As long as the evaluators were on the scene measuring and socializing with the workers, productivity was higher. The intervening variable qualified or interpreted the independent variable.

To conclude this discussion of the statement of the evaluation problem, I suggest that the problem statement include the following: (1) the definition of the object of the evaluation, that is, the activity or status that is to be changed; (2) the definition of the program and other intervening variables, which, by design, should have a stated and measurable effect on the thing being evaluated (the dependent variable); and (3) a statement of how the program should affect the desired changes.

DESIGN

The classic experimental design with random assignment to the experimental and control groups is the ideal evaluation design. Randomization is necessary to ensure that the individuals comprising the two groups are similar at the start of the program or experiment, and the longitudinal dimension allows the evaluator to measure before and after the program. As discussed in the earlier chapter on research designs, the panel, trend, one-shot survey, and case study designs represent compromises to the powerful experimental design and, thus, are relatively less effective in descending order. Evaluation research problems present more than the usual barriers to designing the classic experiment, so often the one-short survey with no controls has to suffice. If you were evaluating the impact of affirmative action on black women, assuredly you would not deliberately and randomly reject one-half of the applicants to an affirmative action program just to get a control group. Be that as it may, the same methodological tools that were presented in earlier chapters, especially in the material on research design, are appropriate for the design of evaluation studies. There is no need to reiterate those strategies, principles, and issues. The "Sesame Street" evaluation study discussed earlier and the "Coleman Report," examined below, are examples of the design strengths and compromises that the real world of evaluation research presents.

THE COLEMAN REPORT

James Coleman and his colleagues (1966) produced the "Coleman Report," one of the most influential evaluation studies ever done. It led courts all over the country to order racial integration of schools through the busing of students, although the study findings implied that busing would not be an especially effective means of creating equality of educational opportunity. The evaluation was both brilliant and seriously flawed in its design, and it serves as a good example of how to do evaluation research and some of the pitfalls in evaluation.

Section 402 of the Civil Rights Act of 1964 reads: "The Commissioner shall conduct a survey and make a report to the President and the Congress, within two years of the enactment of this title, concerning the lack of availability of equal educational opportunities for individual by reason of race, color, religion, or national origin in public educational institutions at all levels in the United States, its territories and possessions, and the District of Columbia." The Office of Education in the Department of Health, Education, and Welfare commissioned Coleman, a quantitative methodologist and sociologist, along with six other evaluators, to do the study and to write the report called for in the law. The Coleman Report resulted.

Conceptually, the evaluation problem was defined nicely:

> Stated in broadest terms, the survey addressed itself to four major questions. The first is the extent to which the racial and ethnic groups are segregated from one another in the public schools. The second question is whether the schools offer equal educational opportunities in terms of a number of other criteria which are regarded as good indicators of educational quality. The attempt to answer this elusive question involves describing many characteristics of the schools. Some of these are tangible, such as numbers of laboratories, textbooks, libraries, and the like. Some have to do with the curriculums offered—academic, commercial, vocational—and with academic practices such as the administering of aptitude and achievement tests and 'tracking' by presumed ability. Other of these aspects are less tangible. They include the characteristics of the teachers found in the schools—such things as their education, amount of teaching experience, salary level, verbal ability, and indications of attitudes. The characteristics of the student bodies are also assessed, so far as is possible within the framework of the study, so that some rough descriptions can be made of the socioeconomic backgrounds of the students, the education of their parents, and the attitudes the pupils have toward themselves and their ability to affect their own destinies, as well as their academic aspirations. Only partial information about equality or inequality of opportunity for education can be obtained by looking at the above characteristics, which might be termed the schools' input. It is necessary to look also at their output—the results they produce. The third major question, then, is addressed to how much the students learn as measured by their performance on standardized achievement tests. Fourth is the attempt to discern possible relationships between the students' achievement, on the one hand, and the kinds of schools they attend on the other.

The dependent variable or evaluation problem was educational attainment, and the independent variables were generally from the realm of the characteristics of the schools, including segregation patterns.

Coleman and his colleagues next presented the basic assumptions underlying the evaluation effort. In summary form, these were: (1) A statistical survey will give the evaluator only "fragmentary evidence" of the school environment of a child. (2) The reams of statistics, especially averages and correlations generated by the evaluation, obscure the diversity they represent. The extreme difference between a particular ghetto school and a wealthy all-white school would remain hidden by statistical analyses based on means and standard deviations, in short, averages. (3) Home and total neighborhood social environments are powerful contributors to the educational and personal growth of children. (4) Cumulative effects are masked by statistical analyses, for example, the statistic "teacher without a college degree" does not reflect the added impact of that teacher having grown up in the neighborhood and thereby sharing the educational deficits with the kids, such as poor vocabulary and negative attitudes toward higher education. (5) Relative deprivation is unmeasured, but it exerts a powerful effect on educational achievement. Just as a dime means more to a poor person than to a rich one, so too will an excellent educational experience mean more to an educationally deprived child than to an educationally blessed one. (6) Unequal educational treatment for blacks in the South carries much greater impact in terms of number of children affected than similar discrimination in the North, due to the large percentage of black school-age children in the South.

Methodologically, the evaluation was based on a stratified two-stage random sample of four thousand public schools representing all the regions of the United States. Questionnaires were mailed to all the teachers, principals, and district superintendents in these schools, along with all the students in the third, sixth, ninth, and twelfth grades, and one half of the first-grade students. Also, these students were administered a standardized achievement test. Roughly 645,000 students were involved in the survey. Questionnaires did not contain any personally identifying characteristics of the respondents. The data on the physical facilities of the schools and the academic and extracurricular activities at the schools were derived from questionnaires filled out by the school personnel. Teachers and administrators also provided information about their own educational background, their philosophy of education, and the socioeconomic characteristics of the neighborhoods surrounding their schools. Data on student socioeconomic background, level of education of their parents, reading materials and other educationally enhancing items in their homes, academic aspirations, and attitudes toward staying in school came from the student questionnaires. The census and the *National Inventory of School Facilities and Personnel* were used as data sources to define the primary sampling units (schools) and to stratify the schools by geographic region and the percentage on nonwhites in the school.

The evaluators found first and foremost that the vast majority of the children studied (almost 100 percent in the South) attended segregated schools, that is, schools where the majority of their peers were of their same race. A similar pattern of segregation held for the teachers, with whites teaching whites, blacks teaching blacks, and whites teaching blacks.

Turning to the quality of education, Coleman and his colleagues concluded that racial segregation had a significant negative impact on the quality of educational output. Black students had fewer of the facilities considered to be related to academic success, such as books and laboratories. Also, schools attended by black students had fewer vocational education and extracurricular enhancement programs and did less intelligence testing. Teacher ability (measured by a thirty-word vocabulary test), the educational level of the teacher's parents, the type of college attended, salary, and years of teaching experience were lower for the average black student. Student intellectual achievement in reading, writing, and problem-solving skills, the dependent variable, was tested. The various parts of this achievement test were analyzed as separate dependent variables, that is, the nonverbal part was used as the dependent variable for one analysis, then the mathematics part for another, the general information test for a third, and so forth. Coleman and his colleagues settled on the verbal test after noting little, if any difference, in any of the other dependent variables and that it showed the highest correlations with the other test scores. Furthermore, they argued that the verbal ability test was the best measure of differences in achievement affected by differences between schools, simply because the test is less directly related to particulars of school curricula. For this, the researchers were roundly, but probably unfairly, criticized (Cain and Watts, 1970). In any case, they found significant school-to-school achievement deficiencies in achievement for black students, and these deficiencies got progressively worse in each higher grade level. Southern blacks had the greatest deficits. Coleman would have liked to have analyzed within school sources of this achievement problem but was unable to because he did not gather the appropriate data on educational quality differences within any particular school, such as the particular set of teachers who had taught a particular child. Other data that were gathered, such as the number of advanced or honor courses a student took, were dependent on achievement, hence could not be considered as independent variables. Unfortunately, the greatest variation in achievement lay within the school, rather than between schools (the variations of individual verbal scores of students in a particular school around the mean score of his or her racial group in the school were greater than the school-to-school or between-school variations). Thus, such school factors as lab facilities could not be very relevant in explaining the achievement differences. Family background and community factors that affected family background emerged as the critical reasons for the inequality in achievement between poor and rich, black and white. The achievement differences were fairly large at grade one, before the particular school factors would have had a chance to influence achievement. The higher achievement of blacks in schools with greater percentages of white students had little to do with better facilities and curricula. Rather, it had to do with teachers' characteristics and the family background characteristics of the students, including the educational levels of the parents and the educational aspirations of the students themselves. As Coleman and his colleagues wrote: "This means that the apparent beneficial effect of a student body with a high proportion of white students comes not from racial composition per se, but from the better educational background and higher educational aspirations that are, on the average, found among white students. The effects of the student body environment upon a student's achievement appear to lie in the educational proficiency possessed by that student body, whatever its racial or ethnic composition" (p. 310).

Coleman and his colleagues urged the members of Congress and other readers of the report to think beyond the scope of the evaluation findings linking integration and academic achievement. They wrote: "An education in integrated schools can be expected to have major effects on attitudes toward members of other racial groups. At its best, it can develop attitudes appropriate to the integrated society these students will live in; at its worst, it can create hostile camps of Negroes and whites in the same school. Thus, there is more to 'school integration' than merely putting Negroes and whites in the same building, and there may be more important consequences of integration than its effect on achievement." They went on to argue: "Yet the analysis of school factors described earlier suggests that in the long run, integration should be expected to have a positive effect on Negro achievement as well. An analysis was carried out to seek such effects on achievement which might appear in the short run. This analysis of the test performance of Negro children in integrated schools indicates positive effects of integration, though rather small ones. . . . Comparing the averages in each row, in every case but one the highest average score is recorded for the Negro pupils where more than half of their classmates the previous year were white. But in reading the rows from left to right, the increase is small and often those Negro pupils in classes with only a few whites score lower than those in totally segregated classes" (p. 29).

The rest of the evaluation consists of detailed qualitative case studies of school integration efforts, including the 1963 California Supreme Court decision in *Jackson v. Pasadena Unified School District,* in which the court accepted the concept of affirmative integration on the grounds that segregated schools were inferior. In the court's words: "Where such [residential] segregation exists, it is not enough for a school board to refrain from affirmative discriminatory conduct. . . . The right to an equal opportunity for education and the harmful consequences of segregation require that school boards take steps, insofar as reasonably feasible, to alleviate racial imbalance in schools regardless of its cause."

■ *Entering the Policy Arena: Some Advice and Warnings*

Cain and Watts (1970) wrote a scathing critique of the Coleman evaluation, something any good evaluator can expect to occur once the judgments have been made. Their main point was that the Coleman evaluation was deficient in theory, a fact they argued that led to Coleman and his colleagues using the percent of variance accounted for by a variable beyond that accounted for by the variables preceding it in a particular set of variables, an inferior procedure to their way of thinking. This in turn rendered the findings suspect and therefore useless to the policymakers, the critics argued. As an alternative, Cain and Watts advocated a type of cost-benefit analysis based on raw linear regression coefficients standardized in dollar terms. Give the most resources to the variable with the highest bet coefficient, the next most to the next highest variable, and so forth. They argued that the absence of an adequate theoretical model rendered the interpretation of the Coleman findings difficult to justify. If the Coleman interpretations are shaky, then it is unwise, perhaps even unethical, to develop or infer policy regarding busing or any other school integration idea predicated on the results of the study. Cain and Watts urged evaluators to do evaluations that are theoretically grounded and policy sound. Theory, if it contains only variables that can be manipulated and changed through various policies, is the best bet for an evaluator, the authors concluded.

This criticism seems unfair on three grounds. One, Coleman and his fellow evaluators used the most appropriate research design given the time and money constraints. Theory about the relationship between segregation or institutional racism and educational opportunities simply did not exist at the time they designed their study. Because of the absence of logically sound, empirically tested theory, Coleman and his colleagues had to rely more on their sociological instincts than established propositions and hypotheses to do the evaluation. It was a politically pressing evaluation problem that hardly afforded the evaluators the luxury of experimentation, pretesting, and theory construction. In light of the situation and the times, the evaluation is a remarkably thorough and focused piece of research. The design cleverly includes a qualitative case study component, and the evaluators are clear in the definition of the problem and in laying out the basic assumptions underlying the study. They are much less rigid and biased than their critics, who urged evaluators to select only policy relevant variables for study. Who is to say that the policy relevant variables of today will be the relevant ones later on? The family background variables that Coleman and his colleagues included turned out to be some of the key factors behind achievement. And yet, family background is hardly policy manipulable in any sense obvious to most of us. Finally, the Coleman evaluation, like most evaluation studies, involves imperfect data replete with sampling and measurement error along with some substantive gaps, for example, data on within-school achievement relevant experiences. In spite of these methodological weaknesses, the study had tremendous impact on research, theory, and public policy. It sounded the start of a veritable avalanche of studies on racially and socioeconomically based inequality in employment, education, housing, and health care. The statistical technique used by Coleman and his colleagues may have been too imprecise to enable the evaluators to attach dollar figures in some rank order to the key policy variables, but that is probably an advantage in evaluation research. Recalling the discussion of cost-benefit evaluation, determining the value of improving teachers' salaries or reducing unemployment so that all childrens' parents who want work have work and rank ordering the costs accordingly is a policy nightmare. The best bet is to do what Coleman and his colleagues did. Define cleanly an evaluation problem that is right on the program target, use a combination of qualitative and quantitative methods, make your basic assumptions clear, use random sampling procedures if at all possible, and write the analysis and conclusions simply in plain English. Do not make a ton of recommendations for the sake of influencing the policy process. Delimit the evaluative judgments that you have the strongest faith in based on the test of your analysis and take a stab at policy recommendations in that case. Otherwise, let the political process operate, but be sure to wrangle invitations to the policy discussions. Play a backstage role in helping the political policymakers sort out the best applications given your evaluation. If they want to bus students, you might caution them against this in terms of its tangential relationship, at best, to family background. Better perhaps to create the same socioeconomic conditions in poor neighborhoods that produce the desired family background characteristics and attract the most competent teachers that the wealthier neighborhoods enjoy.

Unfortunately for the policymakers who initiated desegregation efforts, especially forced busing, on the basis of the Coleman findings, unanticipated consequences of this action derailed the objectives of improved interracial cooperation and understanding. White flight, that is, the rapid migration of whites away from integrated schools either through physical moves or placing their children in private schools, effectively nullified the desegregation efforts. Years after the report was written, Coleman reflected on what had started out as sound public policy but had become flawed because of the failure of the policymakers to take the white flight reaction into consideration. In Coleman's more pessimistic words: "In school integration, there has been a surprising absence of interest on the part of those formulating and implementing the policy about the overall impact—as opposed to the immediate observable effect—of that policy. The results of these analyses show that the indirect consequences are far from negligible and can sharply reduce or perhaps even in the longer run reverse the intended effect of that policy. . . . The extremely strong reaction of individual whites in moving their children out of a large district engaged in rapid desegregation suggests that in the long run the policies that have been pursued will defeat the purpose of increasing overall contact among races in schools" (1976, p. 321).

Be prepared for political controversy that will have almost nothing to do with the evaluation design, methods of analysis, and so forth. As an evaluator, you will inherit deeply rooted ideological and political conflicts that form the context for the programs that might be evaluated. For example, in the United States we do a bit of social experimentation before launching into a full-scale societywide program, but the political advantages of launching full-scale programs are so great that much of the social action programming is massive and essentially untried. The War on Poverty, the Bureau of Reclamation's massive dam building and irrigation efforts over the past thirty years, public subsidies for tobacco, Medicaid, Medicare, the regional medical program, the neighborhood health center program, and the deregulation of the service sector are a few examples of massive actions that had no research basis prior to their implementation. Evaluating one of these massive programs is a political minefield with vested interests galore and perfectly contradictory objectives existing between and within programs. The subsidies to tobacco are in direct conflict with the government's campaign to get people to quit smoking. Water subsidies to farmers in Utah irrigating with incredibly high-cost water are in perfect conflict with subsidies to farmers in Iowa who are paid not to grow on land with plenty of cheap water. And so it goes in a society where rational planning and organization is only a distant glimmer of an idea. Evaluation in these circumstances is likely to produce supporters and critics alike. The best advice is to anticipate the reactions and try to defuse them as much as possible. The ultimate issue, of course, is the consequences that evaluation judgments might have on the vested interests and sacred cows. Perhaps the best way to anticipate this inevitability is to work hard before doing the evaluation to render the results less consequential for the people involved. Establish a climate in which failure is not considered the worst of all possible states but is viewed as a part of organizational life. Talk openly about the possibility that the program will be found lacking in some essential fashion and promote preevaluation policies that will protect the program people as much as possible from losing their jobs or their program, or if termination is required, then have in place some viable options for people to pursue. This takes planning well in advance of doing the evaluation.

Finally, avoid becoming a hired hand type of evaluator, that is, a researcher who hires out his or her skills to the highest bidder. Choose your evaluation projects judiciously and work to establish a contract that ensures that you are independent and free to call the research shots. Beware of research money with a lot of strings attached. Retain the right to publish in the media of your choice. Discussing these issues with the program administrators before signing a contract is the best insurance against finding yourself the unwitting hired-hand researcher.

■ *Conclusions*

Evaluation research is scientific methodology designed to pass judgment on the value of the entity being evaluated by comparing objectives against accomplishments. Cost-benefit analysis and needs assessment are two of several styles of evaluation research that address effectiveness and efficiency, two core dimensions of any program or institution considered valuable or worthwhile.

Evaluation research is unlike all other types of research because it passes judgment on the object of study. This unique feature places the evaluator squarely in the midst of the policy arena, where politics is the main tool of social action. The more politically sensitive or important the evaluation research conclusions are, the greater the chances are that the results will be applied, even misapplied, in the policy arena. The "Coleman Report" is a good example of the tremendous impact evaluation can have on public policy. The report led to desegregation edicts throughout the nation. It led to misuse of the findings as well with forced racial busing. The "Sesame Street" evaluation, one of several major evaluations of the compensatory education programs in the United States, was another example cited to illustrate how a well-designed evaluation can steer the policy process toward protecting a program. The evaluation concluded that "Sesame Street" was effective in accomplishing all of its stated objectives, thereby giving disadvantaged children a much needed academic boost.

Becoming a hired-hand evaluator is a temptation to which lots of researchers have succumbed. The money to do the research is easy to come by relative to the normal, time-consuming competitive grant process. Here the evaluator gets a contract rather than a research grant. The researcher might see it as an opportunity to break new ground, publish, and make a name for himself or herself. But with easy research money are strings pulling the evaluator in directions that suit the grantor. There are circumstances where doing the grantor's bidding does not compromise the scientific merits of the research. But doing evaluations that must be kept secret from the scientific community or having to get approval from the grantor for all publications are two of many ways in which being a hired hand is doing poor evaluation research. Office of the Navy contracts to evaluate Navy training programs could fall into the category of hired-hand research if such restraints were part of the deal.

The greatest challenge of evaluation research is controlling how the evaluative judgments are applied to policy. Because evaluation research is inherently political and controversial, the researcher cannot afford to let the chips fall where they may. A direct hand in the way the findings are used by the policy process is called for. There are few tested models for playing the role of researcher-policymaker, but that should stimulate methodologists to design and evaluate new policy-relevant research roles.

GLOSSARY

evaluation research   is scientific methodology designed to pass judgment on the value of what is being evaluated by comparing objectives against accomplishments.

policy research   affects the principles that govern institutions and programs.

basic research   is considered legitimate, regardless of its potential for being applied.

context   is the setting for what is being evaluated.

content   is the substance of what is being evaluated.

process   is the functioning of what is being evaluated.

output   is the performance level or action level of what is being evaluated.

outcome   is how well what is being evaluated did in reaching the objectives.

benefit   is whether or not achieving the objectives improved things.

cost   is the effort in time, materials, and money to achieve the objectives.

cost-benefit analysis   is a type of evaluation research that defines the ratio of the costs of achieving the objectives to the benefits derived from that achievement.

legitimacy,   a principle of evaluation research, is a collective agreement that an entity is worth protecting and nurturing.

accountability   is the societal expectation that institutions and organizations will evaluate their worthiness and make the results public.

efficiency   is maximizing output while minimizing costs.

marginal costs or **marginal benefits**   are based on increments of change in costs or benefits.

needs assessment   is a type of evaluation research that compares what exists with what ought to be, given specific objectives.

policy   is the process that decides the basic assumptions, principles, and values governing social action at the individual, organizational, and institutional levels.

FOR FURTHER READING

David S. Cordray (Ed.). (1985). *Utilizing Prior Research in Evaluation Planning.* San Francisco: Jossey-Bass.

Policy Studies Review Annual. Published by Transaction Books, New Brunswick, New Jersey. A series of volumes on research in the field of policy studies.

Posavac, Emil J., and Raymond G. Carey. (1985). *Program Evaluation: Methods and Case Studies,* 2d ed. Englewood Cliffs, New Jersey: Prentice-Hall, Inc.

Rutman, Leonard. (1984). *Evaluation Research Methods: A Basic Guide.* Beverly Hills, Calif.: Sage Publications.

Schuerman, John R. (1983). *Research and Evaluation in the Human Services.* New York: Free Press.

Suchman, Edward A. (1967). *Evaluative Research: Principles and Practice in Public Service and Social Action Programs.* New York: Russell Sage Foundation.

Struening, Elmer L., and Marilynn B. Brewer (Eds.). (1983). *The University Edition of the Handbook of Evaluation Research.* Beverly Hills, Calif.: Sage Publications.

Weiss, Carol H. (1972). *Evaluation Research: Methods for Assessing Program Effectiveness.* New York: Prentice-Hall.

REVISED ASA CODE OF ETHICS

PREAMBLE

Sociological research, teaching, and practice, like other social processes, have positive and negative consequences for individuals and institutions; consequently, the work of sociologists must be enhanced and restrained by ethical considerations. Sociological knowledge can be a form of economic and political power, and sociologists therefore need to protect themselves, the discipline, the people they study and teach, their colleagues, and society from abuses of power that may stem from their work.

Agreement on what constitutes abuses of power is not easily reached. In addition, researchers and teachers face inherent ethical dilemmas. On the one hand, they must be responsive and responsible to the truths they uncover in research and promulgate in teaching; they must not distort or manipulate truth to serve untruthful, personal, or institutional ends, and they must make the findings of basic research available in the public domain. On the other hand, however, a first principle of ethics holds that people are always to be considered ends and not means, so that whether they are being studied or taught, their integrity, dignity, and autonomy must be maintained. The possible conflicts between the responsibilities of sociologists to truth and knowledge and to the rights of their subjects, students, associates, and sponsors is therefore one justification for a code of ethics. Another is that, as professionals, sociologists are expected to regulate themselves through individual, peer, and associational action.

This code has several purposes. It establishes feasible requirements for ethical behavior, that is, standards that are neither unachievably utopian nor crassly "realistic." These requirements cover many—but not all—of the potential sources of

Source: *Footnotes* 8(1980): 12–13. Washington, D.C.: American Sociological Association. Reprinted with the permission of the American Sociological Association.

321

ethical conflict that may arise in research, teaching, and practice. Some provisions are "should" statements that represent ideals to strive for; others are "must" statements that represent necessary rules. Most represent *prima facie* obligations that may admit of exceptions but which should stand as principles to be overruled. The Code states an associational consensus about ethical behavior upon which the Committee on Professional Ethics will base its judgments when it must decide whether individual members of the Association have acted unethically in specific instances. More than this, however, the Code is meant to sensitize all sociologists to the ethical issues that may arise in their work and encourage sociologists to educate themselves and their colleagues to behave ethically. To fulfill these purposes, we, the members of the American Sociological Association, affirm and support the following Code of Ethics:

I. RESEARCH

A. Objectivity and Integrity.

Sociologists should strive to maintain objectivity and integrity in the conduct of their research.

Sociologists should be sensitive to the potential for damage to individuals or groups from public disclosure of research based on ungeneralizable samples or unsubstantiated interpretation. Especially where there is the potential to harm groups or individuals, sociological research should adhere to the highest methodological standards.

1. Sociologists must not misrepresent their own abilities, or the competence of their staff, to conduct a particular research project.

2. Sociologists—regardless of their work setting—must present their findings honestly and without distortion. There must be no omission of data from a research report which must significantly modify the interpretation of findings. And sociologists should indicate where and how their own theory, method and research design may bear upon or influence the interpretation.

3. Sociologists must report fully all sources of financial support in their research publications and must note any special relations to the sponsor that might affect the interpretation of findings

4. Sociologists must honor any commitments made to persons or groups in order to gain research access.

5. Sociologists must not accept such grants, contracts, or research assignments as appear likely to require violation of the principles above and should dissociate themselves from the research if they discover a violation and are unable to achieve its correction.

6. The A.S.A. may ask an investigator for clarification of any distortion by a sponsor or consumer of the findings of a research project in which he or she has participated.

7. When financial support for a research project has been accepted, sociologists must make every reasonable effort to carry out the research proposed and to fulfill the reporting requirements of the funding source.

8. When sociologists, including students, are involved in joint research, there should be explicit agreements at the outset with respect to division of work, compensation, access to data, rights of authorship, and other rights and responsibilities. Such agreements must be observed and not thereafter unilaterally changed by any of the participants.

B. Misrepresentation of Research Role.

Sociologists must not knowingly use their research roles as covers to obtain information for other than sociological research purposes.

C. Cross-national Research.

Research conducted in foreign countries raises special ethical issues for the investigator and the profession. Where sociologists undertaking studies in their own countries work as citizens with certain rights and freedoms, in other countries they enter as guests of the host government. Disparities in wealth, power, and political systems between the researcher's country and the host country may create problems of equity in research collaboration, conflicts of interest for the visiting scholar, or personal risks for individuals and groups in the host country. Further, irresponsible actions by a single researcher or research team can eliminate or reduce future access to a country by an entire profession and its allied fields.

1. In relations with their own government and with host governments, sociologists should not serve as double agents or compromise their professional responsibilities in order to conduct research. Specifically, they should not agree to or provide any government with secret research, secret reports, or secret debriefings.

2. Sociologists should not act as recruiting agents for any organization without disclosing that role.

3. In its conceptualization, design, and execution, the research project should show due sensitivity to and respect for local culture and political situations. Field research by foreign sociologists should normally not be undertaken if it is likely to touch off serious international or domestic conflicts or be widely misunderstood. Studies should also avoid research questions or procedures which are ethnocentric or otherwise inappropriate to the society in question.

4. Research should take culturally appropriate steps to secure informed consent and to avoid invasions of privacy. Special actions may be necessary where the individuals studied are illiterate, of very low social status, and/or unfamiliar with social research.

5. While generally adhering to the norm of acknowledging the contribution of all collaborators, sociologists working in foreign areas should be sensitive to harms that may arise from disclosure and respect a collaborator's wish and/or need for anonymity. Full disclosure may be made later if circumstances permit.

6. All research findings, except those likely to cause harm to collaborators and participants, should be made available in the host country, ideally in the language of that country. With repressive governments and in situations of armed conflict, researchers should take particular care to avoid inflicting harm.

D. Work in Nonacademic Settings.

Sociologists who work in government or industry function in an hierarchical organization, usually under the authority of nonacademic leadership. The goals of such organizations are not the pursuit of knowledge per se but rather the formation and implementation of policy relevant to social services, the marketing of commercial products, etc. Thus, the sociologist who accepts such employment necessarily accepts a particular set of values and norms as well.

1. Sociologists accepting employment as sociologists in business, government, and other nonacademic settings should be aware of possible constraints on research and publication in those settings and should negotiate clear understandings about the conditions of their research activity.

2. Sociologists should make every effort to ensure that analyses or research findings in the public domain or directly affecting public debate are reported honestly and without distortion.

E. Respect for the Rights of Research Subjects.

1. Research subjects are entitled to rights of privacy and dignity of treatment.

2. Research must not expose subjects to substantial risk or personal harm in the research process. Where risk or harm is anticipated, full informed consent must be obtained.

3. To the extent possible in a given study, researchers should anticipate potential threats to confidentiality. Such means as the removal of identifiers, the use of randomized responses, and other statistical solutions to problems of privacy should be used where appropriate.

4. Confidential information provided by research participants must be treated as such by sociologists, even when this information enjoys no legal protection or privilege. The obligation to respect confidentiality also applies to members of research organizations (interviewers, coders, clerical staff, etc.) who have access to the information. It is the responsibility of the chief investigator to instruct staff members on this point.

II. PUBLICATIONS AND REVIEW PROCESSES

A. Questions of Authorship and Acknowledgement.

1. Sociologists must acknowledge all persons who contributed significantly to the research and publication processes, including colleagues, student assistants, typists, editors, etc.

2. Claims and ordering of authorship must accurately reflect the contributions of all major participants in the research and writing process, including students. (Where the order of names in a joint-authored piece is ambiguous, a note may be used to explain the ordering.)

3. Material taken verbatim from another person's published or unpublished work must be explicitly identified and referenced to its author. Borrowed ideas or data, even if not quoted, must be explicitly acknowledged.

B. In submission for publication, authors, editors, and referees share coordinate responsibilities.

1. Journal editors must provide prompt decisions to authors of manuscripts submitted for their consideration. They must monitor the work of associate editors and other referees so that delays are few and reviews are conscientious.

2. Editors must promptly acknowledge receipt of manuscripts and inform authors of the progress of the review.

3. An editor's commitment to publish an essay must be binding on the journal. Authors should be given realistic estimates of the likely date of publication of their manuscripts.

4. In striving for fairness in evaluation, editors should (a) be catholic in the choice of associate editors and referees and (b) be especially careful not to dismiss summarily a paper on a novel or undervalued area of investigation.

5. Submission of a manuscript to a professional journal clearly implies a commitment to publish in that journal. Once a paper has been submitted for review to one journal, it must not be submitted to another journal unless the editorial staff of the first journal has not fulfilled its responsibilities as described above; an author is released from the single submission rule where an editor fails to provide some commentary within ninety days of the initial submission.

C. Participation in Review Processes.

Sociologists are frequently asked to provide evaluation of manuscripts or research proposals prepared by colleagues. Few professional obligations are as important, or as subject to abuse, as this, and sociologists should hold themselves to high standards of performance, in several specific ways:

1. Unless requests of evaluations of colleagues' work can be met on time, they should be declined soon after they are received.

2. Sociologists should decline requests for reviews of the work of others where strong conflicts of interest are involved, such as may occur when a person is asked to review work by teachers, personal friends, or colleagues for whom he or she feels an *overriding* sense of obligation, competition, or enmity.

3. Materials sent for review should be read in their entirety and considered carefully. Evaluations should be explicated and justified with explicit reasons, and the reviewer should clearly identify those aspects of his or her own theoretical and methodological perspective that influence the frame of reference from which an evaluation is made (especially when the work being evaluated is based on different theoretical or methodological preferences).

4. It may occasionally happen that a sociologist is solicited to review the same book by the editors of two or more journals. Ideally, books should be reviewed by various sociologists in order to encourage evaluations from a diversity of perspectives. In no case should the same text of a book review be submitted to more than one journal. Furthermore, no sociologist should review the same book more than once without notifying the editors of the journal that solicits the additional review(s). If the prospective reviewer thinks that an additional review by him or her is appropriate, the justification can be presented to the journal editors for their informed consideration.

D. Contractual agreements between sociologists and book publishers must be honored by all parties to those agreements.

III. TEACHING, SUPERVISION, AND THE RIGHTS OF STUDENTS

The routine conduct of faculty responsibilities is treated at length in the faculty codes and the AAUP rules accepted as governing procedures by the various institutions of higher learning. Sociologists in teaching roles should be familiar with the content of the codes in force at their institutions and should perform their responsibilities within their guidelines.

A. Sociologists are obliged to protect the rights of students to fair treatment. Sociologists should perform their instructional duties and responsibility and a commitment to excellence.

1. Where programs are under departmental control, Departments of Sociology must provide students with explicit policies and criteria about recruitment and admission, financial support, and conditions of possible dismissal.

2. Sociologists must provide clear expectations for student performances and make fair evaluations of their work.

3. Sociologists should help to locate employment for students who complete programs.

4. Sociologists should provide students with a fair and honest statement of the scope and perspective of their courses.

B. The rights of students to confidentiality must be recognized.

1. Sociologists must refrain from disclosure of personal information concerning students where such information is not directly relevant to issues of competence or professional ethics.

2. Sociologists must make every effort to honor promises of confidentiality made to students in their teaching or advising roles.

C. Sociologists must refrain from exploiting students.

1. Sociologists must not use faculty or supervisory status to gain sexual or other personal favors from students or other subordinates.

2. Sociologists must not use faculty or supervisory status to gain undue economic or professional advantages at the expense of students or other subordinates.

3. Sociologists must not coerce or deceive students into serving as research subjects.

4. Sociologists must not represent the work of students as their own.

IV. RELATIONSHIPS AMONG SOCIOLOGISTS

A. Sociologists must evaluate the work of colleagues in an objective manner, according to explicit criteria and standards.

B. When evaluations of professional competence occur, sociologists must not disclose personal information about colleagues where such information is not directly relevant to performance or professional ethics.

C. Sociologists must at all times honestly represent their own professional records and credentials.

D. Sociologists must actively defend rights of free inquiry and communication for themselves and all colleagues.

E. Investigators should make reasonable efforts to make their data available to others, at cost of doing so, after they have completed their own analyses, except in cases where confidentiality would be violated in doing so.

F. When a sociologist submits a grant application to a governmental agency which utilizes a peer review system, the applicant must not bring pressure to bear on the review process or engage in subsequent retaliation against reviewers.

TABLE OF RANDOM DIGITS

■ Table of Random Digits

10480	15011	01536	02011	81647	91646	69179	14194	62590	36207	20969	99570	91291	90700
22368	46573	25595	85393	30995	89198	27982	53402	93965	34095	52666	19174	39615	99505
24130	48360	22527	97265	76393	64809	15179	24830	49340	32081	30680	19655	63348	58629
42167	93093	06243	61680	07856	16376	39440	53537	71341	57004	00849	74917	97758	16379
37570	39975	81837	16656	06121	91782	60468	81305	49684	60672	14110	06927	01263	54613
77921	06907	11008	42751	27756	53498	18602	70659	90655	15053	21916	81825	44394	42880
99562	72905	56420	69994	98872	31016	71194	18738	44013	48840	63213	21069	10634	12952
96301	91977	05463	07972	18876	20922	94595	56869	69014	60045	18425	84903	42508	32307
89579	14342	63661	10281	17453	18103	57740	84378	25331	12566	58678	44947	05585	56941
85475	36857	53342	53988	53060	59533	38867	62300	08158	17983	16439	11458	18593	64952
28918	69578	88231	33276	70997	79936	56865	05859	90106	31595	01547	85590	91610	78188
63553	40961	48235	03427	49626	69445	18663	72695	52180	20847	12234	90511	33703	90322
09429	93969	52636	92737	88974	33488	36320	17617	30015	08272	84115	27156	30613	74952
10365	61129	87529	85689	48237	52267	67689	93394	01511	26358	85104	20285	29975	89868
07119	97336	71048	08178	77233	13916	47564	81056	97735	85977	29372	74461	28551	90707
51085	12765	51821	51259	77452	16308	60756	92144	49442	53900	70960	63990	75601	40719
02368	21382	52404	60268	89368	19885	55322	44819	01188	65255	64835	44919	05944	55157
01011	54092	33362	94904	31273	04146	18594	29852	71585	85030	51132	01915	92747	64951
52162	53916	46369	58586	23216	14513	83149	98736	23495	64350	94738	17752	35156	35749
07056	97628	33787	09998	42698	06691	76988	13602	51851	46104	88916	19509	25625	58104
48663	91245	85828	14346	09172	30168	90229	04734	59193	22178	30421	61666	99904	32812
54164	58492	22421	74103	47070	25306	76468	26384	58151	06646	21524	15227	96909	44592
32639	32363	05597	24200	13363	38005	94342	28728	35806	06912	17012	64161	18296	22851
29334	27001	87637	87308	58731	00256	45834	15398	46557	41135	10367	07684	36188	18510
02488	33062	28834	07351	19731	92420	60952	61280	50001	67658	32586	86679	50720	94953

81525	72295	04839	96423	24878	82651	66566	14778	76797	14780	13300	87074	79666	95725
29676	20591	68086	26432	46901	20849	89768	81536	86645	12659	92259	57102	80428	25280
00742	57392	39064	66432	84673	40027	32832	61362	98947	96067	64760	64584	96096	98253
05366	04213	25669	26422	44407	44048	37937	63904	45766	66134	75470	66520	34693	90449
91921	26418	64117	94305	26766	25940	39972	22209	71500	64568	91402	42416	07844	69618
00582	04711	87917	77341	42206	35126	74087	99547	81817	42607	43808	76655	62028	76630
00725	69884	62797	56170	86324	88072	76222	36086	84637	93161	76038	65855	77919	88006
69011	65795	95876	55293	18988	27354	26575	08625	40801	59920	29841	80150	12777	48501
25976	57948	29888	88604	67917	48708	18912	82271	65424	69774	33611	54262	85963	03547
09763	83473	73577	12908	30883	18317	28290	35797	05998	41688	34952	37888	38917	88050
91567	42595	27958	30134	04024	86385	29880	99730	55536	84855	29080	09250	79656	73211
17955	56349	90999	49127	20044	59931	06115	20542	18059	02008	73708	83517	36103	42791
46503	18584	18845	49618	02304	51038	20655	58727	28168	15475	56942	53389	20562	87338
92157	89634	94824	78171	84610	82834	09922	25417	44137	48413	25555	21246	35509	20468
14577	62765	35605	81263	39667	47358	56873	56307	61607	49518	89656	20103	77490	18062
98427	07523	33362	64270	01638	92477	66969	98420	04880	45585	46565	04102	46880	45709
34914	63976	88720	82765	34476	17032	87589	40836	32427	70002	70663	88863	77775	69348
70060	28277	39475	46473	23219	53416	94970	25832	69975	94884	19661	72828	00102	66794
53976	54914	06990	67245	68350	82948	11398	42878	80287	88267	47363	46634	06541	97809
76072	29515	40980	07391	58745	25774	22987	80059	39911	96189	41151	14222	60697	59583
90725	52210	83974	29992	65831	38857	50490	83765	55657	14361	31720	57375	56228	41546
64364	67412	33339	31926	14883	24413	59744	92351	97473	89286	35931	04110	23726	51900
08962	00358	31662	25388	61642	34072	81249	35648	56891	69352	48373	45578	78547	81788
95012	68379	93526	70765	10592	04542	76463	54328	02349	17247	28865	14777	62730	92277
15664	14093	20492	38391	91132	21999	59516	81652	27195	48223	46751	22923	32261	85653
16408	81899	04153	53381	79401	21438	83035	92350	36693	31238	59649	91754	72772	02338
18629	81953	05520	91962	04739	13092	97662	24822	94730	06496	35090	04822	86774	98289
73115	35101	47498	87637	99016	71060	88824	71013	18735	20286	23153	72924	35165	43040
57491	16703	23167	49323	45021	33132	12544	41035	80780	45393	44812	12515	98931	91202
30405	83946	23792	14422	15059	45799	22716	19792	09983	74353	68668	30429	70735	25499
16631	35006	85900	98275	32388	52390	16815	69298	82732	38480	73817	32523	41961	44437
96773	20206	42559	78985	05300	22164	24369	54224	35083	19687	11052	91491	60383	19746
38935	64202	14349	82674	66523	44133	00697	35552	35970	19124	63318	29686	03387	59846
31624	76384	17403	53363	44167	64486	64758	75366	76554	31601	12614	33072	60332	92325
78919	19474	23632	27889	47914	02584	37680	20801	72152	39339	34806	08930	85001	87820
03931	33309	57047	74211	63445	17361	62825	39908	05607	91284	68833	25570	38818	46920
74426	33278	43972	10119	89917	15665	52872	73823	73144	88662	88970	74492	51805	99378
09066	00903	20795	95452	92648	45454	09552	88815	16553	51125	79375	97596	16296	66092
42238	12426	87025	14267	20979	04508	64535	31355	86064	29472	47689	05974	52468	16834
16153	08002	26504	41744	81959	65642	74240	56302	00033	67107	77510	70625	28725	34191
21457	40742	29820	96783	29400	21840	15035	34537	33310	06116	95240	15947	16572	06004
21581	57802	02050	89728	17937	37621	47075	42080	97403	48626	68995	43805	33386	21597
55612	78095	83197	33732	05810	24813	86902	60397	16489	03264	88525	42786	05269	92532
44657	66999	99324	51281	84463	60563	79312	93454	68876	25471	93911	25650	12682	73572
91340	84979	46949	81973	37949	61023	43997	15263	80644	43942	89203	71795	99533	50501

91227	21199	31935	27022	84067	05462	35216	14486	29891	68607	41867	14951	91696	85065
50001	38140	66321	19924	72163	09538	12151	06878	91903	18749	34405	56087	82790	70925
65390	05224	72958	28609	81406	39147	25549	48542	42627	45233	57202	94617	23772	07896
27504	96131	83944	41575	10573	08619	64482	73923	36152	05184	94142	25299	84387	34925
37169	94851	39117	89632	00959	16487	65536	49071	39782	17095	02330	74301	00275	48280
11508	70225	51111	38351	19444	66499	71945	05422	13442	78675	84081	66938	93654	59894
37449	30362	06694	54690	04052	53115	62757	95348	78662	11163	81651	50245	34971	52924
46515	70331	85922	38329	57015	15765	97161	17869	45349	61796	66345	81073	49106	79860
30986	81223	42416	58353	21532	30502	32305	86482	05174	07901	54339	58861	74818	46942
63798	64995	46583	09785	44160	78128	83991	42865	92520	83531	80377	35909	81250	54238
82486	84846	99254	67632	43218	50076	21361	64816	51202	88124	41870	52689	51275	83556
21885	32906	92431	09060	64297	51674	64126	62570	26123	05155	59194	52799	28225	85762
60336	98782	07408	53458	13564	59089	26445	29789	85205	41001	12535	12133	14645	23541
43937	46891	24010	25560	86355	33941	25786	54990	71899	15475	95434	98227	21824	19585
97656	63175	89303	16275	07100	92063	21942	18611	47348	20203	18534	03862	78095	50136
03299	01221	05418	38982	55758	92237	26759	86367	21216	98442	08303	56613	91511	75928
79626	06486	03574	17668	07785	76020	79924	25651	83325	88428	85076	72811	22717	50585
85636	68335	47539	03129	65651	11977	02510	26113	99447	68645	34327	15152	55230	93448
18039	14367	61337	06177	12143	46609	32989	74014	64708	00533	35398	55408	13261	47908
08362	15656	60627	36478	65648	16764	53412	09013	07832	41574	17639	82163	60859	75567
79556	29068	04142	16268	15387	12856	66227	38358	22478	73373	88732	09443	82558	05250
92608	82674	27072	32534	17075	27698	98204	63863	11951	34648	88022	56148	34925	57031
23982	25835	40055	67006	12293	02753	14827	23235	35071	99704	37543	11601	35503	85171
09915	96306	05908	97901	28395	14186	00821	80703	70426	75647	76310	88717	37890	40129
59037	33300	26695	62247	69927	76123	50842	43834	86654	70959	79725	93872	28117	19233
42488	78077	69882	61657	34136	79180	97526	43092	04098	73571	80799	76536	71255	64239
46764	86273	63003	93017	31204	36692	40202	35275	57306	55543	53203	18098	47625	88684
03237	45430	55417	63282	90816	17349	88298	90183	36600	78406	06216	95787	42579	90730
86591	81482	52667	61582	14972	90053	89534	76036	49199	43716	97548	04379	46370	28672
38534	01715	94964	87288	65680	43772	39560	12918	86537	62738	19636	51132	25739	56947

Source: Abridged from Beyer, William H. (Ed.). (1968). *Handbook of Tables for Probability and Statistics*, 2d ed. (Cleveland: The Chemical Rubber Company.) Reproduced by permission of the publishers, The Chemical Rubber Company.

ANTONOVSKY'S SENSE OF COHERENCE QUESTIONNAIRE

21 ....Question 1: "When you talk to people, do you have the feeling that they don't understand you?"

Never have this feeling (1)..(2)..(3)..(4).. (5)..(6)..(7) Always have this feeling
No response (8)
Don't know (9)

22 ....Question 2: "In the past, when you had to do something which depended upon cooperation with others, did you have the feeling that it:"

Surely wouldn't get done (1)..(2)..(3)..(4).. (5)..(6)..(7) Surely would get done
No response (8)
Don't know (9)

23 ....Question 3: "Think of the people with whom you come into contact daily, aside from the ones to whom you feel closest. How well do you know most of them?"

You feel that they're strangers (1)..(2)..(3)..(4).. (5)..(6)..(7) You know them very well
No response (8)
Don't know (9)

24 ....Question 4: "Do you have the feeling that you don't really care about what goes on around you?"

Very seldom or never (1)..(2)..(3)..(4).. (5)..(6)..(7) Very often
No response (8)
Don't know (9)

25 ....Question 5:   "Has it happened in the past that you were surprised by the behavior of people whom you thought you knew well?"

Never happened (1)..(2)..(3)..(4)..
(5)..(6)..(7) Always happened
No response (8)
Don't know (9)

26 ....Question 6:   "Has it happened that people whom you counted on disappointed you?"

Never happened (1)..(2)..(3)..(4)..
(5)..(6)..(7) Always happened
No response (8)
Don't know (9)

27 ....Question 7:   "Life is:"

Full of interest (1)..(2)..(3)..(4)..
(5)..(6)..(7) Completely routine
No response (8)
Don't know (9)

28 ....Question 8:   "Until now, your life has had:"

No clear goals or purpose at all (1)..(2)..(3)..(4)..
(5)..(6)..(7) Very clear goals and purpose
No response (8)
Don't know (9)

29 ....Question 9:   "Do you have the feeling that you're being treated unfairly?"

Very often (1)..(2)..(3)..(4)..
(5)..(6)..(7) Very seldom or never
No response (8)
Don't know (9)

30 ....Question 10:   "In the past ten years, your life has been:"

Full of changes without your knowing what will happen next (1)..(2)..(3)..(4)..
(5)..(6)..(7) Completely consistent and clear
No response (8)
Don't know (9)

31 ....Question 11:   "Most of the things you do in the future will probably be:"

Completely fascinating (1)..(2)..(3)..(4)..
(5)..(6)..(7) Deadly boring
No response (8)
Don't know (9)

32 ....Question 12:   "Do you have the feeling that you are in an unfamiliar situation and don't know what to do?"

Very often (1)..(2)..(3)..(4)..
(5)..(6)..(7) Very seldom or never
No response (8)
Don't know (9)

33 ....Question 13:   "What best describes how you see life?"

One can always find a solution to painful things in life (1)..(2)..(3)..(4)..
(5)..(6)..(7) There is no solution to painful things
No response (8)
Don't know (9)

34 ....Question 14:   "When you think about your life, you very often:"

Feel how good it is to be alive (1)..(2)..(3)..(4)..
(5)..(6)..(7) Ask yourself why you exist at all
No response (8)
Don't know (9)

35 ....Question 15:   "When you face a difficult problem, the choice of a solution is:"

Always confusing and hard to find (1)..(2)..(3)..(4)..
(5)..(6)..(7) Always completely clear
No response (8)
Don't know (9)

36 ....Question 16:   "Doing the things you do every day is:"

A source of deep pleasure and satisfaction (1)..(2)..(3)..(4)..
(5)..(6)..(7) A source of pain and boredom
No response (8)
Don't know (9)

37 ....Question 17:   "Your life in the future will probably be:"

Full of changes without your knowing what will happen next (1)..(2)..(3)..(4)..
(5)..(6)..(7) Completely consistent and clear
No response (8)
Don't know (9)

38 ....Question 18:   "When something unpleasant happened in the past, your tendency was:"

"To eat yourself up" about it (1)..(2)..(3)..(4)..
(5)..(6)..(7) To say "OK, that's that, I have to live with it," and go on
No response (8)
Don't know (9)

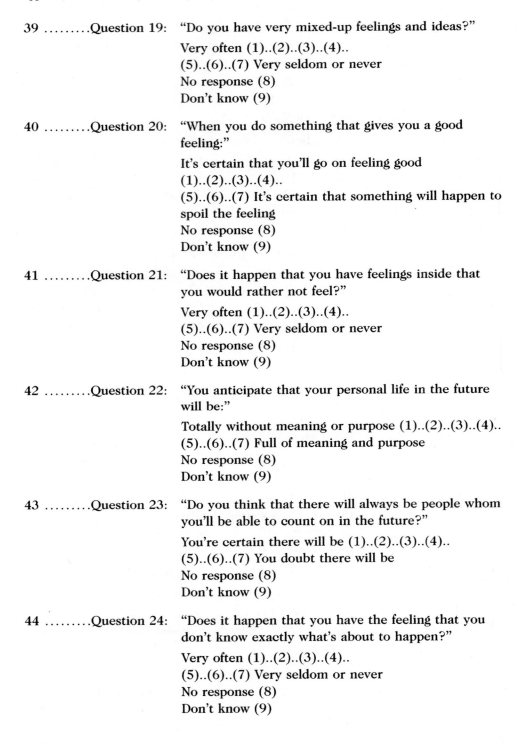

39 ....Question 19: "Do you have very mixed-up feelings and ideas?"

Very often (1)..(2)..(3)..(4)..
(5)..(6)..(7) Very seldom or never
No response (8)
Don't know (9)

40 ....Question 20: "When you do something that gives you a good feeling:"

It's certain that you'll go on feeling good
(1)..(2)..(3)..(4)..
(5)..(6)..(7) It's certain that something will happen to spoil the feeling
No response (8)
Don't know (9)

41 ....Question 21: "Does it happen that you have feelings inside that you would rather not feel?"

Very often (1)..(2)..(3)..(4)..
(5)..(6)..(7) Very seldom or never
No response (8)
Don't know (9)

42 ....Question 22: "You anticipate that your personal life in the future will be:"

Totally without meaning or purpose (1)..(2)..(3)..(4)..
(5)..(6)..(7) Full of meaning and purpose
No response (8)
Don't know (9)

43 ....Question 23: "Do you think that there will always be people whom you'll be able to count on in the future?"

You're certain there will be (1)..(2)..(3)..(4)..
(5)..(6)..(7) You doubt there will be
No response (8)
Don't know (9)

44 ....Question 24: "Does it happen that you have the feeling that you don't know exactly what's about to happen?"

Very often (1)..(2)..(3)..(4)..
(5)..(6)..(7) Very seldom or never
No response (8)
Don't know (9)

45 ....Question 25:   "Many people—even those with a strong character—
sometimes feel like sad sacks (losers) in certain
situations. How often have you felt this way in the
past?"

Never (1)..(2)..(3)..(4)..
(5)..(6)..(7) Very often
No response (8)
Don't know (9)

46 ....Question 26:   "When something happened, have you generally
found that:"

You overestimated or underestimated its importance
(1)..(2)..(3)..(4)..
(5)..(6)..(7) You saw things in the right proportion
No response (8)
Don't know (9)

47 ....Question 27:   "When you think of difficulties you are likely to face
in important aspects of your life, do you have the
feeling that:"

You will always succeed in overcoming the
difficulties (1)..(2)..(3)..(4)..
(5)..(6)..(7) You won't succeed in overcoming the
difficulties
No response (8)
Don't know (9)

48 ....Question 28:   "How often do you have the feeling that there's little
meaning in the things you do in your daily life?"

Very often (1)..(2)..(3)..(4)..
(5)..(6)..(7) Very seldom or never
No response (8)
Don't know (9)

49 ....Question 29:   "How often do you have feelings that you're not sure
you can keep under control?"

Very often (1)..(2)..(3)..(4)..
(5)..(6)..(7) Very seldom or never
No response (8)
Don't know (9)

Appendix D

SAMPLES OF AN RFP AND A PORTION OF A SUCCESSFUL GRANT APPLICATION

DEPARTMENT OF HEALTH & HUMAN SERVICES   Public Health Service

National Institutes of Health
Bethesda, Maryland 20892

EXPLORATORY CENTER GRANT ON THE
HEALTH AND EFFECTIVE FUNCTIONING
OF OLDER RURAL POPULATIONS

NATIONAL INSTITUTE ON AGING

NATIONAL INSTITUTES OF HEALTH

REQUEST FOR APPLICATIONS (AG-90-01) AND GUIDELINES

APPLICATION RECEIPT DATE:

March 20, 1990

TABLE OF CONTENTS

REQUEST FOR APPLICATIONS (AG-90-01)

EXPLORATORY CENTER GRANT ON THE HEALTH AND EFFECTIVE FUNCTIONING OF OLDER RURAL POPULATIONS
NATIONAL INSTITUTE ON AGING

APPLICATION RECEIPT DATE: ???

I.   BACKGROUND

The National Institute on Aging (NIA) invites Exploratory Center Grant applications (P20) to establish a coordinated, multidisciplinary research environment on social, economic, psychological, environmental, and biomedical factors affecting the aging processes and the health and effective functioning of older people in rural areas. Recent governmental and non-governmental reports* highlight the special health-care and other services needs of rural people and especially those who are old. People in rural areas are more likely than their urban counterparts to be in fair or poor health, to suffer from chronic or serious illness, to be without a regular source of health care and health insurance. Moreover, a higher proportion of deaths occur among the nonmetropolitan than the metropolitan population over 65 years of age. The U.S. congress has now called for establishing a center in order to improve the knowledge base necessary for the promotion of health and the prevention of disease among rural older people and for developing and implementing effective, acceptable, and accessible health care and other services.

II.   SPECIFIC OBJECTIVES

A research agenda is needed for examining the life-long experience, the current circumstances, and the special physical and social nature of rural life as they affect the health, well-being, and functioning of nonmetropolitan older people. Although many research topics are worthy of consideration, NIA consultants and staff have identified five as requiring special attention: A) The changing sociodemographic and epidemiologic characteristics of the older rural population, B) the occupational and physicochemical environment, C) the population aging of rural communities, D) the availability, utilization, and quality of health-care and other services, and E) aging rural people as resources. Applications should propose activities relevant to at least two of these broad topics.

The goal of this RFA is to develop a research program at the recipient institutions to facilitate the preparation of competitive research project grant (RO1), program project (P01), or Core

---

*Health Services Research, Special Issue: A Rural Health Services Research Agenda, vol. 23, no. 6, February 1989; The Journal of Rural Health, Special Issue: Rural Geriatrics and Gerontology, vol. 4, no. 3, October 1988; The Rural Health Care Challenge, Staff Report to the Special Committee on Aging, U.S. Senate, October 1988, Serial No. 100-N, U.S. Government Printing Office, Washington, D.C.

Facilities Center (P30) applications during and upon completion of the grant period. (Awards for subsequent P30 grants will depend upon the availability of funds for such Centers.)

A.   CHANGING SOCIODEMOGRAPHIC AND EPIDEMIOLOGIC CHARACTERISTICS OF THE OLDER RURAL POPULATION

In 1980, 25.5 million Americans were 65 or older, and 25% of these lived in rural areas. While older people comprised about 11% of both the urban and rural populations, several aspects of the older rural population reflect its diversity and distinguish it from its urban counterparts. These sources of diversity and distinctiveness need to be considered in regard to their possible effects on aging and the health and effective functioning of older rural residents.,

.   What accounts for the differences between older rural and urban residents in their concentration in particular regions of the country? What are the consequences of such concentration for local communities and regions? For the provision and utilization of health and other services?

.   How does the relative poverty of older rural people in comparison to their urban counterparts affect their health, well-being, and functioning?

.   What role do living arrangements (i.e., household composition) play in rural settings? Why is the proportion of men in the older nonmetropolitan population somewhat higher than in metropolitan areas?

.   Older nonmetropolitan people have less education than older metropolitan people. What impact does this have on their health, functioning, and socioeconomic well-being? What social and psychological mechanisms (e.g., attitudes, beliefs) mediate the effects of education on health, well-being, and functioning? How do the educational differences between older rural people and service providers affect the utilization of services and the quality of services received?

.   Only 11% of all employed rural people are engaged in agriculture, forestry, fisheries, or mining. Indeed, over half of rural workers have occupations in manufacturing, construction, or services. Moreover, increasing numbers of rural workers are moving out of agricultural occupations during their work careers. How does this diversity among rural workers affect their life-long patterns of nutrition, exercise, exposure to chemicals, risk of accidents, and to climatic conditions, and availability of social (e.g., educational) and health services? What are the implications for their health and socioeconomic well-being in old age (i.e., financial resources, housing)?

.   Contradictory information exists about the comparative health status of rural older people. In part, this may reflect differences in definitions of "health" and of "rural" from one study to the next. Research is needed to clarify and specify the relationships among urban-rural residence, aging, and health. Is the health of older rural people poorer or better than that of urban older people? Under which circumstances?

IX.   REVIEW OF APPLICATIONS

A.   REVIEW PROCEDURES

Applications will be received by the NIH Division of Research Grants and assigned to the National Institute on Aging (NIA). Applications judged by NIA to be nonresponsive will not be accepted. If necessitated by a large number of applications, responsive applications may be subjected to triage by a peer-review group to determine their scientific merit relative to the other applications received. Applications judged to be noncompetitive will be administratively inactivated. Those applications judged to be competitive will be fully reviewed for scientific and technical merit by an NIA Initial Review Group (IRG). Following review by the IRG, applications will be evaluated by the National Advisory Council on Aging.

B.   REVIEW CRITERIA

The major review factors listed below will be used in the evaluation of the applications for Exploratory Center Grants:

1.   *Overall Program*

a.   The scientific merit of the program as a whole. The significance of the overall program goals and the development of a well-defined central focus of clear importance and relevance to the goals and mission of the NIA.

b.   The potential of the identified participants to develop research programs of high merit as evidenced by previous accomplishments.

c.   The balance of administrative and planning expenses in comparison to those for conducting the small-scale studies.

2.   *Administration and Planning Core*

a.   The scientific and administrative leadership ability and experience of the Center Director and his/her commitment and ability to devote adequate time to the effective management of the Center.

b.   The proposed administrative organization to conduct the following:

.   Maintenance of internal communication and cooperation among the investigators involved in the Center.

.   Management that includes fiscal administration, procurement, property and personnel management, planning budgets, etc.

.   Mechanism for selecting or replacing professional or technical personnel within the Center.

.   Adequacy of the review committee to assess the scientific merit of the proposed small-scale studies.

    .   Mechanism for reviewing the use of and administration of funds for small-scale studies.

    .   Appropriateness and adequacy of the multidisciplinary teams constituting the Center's members.

c.   Adequacy of the initial research agenda and of the planning mechanism for elaborating a long-term research agenda for the institution.

d.   The appropriateness of the Center budgets for the various components of the Center.

2.   *Small-scale Studies*

a.   The balance in coverage of the topics identified in Section II.

b.   The scientific and technical quality of the initial small-scale studies. (Note: Unlike a Program Project Application, reviewers will not vote on the merit of each study. The overall quality of the proposed small-scale studies will be taken into account in arriving at an evaluation of the application.)

3.   *Institutional Commitment*

a.   The institutional commitment to the program, including lines of responsibility for the Center, and the institution's contribution to the management capabilities of the Center.

b.   The degree of institutional contributions towards the expenses for the Administrative and Planning Core and/or to the Small-scale Studies.

c.   The academic environment and resources in which the activities will be conducted, including the availability of space, equipment, and facilities, and the potential for interaction with scientists from other departments and schools.

d.   The institutional commitment to any newly recruited individuals responsible for conducting essential Center functions and activities.

DUPLICATE COPY - USE IF NEEDED

AA

Form Approved Through 3/31/91
OMB No. 0925-0001

DEPARTMENT OF HEALTH AND HUMAN SERVICES PUBLIC HEALTH SERVICE **GRANT APPLICATION** Follow instructions carefully. Type in the unshaded areas only.	**LEAVE BLANK FOR PHS USE ONLY.**		
	Type	Activity	Number
	Review Group		Formerly
	Council/Board *(Month, Year)*		Date Received

1. TITLE OF PROJECT *(Do not exceed 56 typewriter spaces.)*
A Study of the Independent Rural Elderly in Missouri

2. RESPONSE TO SPECIFIC PROGRAM ANNOUNCEMENT ☒ NO ☐ YES *(If "YES," state RFA number and/or announcement title)*
Number: Title:

3. PRINCIPAL INVESTIGATOR/PROGRAM DIRECTOR   ☐ NEW INVESTIGATOR

3a. NAME *(Last, first, middle)* Hessler, Richard Michael	3b. DEGREE(S) Ph.D.	3c. SOCIAL SECURITY NO. 561-52-9702
3d. POSITION TITLE Professor	3e. MAILING ADDRESS *(Street, city, state, zip code)* Family and Community Medicine University of Missouri–Columbia Columbia, Missouri 65211	
3f. DEPARTMENT, SERVICE, LABORATORY, OR EQUIVALENT Family and Community Medicine & Sociology		
3g. MAJOR SUBDIVISION School of Medicine		
3h. TELEPHONE *(Area code, number, and extension)* (314) 882-6183		

4. HUMAN SUBJECTS				5. VERTEBRATE ANIMALS	If "YES," IACUC approval date	5b. Animal welfare assurance no.
4a. ☐ NO ☒ YES	If "YES," exemption no. or date	IRB approval date	4b. Assurance of compliance no.	5a. ☒ NO ☐ YES		
		7/24/84	1783			

6. DATES OF ENTIRE PROPOSED PROJECT PERIOD		7. COSTS REQUESTED FOR FIRST 12-MONTH BUDGET PERIOD		8. COSTS REQUESTED FOR ENTIRE PROPOSED PROJECT PERIOD	
From (YYMMDD)	Through (YYMMDD)	7a. Direct Costs	7b. Total Costs	8a. Direct Costs	8b. Total Costs
1-1-86	12-31-87	$ 108,317	$	$ 207,116	$

9. PERFORMANCE SITES *(Organizations and addresses)* Department of Family & Community Medicine Behavioral Sciences Med. Sciences Bldg. Un. of Mo. Col. Sociology Department 108 Sociology University of Missouri–Columbia Columbia, Missouri 65211	10. INVENTIONS *(Competing continuation application only)* ☐ NO ☐ YES If "YES," ☐ Previously reported ☐ Not previously reported
	11. NAME OF APPLICANT ORGANIZATION The Curators of the University of Missouri ADDRESS *(Street, city, state, and zip code)* The University of Missouri–Columbia Grants and Contracts Administration 23 Jesse Hall Columbia, Missouri 65211

12. TYPE OF ORGANIZATON ☒ Public: *Specify* ☐ *Federal* ☐ *State* ☐ *Local* ☐ Private Nonprofit ☐ For Profit *(General)* ☐ For Profit *(Small Business)*	13. ENTITY IDENTIFICATION NUMBER 43-600-3859	Congressional District 9th
	14. ORGANIZATIONAL COMPONENT TO RECEIVE CREDIT TOWARDS A BIOMEDICAL RESEARCH SUPPORT GRANT Code: 01 Identification: School of Medicine	

15. NAME OF OFFICIAL IN BUSINESS OFFICE Robert A. Killoren, Jr. TELEPHONE *(Area code, number, and extension)* (314) 882-7569 TITLE Director of Grants and Contracts ADDRESS 23 Jesse Hall University of Missouri–Columbia Columbia, Missouri 65211	16. NAME OF OFFICIAL SIGNING FOR APPLICANT ORGANIZATION TELEPHONE *(Area code, number, and extension)* TITLE ADDRESS

17. PRINCIPAL INVESTIGATOR/PROGRAM DIRECTOR ASSURANCE: I agree to accept responsibility for the scientific conduct of the project and to provide the required progress reports if a grant is awarded as a result of this application. Willful provision of false information is a criminal offense (U.S. Code, Title 18, Section 1001).	SIGNATURE OF PERSON NAMED IN 3a *(In ink. "Per" signature not acceptable.)* *Richard M. Hessler*	DATE 2/27/85
18. CERTIFICATION AND ACCEPTANCE: I certify that the statements herein are true and complete to the best of my knowledge, and accept the obligation to comply with Public Health Service terms and conditions if a grant is awarded as the result of this application. A willfully false certification is a criminal offense *(U.S. Code, Title 18, Section 1001).*	SIGNATURE OF PERSON NAMED IN 16 *(In ink. "Per" signature not acceptable)*	DATE

PHS 398 (Rev. 10/88) (Reprinted 9/89)   **AA**

A.   Specific Aims

This proposed study of 1,650 elderly inhabitants of 64 Missouri towns has four central objectives: (1) to assess the current status of the trends in the degrees of independence and the means of maintaining Independent living, especially social networks, health status, and life satisfaction; (2) to describe via socio-historical analysis the demographic and socio-economic changes within the 64 towns and to relate those changes to the maintenance of independent living; (3) to build a statistically sound model which can predict longevity, problems in maintaining independence, and to establish casual sequences among the key predictors; and (4) to sort out cohorts, aging, and period effects in terms of describing the aging process within and between cohorts, as affected by historical events.

In addition to these primary aims, the study will focus on the following areas relevant to the above four primary aims. These are: (1) attitudes and values of the rural elderly such as self-esteem, life satisfaction, feelings of independence or control, traditional values, and attitudes about death; (2) health status, including physical activities of daily living; (3) voting behavior and political interest; and (4) sociological factors associated with mortality between 1966, 1974, and the proposed 1985 re-study of the surviving panel members.

B.   Significance

The ultimate goal of this proposed study of the rural elderly is to understand longevity and independence from institutional care. The study will shed much needed light on the behavioral predictors of longevity and independent living both in terms of discovering the key variables and in establishing causal sequences among the significantly related variables. Palmore (1980) and his colleagues at the Center for the Study of Aging and Human Development at Duke University have offered convincing evidence through longitudinal research that longevity among the aged primarily is the result of environmental and life-style differences, many of which can be changed. Whatever genetic influences on mortality there are tend to be overwhelmed by socio-environmental factors so that for individuals healthy enough to survive to age 60 and enter Palmore's study, there is no longer any measurable genetic influence on their remaining longevity. In Palmore's words, "Large scale longitudinal studies of the aged may be the ideal method (short of experimentation) to develop better predictors of mortality. In such studies specific age cohorts are followed over a substantial number of years (say 10 or more), so that information gathered at the beginning of the study can be used to predict mortality and longevity for various types of persons. The key point is that we are in a position to capitalize on almost 20 years of longitudinal research on a rural elderly sample together with a new cross-sectional sample from the same 64 small towns in order to develop predictors of longevity and independent living.

Many of the past models of aging have been fairly static presentations of stable and universal stages of development from infancy through old age and death. Recently a multidisciplinary research orientation known as the "life-span perspective" has emerged with the central proposition being that developmental change occurs over the entire course of life. Aging is not considered limited to any part of life, nor is development. From this the "age stratification" model, 1968; 1969; 1972). for an excellent review of the contribution of the life span perspective and longitudinal research over the course of individuals' lives, see Featherman (1981).

The proposed study fits the life span model and contributes, theoretically and substantively, to the body of knowledge about the aging process, taking cohort, aging, and period effects into account as well as possible.

In addition to the disciplinary significance of the proposed study, the focus on the elderly in the small midwestern town was motivated by three practical reasons: (1) the small towns of the North Central Region contain a disproportionate number of elderly people. (The towns selected averaged nearly 20 percent 65 and older compared to 13 percent for the State as a whole.); (2) most studies in social gerontology have focused on urban populations the findings of which may be somewhat inappropriate when applied to persons with rural backgrounds; (3) programs designed to meet the needs of the elderly for health, for social participation, or maintenance of morale, are primarily designed for urban populations and may be ill-suited to the needs of a small town or village population. The small town has an intimacy and neighborliness often lacking in an urban setting. On the other hand, the problem of transportation may be more acute in the small town, particularly in terms of visiting family and friends if separated by many miles.

This proposed study is guided by the remarkable population changes which are sweeping us into the future. Since 1960 the population aged 65 and over has increased by 55 percent (16.7 million to 25.9 million in 1980) while the population under 65 increased 24 percent. More people living longer means that chronic diseases which can only be managed, not cured, have emerged as a major cause of health expenditures and institutionalization of the elderly (National Center for Health Statistics, 1981). High medical care utilization patterns among the elderly reflect problems with their health status. Hospital use, physician visits and commitments to nursing homes are disproportionately high for the elderly (Kovar, 1977). Of the total $219 billion spent in 1980 for personal health care, $64.5 billion (20%) was spent by or on behalf of the elderly population. In contrast, the expenditures for the population under 65 are projected to increase 30 percent (Rice and Feldman, 1983). Furthermore, Missouri is one of seven states in which the percent of persons 65 years and over exceeds 12.5 and many of the 64 small towns in our proposed research have percentages as high as 20.

Recent research has found that the elderly are disproportionately heavy utilizers of medical services (Irelan, et al., 1976). Although currently constituting less than 11 percent of the population in this country, the elderly fill a third of the hospital beds and account for a quarter of health care expenditures (Kart, et al., 1978). Much of the prior health planning and social service delivery to the elderly has been based on using population projections as a guide for the type and number of services to be delivered.

The National Institute on Aging has called for research involving very old persons 85 years and beyond. These persons called "the oldest old" are forecast to be the fastest growing segment of the population. The oldest old are very high users of institutional care, require a lot of social support in order to maintain their independence, and very little sociological and physiological knowledge about this group has been gathered. The longitudinal phase of our proposed research will provide much needed information about the independently living elderly 85 years and over.

Of particular interest is the recent work using longitudinal data reporting that a small portion of those 65 and older account for a disproportionately large share of health care service utilization (Roos, Shapiro, 1981). This finding is consistent with studies using longitudinal data from prepaid health plans (Mulhoony, Freehorn, 1979) and with other earlier work

(Denson, Shapiro, Einhorn, 1969). Butler (1980) has challenged researchers to design studies of older persons which can contribute to a better understanding of the pre-conditions associated with disease and, ultimately, the loss of independence and admission to nursing homes.

It has been shown (Branch, et al., 1981) that utilization of health care services is much more closely related to the older persons' physical and functional status than to their demographic and economic status.

While the study of the elderly's utilization of health care services continues, it is obvious that the combination of "rural and elderly" has not received adequate attention. It has been suggested that differences exist between rural and urban settings in physician use (Chaska, et al., 1980). Although descriptive, these data do not permit conclusions to be drawn as to whether lower utilization of health care resources in rural settings are a function of availability of resources or a function of different health attitudes, social support, and other factors.
McCall and Wai (1983) investigated utilization patterns of the Medicare aged who were enrolled continuously in the program over a 4 year period. Their data supported the earlier findings, and showed that 18 percent of the beneficiaries accounted for 88 percent of the cost of services delivered. We are observing these patterns partly because modern medicine has extended human life. consequently, the numbers of older people are growing and the proportion of the adult life cycle spent in retirement is increasing rapidly. Are older people benefiting from this extension of life? Can older people continue to be independent and productive members of society? What sociological factors contribute to the maintenance of health and independence for retired persons?

As a society we are no longer able to add more and more government programs in response to the aging of our population. for several years we, in the Department of Sociology at UMC, have engaged in an on-going study of the elderly in 64 small Missouri towns. This research is designed to provide information useful to policy-makers and social planners who are searching for means to promote greater self-sufficiency and self-reliance among the growing ranks of the elderly.

Relative to the astronomical costs associated with institutional care, local systems which function to maintain and promote health and independent living for the elderly are extremely valuable. We are proposing to study the factors associated with a decent quality of life for the independently living rural elderly, the ultimate goal being to maintain and promote a high quality of life for the most deserving people in our society.

Indeed, recent research findings are beginning to show that productivity of older persons can be extended and that mental and physical disabilities can be prevented, lessened, and even reversed. However, much of this research is based on cross sectional research designs in which little is known about how older persons change and adapt over the course of their lives. Longitudinal research and comparisons across cross sectional surveys are essential.

Through our research program on the rural elderly, we are in a unique position to understand how individuals and environments change with age and what factors operate to allow older persons to maintain independent and productive living. There is no question that the consequences of not having the above are potentially ruinous, both economically and socially. Today alone, just a 10 percent increase in the number of older persons demanding beds in nursing homes would strain resources, particularly medicare, to the breaking point. We must get on with prospective research capable of describing and analyzing these changes over time. Our present study, the third in eight years of research on the rural elderly moves us in this direction.

Beginning in 1966, the Department of Sociology UMC received a three-year grant from the Division of Chronic Diseases, U.S. Public Health Service, to study the small town elderly of Missouri (see Appendix B, Supporting Data, for a description of the 1966 study). A panel of 1,700 independently living individuals 65 years of age or older was drawn in 64 small Missouri towns in order to understand the factors associated with life satisfaction, health and the maintenance of independence. (Pihlblad and Adams, 1972; Pihlblad, et al., 1967; Pihlblad and Rosencranz, 1968). Interviews were conducted with each of the 1,700 individuals sampled. Again in 1973-74, follow-up interviews with the survivors of the original sample were conducted. Topics covered included: (1) household composition; (2) income; (3) quality of social networks and support; (4) community and institutional participation; (5) voting behavior; (6) feelings about death and dying and contact with programs designed for the elderly. It was possible to obtain complete information from 568 survivors, or about one-third of the original 1,700. (See Appendix B "The Rural Elderly 8 Years Later" for portions of the final report).

The outstanding finding of the 1966 and 1973-74 analyses was the strong feeling of independence of the respondents, their expressed desire to continue living independently, their unwillingness to accept institutional care, and their desire to be independent of their children and family. This attitude and value was threatened by invalidism and illness, some of it preventable. Very low rates of utilization of medical services coupled with negative changes over time in social support and contracts, physical abilities, and life satisfaction placed large numbers of the 1973-74 respondents in grave risk of losing their independence and quite possibly their lives earlier than what might have been given certain programmatic efforts. Other important earlier findings which the 1985 cross-sectional survey would allow us to pursue are: (1) very low residential mobility with the preponderance of women living alone while most of the men were married and living with a spouse. men had a lower life expectancy than women and this was particularly true of single men who had fewer social contracts; (2) the number of persons living alone or living with someone other than a spouse increased with aging and dependence on others increased accordingly. An analysis of marital status revealed that the proportion of married males was substantially larger than for females--one-half of the males were married versus one-fourth of the females. Widowhood increased with age while proportions married for males and females decreased. The increase in widowhood with age was much more rapid and consistent for women than for men. Similarly, the proportion of single, never married, was higher for females in the youngest and oldest cohorts. Given that two-thirds of all the women were widowed with most of them living alone, it is not surprising that 70 percent of the women in the study reported yearly incomes of less than $2,000. Poverty was very much a part of the rural elderly's existence; (3) in 1966, eight percent of income was spent on health care on the average and failure to use medical care resources was blamed most frequently on the expense of services. Many more of the poorest respondents died than did those with higher incomes, thus the 1973-74 sample showed some gains in income but it did not keep pace with inflation. A greater percentage of income was spent on medical care in 1973-74 with those persons reporting a decline in income being much more likely to report deteriorating health, more likely to not be registered for Medicare, and to be non-users of services. the poorest and sickest people tended to die between the two samplings, making this finding more conservative; (4) social networks: in the 1966 study, friends were considered a

PRINCIPAL INVESTIGATOR/PROGRAM DIRECTOR: Richard Hessler

greater source of social support and source of life satisfaction than were children or relatives. About 10 percent of the respondents reported feeling lonely. The 1973-74 findings showed that contact with children was not associated with life satisfaction, that is, that high contact respondents were equally likely to report high life satisfaction as dissatisfaction. One problem to be rectified in the proposed 1985 study, is to measure quality of the contact. Thus, we found that as health deteriorated, life satisfaction dropped and contacts with family increased. We will test for this in the proposed study. One in twenty respondents in 1966 relied on children for help with meals, whereas one in seven did so in 1973-74. Nevertheless, the small town elderly, even at advanced ages, placed great value in, and were successful at, maintaining their independence. Children increased services to their parents in order to extend independence as long as possible. Participation in community formal organizations and with friends were lower in 1973-74, particularly for men. Widowhood had less of an impact on participation than did being a widower. There was clear evidence in 1966 that those individuals with few or no friends or little to no community involvement had life satisfaction respondents did not show as strong a relationship between life satisfaction and contacts, perhaps, we argued, because social contact becomes less important as one gets older, especially if income is relatively high; (5) Religion: In 1966, 85 percent of the respondents belonged to a church with two-thirds actively participating. Membership and regularity of church attendance increased between 1966 and 1973-74. Religious participation played a greater role in the lives of women than of men and this remained constant over time. Thus, religious participation formed a very important central component of the rural elderly's independent life style. Physical health problems cut into this participation in a highly negative fashion.

Anticipating this proposal, Hessler analyzed the 873 panelist who died between the 1966 study and the 1974 re-study. Using the stepwise logistic regression procedure, the variables that best predict mortality between those two time periods, in their order of importance are:

1.   Age   3.   Formal participation in social networks
2.   Sex   4.   General health status

Table 1 shows, as expected, that age in 1966 was the single best predictor of mortality. controlling for age, sex was the next best predictor, with women being much more likely to survive than men. controlling for both age and sex, formal participation was the next variable entered. Persons with zero or low participation scores, hence with weak or non-existent social networks, were more likely to have died than those with extensive formal social networks. General health was the other important predictor of mortality. (See Appendix E for contingency bi-variate tables)

PRINCIPAL INVESTIGATOR/PROGRAM DIRECTOR: Richard Hessler

TABLE 1

Stepwise Logistic Regression Procedure for Predicting Mortality

Dependent Variable: Died N = 873

Final Parameter Estimates

Variable	Beta	Std. Error	Chi-Square	P	R
Intercept	-7.75294760	0.67911093	130.33		
Age	0.10183889	0.00893237	129.99		0.233
Sex	0.55013675	0.11281382	23.78	0.0000	0.096
Formal Participation	1.01043567	0.18109558	31.13	0.0000	0.111
General Health Status	-0.79120997	0.14644425	29.19	0.0000	-0.107
General Health Status	-0.54448448	0.13886416	15.37	0.0001	-0.075
Formal Participation	0.80217701	0.20446105	15.39	0.0001	0.075
Formal Participation	0.49523456	0.14201740	12.16	0.0005	0.066

Fraction of concordant Pairs of Predicted Probabilities and Responses: 0.7243*
Rank correlation Between Predicted Probability and Response:

Note: This model was created from a list of 21 independent variables, which were selected on theoretical grounds prior to establishing their statistical bivariate relationship to the dependent variable died. These final four variables were added one-at-a-time to the model. Thus, age in 1966 was the best predictor of mortality. Then controlling for age, sex was the next variable added, and controlling for age and sex, formal participation in social networks was the next variable in, and so on. The backward procedure was the next variable in, and so on. The backward procedure (all variables in the drop variables one-at-a-time) yielded the very same predictor variable model.

*   Means that 72 percent of the time one would be correct in predicting mortality knowing the variables in the model.

This preliminary analysis lends credence to our longitudinal focus on health and social networks and is supported by recent social epidemiological research on reasons for mortality among the elderly (Kaplan and Camacho, 1983; Blazer 1982; Zuckerman, Kasl, and Ostfeld, 1984; Cicirelli, 1980; Longiono, et al., 1980; Hays, 1981; Mossey and Shapiro, 1982; Kohn, 1982).

Finally, at some later date, the 1985 cross-sectional sample could be re-interviewed thereby constituting another panel which could be used to test the predictive power of social networks, health, and the other psycho-social variables associated with longevity and the maintenance of independent living.

D.   Experimental Design and Methods

In order to continue this productive and unique gerontological research program at UMC, we propose a combination cross-sectional design and a longitudinal design. The cross-sectional survey will involve face-to-face interviews with 1,650 elderly persons 65 years or older living independently in the same 64 small Missouri towns studied in 1966 and again in 1974. In addition, we will re-interview the estimated 100 or so survivors of the original 1966 survey, the youngest of whom will be 85 years old in 1986. Thus we will have two different study populations; (1) the 1,700 individuals interviewed in 1966, the survivors in 1974, and the survivors in 1985; (2) a new cross-sectional sample of 1,550 individuals. This new sample will be drawn from the same 64 towns from whence came the 1,700 panelists in 1966.

With this combination of research designs, we are realizing the analytic benefits of 18 years of time and knowledge accumulated about the towns and the members of the panel, thereby making it possible to analyze the aging process, including socio-environmental factors associated with longevity and the maintenance of independent living. Also, causal sequences among significant variables can be analyzed using the cross-lagged correlation technique. Finally, the new 1985 cross-sectional survey can be compared against the 1966 cross-sectional survey and changes in the 64 towns can be used as macro-level contexts for better understanding the differences between age cohorts across the two surveys. Hopefully, at some later date, the 1985 cross-sectional sample could be re-interviewed thereby constituting another panel through which we could test the predictive power of social networks, health, and the other psycho-social variables associated with longevity and the maintenance of independent living.

The study is divided into the following two stages: (1) socio-historical analysis of the 64 small towns; (2) interviewing the respondents, analysis, and write-up. We believe that the first stage is vitally important for providing a macro-level context through which one can interpret the micro-level responses of the elderly respondents. There is a growing body of literature which demonstrates a relationship between individual responses and the context in which the individuals find themselves (Fernandez and Kubik, 1981; Lazarsfeld and Menzel, 1972).

The Sampling Plan

We will use the four cultural areas of the state of Missouri (Gregory, 1958: See Appendix A, Sampling Plan: The Four Cultural Areas and map of Missouri) and 64 small towns spread throughout those four areas from which a sample of 1,650 elderly residents will be drawn. (See Appendix A, 1985 Sampling Plan: Number, towns and population changes). The 64 small towns are the same ones used in the original study in 1966 (Grant CH 00354, Division of Chronic Diseases, U.S. Public Health Service) and in the re-study in 1974-75 (Grant HEW-SRS-93-P-57673/701, Administration on Aging, HEW and a grant from the Research Council, UMC). The sample of towns included those with populations ranging from 250 to 5,000, and was selected on a stratified cluster basis to contain substantially the same proportion of older people who were living in towns of the same size in the state as a whole. Thus the 64 towns are representative of all Missouri towns whose populations fall within the 250 to 5,000 range.

In addition to sampling proportionately from each of the four areas, subjects in the 1966 study were drawn proportionate to the number of elderly in towns of three size categories: those with populations ranging from 250 to 999, or the second category with populations between 1,000 and 2,499, and the third with populations to 2,500 to 5,000. Approximately one-third of the sample of individuals was drawn from communities of each of these size classes. Each town was enumerated and a list was compiled of all non-institutional residences within the city limits containing at least one person 65 years or older. Subjects then were drawn randomly from those lists. The same selection procedure will be used in the proposed re-study of the 64 towns. We will locate those individuals from the 1974 re-interview who have survived to the present time. Names and address of all 1974 respondents will be sent to the Missouri State Division of Health for a check against the computerized death certificates. In addition, letters will be mailed to the postmasters of each of the towns involved along with a list of the names and address of the 1974 respondents. The postmasters will be asked to verify the addresses and to provide new addresses where changes have occurred or to notify us about deaths. This procedure was used effectively between the 1966 and 1974 re-interviews.

Stage 1: Socio-historical Analysis

During the first six months of the proposed two-year study, the principal investigator and research assistants will utilize secondary data plus conduct one oral history interview in each of the 64 towns in order to describe the ways in which the 64 towns have changed during the 18 year period beginning with the original 1966 study. The changes will be described in terms of the following factors:

(1)   Population age pyramid
(2)   Community economic base
(3)   Health care providers and institutions
(4)   Local, State and Federal assistance programs for the elderly

Stage 2: Interviewing, Analysis, and Write-up

Twelve months will be devoted to interviewing and preliminary analysis. The 1,650 respondents will be interviewed using primarily a structured schedule with some focused, open-ended questions included.

During the Winter of 1984, Dr. Hessler re-designed the 1973-74 interview schedule. Questions measuring variables which did not account for much of the variance in the dependent variables were dropped. New questions were added based on a literature review and knowledge about current issues facing the elderly. (See Appendix D for the schedules). The schedules are reproduced in this proposal for the reviewers to assess the groundwork to date and the work needed to revise and pre-test a valid and reliable instrument. Thus, the schedules are in preliminary form and the SSQ schedule is not integrated into the 1973-74 schedule. The interview schedule will be completed during the first three months of the study and pre-tested in the sixth month.

Once the instruments were designed, two of the original 64 research towns were enumerated. Twenty four interviews were completed and analyzed which served as a re-test of the enumeration procedure and as a pre-test of the interview schedule.

In addition, we tested an exchange methodology procedure (Hessler, 1979) in which the two mayors and the directors of the senior citizen centers were apprised of the study and cooperated by helping us spread publicity and otherwise facilitated our entry into the two communities. In return, we proposed to meet with the senior citizen center members and other interested residents in order to present our findings and to lead a discussion of their policy implications.

This same procedure will be used in other study towns.

We propose to hire as interviewers, UMC graduate students in Marketing, Political Science, History, Journalism, sociology, and Health Services Management, in addition to three older persons living in the most outlying areas of the state.

Upon completing all the interviews in one of the four cultural sampling areas, the core research staff and interviewers will convene in columbia to discuss the strengths and weaknesses of the field work, to re-emphasize the specific areas of the research, and to code and analyze the interview data. We discovered in the recent pre-test that coding was a very effective way to make certain that the interviewers were doing what they had been trained to do. Ambiguities and other problems associated with recording answers were highlighted by coding. also, preliminary analysis can help the researcher sharpen ongoing measurement and even revise the coding categories if need be.

Measurement

Social Structure: The variables which will be used to construct the socio-historical analysis (population age pyramid, community economic base, health care providers and institutions, and local/state/federal assistance programs for the elderly) will be measured as follows:

The U.S. Census will be used to construct the age pyramids. The community economic base analysis will utilize the IBM PC Multiplan program and income and transfer payment data on the 64 Missouri communities (see Appendix C, Report No. 60). Information about the changes in numbers of MD's, DO's, and hospital beds will be derived from the Missouri State Medical Society Registry, and from the yearly Hospital Patient Origin Report, Division of Health, Missouri Center for Health Statistics, local county Missouri Division of Health, Missouri Center for Health Statistics, local county Missouri Division of Aging offices and area Agency on Aging offices will be contracted by letter requesting a chronology of programs and their budgets for the 1966-84 period. A booklet published by the Missouri Department of Social Services Division of Aging listing the addresses and phone numbers of all the offices for every county in the state will be used to facilitate the gathering of these data.

Finally, oral history interviews will be conducted with one elderly informant in each of the 64 towns. A review of the available town newspapers housed in the Missouri State Historical Society, UMC will be conducted as a supplement to the other resources.

There is tremendous variety among rural communities. They are composed of different socio-economic and ethnic groups, rest on different economic bases, have different regional cultures, and vary in terms of their relationships with the larger society. Gallaher (1961) following on West's study of Plainville (Wheatland, Missouri, a small town similar to the other 64 in our proposed study), found that the impact of the larger society was pervasive and powerful. Gallaher listed the conditions that accounted for the changes between the two studies: (1)

disappearance of geographical and cultural isolation; (2) pressure for change from outside; and (3) acceptance of new living standards focused on material comfort and efficiency. The result was as "revolution in expectations" among Plainvillers.

The major process was that of urbanization. Gallaher says, "Plainvillers are entering into relationships drawing them into ever-widening circles of awareness of, participation in, and dependency upon the surrounding urban world" (Gallaher, 1961:226). Gallaher echoes Vidich and Bensman (1958) in his conclusion that the major culture change may be that Plainvillers, "...surrender local authority and responsibility in many decision-making processes to sources outside the community" (Gallaher, 1961:243). The author also makes the point that changes in the community to a great extent are the result of deliberate programs by change-oriented agencies (for example, the agricultural extension service) sponsored by centralized agencies in the larger society (Gallaher, 1961:254).

Paradoxically, along with the penetration of elements of the larger society and dependency on outside agencies, there was an active local politics based on cliques and kinship and a distrust of outside authority.

Vidich and Bensman (1958) in their study of rural Springdale found dependency on outside agencies and, most importantly for our proposed research, that social life was highly organized around informal gatherings and formal associations. The authors counted more than 200 formal associations in this small town of 1,000 people. Many of these associations were church related. The main themes of the small town community studies is the increasing economic dependency of the small towns on the outside world and the strong value of independence and distrust of that outside world held by the local residents. Participation in informal and formal associations is an important valued means of preserving independence and control. (for a more extensive review of this literature, see appendix F).

Data on the following areas will be gathered: (1) identifying data such as income, income source, education, number of years living in town, age, race, sex and marital status; (2) household composition including the sex, age, and relationship to the respondent of each person in the household; (3) housing and household equipment; (4) retirement, reason for retirement and attitudes toward retirement; (5) health status will be measured by using perceived global health ratings ("excellent", "good", "fair", and "poor"), the respondent's report of the occurrence of eight chronic conditions, frequency of physician contact and type of physician, expenditure for medial and hospital care during the past six months, and activities of daily living. Katz (1983) and Shanas (1980)concluded that activities of daily living (ADL) is a valid and important measure of mobility and capacity for self care among the elderly. Functional limitations can be expected to increase with age but if detected and treated, independence can be maintained at higher levels of life satisfaction and morale than if no interventions are conducted. The global health questions are found on P. 9, Q's 1, 2, 3 of the 1973-74 schedule, Appendix D. The activities of daily living questions are on P. 13, Q's 11, 12, 13 and 14. Also, we will use Q's 88 and 93 from the F & CM Questionnaire, appendix D in order to assess the eight chronic conditions and emotional health problems. Kaplan and Camacho's (1983) assessment of the 1965 Human Population Survey of a random sample of 6,928 adults in Alameda County, California, found that the global measure of perceived health was an excellent predictor of mortality, lending support to our proposed use of this measure. There are several major methodological assessments of respondent recall of illness and hospitalization episodes. Perry (1982) reviewed the literature and concluded that the aged are as accurate and reliable as younger respondents. Other research suggests that recall of illness episodes, visits to physicians, and hospitalizations is best if the time frame is six months to one year (DHEW, 1977; 1965). We plan on using six months as the time frame for the health-related recall questions.

Older adults are excellent subjects for studying the relationship between social support and other social factors to health problems. By limiting the age range to older subjects, we are simultaneously controlling for the effect of aging and cohort effects. Certain stressful social events such as loss of loved ones and other degradations of the social environment are much more prevalent in later life. Also, the elderly are more susceptible to stressful environmental events (Caudill, 1958; Lazarus, 1966).

We will analyze the data to see if those individuals who report good or excellent health and who are low utilizers of medical services will report satisfying and extensive social support networks and high life satisfaction scores (Blazer, 1982; Zuckerman, Kasl, and Ostfeld, 1984).

(6) Life satisfaction and other attitudinal factors, including beliefs about older people as a category and death and dying. The death and dying measures toward older people are on p. 17. A review of the recent literature on life satisfaction among the elderly shows that the findings are confounded by research design constraints which make it difficult to determine the sequential role of life satisfaction. For example, Linn and Linn (1980) found a strong relationship between life satisfaction and health, and Longino, McClelland and Peterson (1980) found that social support is important in life satisfaction, while Cicirelli (1980) found that social support and health status can affect life satisfaction in later life.

For example, the relationship between associated variables and life satisfaction among the elderly have been demonstrated in longitudinal studies (Palmore & Kivett, 1977), and cross-sectional surveys of elderly persons alone (Chatfield, 1977; Knapp, 1976; Lohmann, 1977). However, it is not clear which types of variables are associated with and/or predict life satisfaction. social support, the amount of social activity, and health status appear to be exceptions. Kushman and Land (1980), and Snider (1980) found that social support and health status can affect life satisfaction in later life. Kushman and Lane suggested that having only infrequent social contacts with friends or relatives who do not reside in the household has a significant negative influence on psychological well-being and life satisfaction. Edwards and Klemmack (1973) found that the best predictors of life satisfaction are informal participation with nonkinsmen, perceived health status, and socioeconomic status.

The activity theory of aging suggests that there is a possible relationship between activity and life satisfaction and that the greater the role loss, the lower the life satisfaction (Burgess, 1954; Kutner, 1956; Lebo, 1953; Richard, 1976; Markides & Martin, 1979). However, Lemon, Bengston and Peterson (1972) point out the need to both revise and enlarge the theory, including as concepts personality configurations and availability of intimates (confidants).

Therefore, self-conception as a personality configuration of the age identification of the elderly is shown to be an important intervening variable between social activity and life satisfaction, especially for the subsample of older people who prefer to spend time with others their own age (McClelland, 1982). Bultena and Powers (1978) also found that favorable self-evaluations versus age peers were positively correlated with younger self-images, which demonstrates the utility of a reference-group perspective embedded with social activities in explaining diverse psychological adaptions to later-life role changes. Similarly, Blau (1956) found that participation in a friendship group serves to forestall a shift in age identification. These researchers argue that self-conception (Rose, 1962). Longino, McClelland and Peterson (1980) found that residents of an age-segregated community show more positive social integration, an enhanced positive self-conception, and distinctive patterns of preference for interaction with other older people.

Furthermore, Lohman (1977, 1980) found that there is a high level of interrelationship between measures of life satisfaction, morale and adjustment, and that the nominal definitions of the three constructs were typically similar to the point of being indistinguishable. the range of definitions for each construct was no greater than the range of definitions among each of the three constructs. In addition, the most common operational definitions of the constructs (Cavan Attitude Scale, Kutner Morale Scale, Dean Morale Scale, Philadelphia Geriatric Center Morale Scale, Life Satisfaction Index A, Life Satisfaction Index B) when applied to the same population, were found to share a common underlying construct (Lohman, 1980). Therefore, although there may be some aspect of the current operational definitions of these constructs which is unique to one of the three, there is also a major aspect common to all three. Larson (1978) signifies these constructs in terms of a single summary construct, subjective well-being. His research shows reported well-being to be related with degree of social interaction, which follows health and socioeconomic factors. Klug and Sauer (1961) found that social activities, self-conception of age and economic circumstances are related to adjustment of the elderly. Pihlblad and McNamara (1965) also found that well-adjusted elderly are more likely to have a youthful self-conception, good health, higher income, higher social participation (both formal and informal social participation), and a favorable view of community and their place in it. Phillips (1957) suggests that role changes, influenced by age, marital and employment change in social relationships as well as activities, are significantly related to maladjustment. Age identification as "Old" is related to low life satisfaction.

We will be able to follow the changes in life satisfaction relative to the other variables in our study and to determine causal sequences. for the 1984 sampling, however, we will have only associations and we expect to find how life satisfaction associated with perceived health problems, impaired social support, and perceived loneliness. Life satisfaction is measured by a short form of the Newgarten-Havighurst (1961) life satisfaction index.

(7) Widowhood and the problems which the respondents identify as associated with it.

(8) Political voting behavior measured by Q's 1-4, Focused interview schedule, Appendix D.

(9) Social support; the general hypothesis is that social support plays a significant role in mediating adverse health consequences of life stresses and in protecting the health of the elderly. The preliminary logistical regression analysis on the decreased respondents reported above supports the hypothesis that after age and sex are taken into account, the survivors will have scored higher on social support/formal participation measures than those who have died. Also, in the 1985 panel, we expect to find lower levels of social support for the older respondents given the natural attrition of friends and family. Impaired social support networks will be associated with an increase in the utilization of health services, an increase in physical health problems (Blazer, 1982), and reduced life satisfaction.

Social support systems are social networks or sets of persons connected by sets of interactions and ties of emotional and physical support. These systems are of three types: (1) primary groups such as children and other kin; (2) Neighborhood/Community based informal, such as friends and neighbors; (3)Neighborhood/Community based formal, such as church and community professionals. It is through contacts with others, particularly with members of primary groups, that the elderly receive validation of their own value and worth, gain a sense of control over their environments and the will to continue living outside of an institutional setting. Many social science researchers have studied the relationship between social support and mortality. McMahon and Pugh, (1970) found that the estimates of mortality are lowest for the married and Berkman and Syme's (1979) study of social ties and mortality in a 10 year follow-up of 87,000 residents in Alameda County, CA found that the people who lacked social and community ties were more likely to die than those individuals with more contact. DiMatteo and Hays (1981), found that social support is a central psychological issue in maintaining health. Cassel's (1974) classic review of the epidemiological findings relative to social support showed that changes in the immediate social environment, e.g., loss of a spouse, are capable of altering people's resistance to disease.

According to Cassel, social support protects the individual against this process. The elderly particularly are at risk because they face change that entail or threaten the loss of social support itself. Gottleib, (1981), has urged researchers to try to gain a contextual understanding of how people cope with these changes in terms of studying the interplay between the attributes of individuals, the attributes of the support structure in which they are embedded, and the attributes of the sociocultural environment influencing the support structure and the individuals. Appendix D contains the description of the indices of social support, and the 1973-74 interview schedule questions (Family Association, Pps. 6-9, Q's 1-10; Activities and Organizations, Pp. 15-16, Q's 1-5; Friendships, Pp. 18-20, Q's 1-4; Loneliness, P. 21, Q 1). These items tend to yield a quantitative picture of social support. In order to measure satisfaction with the level of support or how the respondents feel about their support structure, we will use the 27 items, Social Support Questionnaire (SSQ; Sarason et al, 1983). Each of the 27 items requires a two-part response. Respondents must (a) list the people they can count on for support in given sets of circumstances and (b) indicate their overall level of satisfaction with these supports. A series of studies has been done to determine the reliability and validity of this measure and the results indicate that the SSQ is a very stable instrument with high internal consistency, however, the validations and checks on reliability have been based on other pencil and paper measures, not observable behaviors.

Use of Health Services and Social Programs

Respondents will be asked if they have a family physician, where he/she is located, the number of miles from home to the physician's office, whether they have changed physicians in the last two years, and reasons for any changes. Also, we will determine when the respondents last saw a physician and the respondents will be asked to assess what they feel is the need for different types of medical specialists plus general practitioners in the community. these questions are in Appendix D, Focused Interview, Q's 6-9.

Hospitalization and the factors influencing the choice of the hospital will be measured. Including the respondents evaluation of the appropriateness of the length of time spent in the hospital. These questions are in Appendix D, Focused Interview, Q's 10-13.

Respondents will be asked how their medical care is paid for and they will be asked to evaluate the responsiveness of government programs to the financial needs of the elderly, particularly Medicare and social Security. Respondents will be asked about their ideas or suggestions for improving health care in their town and they will express their feelings about possibly having to use in-home health care in order to maintain their independence. Along this line of thought, respondents will be asked how they feel about their possibly going to a nursing home, what they fear might happen to their situation that would make it difficult to live in their own homes, and what their community offers by way of services that helps the respondents maintain their independence. These items are in Appendix D, Focused Interview, Q's 15-24.

Analysis

The socio-historical data will be coded and placed in the UMC computer using the CMS file system. Then when the individual respondent data are coded, the socio-historical data on a given town will be added to the computer files of the respondents from that town.

This analysis not only will provide a socio-historical interpretive context but we will be in a position to analyze the rise and fall of social programs for the elderly and the utilization issue from the perspective of the elderly themselves. We will be able to address questions such as, "Is there a relationship between changes in levels of program funding and changes in levels of health or life satisfaction?" Copies of this socio-historical write-up will be given to the Missouri State Historical Society and to the Missouri Cultural Heritage Center, UMC campus.

The open-ended questions will yield qualitative data which will be categorized, labeled, and stored on the Apple III computer. Quotations with their appropriate labels can be called up and printed using the Apple Writer word processing program. These qualitative data will be used to buttress and to lend meaning to the quantitative analysis.

Richard Madsen, statistical analysis consultant, has assisted the project director in setting up the SAS file of the 1966 data reported earlier in this proposal. The CMS system at UMC (EZEDIT) is the one these data are stored in and the same system will be used to code the 1986 study data directly onto the main frame IBM computer. Again, a SAS file will be constructed.

Glen (1981) pointed out that a common error in research on aging has been the assumption that cross sectional differences by age necessarily reflects the effects of aging. For example, if we were to find that the oldest people in our study were lonelier than the youngest people, we might argue that growing older tends to cause people to become more lonely. Heeding Glen's warning, we will attempt in the analysis, to deal with age effects, period effects, and cohort effects. Both our panel and cross-sectional designs contain fairly large and age-heterogeneous samples of elderly persons (65-99) which helps in the analysis of period effects, provides information on how the subjects changed over the almost 20 year span of time, and makes it possible to analyze "life course differences" within age cohorts and differences among cohort via age specific data from the two independent cross-sectional samples (Riley, 1973; Nesseiroode and Baltes, 1979).

Figure 1 presents graphically the period, cohort, and aging effect problems. for example, treating the 1966 sample as cross-sectional survey A and the proposed 1985 survey as cross-section B, we will compare the oldest cohort (80-85; 86-90; 91-95; 96 +) on social networks, life satisfaction, and health levels for 1966 and 1985. This may reveal insight into the period effects particularly given the fact that the two independent cross sectional surveys are from the same 64 small towns about which we will have almost 20 years of socio-historical change data. The differences and similarities in their life situations and attitudes, as well as the other age cohorts, will be described relative to the period changes.

PRINCIPAL INVESTIGATOR/PROGRAM DIRECTOR: Richard Hessler

Age effects can be studied by taking advantage of the 30 years or so of age difference among the respondents. Taking the 1966 point in time, we will compare people of different age groups. We will do the same for 1985 and compare the age groups across cohorts to see if age differences are the same for the two time periods. Also, the longitudinal design enables us to describe age variation within cohorts.

However, cohort composition and cohort membership enter the picture to complicate things. For example, cohort composition is a factor because the older cohorts are more likely to be females and thus are more likely to see doctors, join formal associations, and have contact with friends because they are females not because they are in the 86-90 age group. For this reason, the analysis will "control" for the cohort composition variables. Regarding cohort membership, those respondents born right after the war with Spain and McKinley's assassination (65-69 in 1966 study) and those born during Teddy Roosevelt's's administration may be different in attitudes than those persons who were born during the stock market crash (75-79 in 1985). By means of the longitudinal design which provides for the analysis of the survivors of the original 1966 panel, we can compare one cohort with another over three points in time (decade of the 60's, 70's, and 80's) in order to describe the process of aging for each cohort. thus, we will be in a position to access the aging effect versus the cohort effect of being in a more "economically advantaged" cohort, for example.

It is noted that our use of sophisticated statistical procedures, while providing estimates of the three effects and their combinations, does not solve the problem of their confounding effects. In fact, Glen (1976) has reviewed the "best" analytic strategies and has concluded that purely statistical approaches to analyzing age, cohort, and period effects will be unsuccessful. He argues that socio-historical contexts and their analysis along with the building of theories of aging and development, based on findings, is the most reasonable way to approach the problem of interpreting the statistical models.

The hypotheses will be tested using Stepwise, Forward and Backward analysis of variance as well as the Logistic Regression statistical model. Causal sequences of variables will be tested for the longitudinal sample by using cross-lagged correlation, for example, between changes in social support, life satisfaction, and health. The goal here will be to try and determine if decline in social support, for example, produces lower life satisfaction scores and increases in health problems or does declining health eventually reduce satisfaction with life and contact with formal and informal social networks? (See Figure 2)

In this hypothetical example, the auto and synchronous correlations are relatively large and stable which lends credence to the cross-lagged correlations. According to this example, social networks produces life satisfaction (.60) rather than satisfaction producing networks (.40).

E.   Human Subjects

We will interview face-to-face, 1,650 elderly persons 65 years or older chosen at random from the 64 small towns. Given the age and sex distribution of our two earlier studies, plus the 1984 pre-test, we estimate that age will range from 65 to 95 years and that 65 percent of the sample will be women with about one in seven women being married. Because our sample will be non-institutionalized elderly, we do not anticipate very many instances of severe physical or mental disabilities. Where serious problems are encountered, the interviewer will refer to a list of local physicians and give the names and phone numbers to the respondent. If the situation warrants immediate action, the interviewer, with the consent of the respondent, will call the 911 number and initiate emergency care.

Since we plan to reinterview the respondents in 1990, it is necessary to keep the names and addresses of the respondents on file. This file will be locked at all times and secured in Dr. Hessler's office in the Sociology Department. Al of the computer data will not have names on file. Otherwise, none of the information gathered poses any legal, financial, physical, psychological or social threat to the respondents. This judgement is based on experience with the 1966, 1973-74, and 1984 pre-test interviewing.

At the time of the enumeration, potential respondents will be informed of the possibility that they will be chosen at random for participation on the panel. Once chosen, our experiences has shown that a simple explanation of the aims of the study, its sponsorship, the types of questions, the fact that the respondent will be part of an on-going panel, and that participation involves no financial obligations for the respondents will lead to cooperation. The exchange procedure and UMC identification for the interviewer resulted in 100 percent cooperation during the 1984 pre-test and we anticipate similar results for the proposed study.

Interviewers will be instructed verbally and in writing about the medical assistance procedures and about checking in with the office, by phone, should any problems surrounding rapport and cooperation arise.

PRINCIPAL INVESTIGATOR/PROGRAM DIRECTOR: Richard Hessler

Figure 1: Cohort, Age, and Period Effects

Events
- Older American Act
- Vietnam War
- Medicare
- 1967
- Reagan Land slide

1. Cohort Analysis

	Age 65-69	Age 70-75	Age 76-79	Age 80-85	Age 86-89	Age 90-95	Age 96-99
1966 Cross-sectional Survey	0	0	0	0	0	0	0
1986 Cross-sectional Survey	0	0	0	0	0	0	0

2. Age Effect — Life Course Differences Within a Cohort

3. Period Effect — Responses to the Economic Slowdown Versus Responses Due to Aging per se

RECESSION   ECONOMIC   CONOMIC

		Age 65-69	
1974	1966	73-77	65-69

Panel

PRINCIPAL INVESTIGATOR/PROGRAM DIRECTOR: ___Richard Hessler___

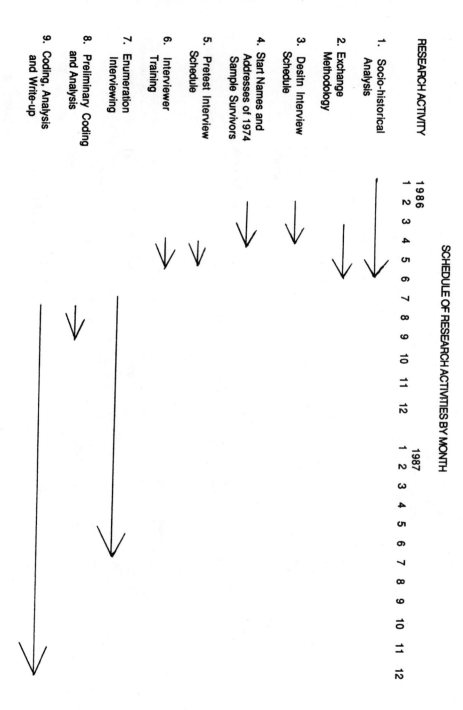

PRINCIPAL INVESTIGATOR/PROGRAM DIRECTOR: Richard Hessler

Figure 2: Cross-lagged Correlation Between Social Networks and Life Satisfaction

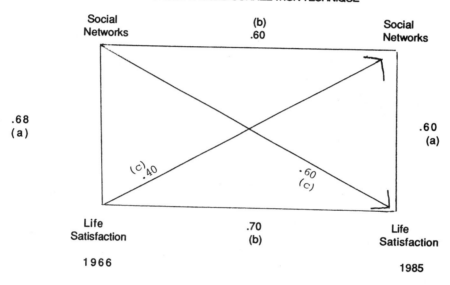

CROSS-LAGGED CORRELATION TECHNIQUE

a.   Synchronous correlations

b.   Autocorrelations

c.   Cross-lagged correlations

General References

Allison, G.T. 1971. *Essence of Decision: Exploring the Cuban Missile Crisis.* Boston, MA: Little, Brown and Embasy.

Antonosky, A. 1979. *Health, Stress, and Coping.* San Francisco, CA: Jossey-Bass Publishers.

Antonucci, T. and H. Akiyama. 1987. "Social Networks in Adult Life and a Preliminary Examination of the Convoy Model," *Journal of Gerontology*, 42(5), pp. 519–527.

Aristotle, *Physics: Books III and IV.* Translated by E. Hussey. 1983. New York, NY: Oxford University Press.

Babbie, E. 1986. *The Practice of Social Research.* Belmont, CA: Wadsworth Publishing Co.

Becker, H. S. 1967. "Whose Side Are We On?" *Social Problems*, 14, Winter, pp. 239–247.

Bernard, S. P. 1971. *Social Research: Strategy and Tactics.* New York, NY: Macmillan.

Biddle, B. J., R. L. Slavings, and D. S. Anderson. 1985. "Panel Studies and Causal Inference," *Journal of Applied Behavorial Science*, Vol. 21(1), pp. 79–93.

Biddle, B. J., B. Bank, and R. Slavings. 1987. "Name Preferences, Identities and Retention Decisions," *Social Psychology Quarterly*, Vol. 50(4), pp. 322–337.

Bishop, G. F., A. J. Tuchfaber, and R. W. Oldendick. 1986. "Opinions on Fictitious Issues: The Pressure to Answer Survey Questions," *Public Opinion Quarterly*, Vol. 50, Summer, pp. 240–250.

Brown, R. 1963. *Explanation in Social Science.* Chicago, IL: Aldine Publishing Co.

Burkman, R. T. 1981. "Association Between Intrauterine Device and Pelvic Inflammatory Disease," *Obstetrics and Gynecology*, Vol. 57 (3), pp. 269–276.

Cain, G. G. and H.W. Watts. 1970. "Problems in Making Policy Inferences from the Coleman Report," *American Sociological Review*, Vol. 35(2), April, pp. 228–242.

Cassel, J. 1978. "Risk and Benefit to Subjects of Fieldwork", *American Sociologist*, 13, pp. 134–143.

Cassel, J. and M. Wax (eds.). 1980. "Ethical Problems of Fieldwork," *Social Problems*, Special Edition, 27(3), February, pp. 259–378.

Chambliss, W. J. 1978. *On the Take: From Petty Crooks to Presidents*. Bloomington, IN: Indiana University Press.

Cohen, M. R. and E. Nagel. 1934. *An Introduction to Logic and Scientific Method*. New York, NY: Harcourt, Brace and Co.

Coleman, J., E. Q. Campbell, C. J. Hobson, J. McParthland, A. M. Mood, F. D. Weinfeld, and R. York. 1966. *Equality of Education Opportunity*. Washington, D.C.: U.S. Government Printing Office, National Center of Educational Statistics.

Coleman, J. S. 1976. "Recent Trends in School Integration," *Evaluation Studies Research Annual*, Vol 1. G. V. Glass (ed.). Beverly Hills, CA: Sage Publications.

Conrad, J. 1983. *Heart of Darkness* and *The Secret Sharer*. New York, NY: Doubleday and Co., Inc.

Cumming, E., and J. Cumming. 1957. *Closed Ranks: An Experiment in Mental Health Education*. Cambridge, MA: Harvard University Press.

Davis, F. 1963. *Passage Through Crisis: Polio Victims and Their Families*. Indianapolis, IN: Bobbs-Merrill Company, Inc.

Deutscher, I. 1973. *What We Say/What We Do*. Glenview, IL: Scott, Foresman and Co.

Gallaher, A., Jr. 1961. *Plainville Fifteen Years Later*. New York, NY: Columbia University Press.

Galliher, J. F. 1980. "Social Scientists' Ethical Responsibilities to Superordinates: Looking Upward Meekly," *Social Problems*, February, 27(3), pp. 298–308.

Galliher, J. F. and R. Hessler. 1983. "Institutional Review Boards and Clandestine Research: An Experimental Test," *Human Organization*, 42, Spring, pp. 82–90.

Glaser, B. and A. Strauss. 1967. *The Discovery of Grounded Theory: Strategies for Qualitative Research*. Chicago, IL: Aldine Publishing Co.

Glazer, M. 1972. *The Research Adventure*. New York, NY: Random House.

Glennan, T. K., Jr. 1972. "Evaluating Federal Manpower Programs," *Notes and Observations in Evaluating Social Programs: Theory, Practice, and Politics*. P. H. Rossi and W. Williams (eds.). New York, NY: Seminar Press, pp. 187–220.

Gold, D. 1969. "Statistical Tests and Substantive Significance," *The American Sociologist*, 4, pp. 42–46.

Gouldner, A. W. 1970. *The Coming Crisis in Western Sociology*. New York, NY: Basic Books.

Goulder, A. W. 1979. *The Future of Intellectuals and the Rise of the New Class.* New York, NY: Seabury Press.

Granberg, D. and S. Holmberg. 1990. "Intention-Behavior Relationship Among U.S. and Swedish Voters," *Social Psychology Quarterly*, 53, pp. 44–54.

Hempel, C. "Fundamentals of Concept Formation in Empirical Science," Vols I & II, *International Encyclopedia of United Science.* Chicago, IL: University of Chicago Press.

Hessler, R. M., S. H. Pazaki, R. W. Madsen, and R. L. Blake. 1990. "Predicting Mortality Among Independently Living Rural Elderly: A Twenty-year Longitudinal Study," *Sociological Quarterly*, Summer.

Hessler, R. M., J. Guinn, D. Huesgen, and L. Wolter. 1989. "Research Entry: a Twenty-year Longitudinal Study of the Rural Elderly," *Qualitative Sociology*, 12(3), pp. 261–277.

Hessler, R. M. 1983. "Institutional Review Boards and Clandestine Research: An Experimental Test," *Human Organization*, 42, no. 1, Spring, pp. 82–87.

Hessler, R. M. 1983. "Reply to Reynolds," *Human Organization*, 42, no. 1, Spring, pp. 89–90.

Hessler, R. M. 1977. "Citizen Participation, Social Organization and Culture: A Neighborhood Health Center for Chicanos," *Human Organization*, 36(2), pp. 124–134.

Hessler, R. M., P. K. New. 1972. "Community Research or Research Commune?" *Proceedings, Environmental Design Research Association III*, January.

Hessler, R. M., P. K. New. 1972. "Research as a Process of Exchange," *The American Sociologist*, 7(1), pp. 13–15.

Hollingshead, A. and F. Redlich, 1958. *Social Class and Mental Illness.* New York, NY: Wiley.

Holzner, B. 1968. *Reality Construction in Society.* Cambridge, MA: Schenkman Publishing Co.

Homans, G. C. 1950. *The Human Group.* New York, NY: Harcourt, Brace and Company, Inc.

Horowitz, I. L. 1974 (revised). *The Rise and Fall of Project Camelot: Studies in the Relationship Between Social Science and Practical Politics.* Cambridge, MA: M.I.T. Press.

Humphreys, A. J. 1966. *New Dubliners: Urbanization and the Irish Family.* New York, NY: Fordham University Press.

Humphreys, I. L. 1970. *Tearoom Trade: Impersonal Sex in Public Places.* Chicago, IL: Aldine Publishing Co.

Kaplan, G. A. 1988. "Social Contacts and Ischaemic Heart Disease," *Annals of Clinical Research*, 20, pp. 131–136.

Kronmal, R. A., C. W. Whitney, and S. D. Mumford. 1991. "The Intrauterine Device and Pelvic Inflamatory Disease: The Women's Health Study Reanalyzed," *Journal of Clinical Epidemiology*, Vol. 44, No. 2, pp. 109–122.

Kuhn, T. S. 1962. *The Structure of Scientific Revolutions.* Chicago, IL: University of Chicago Press.

LaPiere, R. T. 1934 and 1935. "Attitudes vs. Actions," *Social Forces*, 13, October and May, pp. 230–237.

Lazarsfeld, P. F. 1951. "Qualitative Measurement in the Social Sciences," *The Policy Sciences*. D. Lerner and H. D. Lasswell (eds.). Stanford University Press, pp. 155–189.

Lazarsfeld, P. F., and W. Thielens, Jr. 1958. *The Academic Mind: Social Scientists in a Time of Crisis*. Glencoe, IL: The Free Press.

Lazarsfeld, P. F. 1968. "An Episode in the History of Social Research: A Memoir," *The Intellectual Migration: Europe and America 1930–1960*. Cambridge, MA: Harvard University Press.

Lazarsfeld, P. F. 1982. *The Varied Sociology of Paul Lazarsfeld*, P. L. Kendall (Ed.). New York, NY: Columbia University Press, pp. 11–73.

Lazarsfeld, P. F. 1987. "Evidence and Inference in Social Research," *Daedalus*, Fall, pp. 99–130.

Likert, R. 1932. "A Technique for the Measurement of Attitudes," *Archives of Psychology*, 140.

Lincoln, Yvonna and Egon Guba. 1985. *Naturalistic Inquiry*. Beverly Hills, CA: Sage Publications.

Madge, J. 1965. *The Tools of Social Science*. Garden City, NY: Doubleday and Co.

May, J. T., M. L. Durham and P. K. New. 1979. "The Process of Problem Definition," presented at the Society for the Scientific Study of Social Problems. Boston, MA, August.

McDill, E. L., M. S. McDill and T. Sprehe. 1969. *Strategies for Success in Compensatory Education: An Appraisal of Evaluation Research*. Baltimore, MD: Johns Hopkins Press.

Malinowski, B. 1926. *Crime and Custom in Savage Society*. New York, NY: Harcourt, Brace and Co., Inc.

Merton, R. K. 1963. *Social Theory and Social Structure*. New York, NY: Free Press.

Mill, J. S. 1935. *On Liberty*, edited by P. Wheelwright. Garden City, NY: Doubleday, Doran.

Mills, C. W. 1959. *The Sociological Imagination*. New York, NY: Oxford University Press.

Milne, A. A. 1954. *Winnie-the-Pooh*. New York, New York: Dell Publishing Co., Inc.

Nagel, E. 1961. *The Structure of Science: Problems in the Logic of Scientific Explanation*. New York, NY: Harcourt, Brace, and World, Inc.

Namboodiri, N. K., L. Carter, and H. Blalock, Jr. 1975. *Applied Multivariate Analysis and Experimental Design*. New York, NY: McGraw-Hill Co.

Parker, S. and R. Kleiner. 1966. *Mental Illness in the Negro Community*. New York, NY: Free Press.

Popper, K. 1959. *The Logic of Scientific Discovery*. New York, NY: Basic books.

Popper, K. 1964. *The Poverty of Historicism*. London, Rutledge and Kegan Paul.

Popper, K. 1968. *Conjectures and Refutations: The Growth of Scientific Knowledge.* Harper Torchbooks.

Regis, E. 1987. *Who Got Einstein's Office?: Eccentricity and Genius at the Institute for Advanced Study*, Reading, MA: Addison-Wesley.

Roethlisberger, F. J. and W. J. Dickson. 1967. *Management and the Worker: An account of a Research Program Evaluated by the Western Electric Company.* Cambridge, MA: Harvard University Press.

Saffir, W., R. A. Stebbins, and A. Turowetz. 1980. *Fieldwork Experience: Qualitative Approaches to Social Research.* New York, NY: St. Martin's Press.

Salloway, J. C., and C. M. Oberembt. 1976. "Social Aspect of Health Care Utilization," *A Coursebook in Health Care Delivery.* S. S., J. C. Salloway, and C. M. Oberembt (eds.) New York, NY: Appleton-Century-Crofts, pp. 3–21.

Schwartz, R. D. and J. H. Skolnick. 1962. "Two Studies of Legal Stigma," *Social Problems*, 10, Fall, pp. 133–142.

Siegel, K., and B. J. Krauss. 1991. "Living with HIV Infection: Adaptive Tasks of Sero-positive Gay Men," *Journal of Health and Social Behavior.* Vol. 32, March, pp. 17–32.

Stouffer, S. et al. 1949. *The American Soldier*, 4 Vols., Princeton, NJ: Princeton University Press.

Stouffer, S. 1950. "Some Observations on Study Design," *American Journal of Sociology.* Vol. 55, January, pp. 355–361.

Stouffer, S. 1955. *Communism, Conformity, and Civil Liberties: A Cross Section of the Nation Speaks Its Mind.* Garden City, NY: Doubleday.

Strauss, A., L. Schatzman, R. Boucher, D. Ehrilich and M. Sabshin. 1964. *Psychiatric Ideologies and Institutions.* New York Free Press, p. 20.

Strauss, A. 1987. *Qualitative Analysis for Social Scientists.* New York, NY: Cambridge University Press.

Suchman, E. A. 1967. *Evaluative Research: Principles and Practice in Public Service and Social Action Programs*, New York, NY: Russell Sage Foundation.

Suppes, P. 1970. *A Probabalistic Theory of Causality.* Amsterdam: North Holland.

Swigert, V. Lynn, and R. A. Farrell. 1976. *Murder, Inequality, and the Law.* Lexington, MA: Lexington Books.

Thomas, W. I. and F. Znaniecki. 1984. *The Polish Peasant in Europe and America*, (1918–1919) (ed. and abridged by E. Zaretsky). Urbana, IL: University of Illinois Press.

Thurstone, L. and E. Chave. 1929. *The Measurement of Attitude.* Chicago, IL: University of Chicago Press.

Tittle, C. R. and A. R. Rowe. 1973. "Moral Appeal, Sanction Threat, and Deviance: An Experimental Test," *Social Problems*, Spring, 20, pp. 488–498.

Turnbull, C. M. 1972. *The Mountain People.* New York, NY: Simon and Schuster.

Watson, J. B. 1958 (revised). *Behaviorism*. Chicago, Illinois: University of Chicago Press.

Wax, M. 1977. "On Fieldworkers and Those Exposed to Fieldwork: Federal Regulations and Moral Issues, *Human Organizations*, Fall, 36, pp. 321–329.

Wax, M. and J. Cassell. 1979. *Federal Regulations: Ethical Issues and Social Research*. Boulder, CO: Westview Press.

Westie, F. 1957. "Toward Closer Relations Between Theory and Research: A Procedure and An Example," *American Sociological Review*. p. 22.

Withers, C. 1945. *Plainville, U.S.A.* New York, NY: Columbia University Press.

Zimbardo, P., C. W. Banks, C. Haney, and D. Jaffe. 1973. "The Mind is a Formidable Jailer," *The New York Times*, April 8, p. 41.

Name Index

Subject Index

Alameda County Study, 181
action research, 205, 300–301, 310–316
advocacy research, (*see* methodology)
AIDS research, 229–230
American Association of University Professors, 36
American Sociological Association, 31, 32, 37
    code of ethics, 321–328
American Soldier Study, 23
analysis
    collapsing variable, 268–269
    cross tabulation, 268–272
    definition of, 254
    description, 254–255, 256–258
    deviant case, 22
    elaboration, 272–275
    explanation, 255–256
    induction, 255
    multivariate, 269–275
    percentaging, 258–261, 269
    plan, 65, 177–178, 260, 262–263
    principles of, 19, 79
    qualified, 274–275
    spurious relationship, 274
    true relationship, 274
applied sociological research (*see* evaluation research)
applied versus basic research debate, 42, 45, 292–295, 302

artificiality of experiment, 172, 176
artificiality of measurement, 202
assumptions (*see* domain assumptions)

behaviorism
    definition of, 14
bias
    in interviewing, 138, 149, 189, 194–195
    in observational research, 207, 222
    in questionnaire construction, 99–101, 189
    in sampling, 116, 118, 192–195
Bogardus Social Distance Scale, 78, 83
bomb shelter experiment, 172
Boston's Chinatown study, 41–44, 210, 228, 275–276

cancer screening study, 241, 262
case study design, 163, 167, 189–190
causality, 19, 20, 163–167, 183–186, 188, 194, 268, 273–275
causality
    method of agreement, 163–164
    method of difference, 164
Central Intelligence Agency, 43
Central Tendency Measures, 261

classification, (*see* level of measurement)
cluster analysis, 88
code book, 237–242
coders, hiring and training, 242–243
coding
    definition of, 238
    management of, 242–245
    qualitative data, 231, 241–242, 263
    quantitative data, 239–241, 252
    reliability of, 245
Coefficient of Reproducibility, 85
Coleman Report, 310–316
Columbia University, 167
community studies, 228, 231
concept, definition of, 10–12, 21
conceptual definition
    example of, 10, 20, 65, 66, 70
    validity of, 62, 69, 92, 99, 189–190, 195
confidence interval, 119–120
confidence level, 120, 164, 190
confidentiality, 39, 140, 208, 243, 257
control
    as core characteristic of research, 19–20, 164–167, 190–191
    of extraneous factors, 164–165, 178
    of time, 164, 181–182
control group, 167, 191–193

375